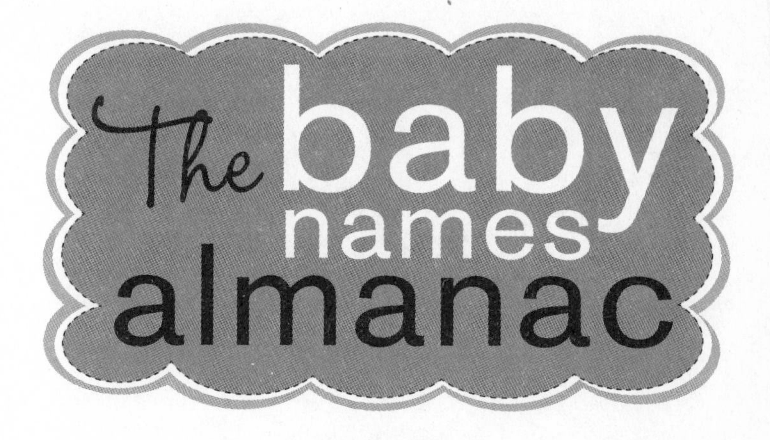

2017

Emily Larson

Cover design by Dawn Adams/Sourcebooks, Inc.

This publication is designed to provide accurate and authoritative information in regard to the subject matter covered. It is sold with the understanding that the publisher is not engaged in rendering legal, accounting, or other professional service. If legal advice or other expert assistance is required, the services of a competent professional person should be sought.—*From a Declaration of Principles Jointly Adopted by a Committee of the American Bar Association and a Committee of Publishers and Associations*

Published by Sourcebooks, Inc.
P.O. Box 4410, Naperville, Illinois 60567-4410
(630) 961-3900
Fax: (630) 961-2168
www.sourcebooks.com

Seventh Edition

Printed and bound in the United States of America.
VP 10 9 8 7 6 5 4 3 2

Contents

Introduction v

Inside the Popularity Charts 1

What's Hot (or Not) Today
(And What Will—and Won't!—Be Tomorrow) 27

Girls' Names 67

Boys' Names 225

Introduction

So, you've got a baby to name.

As if preparing for the arrival of the baby isn't enough, you're dealing with all the pressure of figuring out what, exactly, to call the little bundle of joy. It can be stressful to find a name that will do justice to the hope you have for your child.

After all, names influence first impressions. They can trigger great—or unpleasant—nicknames. They can affect your child's self-esteem. They can be a tangible, lasting link to a family legacy. But let's not forget that they can be fun. And that's what this book is all about.

Remember *The Old Farmer's Almanac*, which comes out annually as a guide to each year's trends, forecasts, and hot spots? Aimed at farmers, of course, the book provides a way to put the year into context, to navigate the shifting seasons, and to understand all the factors swirling in the atmosphere.

The *2017 Baby Names Almanac* aims to be a similar lifeline for parents. With a finger on the pulse of pop culture and an ear to the ground of what's hip, new, and relevant, this book offers you an instant, idiosyncratic snapshot of how the world today is shaping what you may want to name your child tomorrow.

Jam-packed with information and ideas, plus thousands of names to browse, this book analyzes the most recent trends and fads in baby naming, offering up forecasts and predictions. You'll find our take on questions like these (and much more!):

- Which cutting-edge names are on the rise?
- Which popular names are on the decline?
- What influence do celebrities have on names?

  - *Names in music:* Will your child be **Alessia** or **Zayn**?
  - *Names in entertainment:* Will **Finn** or **Rey** be in your child's kindergarten class? Or will you see more *Hamilton*-inspired kids?
  - *Names in current events:* Will Parisian names like **Elodie** and **Jules** inspire? How about the Olympic feats of **Simone**?
- How many babies get the most popular name, anyway?
- Which letter do most girls' names start with? How about boys' names?
- What are the most popular "gender-neutral" names today—and which gender uses each name more often? (If you name your daughter **Sawyer**, will she find herself playing with lots of other little girls named **Sawyer**, or little boys instead?)
- How can you take a trend and turn it into a name you love? (How about a little **Prince** of your own?)

We understand that sometimes this information on trends and popularity is hard to digest, so we've created some easy-to-visualize graphics. Turn to page 4, for example, to see a map of the United States showing where **Emma** reigns and where little **Noah** is king.

And what baby name book would be complete without the names? Flip to page 67 to begin browsing through more than 20,000 names, including entries for the most popular names for girls and boys as reported by the Social Security Administration (www.ssa.gov/OACT/babynames).

A little bit of a mishmash and a screenshot of the world today, *The 2017 Baby Names Almanac* is like no other book out there. Stuffed with ideas on what's hip and hot and how you can take a trend and turn it into a name you love, this book is your all-in-one guide to baby names now.

Inside the Popularity Charts

The Top 10

Let's start with the most popular names in the country. Ranked by the Social Security Administration (SSA), these names are released around Mother's Day each year. (The top 10 names get the most attention, but you may also hear about the top 100. The total number of names widely reported is 1,000.) In 2015 the top 10 names were similar to—but not identical to—the top 10 for 2014. For example, **Emma**, **Olivia**, and **Sophia** remained the top three choices for girls, while **Ava** replaced **Isabella** for the number 4 spot. The boys' list was just as stable, though **Daniel** dropped out and **James** rose two spots in the ranks. **Benjamin** (on the boys' side) and **Harper** (on the girls' side) were new additions to the top 10 lists this year. Here's a quick comparison of 2014 and 2015:

2015 Girls	2014 Girls	2015 Boys	2014 Boys
1. Emma	1. Emma	1. Noah	1. Noah
2. Olivia	2. Olivia	2. Liam	2. Liam
3. Sophia	3. Sophia	3. Mason	3. Mason
4. Ava	4. Isabella	4. Jacob	4. Jacob
5. Isabella	5. Ava	5. William	5. William
6. Mia	6. Mia	6. Ethan	6. Ethan
7. Abigail	7. Emily	7. James	7. Michael
8. Emily	8. Abigail	8. Alexander	8. Alexander
9. Charlotte	9. Madison	9. Michael	9. James
10. Harper	10. Charlotte	10. Benjamin	10. Daniel

Just How Many Emmas Are There, Anyway?

Sure, these names are popular, but what does that mean? Well, it seems that new parents are increasingly looking for off-the-beaten-path names for their little ones, and it shows. According to the SSA, the top 1,000 names represent 73.48 percent of all babies born and named in the United States in 2015—a significant drop from the 77.84 percent recorded in 2000.

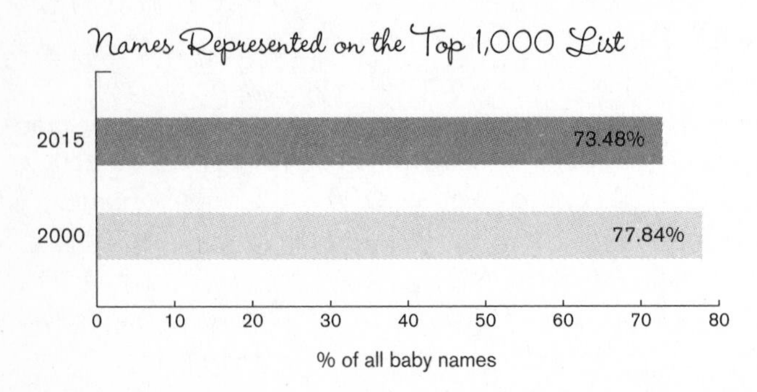

Although parents of either gender have always been looking beyond the top 1,000, parents of boys are more likely to pick a name in that mix—78.81 percent of boys' names are represented on the top 1,000 list, while only 67.90 percent of girls' names are.

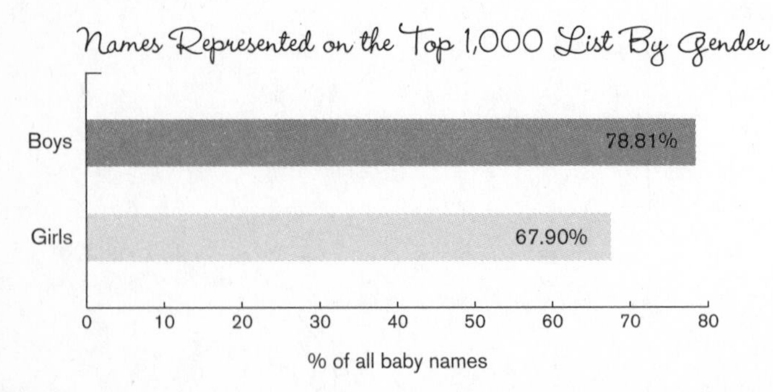

Plus, although it may seem like you know a zillion people with daughters named **Emma** or **Ava**, the most popular names are actually bestowed upon a relatively small number of babies each year. For example, in 2015 only 0.9626 percent of all male babies born in the United States (that's 19,511 little guys total) got the most popular name, **Noah**. There are slightly more girls (20,355) with the most popular name, **Emma**, but even that's only 1.0519 percent of all girls born. Only a fifth of the **Noah** total—4,062 babies—were given the 100th most popular name, **Elias**. The number of babies with the number one name is dropping swiftly—back in 1999, when **Jacob** first hit number one, more than 35,000 boys got that name, which is almost 16,000 more babies than got the top boys' name, **Noah**, in 2015. And back in 1970, 4.48 percent of all male babies (a staggering 85,298 tots) were named **Michael**, the most popular name of that year. So if you've got your heart set on naming your son **Mason** but you're worried that he'll be surrounded by Masons wherever he goes, take heart!

Mary, Mary Quite Contrary

Mary has been the most popular girls' name in the last 100 years, with about 3.6 million babies given the name since 1916. For boys, **James** reigns, with about 4.9 million namesakes in the last century.

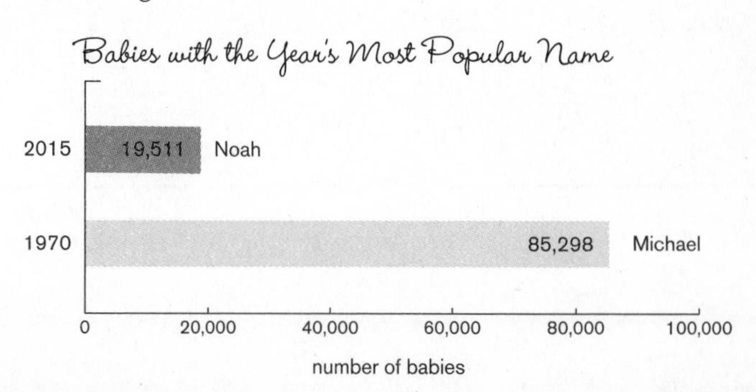

What's Popular in My State?

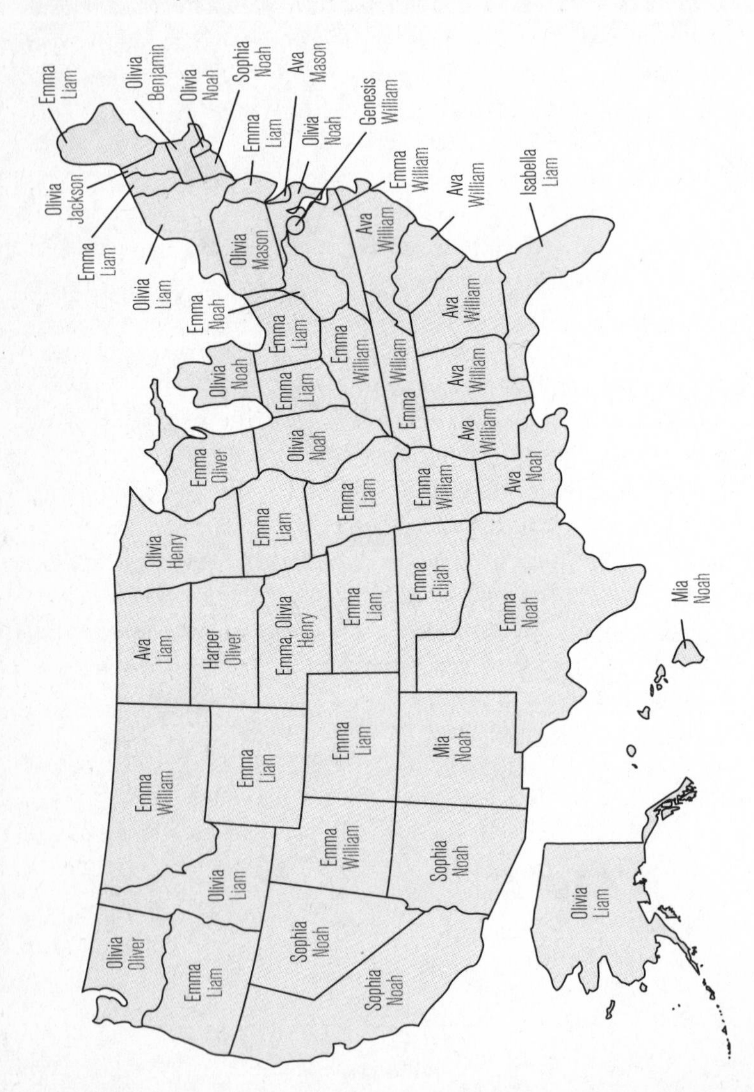

It's interesting to see how some names are more popular in certain states than in others. For example, **Harper** ranks 10th nationally for girls, but in South Dakota, it's the most popular name. Likewise, **Aria** ranks fourth among Hawaii's baby girls, but only 29th in the nation. On the boys' side, **Wyatt** was the third most popular name in Montana, but falls to number 34 across the country.

The following chart lists the top five names for girls and boys for each of the 50 states, and it also shows the actual number of births for each of those names in each state.

Top Five Names by State

State	Girl	Births	Boy	Births
Alabama	Ava	297	William	411
	Emma	285	James	322
	Olivia	258	John	317
	Harper	213	Mason	294
	Elizabeth	186	Elijah	276
Alaska	Olivia	56	Liam	53
	Emma	49	Noah	46
	Aurora	46	James	45
	Amelia	39	William	44
	Ava	39	Oliver	41
Arizona	Sophia	470	Noah	444
	Mia	460	Liam	411
	Emma	447	Alexander	366
	Olivia	413	Michael	339
	Isabella	383	Ethan	335

State	Girl	Births	Boy	Births
Arkansas	Emma	213	William	193
	Olivia	170	Elijah	171
	Ava	165	Mason	169
	Isabella	134	Noah	166
	Harper	120	James	146
California	Sophia	2,942	Noah	2,751
	Mia	2,850	Jacob	2,540
	Emma	2,706	Ethan	2,467
	Olivia	2,507	Daniel	2,460
	Isabella	2,388	Matthew	2,414
Colorado	Emma	353	Liam	305
	Olivia	345	William	275
	Mia	253	Jackson	269
	Evelyn	251	Alexander	256
	Sophia	249	Oliver	255
Connecticut	Sophia	215	Noah	215
	Emma	203	Mason	211
	Olivia	201	Alexander	188
	Isabella	186	Liam	184
	Ava	184	Benjamin	178
Delaware	Ava	69	Mason	60
	Olivia	58	Noah	59
	Sophia	57	Liam	57
	Abigail	46	Jackson	53
	Emma	43	Michael	51
District of Columbia	Genesis	49	William	78
	Ava	47	Henry	74
	Charlotte	47	James	68
	Sofia	45	Alexander	64
	Emma	41	Jacob	61

State	Girl	Births	Boy	Births
Florida	Isabella	1,376	Liam	1,274
	Emma	1,218	Noah	1,236
	Sophia	1,172	Jacob	998
	Olivia	1,151	Mason	985
	Mia	1,029	Ethan	965
Georgia	Ava	634	William	728
	Olivia	559	Noah	610
	Emma	541	Mason	603
	Madison	442	Elijah	557
	Isabella	412	James	530
Hawaii	Mia	73	Noah	77
	Emma	67	Liam	75
	Olivia	62	Mason	65
	Aria	59	Ezekiel	52
	Ava	59	Aiden	51
Idaho	Olivia	115	Liam	109
	Emma	111	William	97
	Evelyn	74	Oliver	87
	Ava	69	James	85
	Harper	69	Wyatt	81
Illinois	Olivia	813	Noah	863
	Emma	808	Liam	709
	Sophia	733	Alexander	703
	Mia	665	Jacob	650
	Isabella	641	William	618
Indiana	Emma	434	Liam	403
	Olivia	413	Noah	402
	Ava	381	Oliver	384
	Harper	332	Elijah	372
	Sophia	318	Mason	355

State	Girl	Births	Boy	Births
Iowa	Emma	198	Liam	212
	Olivia	190	William	176
	Harper	182	Oliver	174
	Evelyn	142	Henry	172
	Sophia	136	Owen	161
Kansas	Emma	215	Liam	179
	Olivia	198	William	170
	Harper	160	Mason	158
	Ava	159	Oliver	149
	Sophia	146	Wyatt	146
Kentucky	Emma	306	William	334
	Olivia	269	Mason	282
	Ava	254	Elijah	274
	Harper	229	James	272
	Isabella	209	Noah	260
Louisiana	Ava	321	Noah	294
	Emma	293	Mason	278
	Olivia	256	Liam	265
	Isabella	193	Elijah	253
	Harper	186	William	230
Maine	Emma	75	Liam	78
	Olivia	67	Owen	78
	Amelia	65	Mason	69
	Abigail	55	Oliver	68
	Harper	54	Wyatt	65
Maryland	Olivia	320	Noah	386
	Ava	307	Logan	323
	Sophia	303	James	321
	Emma	277	Mason	317
	Charlotte	232	Jacob	294

State	Girl	Births	Boy	Births
Massachusetts	Olivia	428	Benjamin	454
	Emma	402	William	445
	Sophia	373	Noah	401
	Isabella	348	Mason	364
	Charlotte	343	James	352
Michigan	Olivia	600	Noah	530
	Ava	570	Liam	520
	Emma	498	Carter	496
	Sophia	418	Mason	494
	Charlotte	404	Lucas	461
Minnesota	Olivia	376	Henry	392
	Emma	323	Oliver	358
	Evelyn	272	William	339
	Ava	265	Liam	321
	Nora	242	Mason	290
Mississippi	Ava	214	William	212
	Emma	164	John	204
	Olivia	139	James	196
	Madison	120	Mason	189
	Brooklyn	118	Elijah	157
Missouri	Emma	395	Liam	380
	Olivia	375	William	360
	Ava	325	Mason	350
	Harper	299	Henry	325
	Charlotte	272	Jackson	307
Montana	Emma	69	William	63
	Olivia	57	Liam	55
	Harper	53	Wyatt	55
	Ava	47	Oliver	54
	Aurora	38	James	51

State	Girl	Births	Boy	Births
Nebraska	Emma	120	Henry	127
	Olivia	120	William	114
	Harper	117	Liam	109
	Charlotte	108	Noah	106
	Ava	102	Oliver	99
Nevada	Sophia	188	Noah	184
	Olivia	169	Liam	183
	Mia	168	Alexander	165
	Isabella	158	Jacob	146
	Emma	156	Anthony	142
New Hampshire	Olivia	91	Jackson	85
	Charlotte	87	Benjamin	74
	Emma	82	Owen	73
	Sophia	66	Mason	71
	Ava	64	Noah	71
New Jersey	Emma	532	Liam	569
	Isabella	518	Michael	539
	Sophia	518	Jacob	531
	Olivia	503	Noah	508
	Mia	488	Mason	500
New Mexico	Mia	121	Noah	131
	Sophia	113	Elijah	123
	Isabella	103	Liam	109
	Ava	97	Michael	91
	Emma	88	Aiden	88
New York	Olivia	1,297	Liam	1,388
	Emma	1,254	Jacob	1,281
	Sophia	1,121	Ethan	1,244
	Isabella	1,066	Noah	1,236
	Mia	1,012	Michael	1,163

State	Girl	Births	Boy	Births
North Carolina	Ava	622	William	702
	Emma	580	Noah	674
	Olivia	563	Mason	597
	Isabella	429	Liam	586
	Sophia	424	James	533
North Dakota	Ava	70	Liam	63
	Emma	69	Oliver	57
	Olivia	64	Carter	52
	Harper	58	Owen	52
	Avery	42	Henry	51
Ohio	Emma	720	Liam	688
	Ava	708	Mason	617
	Olivia	687	Noah	614
	Sophia	541	Carter	585
	Harper	512	William	565
Oklahoma	Emma	264	Elijah	213
	Olivia	237	Jaxon	198
	Ava	186	William	198
	Isabella	172	Liam	197
	Sophia	171	Noah	189
Oregon	Emma	234	Liam	222
	Olivia	218	Henry	207
	Sophia	181	Oliver	190
	Abigail	170	James	181
	Charlotte	165	Noah	181
Pennsylvania	Olivia	780	Mason	790
	Emma	761	Liam	757
	Ava	720	Noah	714
	Sophia	593	Michael	626
	Isabella	528	Jacob	624

State	Girl	Births	Boy	Births
Rhode Island	Olivia	83	Noah	72
	Emma	77	Liam	69
	Sophia	74	Mason	69
	Ava	63	Logan	66
	Isabella	58	Alexander	61
South Carolina	Ava	277	William	357
	Olivia	237	James	293
	Emma	224	Mason	282
	Madison	207	Noah	271
	Elizabeth	200	Elijah	228
South Dakota	Harper	59	Oliver	62
	Emma	58	Owen	56
	Olivia	50	Liam	54
	Ava	46	Jackson	49
	Evelyn	42	Levi	48
Tennessee	Emma	473	William	522
	Ava	412	James	434
	Olivia	412	Elijah	413
	Harper	295	Mason	413
	Isabella	282	Noah	396
Texas	Emma	2,197	Noah	2,147
	Sophia	2,169	Liam	1,739
	Mia	2,036	Jacob	1,680
	Isabella	1,854	Ethan	1,669
	Olivia	1,806	Daniel	1,646
Utah	Emma	281	William	309
	Olivia	277	Oliver	280
	Charlotte	192	James	230
	Evelyn	160	Liam	222
	Harper	157	Lincoln	216

State	Girl	Births	Boy	Births
Vermont	Emma	33	Liam	40
	Ava	29	Oliver	35
	Harper	26	Jackson	34
	Charlotte	25	Mason	33
	Isabella	24	Owen	32
Virginia	Emma	464	William	549
	Ava	456	Noah	516
	Olivia	454	Liam	511
	Charlotte	402	James	494
	Sophia	394	Mason	446
Washington	Olivia	477	Oliver	397
	Emma	420	Noah	364
	Sophia	352	Liam	363
	Ava	305	Benjamin	356
	Evelyn	302	Henry	347
West Virginia	Emma	143	Noah	137
	Ava	108	Liam	127
	Olivia	104	Mason	122
	Harper	86	Hunter	96
	Isabella	78	Levi	95
Wisconsin	Emma	352	Oliver	305
	Olivia	345	Owen	304
	Evelyn	262	Liam	298
	Ava	261	Noah	296
	Charlotte	250	Mason	293
Wyoming	Emma	39	Liam	38
	Harper	35	Mason	37
	Olivia	31	Benjamin	29
	Ava	23	Wyatt	29
	Evelyn	23	Luke	28

What Joined—and Dropped Off—the Hot 100 in 2015?

One of the easiest ways to spot name trends is to watch what joins the Hot 100 and what drops off. For the (young) ladies, several new names joined in 2015: **Hazel**, **Cora**, **Quinn**, **Clara**, **Aurora**, and **Reagan**. A number of these names are following current trends, like Hazel, a nod to a character in popular literature, and Reagan and Quinn, which are also very popular boy names.

Another bunch dropped off the list: **Lauren**, number 21 only ten years ago, lost its Hot 100 spot, as did **Sophie**, **Alexandra**, **London**, **Hadley**, and **Jasmine**. **Jennifer**, which held the number one spot from 1970 to 1984, continued to slide, dropping from 192 in 2013 to 252 in 2015. For the boys, a handful of newcomers joined the Hot 100. **Mateo**, **Ezra**, **Sawyer**, **Theodore**, and **Elias** all continued to rise, while **Brody**, **Justin**, **Juan**, **Luis**, and **Tristan** fell off.

New to the Hot 100

Hazel	Mateo
Aurora	Ezra
Cora	Sawyer
Quinn	Theodore
Clara	Elias
Reagan	

Off the Hot 100

Sophie	Brody
Alexandra	Justin
London	Juan
Lauren	Luis
Hadley	Tristan
Jasmine	

New to the Top 1,000 This Year

These names are fresh faces in the top 1,000 list this year. Some of them have never set foot on the list before, but odds are they'll keep moving up.

Girls

Adaline	364	Sarahi	909	Heavenly	967
Zelda	647	Andi	911	Kensington	971
Alaia	664	Arden	912	Tinley	974
Lennox	740	Dalary	913	Ophelia	975
Royal	755	Aitana	917	Charlize	978
Amaris	789	Vienna	925	Avalyn	980
Adilynn	805	Esperanza	926	Taya	982
Adley	827	Kyndall	934	Lyra	984
Kalani	841	Kaelynn	939	Noor	985
Briar	844	Veda	945	Sariyah	986
Kaya	856	Meilani	950	Giavanna	987
Analia	859	Harmoni	955	Rhea	989
Jayde	861	Luz	959	Zaylee	990
Romina	863	Aislinn	960	Frankie	992
Nathalia	868	Ellis	962	Princess	998
Aminah	902	Elora	963	Alianna	1000

Boys

Canaan	806	Kashton	942	Kye	978
Otis	848	Jabari	945	Todd	980
Shiloh	894	Avi	946	Haiden	984
Denver	900	Sutton	950	Brixton	985
Immanuel	906	Kamren	958	Dangelo	986
Jonael	919	Huxley	962	Juelz	987
Ignacio	925	Wilder	964	Bishop	989
Riaan	926	Louie	967	Freddy	990
Musa	930	Achilles	968	Reagan	991
Ridge	932	Aarush	971	Malaki	993
Jaziel	939	Robin	973	Leroy	997
Boone	940	Yadiel	974	Briar	998
Cairo	941	Yahya	975	Antoine	1000

Biggest Jumper: Alaia and Riaan

The rise of the girls' name **Alaia**, which rose 2,012 slots from 2,676 in 2014 to 664 in 2015, looks to be a variation of another popular girls' name–**Aaliyah**, which has steadily been in the top 100 since 2001 and currently holds the number 48 spot. **Riaan**, which raced 1,360 spots from 2,286 to 926, means "little king" and is continuing to rise in popularity, especially following the birth of Reign Disick, Kourtney Kardashian's son, in 2014.

How Do You Spell Aiden?

When you take into account that the male name **Aiden** has eight spelling variations in the top 1,000 (see the list that follows), that means that this one name actually shows up on the list eight different times! We broke down the top 1,000 names for boys and girls this way, counting all the different spelling variations as one name, and we got some surprising results. Looking from that perspective, there aren't 1,000 unique names at all! We counted roughly 698 unique girls' names and approximately 834 unique boys' names. The girls have fewer unique names, spelled in more ways, whereas parents of boys reach into a bigger pool of names. Let's take a look at some of the names with the most (or most interesting!) variations in the top 1,000.

Note: Some of these names could be pronounced slightly differently from one another. Also, names are listed in order of popularity.

Boys

It's no surprise that the "-ayden" names (such as **Aiden**, **Jayden**, **Brayden**, and **Kayden**) offer lots of spelling variety, but the changes in **Devin** and **Kason** struck us as a little more unusual.

Aiden

1. Aiden
2. Ayden
3. Aidan
4. Aden
5. Adan
6. Aaden
7. Aydin
8. Aydan

Jayden

1. Jayden
2. Jaden
3. Jaiden
4. Jadon
5. Jaydon

Brayden

1. Brayden
2. Braden
3. Braydon
4. Braeden
5. Braiden

Kayden

1. Kayden
2. Kaiden
3. Kaden
4. Caden
5. Cayden
6. Caiden
7. Kaeden

Cameron

1. Cameron
2. Kameron
3. Camron
4. Kamryn
5. Kamron
6. Camren

Connor

1. Connor
2. Conner
3. Conor
4. Konnor

Kason

1. Kason
2. Kayson
3. Cason
4. Kasen
5. Cayson
6. Casen
7. Kaysen
8. Kaison

Devin

1. Devin
2. Devon
3. Davion
4. Davian
5. Davin

Jackson

1. Jackson
2. Jaxon
3. Jaxson
4. Jaxton
5. Jaxen

Girls

Some of these seemed more obvious—**Adalynn**, for one—but others, like **Liliana**, surprised us with their robust variety.

Kaelyn

1. Kaelyn
2. Kaylin
3. Kailyn
4. Kaylynn
5. Kaelynn

Hailey

1. Hailey
2. Haley
3. Haylee
4. Hayley
5. Hallie
6. Hailee
7. Halle

Madelyn

1. Madelyn
2. Madeline
3. Madeleine
4. Madilyn
5. Madelynn
6. Madilynn
7. Madalyn
8. Madalynn

Emily

1. Emily
2. Emely
3. Emilee
4. Emilie
5. Emmalee

Kaitlyn

1. Kaitlyn
2. Katelyn
3. Caitlyn
4. Caitlin
5. Katelynn
6. Kaitlynn

Kayleigh

1. Kayleigh
2. Kaylee
3. Kailey
4. Kailee
5. Caylee
6. Kaylie

Aaliyah

1. Aaliyah
2. Aliyah
3. Aleah
4. Alayah
5. Alia
6. Alaya
7. Aliya

Eliana

1. Eliana
2. Elliana
3. Elianna
4. Aliana
5. Iliana
6. Alianna

Layla

1. Layla
2. Laila
3. Leila
4. Lailah
5. Laylah
6. Leyla

Liliana

1. Liliana
2. Lilliana
3. Lilyana
4. Lilianna
5. Lillianna
6. Lilyanna

Adalynn

1. Adalynn
2. Adalyn
3. Adeline
4. Adelyn
5. Adelynn
6. Addilyn
7. Adaline
8. Addilynn
9. Adilynn

Allison

1. Allison
2. Alison
3. Allyson
4. Alyson
5. Alisson

Carly

1. Carly
2. Karlee
3. Carlee
4. Karlie

Charlie

1. Charlie
2. Charlee
3. Charley
4. Charleigh
5. Charli

Maya

1. Maya
2. Mya
3. Maia
4. Miah
5. Myah
6. Miya

Makayla

1. Makayla
2. Mikayla
3. Michaela
4. Mikaela

Natalie

1. Natalie
2. Nathalie
3. Nathaly
4. Nataly
5. Natalee

Annabelle

1. Annabelle
2. Annabel
3. Anabelle

Top 698 Names, Not Top 1,000

Only 70 percent of the top 1,000 girls' names are unique names. Only 83 percent of the top 1,000 boys' names are unique names. The rest of the names are spelling variations of those names.

Here are the three names with the most spelling variations:

Girls

1. Kayleigh
2. Adalynn
3. Hailey, Madelyn

Boys

1. Aiden, Kason
2. Kayden
3. Cameron

What Do the Most Popular Names Start With?

You may find it surprising, but only seven of the names in the top 1,000 girl baby names for 2015 start with a *W*: **Wendy**, **Whitney**, **Willa**, **Willow**, **Winter**, **Wren**, and **Wynter**. At the same time, you probably won't find it surprising that the most popular letter that girls' names start with is A (176 of the top 1,000), with M as a close second with 99 names. Among the boys' names, 99 start with J, and A names comprise 98 of the total 1,000 names. In 2009, every single letter in the alphabet had at least one boy and girl name, as **Unique** hopped back on the chart (929) for the first time in four years. But in 2015, no U names made it on the girls' list. (The boys, however, are covered, with **Uriah**, **Uriel**, **Urijah**, and **Ulises**). And there was only one Q (**Quinn**) or X (**Ximena**) for girls.

Gender-Neutral Options

Lots of names are popular for both boys and girls, but they're generally more popular for one gender than the other. Here's a list of names that appeared on both the boys' top 1,000 and the girls' top 1,000, plus how they ranked in 2015 for each gender. Some interesting finds here—**Hayden** and **Charlie**, once in the top 100 for boys, are now given to nearly the same number of boys as girls. **Lennon**, relatively new to the top 1,000 for both genders, is also almost equally distributed, and **Frankie** is exactly even, ranking at 992 for both boys and girls. And the sky is the limit for **Skyler**, sitting at 361 for boys and 285 for girls. We'd suggest that 2017 will be a great year for **James** and **Arlo** to hit the girls' list.

Spelling Matters!

If you're going to choose...

Cameron/Camryn/Kamryn: Camryn and Kamryn are the more popular choices for girls, Cameron for boys

Skylar/Skyler: Skylar is more popular for girls, while Skyler wins for boys

Jordan/Jordyn: Jordyn is more popular for girls, Jordan for boys

Nearly Equal

Name	Girl Rank	Boy Rank
Frankie	992	992
Jamie	498	485
Charlie	207	229
Hayden	190	151

More Popular for Girls

Name	Girl Rank	Boy Rank
Harper	10	722
Avery	16	187
Riley	35	194
Skylar	42	708
Peyton	72	260
Taylor	76	462
Alexis	86	343
Quinn	97	354
Reagan	99	991
London	105	605
Morgan	120	674
Jordyn	136	966
Ariel	137	598
Kendall	147	780
Payton	153	693

Name	Girl Rank	Boy Rank
Reese	173	701
Finley	204	326
Charlie	207	229
Marley	218	863
Harley	281	663
Skyler	285	361
Lyric	289	892
Sage	370	649
Tatum	410	590
Justice	452	525
Leighton	473	859
Lennon	516	609
Jessie	617	918
Sutton	672	950
Frankie	992	992

More Popular for Boys

Name	Girl Rank	Boy Rank
Logan	394	14
Jayden	657	20
Carter	533	24
Dylan	397	27
Ryan	474	39
Hunter	786	41
Cameron	530	56
Jordan	262	60
Angel	290	64
Parker	227	72
Sawyer	260	94
Kayden	879	95
Blake	423	96
Micah	834	108
Kai	895	145
Hayden	190	151
Elliot	635	208
Rowan	331	219

Name	Girl Rank	Boy Rank
Zion	899	227
Rylan	877	241
River	350	244
Dallas	562	255
Amari	475	265
Remington	622	299
Phoenix	455	307
Rory	679	378
Ellis	962	419
Royal	755	465
Jamie	498	485
Lennox	740	488
Remy	847	520
Casey	814	551
Oakley	611	567
Azariah	849	699
Landry	918	858
Frankie	992	992

Which Names Are Moving Up—and Falling Down—the Fastest?

The SSA compiles a list of names that have made the biggest moves when compared to their rank the previous year (assuming the name has made the top 1,000 at least once in the last two years). Some of these jumpers have obvious triggers, while the reasons for other jumps and declines are more open to interpretation. Take a look and see what you think.

40 Girls' Names Heating Up

Name	Number of Spots It Moved Up	Name	Number of Spots It Moved Up
Alaia	2,012	Amaris	251
Meilani	1,836	Dalary	237
Aitana	1,721	Kalani	236
Aislinn	1,385	Analia	235
Taya	1,107	Zahra	224
Adaline	1,029	Romina	223
Briar	597	Gwen	213
Zelda	512	Addilyn	208
Adley	495	Magnolia	197
Lennox	416	Addilynn	193
Ariyah	329	Saylor	191
Adilynn	318	Alannah	189
Heavenly	314	Lennon	183
Zaylee	312	Ariah	181
Thea	295	Veda	178
Jessa	295	Kinslee	175
Milani	281	Noa	172
Karter	270	Kori	169
Royal	254	Lorelai	168
Carter	251	Freya	167

40 Girls' Names Cooling Down

Name	Number of Spots It Moved Down
Isis	1,065
Annabell	500
Anabel	500
Cindy	343
Anabella	333
Aranza	324
Anabelle	272
Sherlyn	250
Kiley	235
Danika	225
Miley	221
Denise	213
Bryn	209
Taryn	208
Elsa	201
Mollie	197
Temperance	197
Elin	196
Jasmin	194
Audriana	189

Name	Number of Spots It Moved Down
Kenya	189
Lindsay	188
Abbigail	179
Aubri	177
Ayanna	175
Annabel	174
Monserrat	174
Aryanna	171
Kayden	169
Caylee	167
Kathleen	156
Wendy	154
Angelique	154
Riya	151
Lexie	151
Nataly	151
Danica	150
Rosalyn	150
Maleah	149
Kaleigh	148

40 Boys' Names Heating Up

Name	Number of Spots It Moved Up
Riaan	1,360
Huxley	392
Wilder	360
Jaziel	276
Canaan	271
Kaison	251
Brixton	212
Ridge	204
Omari	198
Jabari	194
Titan	190
Zayn	189
Matteo	182
Dash	182
Haiden	181
Kashton	176
Kyrie	172
Ignacio	169
Yahya	167
Cairo	164

Name	Number of Spots It Moved Up
Killian	163
Otis	160
Denver	155
Achilles	155
Baylor	152
Atlas	149
Shiloh	149
Adriel	148
Mack	145
Legend	144
Ford	143
Ariel	143
Louie	142
Kyree	140
Lachlan	139
Rowen	139
Azariah	135
Augustine	134
Kohen	131
Reyansh	130

40 Boys' Names Cooling Down

Name	Number of Spots It Moved Down
Arnav	666
Jayse	257
Neymar	240
Rylee	228
Johnathon	213
Broderick	195
Brenden	187
Yael	178
Aidyn	173
Gavyn	167
Ulises	159
Giovanny	153
Eliezer	153
Konner	151
Jaydon	147
Menachem	137
Tristian	132
Zackary	132
Kale	131
Ramiro	130
Alfred	127
Markus	125
Randall	123
Gino	123
Gannon	120
Deshawn	119
Davian	116
Keenan	114
Jeffery	113
Jaycob	113
Tristen	111
Jessie	109
Ishaan	107
Jovanni	104
Jaxen	98
Urijah	94
Channing	93
Triston	92
Efrain	92
Marquis	92

What's Hot (or Not) Today
(And What Will—and Won't!—Be Tomorrow)

Now that we've seen the state of baby names today, here's a snapshot of some interesting trends we've spotted, as well as some predictions of who you may be meeting on the playground sometime soon.

You'll notice that certain names are on the rise and others are on the decline, showing how trends are morphing over time (for example, how some religious names like **Jesus** and **Rachel** are on the decline, but others like **Abel** and **Genesis** are climbing the ranks). We've also included some offbeat and unique ways to take each of these trends and find a name that really fits you and your family.

Trends Today

SHORT AND SWEET

In a world where chaos and clutter reign supreme, parents are now making an effort to tidy up—simplicity is key! In a new trend that has swept across Europe and is now making its way over to the United States, short and simple names are becoming increasingly popular, and this trend doesn't seem like it will stop anytime soon. Girls' names like **Liv**, which rose 63 spots to 720 in 2015, and **Elle**, which currently holds the 398 spot, are looking to climb up the top 1,000. Meanwhile, boys' names like **Dax**, which jumped from 602 in 2014 to 549 in 2015, and **Finn**, a steady riser from 835 in 2000 to 209 fifteen years later, are on the move to pass their longer counterparts, **Finnegan** and **Daxton**.

These single syllable names are reminiscent of simpler times, and, as the trend continues, don't be surprised to see names like **Kit**, **Jude**, **Bee**, **Mac**, and **Win** appear on the list in coming years.

FIT FOR A PRINCE

There is no monarchy on American soil, but that doesn't stop some parents from wishful thinking—but don't automatically assume there are names coming out of Kensington Palace. Americans are searching for their own royal treatment, and three names are on the rise. **Royal**, **King**, and **Prince** are contemporary twists that are looking to oust the ruling monarchy of the boys' list: **George**, **Alexander**, and **Louis**. **Royal** debuted at 900 in 2013 and shot up 435 spots to 465 in 2015. **King** jumped from 193 in 2013 to 163 in 2015 (its variant **Kingston** rose from 191 to 142), and **Duke** debuted on the boys' list at 720 in 2013, and this year sits at 603. And don't forget about **Prince**! With the *Purple Rain* singer's passing in April 2016, we predict that the name is going to see a significant increase from its current spot at 387. Its counterpart **Princeton**, at number 431, might see a bump as well. And what about the girls? After a brief hiatus in 2014, **Princess** has climbed back on to the top 1,000 to hold the number 998 spot, and **Jewel** is holding steadily at 887.

What name will rule in 2017? We could see fairy tale favorites **Knight** and **Reign** soon commanding attention in the top 1,000 in the coming years.

MAY THE FORCE BE WITH YOU

The first Star Wars film was released in 1977, but the names from the series are getting new life—perhaps due to the release of the most recent film, which came out at the end of 2015. It seems hard to believe that many parents would want to name their little ones after Darth Vader, but the name **Anakin** had a huge rise in popularity, moving up from 1,258 in 2013 to 957 in 2014, and again to 912 in 2015. **Luke** held steady at 28, and **Leia**, which came back into the top 1,000 in 2006 (its other two appearances were in 1978 and 1980, no doubt due to the film), rose to 421 in 2015, its highest rank yet. And let's not forget about the new faces in the Star Wars universe! With *Star Wars: The Force Awakens* grossing over two billion in the box office and the much anticipated sequel premiering in 2017, it won't be a surprise to see characters like **Rey**, **Kylo**, **Finn**, and **Poe** storm-troopering on to our lists.

GREAT SCOT!

For decades, American parents have been looking across the Atlantic for baby names, borrowing popular monikers from **Patrick** and **Liam** to **Erin** and **Claire** from the Irish and English. But now, it seems that Scottish choices are on the rise, and parents are looking toward the highlands to name their new bairns. We're predicting an increase of little Scots invading in 2017, especially classic favorites like **Isla**, which is ranked at 141 on the girls' side, and **Lachlan**, which jumped 139 spots on the boys' list in 2015. This trend may be due to the huge popularity of the hit Starz show *Outlander*, which premiered in 2014, and now Scottish names are in high demand. Here's a look at how some of the names straight from bonnie Scotland are doing on the top 1,000:

Girls' Names	2014	2015
Isla	150	141
Finley	223	204
Maisie	653	624
Esme	810	682
Rory	840	679

Ways to Make This Trend Your Own

Options still off the radar: Agnes, Mairi, Ailsa, Greer, Nessa

Boys' Names	2014	2015
Callum	730	683
Lachlan	907	768
Graham	199	176
Lennox	584	488
Magnus	974	860

Ways to Make This Trend Your Own
Options still off the radar: Fergus, Blair, Arran, Angus, Innes

TO DIE FOR DIGRAPHS

Instead of one consonant ruling the schools, we're looking at the digraph *th* sound to be popular in playgrounds in the coming years. With th names rising in the top 1,000, we think that the digraph will be a thrilling thing in 2017. Already rising in the ranks on the girls' side are popular names like **Thalia**, at number 792, **Dorothy**, which has been rising since 2006 at 981 to 714 in 2015, and **Thea**, which jumped from 776 last year to 464 today. Boys are dominating the softer th names as well, with **Theo** climbing from 509 to 408 in 2015, **Thiago** landing at 333, its highest rank to date, and **Thaddeus** making a steady rise since 2010 to hold the 703 spot.

Ways to Make This Trend Your Own
Options still off the radar: Theodosia, Thayer, Matthias, Edith, Ruth, Seth

T-SWIFT SQUAD GOALS

In 2015 Taylor Swift's "Bad Blood" music video premiered at the Billboard Music Awards, and "squad goals" were born. Soon enough, Taylor's posse of famous models, singers, and actors were making headlines around the world, and the phrase "squad goals" emerged across various platforms, suddenly a part of the vernacular. With 2015 being a banner year for Swift and the Bad Blood squad, we're predicting a possible rise in the polls for **Taylor**, which currently holds the 76 spot on the girls' side, a one bump increase from 2014, and ranks 462 for the boys. Other favorites are likely to see a jump as well, like **Selena** which holds the 321 spot, a 26 spot increase from 2014, and **Karlie**, which rose 69 spots to 815 in 2015. Boys are included in this trend as well, with superstar (and recent ex) **Calvin** standing strong at 171 and **Edward** on the rise from 162 in 2014 to 158. With this mega-superstar squad, it's likely we'll see many "name goals" appearing in the coming years.

Girls' Names	Squad Member	2015 Rank
Abigail	Abigail Anderson	7
Ella	Ella O'Connor (Lorde)	18
Lily	Lily Aldridge	25
Taylor	Taylor Swift	76
Lena	Lena Dunham	272
Selena	Selena Gomez	321
Zendaya	Zendaya Coleman	801
Karlie	Karlie Kloss	815

Boys' Names	Squad Member	2015 Rank
Austin	Austin Swift	69
Edward	Edward (Ed) Sheeran	158
Calvin	Calvin Harris	171
Taylor	Taylor Swift	462
Benson	Olivia Benson	470
Lamar	Kendrick Lamar	819

Ways to Make This Trend Your Own

Options still off the radar: Gigi, Camila, Serayah, Swift, Harris

LITERARY INSPIRATION

Been noticing a lot of Holdens and Eloises in the sandbox lately? Names from classic children's books have been heating up, perhaps because parents have such fond memories and associations with these popular characters from their own youth. On the boys' side, **Holden** (of *The Catcher in the Rye*'s Holden Caulfield), **Rhett** (of *Gone with the Wind* fame), **Milo** (from *The Phantom Tollbooth*), **Sawyer** and **Finn** (the last names of popular Mark Twain heroes Tom Sawyer and Huckleberry Finn), and author inspirations like **Emerson** (Ralph Waldo Emerson) and **Beckett** (Samuel Beckett) have all been climbing the charts.

For girls, our eyes are on **Matilda** (from the Roald Dahl classic), **Frances** (the full name of *A Tree Grows in Brooklyn*'s Francie Nolan), **Eloise** (from Kay Thompson's popular series about a young girl who lives at the Plaza Hotel), **Josephine** (the full name of *Little Women*'s Jo March), **Amelia** (from the children's series *Amelia Bedelia*), and **Alice** (of Wonderland). Some beloved authors like **Maya** (Maya Angelou) and **Charlotte** (Charlotte Bronte) are sure to make a strong showing as well. Take a look at this chart to see how these literary namesakes have been trending over the past six years.

Name	2009	2010	2011	2012	2013	2014	2015
Holden	333	316	299	296	288	292	291
Charlie	274	244	236	233	233	225	229
Rhett	658	607	564	507	425	338	274
Sawyer	202	172	172	147	120	110	94
Finn	342	300	302	291	250	234	209
Milo	450	423	358	326	311	311	288

Name	2009	2010	2011	2012	2013	2014	2015
Dorian	513	501	522	559	546	538	563
Emerson	437	430	387	363	329	323	301
Beckett	411	356	330	314	280	244	218
Matilda	757	799	769	658	645	583	535
Frances	797	766	780	763	693	602	514
Eloise	913	528	449	364	338	300	256
Josephine	201	185	182	160	160	147	131
Amelia	55	41	30	23	17	15	12
Alice	258	172	142	127	107	97	87
Charlotte	68	45	27	19	11	10	9
Maya	61	66	64	63	72	74	69
Scarlett	170	115	80	61	42	30	22

Ways to Make This Trend Your Own

Options still off the radar: Huck (Finn), Marius (Pontmercy), Abra (Bacon), Pip (Pirrup), Scout (Finch)

WHAT ABOUT HARPER?

Back in 2004, **Harper** burst on to the top 1,000 girls' list at number 887, and since then, its popularity has skyrocketed for both boys and girls, mostly due to the popularity of Harper Lee's American classic *To Kill a Mockingbird*. Holding the number 722 spot on the boys list and the number 10 spot for the girls, this literary inspiration represented 0.529 percent of total female births in 2015 and 0.017 of boys. But what does the future of Harper look like now? We're expecting a drop in Harper's popularity, and other Lee-inspired favorites like **Atticus**, which sits at 350 on the boys' list, in the coming years. This is mostly due to the racist undertones of Lee's *Go Set a Watchman* manuscript, which was discovered in 2011 and published in 2015 to mixed reception.

END IN AN O

Typically, we're used to seeing boys' names rounding off with an O, but now we're thinking that little girls are about to start jumping on this trend. While classics like Milo, at number 288, and Theo, at number 408, are staples of the boys' list, we're now seeing rising girls' names ending in the long O sound. Harlow jumped from 508 to 422 in 2015, and Margo is on its tail, making a huge climb from 738 in 2014 to 593 in 2015. Other little girls' names like Willow, Margot, Shiloh, and Juno are bound to make the list in the coming years.

TEN-DOLLAR FOUNDING FATHER

With the cultural phenomenon *Hamilton*, a musical based on the life of first U.S. Treasury Secretary Alexander Hamilton, sweeping the Broadway box offices, we're expecting both *Hamilton* and other founding father–inspired names to rise up and conquer the top 1,000. With **Alexander** already holding the number 8 spot since 2013, we're expecting **Eliza** (Hamilton), **George** (Washington), **Angelica** (Schulyer), **Jefferson** (Thomas), and **Aaron** (Burr) to duel it out in the coming years. And we can see this trend extending past *Hamilton*'s Broadway stage. Presidential options are popping up everywhere for both sexes—**Ford** entered the boys' top 1,000 in 2014 and rose to 741 in 2015, and **Hayes** (also for boys) sits comfortably at 539. **Carter** appeared on the girls' list for the first time in 2013 and shot up to 254 spots in 2015 to a 533 rank. Take a look at these other presidential name nominations over the years:

Girls' Names	2000 Rank	2015 Rank
Eliza (Hamilton)	379	175
Angelica (Schulyer)	138	425
Madison (James)	3	11

Girls' Names	2000 Rank	2015 Rank
Kennedy (John F.)	139	57
Taylor (Zachary)	10	76
Reagan (Ronald)	286	99
McKinley (William)	–	380
Monroe (James)	–	716

Ways to Make This Trend Your Own

Options still off the radar: Martha (Washington), Jackson (Andrew), Schuyler (pronounced Skylar), Theodosia (Burr Alston)

Boys' Names	2000 Rank	2015 Rank
Alexander (Hamilton)	20	8
Jefferson (Thomas)	717	670
Aaron (Burr)	41	52
George (Washington)	130	136
Jackson (Andrew)	72	17
Tyler (John)	10	81
Lincoln (Honest Abe)	710	66
Harrison (Benjamin or William Henry)	184	119
Grant (Ulysses)	123	177
Pierce (Franklin)	498	466
Hayes (Rutherford)	–	539
Wilson (Woodrow)	526	620
Carter (Jimmy)	152	24
Ford (Gerald)	–	741
Truman (Harry S.)	–	981

Ways to Make This Trend Your Own

Options still off the radar: Madison (James), Fillmore (Millard), Garfield (James), Roosevelt (Theodore and Franklin Delano)

PARIS IS ALWAYS A GOOD IDEA

Current events always seem to affect current trends, and that's what we're predicting in 2017 for popular French names. With the world looking toward Paris after the 2015 Paris attacks, there is fresh attention on French names, and we're predicting a rise in already common names in the U.S. like **Leo**, which sits at 91, and **Theo** at 408, along with a bump in those that have yet to hit our lists, like **Elodie** and **Jules**. Take a look at other names on our list that shout "*vive la* France!"

KEEPING UP WITH THE KARDASHIANS

There's no question that the oldest Kardashian sister, Kourtney, bears responsibility for the rise of **Mason**. Mason Dash Disick, Kourtney's older son, was born December 14, 2009. Since his birth, the name Mason has shot up from number 34 in 2009 to number 12 in 2010 and then all the way to number 2 in 2011. Today it sits at number 3—pretty impressive! **Dash** has also made it into the top 1,000, debuting at 948 in 2014 and then skyrocketing to hold the 766 spot just a year later. Kourtney's daughter, Penelope, was born July 8, 2012. **Penelope** climbed the name ranks from 168 in 2011 to 125 in 2012, and it rose to 34 in 2015. (Its variant **Penny** is on the climb too, entering the top 1,000 in 2013 and jumping to 754 in 2015.) In 2015, Kourtney gave birth to her third child, baby boy Reign Aston. While **Reign** isn't in the top 1,000 names yet, it's totally on trend with its royal undertones. Look for it, and its middle name counterpart **Aston**, to hit the list soon.

All eyes are on the name **Saint** as we wait for the newest Kardashian moniker to emerge on the top 1,000 in the coming years after Kim gave birth to her second child at the end of 2015. While her first daughter's name, **North**, hasn't hit the list yet, we expect it (and the nickname **Nori**) to arrive soon.

POP MUSIC INSPIRING NAMES—AND NOT

Some of the fastest-rising names in popularity are thanks to pop stars...but so too are the fastest fallers. **Zendaya**, the one-named singer and actress, most definitely deserves credit for the rise of her name, which appeared in 2014 and has shot up a whopping 511 spots in the charts to hold the 801 spot this year. **Adele**, an ode to the soulful British singer, skyrocketed 114 spots in 2015 and now sits at 652, and **Camila**, as in Fifth Harmony's Camila Cabello, sits high at the number 43 spot. And One Direction fans are probably to thank for the remarkable rise of **Zayn**, which jumped 189 spots in 2015 to 644, making it the twelfth-fastest riser of the year. Rock fans also probably helped with **Hendrix**, like Jimi, which climbed 301 spots in 2014 and 2015, peaking at 444 this year. But perhaps more notable is the negative effect some pop stars have had on their names' popularity. The biggest faller of recent years was **Miley**, no doubt a nod to Miley Cyrus. The name entered the list in 2007 at 278, peaked in 2009 at 189, but in 2014 sat at 793 and dropped off the top 1,000 in 2015. **Rihanna** also followed suit, peaking at 312 in 2008 and falling off the top 1,000 list in 2014. Now all we can do is wait for the next comeback tour.

THE RISE AND FALL OF MILEY

Year	Rank
2007	278
2008	128
2009	189
2010	218

Year	Rank
2011	316
2012	341
2013	388
2014	793
2015	1,016

DESTINATION NAMES

Ten years ago, naming a child after a location was quite unusual. Now, **Brooklyn** is number 31 on the list for girls! Naming tots after places is a hot idea these days—and it's even a big trend among celebrities. Country singer Eric Church welcomed his second son, **Tennessee**, in 2015. Singer Shakira named her son **Milan**, Rosie O'Donnell named her daughter **Dakota**, country singer Joe Nichols welcomed daughter **Georgia**, and actress Jemima Kirke named her son **Memphis**. Here are some place names on the rise.

Girls' Names	2000 Rank	2015 Rank
Adelaide (Australia)	–	273
Aspen (Colorado)	570	372
Brooklyn (New York)	177	31
Charlotte (North Carolina)	289	9
Georgia	334	230
Holland	–	845
Ireland	–	983
London (England)	828	105
Malaysia	479	438
Milan (Italy)	–	424
Paris (France)	473	263

Ways to Make This Trend Your Own

Options still off the radar: Orleans (New Orleans, Louisiana), Helena (Montana), Geneva (Wisconsin), Juneau (Alaska), Vienna (Austria), Dublin (Ireland), Pristina (Kosovo)

Boys' Names	2000 Rank	2015 Rank
Boston (Massachusetts)	–	607
Jackson (Mississippi)	72	17
Kingston (Jamaica)	–	142
Lincoln (Nebraska)	710	66
London (England)	895	605
Milan (Italy)	–	424
Phoenix (Arizona)	876	307
Santiago (Chile)	359	127

Ways to Make This Trend Your Own

Options still off the radar: Richmond (Virginia), Memphis (Tennessee), Montgomery (Alabama), Wellington (New Zealand), Essex (England), Cairo (Egypt)

GAME OF THRONES REIGNS

Ever met a Daenerys, Cersei, or Tyrion? You might soon! The popular HBO series, *Game of Thrones,* based on the *A Song of Ice and Fire* novels by George R. R. Martin, is a pop culture phenomenon with a legion of loyal fans—and unusual names! The TV show premiered in 2011, and in 2012, the name **Arya**—also the name of one of the series' most popular characters—shot up from number 714 to 412. In 2013, it flew another 134 slots to 278, and in 2015 it landed at 201. Variants of Arya are on the rise too: **Aria** rose from 91 in 2012 to 40 in 2013 to 31 in 2014, and finally to 29 in 2015, and **Ariya** debuted at 918 in 2013 and has risen to 692 in 2015.

While the popular character Margaery Tyrell, with its uncommon spelling, hasn't inspired any namesakes in the top 1,000, the more common spelling, **Marjorie**, debuted at 912 in 2013 and rose to 799 in 2015. The actress who plays Daenerys Targaryen, Emilia Clarke, is another name inspiration. **Emilia** climbed from 164 in 2014 to 145 in 2015, while **Khaleesi** (the fictional royal title given to her character) debuted on the list in 2014 and now holds the 816 rank. But plenty of names from this fantasy world are still off the radar. Try Missandei, Sansa, Ygritte, Catelyn, or Daenerys for girls, or Tyrion, Rickon, Gendry, Bran, Loras, or Theon for boys, and your little one will have a unique—but on-trend!—name.

ANYTHING YOU CAN DO, I CAN DO BETTER

We've already talked about gender-neutral names, but let's just focus on the girls for a moment. Lately, girls have been reclaiming typical boys' names and making them their own, and we don't see this gender-bending trend stopping anytime soon. With celebs like Blake Lively and Ryan Reynolds naming their daughter **James**, and Leighton Meester and Adam Brody and their new little girl **Arlo**, classically masculine names are about to become a huge trend for girls' names. **Ryan**, a typical boys' name, has risen on the girls' list from 642 in 2013 to 474 in 2015, and **Charlie** is following suit, jumping from 959 in 2005 to 207 just ten years later! Even **Sawyer**, which is at 94 on the boys' list, has jumped 84 spots in 2015 to land at 260 on the girls' side. And we're predicting even more typical boys' names like James, Arlo, Austin, Flynn, Quincy, Ira, Lyle, Wylie, Spencer, and August to be hitting the girls' top 1,000 soon.

NAMES FROM THE ANCIENT GREEKS AND ROMANS

When we say these names are old, we're not kidding. They have been around for a long, long time...and while many girls' names are becoming more popular (with some traditional exceptions—**Daphne** and **Helen** are on the slide), the boys' names are surprisingly less popular (and perfect for someone looking for the cutting edge).

Girls' Names	1998 Rank	2015 Rank
Ariadne	–	765
Athena	550	157
Chloe	87	17
Daphne	757	378
Diana	83	295
Freya	–	417
Helen	349	419
Maeve	881	450
Paris	457	263
Phoebe	606	287

Ways to Make This Trend Your Own

Options still off the radar: Artemis, Antigone, Aphrodite, Calliope, Circe, Cleopatra, Echo, Electra, Eurydice, Euterpe, Gaia, Halcyone, Ione, Juno, Lavinia, Medea, Minerva, Persephone, Psyche, Rhea, Selene, Venus

Boys' Names	1998 Rank	2015 Rank
Alexander	22	8
Apollo	–	751
Atlas	–	490
Cassius	–	646
Jason	40	86
Titan	–	640

Ways to Make This Trend Your Own

Options still off the radar: Achilles, Aeneas, Cadmus, Dionysus, Endymion, Hercules, Hermes, Hyperion, Icarus, Janus, Mercury, Midas, Minos, Morpheus, Odysseus, Orpheus, Pegasus, Perseus, Prometheus, Ptolemy, Theseus, Vulcan, Zeus

OUT OF THIS WORLD

It's time to look to the stars, and for once we're not talking about the celebrity variety. Girls' names like **Luna** and **Aurora** are shooting across the top 1,000, and the boys aren't far behind. With **Atlas** debuting at 778 in 2013 and climbing to 490 in 2015, and **Leo** reaching the 91 spot, we're expecting these celestial baby names to be out of this world popular in the coming years. Take a look at some other names rocketing across our lists:

Girls' Names	2012 Rank	2013 Rank	2014 Rank	2015 Rank
Luna	223	183	143	110
Sky	857	882	742	773
Nova	620	529	287	215
Celeste	470	469	466	499
Aurora	166	146	116	79
Stella	62	70	66	51
Selena	304	345	347	321

Ways to Make This Trend Your Own

Options still off the radar: Lyra, Cassiopeia, Venus, Io, Star

Boys' Names	2012 Rank	2013 Rank	2014 Rank	2015 Rank
Atlas	–	778	639	490
Leo	134	112	97	91
Orion	419	396	381	368

Ways to Make This Trend Your Own

Options still off the radar: Aries, Jupiter, Sirius, Oberon, Rocket

NOT YOUR GRANDMA'S NAME

Names like **Mabel**, **Walter**, **Pearl**, and **Henry** might sound like old-fashioned monikers more fit for your grandparents than your kids, but these names—all of which were in the top 100 in 1915—were on the rise in 2015. New parents paying tribute to their greatest generation grandparents are probably the culprit, and also the reason why popular baby boomer names are falling off the charts. Take a look at these "old-fashioned" names (not anymore!) that were popular a century ago and are suddenly climbing again.

Girls' Names	1915 Rank	2015 Rank
Frances	9	514
Lillian	15	26
Eleanor	28	60
Clara	38	98
Elsie	41	386
Pearl	56	628
Mabel	62	578
Stella	64	51
Lena	77	272
Mae	89	589

Ways to Make This Trend Your Own

Options still off the radar: Ida, Minnie, Cecily, Beatrice, Florence

Boys' Names	1915 Rank	2015 Rank
Walter	11	308
Henry	14	29

Boys' Names	1915 Rank	2015 Rank
Arthur	18	292
Vincent	65	109
Clyde	63	804
Theodore	64	99
Charlie	75	229
Leon	82	314
Harvey	95	439
Everett	89	135

Ways to Make This Trend Your Own

Options still off the radar: Chester, Ralph, Albert, Thaddeus

LAST NAMES FIRST

We've already looked at gender-neutral names, and the surname-as-first-name fad is a deeper twist on that. In fact, perhaps due to women naming their children with their maiden names, using last names as first names is one of the biggest trends of the past ten years—especially for boys. One of the more unusual recent celebrity takes on this was actor Scott Porter's son McCoy. Take a look at some of the more popular last-name choices for boys and girls.

Girls' Names	2015 Rank
Avery	16
Riley	35
Kennedy	57
Mackenzie	73
Presley	187
Delaney	243

Girls' Names	2015 Rank
Monroe	716
Collins	704

Ways to Make This Trend Your Own

Options still off the radar: Golden, Sheridan, Easton, Smith, Jones

Boys' Names	2015 Rank
Logan	14
Jackson	17
Carter	24
Hunter	41
Landon	46
Grayson	47
Connor	54
Parker	72
Chase	74
Cooper	77
Easton	78
Carson	89
Bentley	93
Brody	105
Braxton	122
Preston	169
Brooks	232
Cohen	336
Ford	741
Miller	825

Ways to Make This Trend Your Own
Options still off the radar: Albee, Burroughs, Pelham, Wilder, Barnes, Hopper, Callahan

REVERING A LEGEND

Many parents are looking to superstar musicians and actors' last names to find inspiration for their tots. For example, **Lennon** (for John) is on the rise for boys (up 83 spots to 609 in 2015) and landed on the girls' list for the first time in 2013, at 923 and has climbed 413 spots to 510 in 2015, making Lennon basically a gender-neutral name. **Monroe** (for Marilyn) debuted on the girls' list in 2012 and sits at 716 in 2015. **Marley** (in honor of Bob) is a popular choice for girls (218 in 2015), while **Jackson** (for Michael) is a big hit for boys (17 in 2015). **Presley** (for Elvis, of course) hit 187 for girls—though **Elvis** fell off the list entirely in 2012. Even the name **Legend** itself is having a moment—it rose 144 spots to 392 for boys in 2015! Other notable names looking to climb the list: Prince, Judy (Garland), Jimi (Hendrix), Olivier (for Lawrence), Ingrid (Bergman).

RELIGIOUS NAMES

Religious names have become quite a bit more popular in recent years, and the trend is reflected in the different types of religious names that are popular now versus years ago. As a prime example, **Mary** rings in at 124 but **Nevaeh** (heaven backward) settles in at 70. Even though the overall popularity of these names has fallen slightly (and at a similar pace), Nevaeh, the name with a newer or unique take on a classic, remains hotter. Here's a look at some religious names and how they've changed in popularity over the past fifteen years.

Girls' Names	2000 Rank	2015 Rank
Sarah	5	58
Nevaeh	–	70
Genesis	247	65
Trinity	74	130
Mary	46	124
Eden	521	156
Rachel	21	167
Rebecca	39	188
Heaven	340	351
Miracle	524	414
Eve	539	476
Hadassah	–	706

Ways to Make This Trend Your Own

Options still off the radar: Khadija, Dinah, Seraphina

Boys' Names	2000 Rank	2015 Rank
Noah	27	1
Daniel	9	12
Benjamin	26	10
Gabriel	44	22
Joshua	4	33
Isaac	53	31
Isaiah	47	49
Adam	45	73
Jesus	76	128
Abel	352	125

Boys' Names	2000 Rank	2015 Rank
Zion	300	227
Messiah	–	243
Muhammad	621	365
Moses	459	471
Cain	–	743

Ways to Make This Trend Your Own
Options still off the radar: Aasif, Esau, Tabor

FLOWER CHILDREN

Are you a nature lover? Are you planning to make your little one a part of your outdoorsy lifestyle? Perhaps the rise in eco-consciousness should get the credit for the explosion of nature names, especially for girls. Actress Poppy Montgomery, named for a flower herself (as are her sisters Lilly Belle, Rosie Thorn, Daisy Yellow, and Marigold Sun), was right on trend when she named her daughter, born in April 2013, Violet Grace. As was Dallas Cowboys quarterback Tony Romo, who named his newest addition Rivers.

Girls' Names	2011 Rank	2012 Rank	2013 Rank	2014 Rank	2015 Rank
Azalea	–	906	631	527	581
Cataleya	–	479	446	461	434
Hunter	–	–	931	766	786
Iris	303	282	253	245	217
Ivy	267	187	152	146	129
Juniper	953	875	648	490	429
Magnolia	–	–	981	831	633
Meadow	891	949	974	757	677

Girls' Names	2011 Rank	2012 Rank	2013 Rank	2014 Rank	2015 Rank
Oakley	–	–	929	768	611
Rose	291	261	224	194	166
Sky	986	859	882	740	773
Skye	480	447	427	368	385
Violet	101	89	69	67	50
Willow	200	171	155	138	111
Wren	–	–	807	704	712

Ways to Make This Trend Your Own

Options still off the radar: Blossom, Lake, Evergreen, Everest, Poppy, Petunia

Boys' Names	2011 Rank	2012 Rank	2013 Rank	2014 Rank	2015 Rank
River	423	407	372	287	244
Hunter	55	45	36	40	41
Oakley	995	879	769	657	567
Forrest	–	–	841	719	659

Ways to Make This Trend Your Own

Options still off the radar: Ranger, Trail, Trek, Cliff, Scout, Summit

PAIRING SIBLING NAMES

So you've picked the perfect baby name, but now you're stuck with the question—what about the next one? Over the years, choosing sibling names that "go together" has been very on trend, and while the days of sibling names with matching first consonants may feel dated, there are some other surefire tricks to make sure your baby monikers match. The most important factor in creating cohesive sibling names is consistency: consistency in the style, the tradition, and sex of the names you're choosing.

For example, if you're naming your child the more traditional **Christopher**, you may stick on the same straight and narrow for your second born **Mary**. On the other hand, a new baby **Willow** can definitely stand alongside the more unconventional **Saylor**. And what about the gender-neutral names? If you're looking to name a little girl the traditionally male **Riley**, you may want to stick with something equally gender-ambiguous for the second as well, pairing Riley with a name like **Hayden**, instead of going full-feminine with **Isabella**. Keeping the style, sex, and tradition of names consistent will make sure your kids are the perfect pair.

Predictions: Hot Names

Okay, so you've read about the trends. But what other names might be taking off in the near future? Here are some we think could be gaining ground.

GIRLS

Luna

In 2003 the fifth Harry Potter book was published, and with it came the popular girls' name **Luna**, which debuted on the top 1,000 list that same year at number 889. Since then, Luna has climbed up the ranks, moving from 889 in '03, to 324 in '09, to finally land at its peak spot—110 in 2015. Completely on-trend with space-themed names this year, we're predicting Luna to go sky-high in our ranks, especially after celebrity parents Chrissy Teigen and John Legend welcomed their baby Luna Simone in April of 2016.

Briar

Making a strong debut in 2015, **Briar** appeared for the first time in history on the top 1,000! Ranking at 844, it was the 7th fastest rising girl's name, jumping 597 spots from 1,441 this year. With actors Rachel Bilson and Hayden Christensen naming their daughter Briar Rose in 2014, we're expecting this name to continue to climb the trellis in 2017.

Saylor

Looking for a little girl's name that projects strength? Why not hit the high seas with this newest trendsetter—**Saylor**. Debuting on our list at 908 in 2013, Saylor has only risen in the ranks, landing at 799 in 2014 and reaching its peak at 608 in 2015. We're predicting a huge swell in popularity in the coming years, especially on the toes of Kristin Cavallari and Jay Cutler's newest arrival in November 2015, Saylor James.

Aurora

For a name that's been on the top 1,000 since the 1900s, it's incredible that 2015 brought new life to **Aurora**. After hitting its second highest peak in 1929 at 348, Aurora seemed to slip up and down the ranks. That is, until 2004 when Aurora rose past 348 and has been climbing ever since. Rising 37 spots in 2015, Aurora has reached its highest ranking to date, breaking in to the top 100 for the first time at number 79. We think that with Aurora's momentum and lasting power, it's going to be a big name in 2017.

Aurora	
Year	**Rank**
1900	806
1910	522

Aurora	
Year	Rank
1920	398
1930	377
1940	556
1950	568
1960	767
1970	832
1980	792
1990	715
2000	488
2010	203
2015	79

More 2017 Forecasts: Getting Hotter

Simone: With the Summer Olympics having taken place in Rio de Janeiro, Brazil, is the name Simone set to go for gold? U.S. gymnast Simone Biles rose to international fame after her stunning Rio performances in August 2016, winning four Olympic gold medals that set a new American record and sparked a rising fandom. What's more, U.S. swimmer Simone Manuel won two gold and two silver medals in Rio and became the first African American woman to win an individual Olympic gold medal in swimming. But what does that mean for the name **Simone** in coming years? Currently sitting at number 821 on our girls' list, its lowest rank in 15 years, we predict that this unique and powerful name is poised to rise and take the podium in 2017.

Arlo: Gender-neutral names have long enjoyed popularity, but lately parents are giving their little girls names that have long been considered classic boy monikers. Ashton Kutcher and Mila Kunis had little girl **Wyatt**, and Blake Lively and Ryan Reynolds went with the even more masculine **James**. Now, Leighton Meester and Adam Brody have joined the club, naming their little girl **Arlo**. Though it sits at 502 for boys, Arlo has yet to crack the girls' list. However, with a celebrity namesake like the daughter of TV stars Meester and Brody, Arlo is likely to appear on the list in the coming years.

Hazel: When *The Fault in Our Stars* premiered in 2014, we knew that characters Hazel and Augustus were going to have banner years in 2015. However, after reaching its lowest ranking in 1975 at 945, we weren't expecting **Hazel** to climb this high, breaking in to the top 100 for the first time since 1936! Now Hazel sits at number 63 on our list.

Lennox: The male counterpart has now spent its fifth year on the boys' list, and this year **Lennox** appeared on the girls' list for the first time ever as the 10th fastest rising girl's name of the year. Given the popularity of boys' names for girls, and its high 740 debut, we expect to see it pop up more and more in classrooms over the years!

BOYS

Tobias

The 2014 film series *Divergent* (and the bestselling YA books they're based on) might have something to do with the rise of **Tobias**, the name of one of the book's main characters. It's a

powerful name—Tobias is derived from Hebrew and means "the goodness of God," after all—with an adorable nickname to boot. With the name currently at number 316 for boys (it was 419 in 2014), we think the future is bright for Tobias!
Variants: Toby

Prince

With the sudden passing of the pop icon in 2016, we're predicting that **Prince** is going to be a huge name in the coming years, maybe even breaking into the top 100—an unheard of rank for this moniker. Prince has been up and down the charts since the 1900s, but on the heels of the royal names trend, Prince has been seeing a resurgence in the last ten years. Reaching its highest rank since 1903, Prince now sits at 387 in 2015, and we think that number will continue to rise as parents remember the iconic artist.

The Prince of Pop

Year	Rank
1900	510
1910	451
1920	730
1930	823
1940	807
1950	969
1960	980
1970	–
1980	768
1990	916

The Prince of Pop	
2000	891
2010	510
2015	387

Boomer

Super-swimmer father Michael Phelps and fiancée Nicole Johnson welcomed baby Boomer Robert this year, and that's just the kind of star power the name needs to burst onto the top 1,000. **Boomer** is very on trend right now alongside other action names like **Dash** and **Blaze**, which have both reached new peaks, 766 and 706, in 2015. As the years go on, we're predicting big things for baby Boomers.

Killian

Since its brief stint from 1995 to 1998, **Killian** had disappeared from the top 1,000 names, only to come back in a big way. Reemerging at 836 in 2007, Killian has skyrocketed up the charts, jumping from 767 in 2013, to 348 in 2015. One of the fastest risers of 2015, this increase is partly due to the huge popularity of ABC's hit show *Once Upon a Time,* and the character Killian Jones, Captain Hook's alter-ego—who also stars as the hunky hero of the show.

More 2017 Forecasts: Getting Hotter

Tennessee: With the destination trend going strong—especially city and state names from down south—it's no surprise country crooner Eric Church and his wife Katherine named their second son, born in 2015, Tennessee Hawkins. With **Tennessee** on the pop culture radar, we're expecting it to make its debut appearance on the top 1,000 in the future.

Kyrie: With the popularity of NBA baller Kyrie Irving, who was drafted by the Cleveland Cavaliers in 2011, we've seen a huge rise in **Kyrie** on our list in recent years. Debuting at 836 in 2007, Kyrie got a jolt in 2014, jumping all the way to 511. At 348 in 2015 and with the Cavaliers winning the NBA championship in 2016, we're expecting this name to continue to make huge strides on our list.

Silas: Growing from 602 in 2000 to 129 in 2015, **Silas** is one of our steady risers on the list, and next year we're predicting that this name will break on to the top 100—especially with celebrity endorsers Justin Timberlake and Jessica Biel, who welcomed their son Silas Randall in April 2015.

Hidden Climbers

These names aren't necessarily the biggest jumpers in popularity, and we've mentioned some of them already, but we wanted to bring them to your attention because they have steadily climbed the charts over the past few years. Look for them to gain even more ground in 2017.

Girls

Adalyn
Adelaide
Adeline
Amira
Aria
Ayla
Blair
Brinley
Catalina
Cecilia
Clara
Cora
Dallas
Daniella
Elena
Eliana
Eloise
Emerson
Emery
Everly
Georgia
Harlow
Hazel
Isla
Ivy
Jane
Josephine
June
Kinsley
Laurel
Leona
Lilith
Luna
Mabel
Margaret
Millie
Nia
Norah
Piper
Quinn
Ryan
Saylor
Tessa
Vera
Willow
Ximena

Hidden Climbers

Boys

Adriel
Ali
Amir
Archer
Atlas
Axel
Beckett
Benson
Calvin
Daxton
Elias
Emmanuel
Enzo
Everett
Ezekiel
Ezra
Finnegan
Gideon
Griffin
Hank
Hayes
Iker
Jasper
Jayce
Jeremiah
Kai
Karter
Kian
Knox
Luca
Maddox
Malcolm
Mateo
Maximus
Milo
Nash
Parker
Remy
Rowan
Samson
Sawyer
Theodore
Wade
Wesley
Weston
Zeke

Predictions: The Coldest Baby Names

We think these names are over with a capital O. In some cases, they became really hot really fast, and now they're oh so out of style. Others are surprisingly low in popularity considering their perceived "commonality." Perhaps you may want to consider some of these options if you want your baby to stand out in a crowd. See if you agree.

BOYS

Channing: Just a few years ago we were celebrating the rise of actor Channing Tatum and his trendy name, but after debuting at 645 in 2010 and peaking at 514 in 2012, we think its time has passed. In 2015, Channing landed at 784.

Neymar: Even the soccer superstar can't save this falling name. It arrived on the list in 2012 at number 702 and quickly peaked in 2014 at 550. In 2015, Neymar was the third fastest falling name on the boys' list, kicking around at 790.

Kale: At 990 in 2000, Kale steadily rose during the health food craze, peaking in 2008 at 504. Six years later, Kale had declined to 969 in 2014 before finally falling off the list in 2015, sitting below the top 1,000 at 1,100.

Chevy: The US car brand had only a brief stint on the top 1,000 boys' list, debuting in 2014 at 903 before sinking to 982 in 2015. We wouldn't be surprised to see this name drive right off the list in the next year.

GIRLS

Isis: Not surprisingly, this name—which was at 535 in 2013, dropped to 706 only a year later and completely left the top 1,000 in 2015. Considering its current political association, we'd be surprised to see Isis make the list in the coming years.

Denise: How very '90s. This name—which gained popularity in the late '80s and stayed relevant (thank you, Denise Richards) throughout the '90s and early 2000s—plummeted from 778 in 2014 to 991 in 2015. Just nine years ago, it was 298.

Elsa: Names that rise quickly seem to fall just as fast. Elsa, at 527 in 2013, rose to 286 a year later, due to the huge popularity of Disney's *Frozen*. But it looks like it's time to "let it go"—in 2015, the name was back down to 487 and was the 15th fastest faller for girls.

Anabelle: Anabelle, and its many spelling variations, make up four of the top ten fastest falling girls' names in 2015, with Annabell and Anabel plummeting 500 spots, Anabella 333, and Anabelle 272. It seems that the only spelling variation with lasting power is Annabelle, which still holds the 92 spot. Overall though, we're predicting a drop in all things Anabelle.

Catching Z's

The latest fashion in baby naming might be throwing in one of the least common letters: Z. Sure there are some common cases—like **Zachary**, but the rising stars of this trend are more unexpected—think **Zeke** for boys, **Zendaya** for girls. We love the nod to the end of the alphabet!

Girls' Name	2015 Rank
Aliza	675
Aranza	931
Azalea	581
Azaria	938
Azariah	849
Eliza	175
Elizabeth	13

Boys' Name	2015 Rank
Alexzander	808
Alonzo	526
Azariah	699
Blaze	706
Eliezer	870
Enzo	330
Ezekiel	148

Girls' Name	2015 Rank
Hazel	63
Itzel	492
Izabella	234
Jazlyn	503
Jazlynn	770
Jazmin	431
Jazmine	449
Kenzie	277
Lizbeth	832
Mackenzie	73
Makenzie	210
Mckenzie	151
Yaretzi	400
Yaritza	937
Zahra	690
Zainab	941
Zaniyah	826
Zara	402
Zaria	872
Zariah	506
Zariyah	745
Zendaya	801
Zion	899
Zoe	33
Zoie	764
Zoey	23
Zuri	443

Boys' Name	2015 Rank
Ezequiel	573
Ezra	92
Hamza	615
Hezekiah	678
Izaiah	535
Joziah	753
Lorenzo	216
Vincenzo	815
Xzavier	729
Zachariah	422
Zachary	88
Zackary	750
Zaid	888
Zaiden	372
Zaire	873
Zander	249
Zane	233
Zavier	864
Zayden	193
Zayn	644

Celebrity-Inspired Names on the Rise

Isla (Fisher): Debuted in 2008 at 622, now at 141.
Harrison (Ford): Was 241 in 2009, now at 119.
Kellan (Lutz): Debuted in 2007 at 883, now at 398.
Blake (Lively): Debuted in 2011 and now sits at 423 on the girls' list.
Harlow (Jean): Debuted in 2009 at 901, now ranks 422.
Leighton (Meester): Sits at 859 on the boys' side.
Joaquin (Phoenix):Was at 563 in 2000, now at 321.
Piper (Perabo): Debuted in 2000 at 509, now at 68.
Hugh (Jackman): Was at 991 in 2009, now sits at 849.

Recent Celebrity Babies

Here's a quick overview of what the celebustork has dropped off.

Alayna Madaleine (Kerri Strug and Robert Fischer)
Alexandra Kalliope (Debbie Matenopoulos and Jon Falcone)
Aman Tyler (Gelila Bekele and Tyler Perry)
Amélie Moon (Sandra Cho Durand and Kevin Durand)
Anders Reyn (Angela and Alfonso Ribeiro)
Arlo Day (Leighton Meester and Adam Brody)
Art (Dawn O'Porter and Chris O'Dowd)
Augustus Juppiter (Chloe Mendel and Billy Corgan)
Ava Grace (Stacy Keibler and Jared Pobre)
Avri Roel (Susan and Robert Downey Jr.)
Blues Anthony (Jessica Paré and John Kastner)
Bodhi Ryan (Noureen DeWulf and Ryan Miller)
Boomer Robert (Nicole Johnson and Michael Phelps)
Bosley Jo (Bill Horn and Scout Masterson)
Bowie Ezio (Zoe Saldana and Marco Perego)
Brexton Locke (Samantha and Kyle Busch)
Briar Rose (Rachel Bilson and Hayden Christensen)
Brooklyn Elisabeth (Vanessa and Nick Lachey)

Cadence Gaelle (Eudoxie Mbouguiyengue and Ludacris)
Calder Allan William (Meghan Mikkelson and Scott Reid)
Carey (Julia Carey and James Corden)
Caroline Olivia (Abby and Eli Manning)
Cash Van (Kelli Cashiola and Dave Haywood)
Chanel Nicole (Coco Austin and Ice-T)
Charlie Ocean (Emilie Livingston and Jeff Goldblum)
Chosen Sebastian (Kia Proctor and Cam Newton)
Christopher Carlton (Sophie Hunter and Benedict Cumberbatch)
Coco (Terri Seymour and Clark Mallon)
Conrad (Elspeth Keller and Reid Scott)
Cooper Blue (Dylan Lauren and Paul Arrouet)
Cy Aridio (Zoe Saldana and Marco Perego)
Daenerys Josephine (Gina Glocksen and Joe Ruzicka)
Dashiel Edon (Milla Jovovich and Paul W. S. Anderson)
Dashiell Julius William (Michelle Clunie and Bryan Singer)
Declan (Elisa Yao and Patrick Stump)
Della Rose (Alexis and Billy Joel)
Delta Bell (Kristen Bell and Dax Shepard)
Edie (Keira Knightley and James Righton)
Edith Vivian Patricia (Cate Blanchett and Andrew Upton)
Elizabella Dylan (Alyssa Milano and David Bugliari)
Elsie Otter (Zooey Deschanel and Jacob Pechenik)
Esmeralda Amada (Eva Mendes and Ryan Gosling)
Ever Belle (Gigi Yallouz and Owain Yeoman)
Florence May (Candice Accola and Joe King)
Ford (David Miller and Ryan Murphy)
Fordham Rhys (Ashley Hebert and J. P. Rosenbaum)
Frances Cole (Nancy Juvonen and Jimmy Fallon)
Genesis Ali (Alicia Keys and Swizz Beatz)
Gus Monroe (Poppy Montgomery and Shawn Sanford)
Gus Williams (Ashley Williams and Neal Dodson)

Hank (Brooklyn Decker and Andy Roddick)
Hannah Mali Rose (Sarah Drew and Peter Lanfer)
Harlow Monroe (Kimberly Caldwell and Jordan Harvey)
Harper (Elizabeth Chambers and Armie Hammer)
Henry Peet Friedman (Amanda Peet and David Benioff)
Holland Marysia Walker (Courtney Hansen and Jay Hartington)
Holt Fisher (Tiffani Thiessen and Brady Smith)
Hutton Michael (Beverly Mitchell and Michael Cameron)
Ilya Vue (Ashley Scott and Steve Hart)
Indigo (Alexandra Baretto and Rider Strong)
Ioni James (Coco Rocha and James Conran)
Isaiah Michael (Carrie Underwood and Mike Fisher)
Isley Ray (Jill Latiano and Glenn Howerton)
Jack Lion (Amy Lee and Josh Hartzler)
Jagger Snow (Ashlee Simpson and Evan Ross)
James (Blake Lively and Ryan Reynolds)
Jasmine (Lauren Hashian and Dwayne Johnson)
Jax Bracy (Renee Oteri and Bracy Maynard)
Jolie Rae (Jana Kramer and Michael Caussin)
Jonathan Rosebanks (Anne Hathaway and Adam Shulman)
Josey Hollis (Naya Rivera and Ryan Dorsey)
Kane Alexander (Meghan McDermott and Theo Rossi)
Kaya Evdokia (Hayden Panettiere and Wladimir Klitschko)
Kellen William (Kelly Stables and Kurt Patino)
Kenric Justin (Sonequa Martin-Green and Kenric Green)
Kingsley Rainbow (Dylan Lauren and Paul Arrouet)
Kinzee Cruz (Heidi Lowe and James Durbin)
Knox Blue (Sarah Shahi and Steve Howey)
Konrad (Marika Dominczyk and Scott Foley)
Lachlyn Hope (Catriona McGinn and Mark-Paul Gosselaar)
Larkin Zouey (Mireille Enos and Alan Ruck)
Leo Thames (Jaime King and Kyle Newman)

London Rose (Siri Pinter and Carson Daly)
Luna Mae (Leonor Varela and Lucas Akoskin)
Luna Simone Stephens (Chrissy Teigen and John Legend)
Matteo Oliver (Felicity Blunt and Stanley Tucci)
McCoy Lee (Kelsey Mayfield and Scott Porter)
Montgomery Moses Brian (Isla Fisher and Sacha Baron Cohen)
Myllena Mae (Doutzen Kroes and Sunnery James)
Nash Skan (Morgan Beck and Bode Miller)
Olive Mae (Marla Sokoloff and Alec Puro)
Ophelia Saint (Jordyn Blum and Dave Grohl)
Owen Bartlett (Heather Morris and Taylor Hubbell)
Paulina Kathleen (Kelly and Mike Myers)
Pauline (Paloma Jimenez and Vin Diesel)
Phoenix Sky (A.J. Cook and Nathan Anderson)
Poppy (Nate Berkus and Jeremiah Brent)
Qirin Love (Miranda and Terrence Howard)
Quinn Lily (Jenna Wolfe and Stephanie Gosk)
Rafael Thomas (Hilaria and Alec Baldwin)
Reign Aston (Kourtney Kardashian and Scott Disick)
Remington Alexander (Kelly Clarkson and Brandon Blackstock)
Rhodes Emilio (Sara Gilbert and Linda Perry)
Ripley Dorothy (Robyn Lawley and Everest Schmidt)
Rocket Zot (Lara Bingle and Sam Worthington)
Rose Dorothy (Scarlett Johansson and Romain Dauriac)
Ryan Ava Erhard (Haylie Duff and Matt Rosenberg)
Ryan Carson (Ayesha and Steph Curry)
Rylen Judith (Brittany and Drew Brees)
Sailor Gene (Liv Tyler and David Garner)
Saint (Kim Kardashian and Kanye West)
Saint Lazslo (Meagan Camper and Pete Wentz)
Samuel Hawke (Jennifer and Josh Turner)
Sasha (Shakira and Gerard Piqué)

Saylor James (Kristin Cavallari and Jay Cutler)
Scarlett May (Molly Sims and Scott Stuber)
Sebastian Lopeti (Agnes Bruckner and Alefaio Brewer)
Sidney Aoibheann (Vanessa Carlton and John McCauley)
Sienna May (Ellen Pompeo and Chris Ivery)
Silas Randall (Jessica Biel and Justin Timberlake)
Simcha "Simi" (Randi Zuckerberg and Brent Tworetzky)
Sistine Sabella (Steffiana de la Cruz and Kevin James)
Stefan (Jelena and Novak Djokovic)
Stella June (Holly Williams and Chris Coleman)
Story (Soleil Moon Frye and Jason Goldberg)
Summer Rain (Christina Aguilera and Matt Rutler)
Tatum (Paulina Gretzky and Dustin Johnson)
Tennessee Hawkins (Katherine and Eric Church)
Theodore Vigo Sullivan (Rachael Leigh Cook and Daniel Gillies)
Titan Jewell (Kelly Rowland and Tim Witherspoon)
Tobias (Bethany Hamilton and Adam Dirks)
Vale Guthrie (Savannah Guthrie and Michael Feldman)
Vera Audrey (Emilie de Ravin and Eric Bilitch)
Victoria Isabella (Leyicet and Danny Gokey)
Viola Philomena (Megan Hilty and Brian Gallagher)
Violet Moon (Sarah Shahi and Steve Howey)
Vivienne Margaret (Ali Larter and Hayes MacArthur)
Wilder (Jocelyn Towne and Simon Helberg)
Wilder Frances (CaCee Cobb and Donald Faison)
Wolfe (Kimora Lee Simmons and Tim Leissner)
Wyatt Isabelle (Mila Kunis and Ashton Kutcher)
York (Tyra Banks and Erik Asla)
Zephyr Emerson (Alexandra and Sean Parker)
Zhuri Nova (Savannah and LeBron James)

⋆ — *All names with a ⋆ in the text denote Top 100 Names of 2015.*

^ — *All names with a ^ in the text denote hot names rising in popularity in 2015.*

Aadi (Hindi) Child of the beginning
Aadie, Aady, Aadey, Aadee, Aadea, Aadeah, Aadye

★**Aaliyah** (Arabic) An ascender, one having the highest social standing
Aaleyah, Aaliya, Aliyah, Alliyah, Alieya, Aliyiah, Alliyia, Aleeya, Alee, Aleiya, Alia, Aleah, Alea, Aliya

Aaralyn (American) Woman with song
Aaralynn, Aaralin, Aaralinn, Aaralinne, Aralyn, Aralynn

Aba (African) Born on a Thursday
Abah, Abba, Abbah

Abarrane (Hebrew) Feminine form of Abraham; mother of a multitude; mother of nations
Abarrayne, Abarraine, Abarane, Abarayne, Abaraine, Abame, Abrahana

Abena (African) Born on a Tuesday
Abenah, Abeena, Abyna, Abina, Abeenah, Abynah, Abinah

Abiela (Hebrew) My father is Lord
Abielah, Abiella, Abiellah, Abyela, Abyelah, Abyella, Abyellah

★**Abigail** (Hebrew) The source of a father's joy
Abagail, Abbigail, Abigael, Abigale, Abbygail, Abygail, Abygayle, Abbygayle, Abbegale, Abby, Abbagail, Abbey, Abbie, Abbi, Abigayle

Abijah (Hebrew) My father is Lord
Abija, Abisha, Abishah, Abiah, Abia, Aviah, Avia

Abila (Spanish) One who is beautiful
Abilah, Abyla, Abylah

Abilene (American / Hebrew) From a town in Texas / resembling grass
Abalene, Abalina, Abilena, Abiline, Abileene, Abileen, Abileena, Abilyn

Abir (Arabic) Having a fragrant scent
Abeer, Abyr, Abire, Abeere, Abbir, Abhir

Abira (Hebrew) A source of strength; one who is strong
Abera, Abyra, Abyrah, Abirah, Abbira, Abeerah

Abra (Hebrew / Arabic) Feminine form of Abraham; mother of a multitude; mother of nations / lesson; example
Abri, Abrah, Abree, Abria, Abbra, Abrah, Abbrah

Abril (Spanish / Portuguese) Form of April, meaning opening buds of spring

Academia (Latin) From a community of higher learning
Akademia, Academiah, Akademiah

Acantha (Greek) Thorny; in mythology, a nymph who was loved by Apollo
Akantha, Ackantha, Acanthah, Akanthah, Ackanthah

Accalia (Latin) In mythology, the foster mother of Romulus and Remus
Accaliah, Acalia, Accalya, Acalya, Acca, Ackaliah, Ackalia

Adah (Hebrew) Ornament; beautiful addition to the family
Adda, Adaya, Ada

Adanna (African) Her father's daughter; a father's pride
Adana, Adanah, Adannah, Adanya, Adanyah

Adanne (African) Her mother's daughter; a mother's pride
Adane, Adayne, Adaine, Adayn, Adain, Adaen, Adaene

Adara (Greek / Arabic) Beautiful girl / chaste one; virgin
Adair, Adare, Adaire, Adayre, Adarah, Adarra, Adaora, Adar

Addin (Hebrew) One who is adorned; voluptuous
Addine, Addyn, Addyne

***Addison** (English) Daughter of Adam
Addeson, Addyson, Adison, Adisson, Addisyn, Adyson

Adeen (Irish) Little fire shining brightly
Adeene, Adean, Adeane, Adein, Adeine, Adeyn, Adeyne

Adela (German) Of the nobility; serene; of good humor
Adele, Adelia, Adella, Adelle, Adelie, Adelina, Adali

^**Adelaide** (German) Of the nobility; serene; of good humor
Adelaid

^**Adeline** (German) Form of Adela, meaning of the nobility
Adalyn, ***Adalynn****, Adelyn, Adelynn*

Adianca (Native American) One who brings peace
Adianka, Adyanca, Adyanka

Adira (Hebrew / Arabic) Powerful, noble woman / having great strength
Adirah, Adeera, Adyra, Adeerah, Adyrah, Adeira, Adeirah, Adiera

Admina (Hebrew) Daughter of the red earth
Adminah, Admeena, Admyna, Admeenah, Admynah, Admeina

Adoración (Spanish) Having the adoration of all

Adra (Arabic) One who is chaste; a virgin

Adriana (Greek) Feminine form of Adrian; from the Adriatic Sea region; woman with dark features
Adria, Adriah, Adrea, Adreana, Adreanna, Adrienna, Adriane, Adriene, Adrie, Adrienne, Adrianna, Adrianne, Adriel

Adrina (Italian) Having great happiness
Adrinna, Adreena, Adrinah, Adryna, Adreenah, Adrynah

Aegea (Latin / Greek) From the Aegean Sea / in mythology, a daughter of the sun who was known for her beauty

Aegina (Greek) In mythology, a sea nymph
Aeginae, Aegyna, Aegynah

Aelwen (Welsh) Woman with a fair brow
Aelwenn, Aelwenne, Aelwin, Aelwinn, Aelwinne, Aelwyn, Aelwynn, Aelwynne

Aerwyna (English) A friend of the ocean

Afra (Hebrew / Arabic) Young doe / white; an earth color
Affra, Affrah, Afrah, Afrya, Afryah, Afria, Affery, Affrie

Afrodille (French) Daffodil; showy and vivid
Afrodill, Afrodil, Afrodile, Afrodilla, Afrodila

Afton (English) From the Afton river

Agave (Greek) In mythology, a queen of Thebes

Agnes (Greek) One who is pure; chaste
Agneis, Agnese, Agness, Agnies, Agnus, Agna, Agne, Agnesa, Nessa, Oona

Agraciana (Spanish) One who forgives
Agracianna, Agracyanna, Agracyana, Agraciann, Agraciane, Agracyann, Agracyane, Agracianne

Agrona (Celtic) In mythology, the goddess of war and death
Agronna, Agronia, Agrone

Ahelia (Hebrew) Breath; a source of life
Ahelie, Ahelya, Aheli, Ahelee, Aheleigh, Ahelea, Aheleah, Ahely

Ahellona (Greek) Woman who has masculine qualities
Ahelona, Ahellonna, Ahelonna

Ahinoam (Hebrew) In the Bible, one of David's wives

Ahuva (Hebrew) One who is dearly loved
Ahuvah, Ahuda, Ahudah

Aida (English / French / Arabic) One who is wealthy; prosperous / one who is helpful / a returning visitor
Ayda, Aydah, Aidah, Aidee, Aidia, Aieeda, Aaida

Aidan (Gaelic) One who is fiery; little fire
Aiden, Adeen, Aden, Aideen, Adan, Aithne, Aithnea, Ajthne

Aiko (Japanese) Little one who is dearly loved

Ailbhe (Irish) Of noble character; one who is bright

Aileen (Irish / Scottish) Light bearer / from the green meadow
Ailean, Ailein, Ailene, Ailin, Aillen, Ailyn, Alean, Aleane

Ailis (Irish) One who is noble and kind
Ailish, Ailyse, Ailesh, Ailisa, Ailise

Ailna (German) One who is sweet and pleasant; of the nobility
Ailne

Ain (Irish / Arabic) In mythology, a woman who wrote laws to protect the rights of women / precious eye

Aine (Celtic) One who brings brightness and joy

Aingeal (Irish) Heaven's messenger; angel
Aingealag

Ainsley (Scottish) One's own meadow
Ainslie, Ainslee, Ainsly, Ainslei, Aynslie, Aynslee, Aynslie, Ansley

Aionia (Greek) Everlasting life
Aioniah, Aionea, Aioneah, Ayonia, Ayoniah, Ayonea, Ayoneah

Airic (Celtic) One who is pleasant and agreeable
Airick, Airik, Aeric, Aerick, Aerik

Aisha (Arabic / African) lively / womanly
Aiesha, Ayisha, Myisha

Aisling (Irish) A dream or vision; an inspiration
Aislin, Ayslin, Ayslinn, Ayslyn, Ayslynn, Aislyn, Aisylnn, Aislinn, Isleen

Aitheria (Greek) Of the wind
Aitheriah, Aitherea, Aithereah, Aytheria, Aytheriah, Aytherea, Aythereah

Ajaya (Hindi) One who is invincible; having the power of a god
Ajay

Aka (Maori / Turkish) Affectionate one / in mythology, a mother goddess
Akah, Akka, Akkah

Akili (Tanzanian) Having great wisdom
Akilea, Akilee, Akilie, Akylee, Akylie, Akyli, Akileah

Akilina (Latin) Resembling an eagle
Akilinah, Akileena, Akilyna, Akilinna, Ackilina, Acilina, Akylina, Akylyna

Akira (Scottish) One who acts as an anchor
Akera, Akerra, Akiera, Akirah, Akiria, Akyra, Akirrah, Akeri, Akeira, Akeara

Aksana (Russian) Form of Oksana, meaning "hospitality"
Aksanna, Aksanah, Aksannah

Alaia (Arabic / Basque) One who is majestic, of high worth joy
Alaya, Alayah, Alaiah

Alaina (French) Beautiful and fair woman; dear child
Alayna, Alaine, Alayne, Alainah, Alana, Alanah, Alanna, Alannah, Alanis, Alyn, Alani, Alanni, Alaney; Alanney; Alanie

Alair (French) One who has a cheerful disposition
Alaire, Allaire, Allair, Aulaire, Alayr, Alayre, Alaer

Alanza (Spanish) Feminine form of Alonzo; noble and ready for battle

Alarice (German) Feminine form of Alaric; ruler of all
Alarise, Allaryce, Alarica, Alarisa, Alaricia, Alrica

Alcina (Greek) One who is strong-willed and opinionated
Alceena, Alcyna, Alsina, Alsyna, Alzina, Alcine, Alcinia, Alcyne

Alda (German / Spanish) Long-lived, old / wise; an elder
Aldah, Aldine, Aldina, Aldinah, Aldene, Aldona

Aldis (English) From the ancient house
Aldys, Aldiss, Aldisse, Aldyss, Aldysse

Aldonsa (Spanish) One who is kind and gracious
Aldonza, Aldonsia, Aldonzia

Aleah (Arabic) Exalted
Alea, Alia, Aliah, Aliana, Aleana

Aleen (Celtic) Form of Helen, meaning "the shining light"
Aleena, Aleenia, Alene, Alyne, Alena, Alenka, Alynah, Aleine

Alegria (Spanish) One who is cheerful and brings happiness to others
Alegra, Aleggra, Allegra, Alleffra, Allecra

Alera (Latin) Resembling an eagle
Alerra, Aleria, Alerya, Alerah, Alerrah

Alethea (Greek) One who is truthful
Altheia, Lathea, Lathey, Olethea

⋆**Alexa** (Greek) Form of Alexandra, meaning "helper and defender of mankind"
Aleka, Alexia

^⋆**Alexandra** (Greek) Feminine form of Alexander; a helper and defender of mankind
Alexandria, Alexandrea, Alixandra, ***Alessandra****,* ***Alexis****, Alondra, Aleksandra, Alejandra, Sandra, Sandrine, Sasha*

⋆**Alexis** (Greek) Form of Alexandra, meaning "helper and defender of mankind"
Alexus, Alexys, Alexia

Ali (English) Form of Allison or Alice, meaning "woman of the nobility"
Allie, Alie, Alli, Ally

Aliana (English) Form of Eliana, meaning "the Lord answers our prayers"
Alianna

^⋆**Alice** (German) Woman of the nobility; truthful; having high moral character
Ally, Allie, Alyce, Alesia, Aleece

Alicia (Spanish) Form of Alice, meaning "woman of the nobility"
Alecia, Aleecia, Aliza, Aleesha, Alesha, Alisha, Alisa

Alika (Hawaiian) One who is honest
Alicka, Alicca, Alyka, Alycka, Alycca

Alina (Arabic / Polish) One who is noble / one who is beautiful and bright
Aline, Aleena, Alena, Alyna

Alivia (Spanish) Form of Olivia, meaning of the olive tree

*****Allison** (English) Form of Alice, meaning "woman of the nobility, truthful; having high moral character"
Alisanne, Alison, Alicen, Alisen, Alisyn, Allyson, Alyson, Allisson

Alma (Latin / Italian) One who is nurturing and kind / refers to the soul
Almah

Almira (English) A princess; daughter born to royalty
Almeera, Almeira, Almiera, Almyra, Almirah, Almeerah, Almeirah

Aloma (Spanish) Form of Paloma, meaning "dove-like"
Alomah, Alomma, Alommah

Alondra (Spanish) Form of Alexandra, meaning "helper and defender of mankind"

Alpha (Greek) The firstborn child; the first letter of the Greek alphabet

Alphonsine (French) Feminine form of Alphonse; one who is ready for battle
Alphonsina, Alphonsyne, Alphonsyna, Alphonseene, Alphonseena, Alphonseane, Alphonseana, Alphonsiene

Alura (English) A divine counselor
Allura, Alurea, Alhraed

Alvera (Spanish) Feminine of Alvaro; guardian of all; speaker of the truth
Alveria, Alvara, Alverna, Alvernia, Alvira, Alvyra, Alvarita, Alverra

*****Alyssa** (German) Form of Alice, meaning "woman of the nobility, truthful; having high moral character"
Alisa, Alissya, Alyssaya, Alishya, Alisia, Alissa, Allisa, Allyssa, Alysa, Alysse, Alyssia

Amada (Spanish) One who is loved by all
Amadia, Amadea, Amadita, Amadah

Amadea (Latin) Feminine form of Amedeo; loved by God
Amadya, Amadia, Amadine, Amadina, Amadika, Amadis

Amadi (African) One who rejoices
Amadie, Amady, Amadey, Amadye, Amadee, Amadea, Amadeah

Amalia (German) One who is industrious and hardworking
***Amelia**, Amalya, Amalie, Amalea, Amylia, Amyleah, Amilia, Neneca*

Amalthea (Greek) One who soothes; in mythology, the foster mother of Zeus
Amaltheah, Amalthia, Amalthya

Amanda (Latin) One who is much loved
Amandi, Amandah, Amandea, Amandee, Amandey, Amande, Amandie, Amandy, Mandy

Amani (African / Arabic) One who is peaceful / one with wishes and dreams
Amanie, Amany, Amaney, Amanee, Amanye, Amanea, Amaneah

Amara (Greek) One who will be forever beautiful
Amarah, Amarya, Amaira, Amaria, Amar

Amari (African) Having great strength, a builder
Amaree, Amarie

Amaya (Japanese) Of the night rain
Amayah, Amaia, Amaiah

Amber (French) Resembling the jewel; a warm honey color
Ambur, Ambar, Amberly, Amberlyn, Amberli, Amberlee, Ambyr, Ambyre

Ambrosia (Greek) Immortal; in mythology, the food of the gods
Ambrosa, Ambrosiah, Ambrosyna, Ambrosina, Ambrosyn, Ambrosine, Ambrozin, Ambrozyn, Ambrozyna, Ambrozyne, Ambrozine, Ambrose, Ambrotosa, Ambruslne, Amhrosine

***Amelia** (German) Form of Amalia or (Latin) form of Emily, meaning "one who is industrious and hardworking"
Amelie, Amelita, Amylia, Amely

America (Latin) A powerful ruler
Americus, Amerika, Amerikus

^**Amina** (Arabic) A princess, one who commands; truthful, trustworthy
Amirah, Ameera, Amyra, Ameerah, Amyrah, Ameira, Ameirah, Amiera

Amissa (Hebrew) One who is honest; a friend
Amisa, Amise, Amisia, Amiza, Amysa, Amysia, Amysya, Amyza

Amiyah (American) Form of Amy, meaning "beloved"
Amiah, Amiya, Amya

Amrita (Hindi) Having immortality; full of ambrosia
Amritah, Amritta, Amryta, Amrytta, Amrytte, Amritte, Amryte, Amreeta

Amser (Welsh) A period of time

Amy (Latin) Dearly loved
Aimee, Aimie, Aimi, Aimy, Aimya, Aimey, Amice, Amicia

Anaba (Native American) A woman returning from battle
Anabah, Annaba, Annabah

Anabal (Gaelic) One who is joyful
Anaball, Annabal, Annaball

Anahi (Latin) Immortal

Analia (Spanish) Combination of Ana and Lea or Lucia
Annalee, Annali, Annalie, Annaleigh, Annalea, Analeigh, Anali, Analie, Annalina, Anneli, Annaleah, Annaliese, Annalise, Annalisa, Analise, Analiese, Analisa

Anarosa (Spanish) A graceful rose
Annarosa, Anarose, Annarose

Anastasia (Greek) One who shall rise again
Anastase, Anastascia, Anastasha, Anastasie, Stacia, Stasia, Stacy, Stacey

Ancina (Latin) Form of Ann, meaning "a woman graced with God's favor"
Ancyna, Anncina, Anncyna, Anceina, Annceina, Anciena, Annciena, Anceena

Andrea (Greek / Latin) Courageous and strong / feminine form of Andrew; womanly
Andria, Andrianna, Andreia, Andreina, Andreya, Andriana, Andreana, Andera

Angel (Greek) A heavenly messenger

^**Angela** (Greek) A heavenly messenger; an angel
*Angelica, **Angelina**, **Angelique**, Anjela, Anjelika, Angella, Angelita, Angeline, Angie, Angy*

Angelina (Greek) Form of Angela, meaning "a heavenly messenger, an angel"
Angeline, Angelyn, Angelene, Angelin

Ani (Hawaiian) One who is very beautiful
Aneesa, Aney, Anie, Any, Aany, Aanye, Anea, Aneah

Aniceta (French) One who is unconquerable
Anicetta, Anniceta, Annicetta

Aniya (American) Form of Anna, meaning "a woman graced with God's favor"
Aniyah, Anaya

⋆**Anna** (Latin) A woman graced with God's favor
Annah, Ana, Ann, Anne, Anya, Ane, Annika, Anouche, Annchen, Ancina, Annie, Anika

^**Annabel** (Italian) Graceful and beautiful woman
***Annabelle**, Annabell, **Annabella**, Annabele, Anabel, Anabell, Anabelle, Anabella*

Annabeth (English) Graced with God's bounty
Anabeth, Annabethe, Annebeth, Anebeth, Anabethe

Annalynn (English) From the graceful lake
Analynn, Annalyn, Annaline, Annalin, Annalinn, Analyn, Analine, Analin

Annmarie (English) Filled with bitter grace
Annemarie, Annmaria, Annemaria, Annamarie, Annamaria, Anamarie, Anamaria, Anamari

Annora (Latin) Having great honor
Anora, Annorah, Anorah, Anoria, Annore, Annorya, Anorya, Annoria

Anouhea (Hawaiian) Having a soft, cool fragrance

Ansley (English) From the noble's pastureland
Ansly, Anslie, Ansli, Anslee, Ansleigh, Anslea, Ansleah, Anslye, Ainsley

Antalya (Russian) Born with the morning's first light
Antaliya, Antalyah, Antaliyah, Antalia, Antaliah

Antea (Greek) In mythology, a woman who was scorned and committed suicide
Anteia, Anteah

Antje (German) A graceful woman

Antoinette (French) Praiseworthy
Toinette

Anwen (Welsh) A famed beauty
Anwin, Anwenne, Anwinne, Anwyn, Anwynn, Anwynne, Anwenn, Anwinn

Anya (Russian) Form of Anna, meaning "a woman graced with God's favor"

Aphrah (Hebrew) From the house of dust
Aphra

Aphrodite (Greek) Love; in mythology, the goddess of love and beauty
Afrodite, Afrodita, Aphrodita, Aphrodyte, Aphhrodyta, Aphrodytah

Aponi (Native American) Resembling a butterfly
Aponni, Apponni, Apponi

Apphia (Hebrew) One who is productive
Apphiah

Apple (American) Sweet fruit; one who is cherished
Appel, Aple, Apel

April (English) Opening buds of spring, born in the month of April
Avril, Averel, Averill, Avrill, Apryl, Apryle, Aprylle, Aprel, Aprele, Aprila, Aprile, Aprili, Aprilla, Aprille, Aprielle, Aprial, Abrielle, Avrielle, Avrial, Abrienda, Avriel, Averyl, Averil, Avryl, Apryll

Aquene (Native American) One who is peaceful
Aqueena, Aqueene, Aqueen

Arabella (Latin) An answered prayer; beautiful altar
Arabela, Arabel, Arabell

Araceli (Spanish) From the altar of heaven
Aracely, Aracelie, Areli, Arely

Aranka (Hungarian) The golden child

Ararinda (German) One who is tenacious
Ararindah, Ararynda, Araryndah

Arava (Hebrew) Resembling a willow; of an arid land
Aravah, Aravva, Aravvah

Arcadia (Greek / Spanish) Feminine form of Arkadios; woman from Arcadia / one who is adventurous
Arcadiah, Arkadia, Arcadya, Arkadya, Arckadia, Arckadya

Ardara (Gaelic) From the stronghold on the hill
Ardarah, Ardarra, Ardaria, Ardarrah, Ardariah

Ardel (Latin) Feminine form of Ardos; industrious and eager
Ardelle, Ardella, Ardele, Ardelia, Ardelis, Ardela, Ardell

Arden (Latin / English) One who is passionate and enthusiastic / from the valley of the eagles
Ardin, Ardeen, Ardena, Ardene, Ardan, Ardean, Ardine, Ardun

Ardra (Celtic / Hindi) One who is noble / the goddess of bad luck and misfortune

Argea (Greek) In mythology, the wife of Polynices
Argeia

^**Aria** (English) A beautiful melody
Ariah

***Ariana** (Welsh / Greek) Resembling silver / one who is holy
Ariane, Arian, ***Arianna****, Arianne, Aerian, Aerion, Arianie, Arieon, Aryana, Aryanna*

Ariel (Hebrew) A lionness of God
Arielle, Ariele, Airial, Ariela, Ariella, Aryela, Arial, Ari, Ariely, Arely, Arieli, Areli

Arietta (Italian) A short but beautiful melody
Arieta, Ariete, Ariet, Ariett, Aryet, Aryeta, Aryetta, Aryette

Arin (English) Form of Erin, meaning "woman of Ireland"
Aryn

Arisje (Danish) One who is superior

Arissa (Greek) One who is superior
Arisa, Aris, Aryssa, Arysa, Arys

Arizona (Native American) From the little spring / from the state of Arizona

Armani (Persian) One who is desired
Armanee, Armahni, Armaney, Armanie, Armaney

Arnette (English) A little eagle
Arnett, Arnetta, Arnete, Arneta, Arnet

Aroha (Maori) One who loves and is loved

Arona (Maori) One who is colorful and vivacious
Aronah, Aronnah, Aronna

Arrosa (Basque) Sprinkled with dew from heaven; resembling a rose
Arrose

Artis (Irish / English / Icelandic) Lofy hill; noble / rock / follower of Thor
Artisa, Artise, Artys, Artysa, Artyse, Artiss, Arti, Artina

Arusi (African) A girl born during the time of a wedding
Arusie, Arusy, Arusey, Arusee, Arusea, Aruseah, Arusye

Arwa (Arabic) A female mountain goat

Arya (Indian) One who is noble and honored
Aryah, Aryana, Aryanna, Aryia

Ascención (Spanish) Refers to the Ascension

Ashby (English) Home of the ash tree
Ashbea, Ashbie, Ashbeah, Ashbey, Ashbi, Ashbee

Asherat (Syrian) In mythology, goddess of the sea

Ashima (Hebrew) In the Bible, a deity worshipped at Hamath
Ashimah, Ashyma, Asheema, Ashimia, Ashymah, Asheemah, Asheima, Asheimah

Ashira (Hebrew) One who is wealthy; prosperous
Ashyra, Ashyrah, Ashirah, Asheera, Asheerah, Ashiera, Ashierah, Asheira

***Ashley** (English) From the meadow of ash trees
Ashlie, Ashlee, Ashleigh, Ashly, Ashleye, Ashlya, Ashala, Ashleay

Ashlyn (American) Combination of Ashley and Lynn
Ashlynn, Ashlynne

Asia (Greek / English) Resurrection / the rising sun; in the Koran, the woman who raised Moses; a woman from the east
Aysia, Asya, Asyah, Azia, Asianne

Asis (African) Of the sun
Asiss, Assis, Assiss

Asli (Turkish) One who is genuine and original
Aslie, Asly, Asley, Aslee, Asleigh, Aslea, Asleah, Alsye

Asma (Arabic) One of high status

Aspen (English) From the aspen tree
Aspin, Aspine, Aspina, Aspyn, Aspyna, Aspyne

Assana (Irish) From the waterfall
Assane, Assania, Assanna, Asanna, Asana

Astra (Latin) Of the stars; as bright as a star
Astera, Astrea, Asteria, Astrey, Astara, Astraea, Astrah, Astree

Astrid (Scandinavian / German) One with divine strength
Astryd, Estrid

Asunción (Spanish) Refers to the Virgin Mary's assumption into heaven

^**Athena** (Greek) One who is wise; in mythology, the goddess of war and wisdom
Athina, Atheena, Athene

^*__Aubrey__ (English) One who rules with elf-wisdom
***Aubree**, Aubrie, Aubry, Aubri, Aubriana*

*__Audrey__ (English) Woman with noble strength
*Audree, Audry, Audra, Audrea, Adrey, Audre, Audray, Audrin, **Audrina***

Augusta (Latin) Feminine form of Augustus; venerable, majestic
Augustina, Agustina, Augustine, Agostina, Agostine, Augusteen, Augustyna, Agusta

Aulis (Greek) In mythology, a princess of Attica
Auliss, Aulisse, Aulys, Aulyss, Aulysse

Aurora (Latin) Morning's first light; in mythology, the goddess of the dawn
Aurore, Aurea, Aurorette

*__Autumn__ (English) Born in the fall
Autum

^*__Ava__ (German / Iranian) A birdlike woman / from the water
*Avah, Avalee, Avaleigh, Avali, Avalie, Avaley, Avelaine, Avelina, **Ayva, Avalynn***

Avasa (Indian) One who is independent
Avasah, Avassa, Avasia, Avassah, Avasiah, Avasea, Avaseah

Avena (English) From the oat field
Avenah, Aviena, Avyna, Avina, Avinah, Avynah, Avienah, Aveinah

Avera (Hebrew) One who transgresses
Averah, Avyra, Avira

***Avery** (English) One who is a wise ruler; of the nobility
Avrie, Averey, Averie, Averi, Averee, Averea, Avereah

Aviana (Latin) Blessed with a gracious life
Avianah, Avianna, Aviannah, Aviane, Avianne, Avyana, Avyanna, Avyane

Aviva (Hebrew) One who is innocent and joyful; resembling springtime
Avivi, Avivah, Aviv, Avivie, Avivice, Avni, Avri, Avyva

Awel (Welsh) One who is as refreshing as a breeze
Awell, Awele, Awela, Awella

Awen (Welsh) A fluid essence; a muse; a flowing spirit
Awenn, Awenne, Awin, Awinn, Awinne, Awyn, Awynn, Awynne

^**Axelle** (German / Latin / Hebrew) Source of life; small oak / ax / peace
Axella, Axell, Axele, Axl, Axela, Axelia, Axellia

^**Ayala** (Hebrew) Resembling a gazelle
Ayalah, Ayalla, Ayallah, ***Aylin****, Ayleen, Ayline, Aileen*

Ayanna (Hindi / African) One who is innocent / resembling a beautiful flower
Ayana, Ayania, Ahyana, Ayna, Anyaniah, Ayannah, Aiyanna, Aiyana

Ayla (Hebrew) From the oak tree
Aylah, Aylana, Aylanna, Aylee, Aylea, Aylene, Ayleena, Aylena, Aylin, Ayleen, Ayline, Aileen

Aza (Arabic / African) One who provides comfort / powerful
Azia, Aiza, Aizia, Aizha

Azana (African) One who is superior
Azanah, Azanna, Azannah

Azar (Persian) One who is fiery; scarlet
Azara, Azaria, Azarah, Azarra, Azarrah, Azarr

Aznii (Chechen) A famed beauty
Azni, Aznie, Azny, Azney, Aznee, Aznea, Azneah

Azriel (Hebrew) God is my helper
Azrael, Azriell, Azrielle, Azriela, Azriella, Azraela

Azul (Spanish) Blue

B

Badia (Arabic) An elegant lady; one who is unique
Badiah, Badi'a, Badiya, Badea, Badya, Badeah

Bahija (Arabic) A cheerful woman
Bahijah, Bahiga, Bahigah, Bahyja, Bahyjah, Bahyga, Bahygah

Bailey (English) From the courtyard within castle walls; a public official
Bailee, Bayley, Baylee, Baylie, Baili, Bailie, Baileigh, Bayleigh

Baka (Indian) Resembling a crane
Bakah, Bakka, Backa, Bacca

Baligha (Arabic) One who is forever eloquent
Balighah, Baleegha, Balygha, Baliegha, Baleagha, Baleigha

Banba (Irish) In mythology, a patron goddess of Ireland

Bansuri (Indian) One who is musical
Bansurie, Bansari, Banseri, Bansurri, Bansury, Bansurey, Bansuree

Bara (Hebrew) One who is chosen
Barah, Barra, Barrah

Barbara (Latin) A traveler from a foreign land; a stranger
Barbra, Barbarella, Barbarita, Baibin, Babette, Bairbre, Barbary, Barb

Barika (African) A flourishing woman; one who is successful
Barikah, Baryka, Barikka, Barykka, Baricka, Barycka, Baricca, Barycca

Barr (English) A lawyer
Barre, Bar

Barras (English) From among the trees

Beatrice (Latin) One who blesses others
Beatrix, Beatriz, Beatriss, Beatrisse, Bea, Beatrize, Beatricia, Beatrisa

Becky (English) Form of Rebecca, meaning "one who is bound to God"
Beckey, Becki, Beckie, Becca, Becka, Bekka, Beckee, Beckea

Bel (Indian) From the sacred wood

Belen (Spanish) Woman from Bethlehem

Belinda (English) A beautiful and tender woman
Belindah, Belynda, Balynda, Belienda, Bleiendah, Balyndah, Belyndah

Belisama (Celtic) In mythology, a goddess of rivers and lakes
Belisamah, Belisamma, Belysama, Belisma, Belysma, Belesama

*****Bella** (Italian) A woman famed for her beauty
Belle, Bela, Bell, Belita, Bellissa, Belia, Bellanca, Bellany

Bena (Native American) Resembling a pheasant
Benah, Benna, Bennah

Benigna (Spanish) Feminine form of Benigno; one who is kind; friendly

Bernice (Greek) One who brings victory
Berenisa, Berenise, Berenice, Bernicia, Bernisha, Berniss, Bernyce, Bernys

Bertha (German) One who is famously bright and beautiful
Berta, Berthe, Berth, Bertina, Bertyna, Bertine, Bertyne, Birte

Bertilda (English) A luminous battle maiden
Bertilde, Bertild

Beryl (English) Resembling the pale-green precious stone
Beryll, Berylle, Beril, Berill, Berille

Bess (English) Form of Elizabeth, meaning "my God is bountiful; God's promise"
Besse, Bessi, Bessie, Bessy, Bessey, Bessee, Bessea

Beth (English) Form of Elizabeth, meaning "my God is bountiful; God's promise"
Bethe

Bethany (Hebrew) From the house of figs
Bethan, Bethani, Bethanie, Bethanee, Bethaney, Bethane, Bethann, Bethanne

Beyonce (American) One who surpasses others
Beyoncay, Beyonsay, Beyonsai, Beyonsae, Beyonci, Beyoncie, Beyoncee, Beyoncea

Bianca (Italian) A shining, fair-skinned woman
Bianka, Byanca, Byanka

Bibiana (Italian) Form of Vivian, meaning "lively woman"
Bibiane, Bibianna

Bijou (French) As precious as a jewel

Billie (English) Feminine form of William; having a desire to protect
Billi, Billy, Billey, Billee, Billeigh, Billea, Billeah

Blaine (Scottish / Irish) A saint's servant / a thin woman
Blayne, Blane, Blain, Blayn, Blaen, Blaene

Blair (Scottish) From the field of battle
Blaire, Blare, Blayre, Blaer, Blaere, Blayr

Blake (English) A dark beauty
Blayk, Blayke, Blaik, Blaike, Blaek, Blaeke

Blue (English) A color, lighter than purple-indigo but darker than green

Blythe (English) Filled with happiness
Blyth, Blithe, Blith

Bonamy (French) A very good friend
Bonamey, Bonami, Bonamie, Bonamee, Bonamei, Bonamea, Bonameah

^**Bonnie** (English) Pretty face
Boni, Bona, Bonea, Boneah, Bonee

Brady (Irish) A large-chested woman
Bradey, Bradee, Bradi, Bradie, Bradea, Bradeah

Braelyn (American) Combination of Braden and Lynn
Braylin, Braelin, Braylyn, Braelen, Braylen

Braima (African) Mother of multitudes
Braimah, Brayma, Braema, Braymah, Braemah

Brandy (English) A woman wielding a sword; an alcoholic drink
Brandey, Brandi, Brandie, Brandee, Branda, Brande, Brandelyn, Brandilyn

Brazil (Spanish) Of the ancient tree
Brasil, Brazile, Brazille, Brasille, Bresil, Brezil, Bresille, Brezille

Brencis (Slavic) Crowned with laurel

Brenda (Irish) Feminine form of Brendan; a princess; wielding a sword
Brynda, Brinda, Breandan, Brendalynn, Brendolyn, Brend, Brienda

Brenna (Welsh) A raven-like woman
Brinna, Brenn, Bren, Brennah, Brina, Brena, Brenah

⋆**Brianna** (Irish) Feminine form of Brian; from the high hill; one who ascends
Breanna, Breanne, Breana, Breann, Breeana, Breeanna, Breona, Breonna, Bryana, Bryanna, Briana

Brice (Welsh) One who is alert; ambitious
Bryce

Bridget (Irish) A strong and protective woman; in mythology, goddess of fire, wisdom, and poetry
Bridgett, Bridgette, Briget, Brigette, Bridgit, Bridgitte, Birgit, Birgitte

Brie (French) Type of cheese
Bree, Breeyah, Bria, Briya, Briah, Briyah, Brya

^**Briella** (Italian / Spanish) Form of Gabriella, meaning "heroine of God"

Brielle (French) Form of Brie, meaning "type of cheese"

Brilliant (American) A dazzling and sparkling woman

^**Brisa** (Spanish) Beloved
Brisia, Brisha, Brissa, Briza, Bryssa, Brysa

^**Bristol** (English) From the city in England
Brystol, Bristow, Brystow

Brittany (English) A woman from Great Britain
Britany, Brittanie, Brittaney, Brittani, Brittanee, Britney, Britnee, Britny

⋆**Brook** (English) From the running stream
***Brooke**, Brookie*

⋆**Brooklyn** (American) Borough of New York City
Brooklin, Brooklynn, Brooklynne

Brylee (American) Variation of Riley
Brilee, Brylie, Briley, Bryli

^**Brynley** (English) From the burnt meadow
***Brynlee**, Brynly, Brinley, Brinli, Brynlie*

^**Brynn** (Welsh) Hill
Brin, Brinn, Bryn, Brynlee, Brynly, Brinley, Brinli, Brynlie

Bryony (English) Of the healing place
Briony, Brionee

C

Cabrina (American) Form of Sabrina, meaning "a legendary princess"
Cabrinah, Cabrinna

Cabriole (French) An adorable girl
Cabriolle, Cabrioll, Cabriol, Cabryole, Cabryolle, Cabryoll, Cabryol, Cabriola

Cacalia (Latin) Resembling the flowering plant
Cacaliah, Cacalea, Cacaleah

Caden (English) A battle maiden
Cadan, Cadin, Cadon

Cadence (Latin) Rhythmic and melodious; a musical woman
Cadena, Cadenza, Cadian, Cadienne, Cadianne, Cadiene, Caydence, Cadencia, Kadence, Kaydence

Caia (Latin) One who rejoices
Cai, Cais

Cailyn (Gaelic) A young woman
Cailin

Cainwen (Welsh) A beautiful treasure
Cainwenn, Cainwenne, Cainwin, Cainwinn, Cainwinne, Cainwyn, Cainwynn, Cainwynne

Cairo (African) From the city in Egypt

Caitlin (English) Form of Catherine, meaning one who is pure, virginal
Caitlyn, Catlin, Catline, Catlyn, Caitlan, Caitlinn, Caitlynn

Calais (French) From the city in France

Cale (Latin) A respected woman
Cayl, Cayle, Cael, Caele, Cail, Caile

Caledonia (Latin) Woman of Scotland
Caledoniah, Caledoniya, Caledona, Caledonya, Calydona

California (Spanish) From paradise; from the state of California
Califia

Calise (Greek) A gorgeous woman
Calyse, Calice, Calyce

Calista (Greek) Most beautiful; in mythology, a nymph who changed into a bear and then into the Great Bear constellation
Calissa, Calisto, Callista, Calyssa, Calysta, Calixte, Colista, Collista

Calla (Greek) Resembling a lily; a beautiful woman
Callah

Callie (Greek) A beautiful girl
Cali, Callee, Kali, Kallie

Calypso (Greek) A woman with secrets; in mythology, a nymph who captivated Odysseus for seven years

Camassia (American) One who is aloof
Camassiah, Camasia, Camasiah, Camassea, Camasseah, Camasea, Camaseah

Cambay (English) From the town in India
Cambaye, Cambai, Cambae

Cambria (Latin) A woman of Wales
Cambriah, Cambrea, Cambree, Cambre, Cambry, Cambrey, Cambri, Cambrie, Cambreah

Camdyn (English) Of the enclosed valley
Camden, Camdan, Camdon, Camdin

Cameron (Scottish) Having a crooked nose
Cameryn, Camryn, Camerin, Camren, Camrin, Camron

*__Camila__ (Italian) Feminine form of Camillus; a ceremonial attendant; a noble virgin
Camile, Camille, Camilla, Camillia, Caimile, Camillei, Cam, Camelai

Campbell (Scottish) Having a crooked mouth
Campbel, Campbelle, Campbele

Candace (Ethiopian / Greek) A queen / one who is white and glowing
Candice, Candiss, Candyce, Candance, Candys, Candyss, Candy

Candida (Latin) White-skinned

Candra (Latin) One who is glowing

Candy (English) A sweet girl; form of Candida, meaning "white-skinned"; form of Candace, meaning "a queen / one who is white and glowing"
Candey, Candi, Candie, Candee, Candea, Candeah

Caneadea (Native American) From the horizon
Caneadeah, Caneadia, Caneadiah

Canika (American) A woman shining with grace
Canikah, Caneeka, Canicka, Canyka, Canycka, Caneekah, Canickah, Canykah

Canisa (Greek) One who is very much loved
Canisah, Canissa, Canysa, Caneesa, Canyssa

Cannes (French) A woman from Cannes

Cantabria (Latin) From the mountains
Cantabriah, Cantebria, Cantabrea, Cantebrea

Caprina (Italian) Woman of the island Capri
Caprinah, Caprinna, Capryna, Capreena, Caprena, Capreenah, Caprynah, Capriena

Cara (Italian / Gaelic) One who is dearly loved / a good friend
Carah, Caralee, Caralie, Caralyn, Caralynn, Carrah, Carra, Chara

Carina (Latin) Little darling
Carinna, Cariana, Carine, Cariena, Caryna, Carinna, Carynna

Carissa (Greek) A woman of grace
Carisa, Carrisa, Carrissa, Carissima

Carla (Latin) Feminine form of Carl; a free woman
Carlah, Carlana, Carleen, Carlena, Carlene, Carletta

Carlessa (American) One who is restless
Carlessah, Carlesa, Carlesah

Carly (American) Form of Carla, meaning "a free woman"
Carlee, Carleigh, Carli, Carlie, Carley

Carmel (Hebrew) Of the fruitful orchid
Carmela, Carmella, Karmel

Carmen (Latin) A beautiful song
Carma, Carmelita, Carmencita, Carmia, Carmie, Carmina, Carmine, Carmita

Carna (Latin) In mythology, a goddess who ruled the heart

Carni (Latin) One who is vocal
Carnie, Carny, Carney, Carnee, Carnea, Carneah, Carnia, Carniah

Carol (English) Form of Caroline, meaning "joyous song"; feminine form of Charles; a small, strong woman
Carola, Carole, Carolle, Carolla, Caroly, Caroli, Carolie, Carolee

*__Caroline__ (Latin) Joyous song; feminine form of Charles; a small, strong woman
Carol, Carolina, Carolyn, Carolann, Carolanne, Carolena, Carolene, Carolena, Caroliana

Carrington (English) A beautiful woman; a woman of Carrington
Carington, Carryngton, Caryngton

Carson (Scottish) Son of the marshland
Carsan, Carsen, Carsin, Carsyn

Carys (Welsh) One who loves and is loved
Caryss, Carysse, Caris, Cariss, Carisse, Cerys, Ceryss, Cerysse

Casey (Greek / Irish) A vigilant woman
Casie, Casy, Caysie, Kasey

Cason (Greek) A seer
Cayson, Caison, Caeson

Cassandra (Greek) An unheeded prophetess; in mythology, King Priam's daughter who foretold the fall of Troy
Casandra, Cassandrea, Cassaundra, Cassondra, Cass, Cassy, Cassey, Cassi, Cassie

Cassidy (Irish) Curly-haired girl
Cassady, Cassidey, Cassidi, Cassidie, Cassidee, Cassadi, Cassadie, Cassadee, Casidhe, Cassidea, Cassadea

Casta (Spanish) One who is pure; chaste
Castah, Castalina, Castaleena, Castaleina, Castaliena, Castaleana, Castalyna, Castara

Catherine (English) One who is pure; virginal
Catharine, Cathrine, Cathryn, Catherin, Catheryn, Catheryna, Cathi, Cathy, Katherine, Catalina

Catrice (Greek) A wholesome woman
Catrise, Catryce, Catryse, Catreece, Catreese, Catriece

Cayenne (French) Resembling the hot and spicy pepper

Cayla (American) Form of Kaila, meaning "crowned with laurel"
Caila, Caylah, Cailah

Caylee (American) Form of Kayla, meaning "crowned with laurel"
Caleigh, Caley, Cayley, Cailey, Caili, Cayli

Cecilia (Latin) Feminine form of Cecil; one who is blind; patron saint of music
Cecelia, Cecile, Cecilee, Cicely, Cecily, Cecille, Cecilie, Cicilia, Sheila, Silka, Sissy, Celia

Celand (Latin) One who is meant for heaven
Celanda, Celande, Celandia, Celandea

Celandine (English) Resembling a swallow
Celandyne, Celandina, Celandyna, Celandeena, Celandena, Celandia

Celeste (Latin) A heavenly daughter
Celesta, Celestia, Celisse, Celestina, Celestyna, Celestine

Celia (Latin) Form of Cecelia, meaning patron saint of music

Celina (Latin) In mythology, one of the daughters of Atlas who was turned into a star of the Pleiades constellation; of the heavens; form of Selena, meaning "of the moon"
Celena, Celinna, Celene, Celenia, Celenne, Celicia

Celosia (Greek) A fiery woman; burning; aflame
Celosiah, Celosea, Celoseah

Cera (French) A colorful woman
Cerah, Cerrah, Cerra

Cerina (Latin) Form of Serena, meaning "having a peaceful disposition"
Cerinah, Ceryna, Cerynah, Cerena, Cerenah, Ceriena

Cerise (French) Resembling the cherry
Cerisa

Chadee (French) A divine woman; a goddess
Chadea, Chadeah, Chady, Chadey, Chadi, Chadie

Chai (Hebrew) One who gives life
Chae, Chaili, Chailie, Chailee, Chaileigh, Chaily, Chailey, Chailea

Chailyn (American) Resembling a waterfall
Chailynn, Chailynne, Chaelyn, Chaelynn, Chaelynne, Chaylyn

Chakra (Arabic) A center of spiritual energy

Chalette (American) Having good taste
Chalett, Chalet, Chalete, Chaletta, Chaleta

Chalina (Spanish) Form of Rosalina, meaning "resembling a gentle horse / resembling the beautiful and meaningful flower"
Chalinah, Chalyna, Chaleena, Chalena, Charo, Chaliena, Chaleina, Chaleana

Chameli (Hindi) Resembling jasmine
Chamelie, Chamely, Chameley, Chamelee

Chan (Sanskrit) A shining woman

Chana (Hebrew) Form of Hannah, meaning "having favor and grace"
Chanah, Channa, Chaanach, Chaanah, Chanach, Channah

Chance (American) One who takes risks
Chanci, Chancie, Chancee, Chancea, Chanceah, Chancy, Chancey

Chanda (Sanskrit) An enemy of evil
Chandy, Chaand, Chand, Chandey, Chandee, Chandi, Chandie, Chandea

Chandra (Hindi) Of the moon; another name for the goddess Devi
Chandara, Chandria, Chaundra, Chandrea, Chandreah

Chanel (French) From the canal; a channel
Chanell, Chanelle, Channelle, Chenelle, Chenel, Chenell

Channary (Cambodian) Of the full moon
Channarie, Channari, Channarey, Channaree, Chantrea, Chantria

Chantrice (French) A singer
Chantryce, Chantrise, Chantryse

Charisma (Greek) Blessed with charm
Charismah, Charizma, Charysma, Karisma

Charity (Latin) A woman of generous love
Charitey, Chariti, Charitie, Charitee

Charlesia (American) Feminine form of Charles; small, strong woman
Charlesiah, Charlesea, Charleseah, Charlsie, Charlsi

^**Charlie** (English) Form of Charles, meaning "one who is strong"
***Charlee**, Charli, Charley, Charlize, Charlene, Charlyn, Charlaine, Charlisa, Charlena*

*__Charlotte__ (French) Form of Charles, meaning "a small, strong woman"
Charlize, Charlot, Charlotta

Charlshea (American) Filled with happiness
Charlsheah, Charlshia, Charlshiah

Charnee (American) Filled with joy
Charny, Charney, Charnea, Charneah, Charni, Charnie

Charnesa (American) One who gets attention
Charnessa, Charnessah

Charsetta (American) An emotional woman
Charsett, Charsette, Charset, Charsete, Charseta

Chartra (American) A classy lady
Chartrah

Charu (Hindi) One who is gorgeous
Charoo, Charou

Chasia (Hebrew) One who is protected; sheltered
Chasiah, Chasea, Chaseah, Chasya, Chasyah

Chasidah (Hebrew) A religious woman; pious
Chasida, Chasyda, Chasydah

Chavi (Egyptian) A precious daughter
Chavie, Chavy, Chavey, Chavee, Chavea, Chaveah

Chaya (Hebrew) Life
Chaia

Chedra (Hebrew) Filled with happiness
Chedrah

Cheer (American) Filled with joy
Cheere

Chekia (American) A saucy woman
Cheekie, Checki, Checkie, Checky, Checkey, Checkee, Checkea, Checkeah

Chelone (English) Resembling a flowering plant

Chelsea (English) From the landing place for chalk
Chelcie, Chelsa, Chelsee, Chelseigh, Chelsey, Chelsi, Chelsie, Chelsy

Chemarin (French) A dark beauty
Chemarine, Chemaryn, Chemareen, Chemarein, Chemarien

Chemda (Hebrew) A charismatic woman
Chemdah

Chenille (American) A soft-skinned woman
Chenill, Chenil, Chenile, Chenilla, Chenila

Cherika (French) One who is dear
Chericka, Cheryka, Cherycka, Cherieka, Cheriecka, Chereika, Chereicka, Cheryka

Cherish (English) To be held dear, valued

Cherry (English) Resembling a fruit-bearing tree
Cherrie, Cherri, Cherrey, Cherree, Cherrea, Cherreah

Chesney (English) One who promotes peace
Chesny, Chesni, Chesnie, Chesnea, Chesneah, Chesnee

Cheyenne (Native American) Unintelligible speaker
Chayanne, Cheyane, Cheyene, Shayan, Shyann

Chiante (Italian) Resembling the wine
Chianti, Chiantie, Chiantee, Chianty, Chiantey, Chiantea

Chiara (Italian) Daughter of the light
Chiarah, Chiarra, Chiarrah

Chiba (Hebrew) One who loves and is loved
Chibah, Cheeba, Cheebah, Cheiba, Cheibah, Chieba, Chiebah, Cheaba

Chidi (Spanish) One who is cheerful
Chidie, Chidy, Chidey, Chidee, Chidea, Chideah

Chidori (Japanese) Resembling a shorebird
Chidorie, Chidory, Chidorey, Chidorea, Chidoreah, Chidoree

Chikira (Spanish) A talented dancer
Chikirah, Chikiera, Chikierah, Chikeira, Chikeirah, Chikeera, Chikeerah, Chikyra

Chiku (African) A talkative girl

Chinara (African) God receives
Chinarah, Chinarra, Chinarrah

Chinue (African) God's own blessing
Chinoo, Chynue, Chynoo

Chiriga (African) One who is triumphant
Chyriga, Chyryga, Chiryga

Chislaine (French) A faithful woman
Chislain, Chislayn, Chislayne, Chislaen, Chislaene, Chyslaine, Chyslain, Chyslayn

Chitsa (Native American) One who is fair
Chitsah, Chytsa, Chytsah

Chizoba (African) One who is well-protected
Chizobah, Chyzoba, Chyzobah

⋆**Chloe** (Greek) A flourishing woman; blooming
Clo, Cloe, Cloey, Chloë

Christina (English) Follower of Christ
Christinah, Cairistiona, Christine, Christin, Christian, Christiana, Christiane, Christianna, Kristina, Cristine, Christal, Crystal, Chrystal, Cristal

Chula (Native American) Resembling a colorful flower
Chulah, Chulla, Chullah

Chulda (Hebrew) One who can tell fortunes
Chuldah

Chun (Chinese) Born during the spring

Chyou (Chinese) Born during autumn

Ciara (Irish) A dark beauty
Ceara, Ciaran, Ciarra, Ciera, Cierra, Ciere, Ciar, Ciarda

Cidrah (American) One who is unlike others
Cidra, Cydrah, Cydra

Cinnamon (American) Resembling the reddish-brown spice
Cinnia, Cinnie

Ciona (American) One who is steadfast
Cionah, Cyona, Cyonah

Claennis (Anglo-Saxon) One who is pure
Claenis, Claennys, Claenys, Claynnis, Claynnys, Claynys, Claynyss

⋆**Claire** (French) Form of Clara, meaning "famously bright"
Clare, Clair

Clancey (American) A lighthearted woman
Clancy, Clanci, Clancie, Clancee, Clancea, Clanceah

*Clara** (Latin) One who is famously bright
Clarie, Clarinda, Clarine, Clarita, Claritza, Clarrie, Clarry, Clarabelle, ***Claire,*** *Clarice*

Clarice (French) A famous woman; also a form of Clara, meaning "one who is famously bright"
Claressa, Claris, Clarisa, Clarise, Clarisse, Claryce, Clerissa, Clerisse, Clarissa

Claudia (Latin / German / Italian) One who is lame
Claudelle, Gladys

Clelia (Latin) A glorious woman
Cloelia, Cleliah, Clelea, Cleleah, Cloeliah, Cloelea, Cloeleah

Clementine (French) Feminine form of Clement; one who is merciful
Clem, Clemence, Clemency, Clementia, Clementina, Clementya, Clementyna, Clementyn

Cleodal (Latin) A glorious woman
Cleodall, Cleodale, Cleodel, Cleodell, Cleodelle

Cleopatra (Greek) A father's glory; of the royal family
Clea, Cleo, Cleona, Cleone, Cleonie, Cleora, Cleta, Cleoni

Clever (American) One who is quick-witted and smart

Cloris (Greek) A flourishing woman; in mythology, the goddess of flowers
Clores, Clorys, Cloriss, Clorisse, Cloryss, Clorysse

Cloud (American) A light-hearted woman
Cloude, Cloudy, Cloudey, Cloudee, Cloudea, Cloudeah, Cloudi, Cloudie

Clydette (American) Feminine form of Clyde, meaning "from the river"
Clydett, Clydet, Clydete, Clydetta, Clydeta

Clymene (Greek) In mythology, the mother of Atlas and Prometheus
Clymena, Clymyne, Clymyn, Clymyna, Clymeena, Clymeina, Clymiena, Clymeana

Clytie (Greek) The lovely one; in mythology, a nymph who was changed into a sunflower
Clyti, Clytee, Clyty, Clytey, Clyte, Clytea, Clyteah

Coby (Hebrew) Feminine form of Jacob; the supplanter
Cobey, Cobi, Cobie, Cobee, Cobea, Cobeah

Coffey (American) A lovely woman
Coffy, Coffe, Coffee, Coffea, Coffeah, Coffi, Coffie

Coira (Scottish) Of the churning waters
Coirah, Coyra, Coyrah

Colanda (American) Form of Yolanda, meaning "resembling the violet flower; modest"
Colande, Coland, Colana, Colain, Colaine, Colane, Colanna, Corlanda, Calanda, Calando, Calonda, Colantha, Colanthe, Culanda, Culonda, Coulanda, Colonda

Cole (English) A swarthy woman; having coal-black hair
Col, Coal, Coale, Coli, Colie, Coly, Coley, Colee

Colette (French) Victory of the people
Collette, Kolette

Coligny (French) Woman from Cologne
Coligney, Colignie, Coligni, Colignee, Colignea, Coligneah

Colisa (English) A delightful young woman
Colisah, Colissa, Colissah, Colysa, Colysah, Colyssa, Colyssah

Colola (American) A victorious woman
Colo, Cola

Comfort (English) One who strengthens or soothes others
Comforte, Comfortyne, Comfortyna, Comforteene, Comforteena, Comfortene, Comfortena, Comfortiene

Conary (Gaelic) A wise woman
Conarey, Conarie, Conari, Conaree, Conarea, Conareah

Concordia (Latin) Peace and harmony; in mythology, goddess of peace
Concordiah, Concordea, Concord, Concorde, Concordeah

Constanza (American) One who is strong-willed
Constanzia, Constanzea

Consuela (Spanish) One who provides consolation
Consuelia, Consolata, Consolacion, Chela, Conswela, Conswelia, Conswelea, Consuella

Contessa (Italian) A titled woman; a countess
Countess, Contesse, Countessa, Countesa, Contesa

Cooper (English) One who makes barrels
Couper

Copper (American) A red-headed woman
Coper, Coppar, Copar

^**Cora** (English) A young maiden
Corah, Coraline, Corra

Coral (English) Resembling the semiprecious sea growth; from the reef
Coralee, Coralena, Coralie, Coraline, Corallina, Coralline, Coraly, Coralyn

Corazon (Spanish) Of the heart
Corazana, Corazone, Corazona

^**Cordelia** (Latin) A good-hearted woman; a woman of honesty
Cordella, Cordelea, Cordilia, Cordilea, Cordy, Cordie, Cordi, Cordee

Corey (Irish) From the hollow; of the churning waters
Cory, Cori, Coriann, Corianne, Corie, Corri, Corrianna, Corrie

Corgie (American) A humorous woman
Corgy, Corgey, Corgi, Corgee, Corgea, Corgeah

Coriander (Greek) A romantic woman; resembling the spice
Coryander, Coriender, Coryender

Corina (Latin) A spear-wielding woman
Corinne, Corine, Corinna, Corrinne, Corryn, Corienne, Coryn, Corynna

Corinthia (Greek) A woman of Corinth
Corinthiah, Corinthe, Corinthea, Corintheah, Corynthia, Corynthea, Corynthe

Cornelia (Latin) Feminine form of Cornelius; referring to a horn
Cornalia, Corneelija, Cornela, Cornelija, Cornelya, Cornella, Cornelle, Cornie

Cota (Spanish) A lively woman
Cotah, Cotta, Cottah

Coty (French) From the riverbank
Cotey, Coti, Cotie, Cotee, Cotea, Coteah

Courtney (English) A courteous woman; courtly
Cordney, Cordni, Cortenay, Corteney, Cortland, Cortnee, Cortneigh, Cortney, Courteney

Covin (American) An unpredictable woman
Covan, Coven, Covyn, Covon

Coy (English) From the woods, the quiet place
Coye, Coi

Cree (Native American) A tribal name
Crei, Crey, Crea, Creigh

Cressida (Greek) The golden girl; in mythology, a woman of Troy
Cressa, Criseyde, Cressyda, Crissyda

Cristos (Greek) A dedicated and faithful woman
Crystos, Christos, Chrystos

Cwen (English) A royal woman; queenly
Cwene, Cwenn, Cwenne, Cwyn, Cwynn, Cwynne, Cwin, Cwinn

Cylee (American) A darling daughter
Cyleigh, Cyli, Cylie, Cylea, Cyleah, Cyly, Cyley

Cynthia (Greek) Moon goddess
Cinda, Cindy, Cinthia, Cindia Cinthea

Cyrene (Greek) In mythology, a maiden-huntress loved by Apollo
Cyrina, Cyrena, Cyrine, Cyreane, Cyreana, Cyreene, Cyreena

Czigany (Hungarian) A gypsy girl; one who moves from place to place
Cziganey, Czigani, Cziganie, Cziganee

D

Dacey (Irish) Woman from the south
Daicey, Dacee, Dacia, Dacie, Dacy, Daicee, Daicy, Daci

Daffodil (French) Resembling the yellow flower
Daffodill, Daffodille, Dafodil, Dafodill, Dafodille, Daff, Daffodyl, Dafodyl

Dagmar (Scandinavian) Born on a glorious day
Dagmara, Dagmaria, Dagmarie, Dagomar, Dagomara, Dagomaria, Dagmarr, Dagomarr

Dahlia (Swedish) From the valley; resembling the flower
Dahlea, Dahl, Dahiana, Dayha, Daleia, Dalia

Daira (Greek) One who is well-informed
Daeira, Danira, Dayeera

Daisy (English) Of the day's eye; resembling a flower
Daisee, Daisey, Daisi, Daisie, Dasie, Daizy, Daysi, Deysi

Dakota (Native American) A friend to all
Dakotah, Dakotta, Dakoda, Dakodah

Damali (Arabic) A beautiful vision
Damalie, Damaly, Damaley, Damalee, Damaleigh, Damalea

Damani (American) Of a bright tomorrow
Damanie, Damany, Damaney, Damanee, Damanea, Damaneah

Damaris (Latin) A gentle woman
Damara, Damaress, Damariss, Damariz, Dameris, Damerys, Dameryss, Damiris

Dana (English) Woman from Denmark
Danna, Daena, Daina, Danaca, Danah, Dane, Danet, Daney, Dania

Danica (Slavic) Of the morning star
Danika

Daniela (Spanish) Form of Danielle, meaning "God is my judge"
Daniella

Danielle (Hebrew) Feminine form of Daniel; God is my judge
Daanelle, Danee, Danele, Danella, Danelle, Danelley, Danette, Daney

^**Danna** (American) Variation of Dana, meaning woman from Denmark
Dannah

Daphne (Greek) Of the laurel tree; in mythology, a virtuous woman transformed into a laurel tree to protect her from Apollo
Daphna, Daphney, Daphni, Daphnie, Daffi, Daffie, Daffy, Dafna

Darby (English) Of the deer park
Darb, Darbee, Darbey, Darbie, Darrbey, Darrbie, Darrby, Derby, Larby

Daria (Greek) Feminine form of Darius; possessing good fortune; wealthy
Dari, Darian, Dariane, Darianna, Dariele, Darielle, Darien, Darienne

Daring (American) One who takes risks; a bold woman
Daryng, Derring, Dering, Deryng

Darlene (English) Our little darling
Dareen, Darla, Darleane, Darleen, Darleena, Darlena, Darlenny, Darlina

Daryn (Greek) Feminine form of Darin; a gift of God
Darynn, Darynne, Darinne, Daren, Darenn, Darene

Dawn (English) Born at daybreak; of the day's first light
Dawna, Dawne, Dawnelle, Dawnetta, Dawnette, Dawnielle, Dawnika, Dawnita

Day (American) A father's hope for tomorrow
Daye, Dai, Dae

Daya (Hebrew) Resembling a bird of prey
Dayah, Dayana, Dayanara, Dayania, Dayaniah, Dayanea, Dayaneah

Dayton (English) From the sunny town
Dayten, Daytan

Dea (Greek) Resembling a goddess
Deah, Diya, Diyah

Deborah (Hebrew) Resembling a bee; in the Bible, a prophetess
Debbera, Debbey, Debbi, Debbie, Debbra, Debby

Deidre (Gaelic) A brokenhearted or raging woman
Deadra, Dede, Dedra, Deedra, Deedre, Deidra, Deirdre, Deidrie

Deiondre (American) From the lush valley
Deiondra, Deiondria, Deiondrea, Deiondriya

Deja (French) One of remembrance
Dayja, Dejah, Daejah, Daijia, Daija, Daijah, Deijah, Deija

Dekla (Latvian) In mythology, a trinity goddess
Decla, Deckla, Deklah, Decklah, Declah

Delaney (Irish / French) The dark challenger / from the elder-tree grove
Delaina, Delaine, Delainey, Delainy, Delane, Delanie, Delany, Delayna

Delaware (English) From the state of Delaware
Delawair, Delaweir, Delwayr, Delawayre, Delawaire, Delawaer, Delawaere

Delilah (Hebrew) A seductive woman
Delila, Delyla, Delylah

Delta (Greek) From the mouth of the river; the fourth letter of the Greek alphabet
Dellta, Deltah, Delltah

Delyth (Welsh) A pretty young woman
Delythe, Delith, Delithe

Demeter (Greek) In mythology, the goddess of the harvest
Demetra, Demitra, Demitras, Dimetria, Demetre, Demetria, Dimitra, Dimitre

Demi (Greek) A petite woman
Demie, Demee, Demy, Demiana, Demianne, Demianna, Demea

Denali (Indian) A superior woman
Denalie, Denaly, Denally, Denalli, Denaley, Denalee, Denallee, Denallie

Dendara (Egyptian) From the town on the river
Dendera, Dendaria, Denderia, Dendarra

Denise (French) Feminine form of Dennis; a follower of Dionysus
Denese, Denyse, Denice, Deniece, Denisa, Denissa, Denize, Denyce, Denys

Denver (English) From the green valley

Derora (Hebrew) As free as a bird
Derorah, Derorra, Derorit, Drora, Drorah, Drorit, Drorlya, Derorice

Derry (Irish) From the oak grove
Derrey, Derri, Derrie, Derree, Derrea, Derreah

Deryn (Welsh) A birdlike woman
Derran, Deren, Derhyn, Deron, Derrin, Derrine, Derron, Derrynne

Desiree (French) One who is desired
Desaree, Desirae, Desarae, Desire, Desyre, Dezirae, Deziree, Desirat

*__Destiny__ (English) Recognizing one's certain fortune; fate
Destanee, Destinee, Destiney, Destini, Destinie, Destine, Destina, Destyni

Deva (Hindi) A divine being
Devi, Daeva

Devera (Latin) In mythology, goddess of brooms
Deverah

Devon (English) From the beautiful farmland; of the divine
Devan, Deven, Devenne, Devin, Devona, Devondra, Devonna, Devonne, Devyn

Dextra (Latin) Feminine form of Dexter; one who is skillful
Dex

Dharma (Hindi) The universal law of order
Darma

Dhisana (Hindi) In Hinduism, goddess of prosperity
Dhisanna, Disana, Disanna, Dhysana

Dhyana (Hindi) One who meditates

Diamond (French) Woman of high value
Diamanta, Diamonique, Diamante

Diana (Latin) Of the divine; in mythology, goddess of the moon and the hunt
Dianna, Dayanna, Dayana, Deanna

Diane (Latin) Form of Diana, meaning "of the divine"
Dayann, Dayanne, Deana, Deane, Deandra, Deann

Diata (African) Resembling a lioness
Diatah, Dyata, Diatta, Dyatah, Dyatta, Diattah, Dyattah

Dido (Latin) In mythology, the queen of Carthage who committed suicide
Dydo

Dielle (Latin) One who worships God
Diele, Diell, Diella, Diela, Diel

Dimity (English) Resembling a sheer cotton fabric
Dimitee, Dimitey, Dimitie, Dimitea, Dimiteah, Dimiti

Dimona (Hebrew) Woman from the south
Dimonah, Dymona, Demona, Demonah, Dymonah

Disa (English) Resembling an orchid

Discordia (Latin) In mythology, goddess of strife
Dyscordia, Diskordia, Dyskordia

Diti (Hindi) In Hinduism, an earth goddess
Dyti, Ditie, Dytie, Dity, Dyty, Ditey, Dytey, Ditee

Dixie (English) Woman from the South
Dixi, Dixy, Dixey, Dixee

Dolores (Spanish) Woman of sorrow; refers to the Virgin Mary
Dalores, Delora, Delores, Deloria, Deloris, Dolorcita, Dolorcitas, Dolorita

Domina (Latin) An elegant lady
Dominah, Domyna, Domynah

Dominique (French) Feminine form of Dominic; born on the Lord's day
Domaneke, Domanique, Domenica, Domeniga, Domenique, Dominee, Domineek, Domineke

Doreen (French / Gaelic) The golden one / a brooding woman
Dorene, Doreyn, Dorine, Dorreen, Doryne, Doreena, Dore, Doirean, Doireann, Doireanne, Doireana, Doireanna

Dorothy (Greek) A gift of God
Dasha, Dasya, Dodie, Dody, Doe, Doll, Dolley, Dolli

Dove (American) Resembling a bird of peace
Duv

Drisana (Indian) Daughter of the sun
Dhrisana, Drisanna, Drysana, Drysanna, Dhrysana, Dhrisanna, Dhrysanna

Drury (French) One who is greatly loved
Drurey, Druri, Drurie, Druree, Drurea, Drureah

Duana (Irish) Feminine form of Dwayne; little, dark one
Duane, Duayna, Duna, Dwana, Dwayna, Dubhain, Dubheasa

Duena (Spanish) One who acts as a chaperone

Dulce (Latin) A very sweet woman
Dulcina, Dulcee, Dulcie

Dumia (Hebrew) One who is silent
Dumiya, Dumiah, Dumiyah, Dumea, Dumeah

Duvessa (Irish) A dark beauty
Duvessah, Duvesa, Dubheasa, Duvesah

^**Dylan** (Welsh) Daughter of the waves
Dylana, Dylane, Dyllan, Dyllana, Dillon, Dillan, Dillen, Dillian

Dympna (Irish) Fawn; the patron saint of the insane
Dymphna, Dimpna, Dimphna

Dyre (Scandinavian) One who is dear to the heart

Dysis (Greek) Born at sunset
Dysiss, Dysisse, Dysys, Dysyss, Dysysse

E

Eadlin (Anglo-Saxon) Born into royalty
Eadlinn, Eadlinne, Eadline, Eadlyn, Eadlynn, Eadlynne, Eadlina, Eadlyna

Eadrianne (American) One who stands out
Eadrian, Eadriann, Edriane, Edriana, Edrianna

Eara (Scottish) Woman from the east
Earah, Earra, Earrah, Earia, Earea, Earie, Eari, Earee

Earla (English) A great leader
Earlah

Earna (English) Resembling an eagle
Earnah, Earnia, Earnea, Earniah, Earneah

Easter (American) Born during the religious holiday
Eastere, Eastre, Eastir, Eastar, Eastor, Eastera, Easteria, Easterea

Easton (American) A wholesome woman
Eastan, Easten, Eastun, Eastyn

Eathelin (English) Noble woman of the waterfall
Eathelyn, Eathelinn, Eathelynn, Eathelina, Eathelyna, Ethelin, Ethelyn, Eathelen

Eber (Hebrew) One who moves beyond

Ebere (African) One who shows mercy
Eberre, Ebera, Eberia, Eberea, Eberria, Eberrea, Ebiere, Ebierre

Ebony (Egyptian) A dark beauty
Eboni, Ebonee, Ebonie, Ebonique, Eboney, Ebonea, Eboneah

Ebrill (Welsh) Born in April
Ebrille, Ebril, Evril, Evrill, Evrille

Edana (Irish) Feminine form of Aidan; a fiery woman
Edanah, Edanna, Ena, Eideann, Eidana

Eden (Hebrew) Place of pleasure
Edan, Edin, Edon

Edith (English) The spoils of war; one who is joyous; a treasure
Edyth, Eda, Edee, Edie, Edita, Edelina, Edeline, Edelyne, Edelynn, Edalyn, Edalynn, Edita, Edyta, Eydie

Edna (Hebrew) One who brings pleasure; a delight
Ednah, Edena, Edenah

Edra (English) A powerful and mighty woman
Edrah, Edrea, Edreah, Edria, Edriah

Eduarda (Portugese) Feminine form of Edward; a wealthy protector
Eduardia, Eduardea, Edwarda, Edwardia, Edwardea, Eduardina, Eduardyna, Edwardina

Edurne (Basque) Feminine form of Edur; woman of the snow
Edurna, Edurnia, Edurnea, Edurniya

Egan (American) A wholesome woman
Egann, Egen, Egun, Egon

Egeria (Latin) A wise counselor; in mythology, a water nymph
Egeriah, Egerea, Egereah, Egeriya, Egeriyah

Eileen (Gaelic) Form of Evelyn, meaning "a birdlike woman"
Eila, Eileene, Eilena, Eilene, Eilin, Eilleen, Eily, Eilean

Eiluned (Welsh) An idol worshipper
Luned

Eilwen (Welsh) One with a fair brow
Eilwenne, Eilwin, Eilwinne, Eilwyn, Eilwynne

Eirene (Greek) Form of Irene, meaning "a peaceful woman"
Eireen, Eireene, Eiren, Eir, Eireine, Eirein, Eirien, Eiriene

Eires (Greek) A peaceful woman
Eiress, Eiris, Eiriss, Eirys, Eiryss

Eirian (Welsh) One who is bright and beautiful
Eiriann, Eiriane, Eiriana, Eirianne, Eirianna

Ekron (Hebrew) One who is firmly rooted
Eckron, Ecron

Elaine (French) Form of Helen, meaning "the shining light"
Ellaine, Ellayne, Elaina, Elayna, Elayne, Elaene, Elaena, Ellaina

Elana (Hebrew) From the oak tree
Elanna, Elanah, Elanie, Elani, Elany, Elaney, Elanee, Elan

Elata (Latin) A high-spirited woman
Elatah, Elatta, Elattah, Elatia, Elatea, Elatiah, Elateah

Elath (Hebrew) From the grove of trees
Elathe, Elatha, Elathia, Elathea

Eldora (Greek) A gift of the sun
Eleadora, Eldorah, Eldorra, Eldoria, Eldorea

Eldoris (Greek) Woman of the sea
Eldorise, Eldoriss, Eldorisse, Eldorys, Eldoryss, Eldorysse

Eleacie (American) One who is forthright
Eleaci, Eleacy, Eleacey, Eleacee, Eleacea

⋆**Eleanor** (Greek) Form of Helen, meaning "the shining light"
Eleanora, Eleni, Eleonora, Eleonore, Elinor, Elnora, Eleanore, Elinora, Nora

Elena (Spanish) Form of Helen, meaning "the shining light"
Elenah, Eleena, Eleenah, Elyna, Elynah, Elina, Elinah, Eleni, Eliana

Eliana (Hebrew) The Lord answers our prayers
Eleana, Elia, Eliane, Elianna, Elianne, Eliann, Elyana, Elyanna, Elyann, Elyan, Elyanne

Elica (German) One who is noble
Elicah, Elicka, Elika, Elyca, Elycka, Elyka, Elsha, Elsje

Elida (English) Resembling a winged creature
Elidah, Elyda, Eleeda, Eleda, Elieda, Eleida, Eleada

Elika (Hebrew) God will judge
Elikah, Elyka, Elicka, Elycka, Elica, Elyca

^**Elisa** (English) Form of Elizabeth, meaning "my God is bountiful"
Elisha, Elishia, Elissa, Elisia, Elysa, Elysha, Elysia, Elyssa

Elise (English) Form of Elizabeth, meaning "my God is bountiful"
Elle, Elice, Elisse, Elyse, Elysse, Ilyse

Elita (Latin) The chosen one
Elitah, Elyta, Elytah, Eleta, Eletah, Elitia, Elitea, Electa

^*__Elizabeth__ (Hebrew) My God is bountiful; God's promise
Liz, Elisabet, Elisabeth, Elisabetta, Elissa, Eliza, Elizabel, Elizabet, Elsa, Beth, Babette, Libby, Lisa, Itzel, Ilsabeth, Ilsabet

*__Ella__ (German) From a foreign land
Elle, Ellee, Ellesse, Elli, Ellia, Ellie, Elly, Ela

Ellen (English) Form of Helen, meaning "the shining light"
Elin, Elleen, Ellena, Ellene, Ellyn, Elynn, Elen, Ellin

Ellery (English) Form of Hilary, meaning "a cheerful woman"
Ellerey, Elleri, Ellerie, Elleree, Ellerea, Ellereah

Elliana (Hebrew) The Lord answers our prayers
Eliana

*__Ellie__ (English) Form of Eleanor, meaning "the shining light"
Elli, Elly, Elley, Elleigh

^**Ellyanne** (American) A shining and gracious woman
Ellianne, Ellyanna, ***Ellianna****, Ellyann, Elliann, Ellyan, Ellian*

Elma (German) Having God's protection
Elmah

^**Eloisa** (Latin) Form of Louise, meaning "a famous warrior"
Eloise*, Eloiza, Eloisee, Eloize, Eloizee, Aloisa, Aloise*

Elrica (German) A great ruler
Elricah, Elrika, Elrikah, Elryca, Elrycah, Elryka, Elrykah, Elrick

^**Elsie** (English) Form of Elizabeth, meaning "my god is bountiful"

Elvia (Irish) A friend of the elves
Elva, Elvie, Elvina, Elvinia, Elviah, Elvea, Elveah, Elvyna

Elvira (Latin) A truthful woman; one who can be trusted
Elvera, Elvita, Elvyra

Ema (Polynesian / German) One who is greatly loved / a serious woman

Ember (English) A low-burning fire
Embar, Embir, Embyr

Emerson (German) Offspring of Emery
Emmerson, Emyrson

Emery (German) Industrious
Emeri, Emerie, Emori, Emorie, Emory

*****Emily** (Latin) An industrious and hardworking woman
Emilee, Emilie, Emilia, Emelia, Emileigh, Emeleigh, Emeli, Emelie, Emely, Emmalee

*****Emma** (German) One who is complete; a universal woman
Emmy, Emmajean, Emmalee, Emmi, Emmie, Emmaline, Emelina, Emeline

Emmylou (American) A universal ruler
Emmilou, Emmielou, Emylou, Emilou, Emielou

Ena (Irish) A fiery and passionate woman
Enah, Enat, Eny, Enya

Encarnación (Spanish) Refers to the Incarnation festival

Engracia (Spanish) A graceful woman
Engraciah, Engracea, Engraceah

Enslie (American) An emotional woman
Ensli, Ensley, Ensly, Enslee, Enslea, Ensleigh

Eranthe (Greek) As delicate as a spring flower
Erantha, Eranth, Eranthia, Eranthea

Erasta (African) A peaceful woman

Ercilia (American) One who is frank
Erciliah, Ercilea, Ercileah, Ercilya, Ercilyah, Erciliya, Erciliyah

Erendira (Spanish) Daughter born into royalty
Erendirah, Erendiria, Erendirea, Erendyra, Erendyria, Erendyrea, Erendeera, Erendiera

Erica (Scandinavian / Latin) Feminine form of Eric; ever the ruler / resembling heather
Erika, Ericka, Erikka, Eryka, Erike, Ericca, Erics, Eiric, Rica

Erimentha (Greek) A devoted protector
Erimenthe, Erimenthia, Erimenthea

Erin (Gaelic) Woman from Ireland
Erienne, Erina, Erinn, Erinna, Erinne, Eryn, Eryna, Erynn, Arin

Ernestina (German) Feminine form of Ernest; one who is determined; serious
Ernesta, Ernestine, Ernesha

Esdey (American) A warm and caring woman
Essdey, Esdee, Esdea, Esdy, Esdey, Esdi, Esdie, Esday

Eshah (African) An exuberant woman
Esha

Eshe (African) Giver of life
Eshey, Eshay, Esh, Eshae, Eshai

Esme (French) An esteemed woman
Esmai, Esmae, Esmay, Esmaye, Esmee

Esmeralda (Spanish) Resembling a prized emerald
Esmerald, Emerald, Emeralda, Emelda, Esma

Esne (English) Filled with happiness
Esnee, Esney, Esnea, Esni, Esnie, Esny

Essence (American) A perfumed woman
Essince, Esense, Esince, Essynce, Esynce

Esthelia (Spanish) A shining woman
Estheliah, Esthelea, Estheleah, Esthelya, Esthelyah, Estheliya, Estheliyah

Esther (Persian) Resembling the myrtle leaf
Ester, Eszter, Eistir, Eszti

Estrella (Spanish) Star
Estrela

Estrid (Norse) Form of Astrid, meaning "one with divine strength"
Estread, Estreed, Estrad, Estri, Estrod, Estrud, Estryd, Estrida

Etana (Hebrew) A strong and dedicated woman
Etanah, Etanna, Etannah, Etania, Etanea, Ethana, Ethanah, Ethania

Etaney (Hebrew) One who is focused
Etany, Etanie, Etani, Etanee, Etanea

Eternity (American) Lasting forever
Eternitie, Eterniti, Eternitey, Eternitee, Eternyty, Eternyti, Eternytie, Eternytee

Ethna (Irish) A graceful woman
Ethnah, Eithne, Ethne, Eithna, Eithnah

Eudlina (Slavic) A generous woman
Eudlinah, Eudleena, Eudleenah

Eudocia (Greek) One who is esteemed
Eudociah, Eudocea, Eudoceah

Eugenia (Greek) A well-born woman
Eugenie, Gina, Zenechka

Eulanda (American) A fair woman
Eulande, Euland, Eulandia, Eulandea

Eunice (Greek) One who conquers
Eunise, Eunyce, Eunis, Euniss, Eunyss, Eunysse

Eurybia (Greek) In mythology, a sea goddess and mother of Pallas, Perses, and Astraios
Eurybiah, Eurybea, Eurybeah

Eurynome (Greek) In mythology, the mother of the Graces
Eurynomie, Eurynomi

Euvenia (American) A hardworking woman

⋆**Eva** (Hebrew) Giver of life; a lively woman
Eve, Evetta, Evette, Evia, Eviana, Evie, Evita, Eeva

^**Evangeline** (Greek) A bringer of good news
Evangelina, Evangelyn

⋆**Evelyn** (German) A birdlike woman
Evaleen, Evalina, Evaline, Evalyn, Evelin, Evelina, Eveline, Evelyne, Eileen, Evelynn

Evline (French) One who loves nature
Evleen, Evleene, Evlean, Evleane, Evlene, Evlyn, Evlyne

^**Everly** (English) Boar in a wild field
Everleigh, Everley, Everlie, Everlee

F

Fairly (English) From the far meadow
Fairley, Fairlee, Fairleigh, Fairli, Fairlie, Faerly, Faerli, Faerlie

*__Faith__ (English) Having a belief and trust in God
Faythe, Faithe, Faithful, Fayana, Fayanna, Fayanne, Fayane, Fayth

Fakhira (Arabic) A magnificent woman
Fakhirah, Fakhyra, Fakhyrah, Fakheera, Fakira, Fakirah, Fakeera, Fakyra

Fala (Native American) Resembling a crow
Falah, Falla, Fallah

Fallon (Irish) A commanding woman
Fallyn, Faline, Falinne, Faleen, Faleene, Falynne, Falyn, Falina

Fantasia (Latin) From the fantasy land
Fantasiah, Fantasea, Fantasiya, Fantazia, Fantazea, Fantaziya

Farley (English) From the fern clearing
Farly, Farli, Farlie, Farlee, Farleigh, Farlea, Farleah

Fate (Greek) One's destiny
Fayte, Faite, Faete, Faet, Fait, Fayt

Fatima (Arabic) The perfect woman
Fatimah, Fahima, Fahimah

Fatinah (Arabic) A captivating woman
Fatina, Fateena, Fateenah, Fatyna, Fatynah, Fatin, Fatine, Faatinah, Fateana, Fateanah, Fatiena, Fatienah, Fateina, Fateinah

Favor (English) One who grants her approval
Faver, Favar, Favorre

Fay (English) From the fairy kingdom; a fairy or an elf
Faye, Fai, Faie, Fae, Fayette, Faylinn, Faylyn, Faylynn

Fayina (Russian) An independent woman
Fayinah, Fayena, Fayeena, Fayeana, Fayiena, Fayeina

February (American) Born in the month of February
Februari, Februarie, Februarey, Februaree, Februarea

Feechi (African) A woman who worships God
Feechie, Feechy, Feechey, Feechee, Fychi, Fychie, Fychey, Fychy

Felicity (Latin) Form of Felicia, meaning "happy"
Felicy, Felicie, Felisa

Femi (African) God loves me
Femmi, Femie, Femy, Femey, Femee, Femea, Femeah

Fenia (Scandinavian) A gold worker
Feniah, Fenea, Feneah, Feniya, Feniyah, Fenya, Fenyah, Fenja

Fernanda (Spanish) Feminine form of Fernando; an adventurous woman

Fernilia (American) A successful woman
Ferniliah, Fernilea, Fernileah, Fernilya, Fernilyah

Fia (Portuguese / Italian / Scottish) A weaver / from the flickering fire / arising from the dark of peace
Fiah, Fea, Feah, Fya, Fiya, Fyah, Fiyah

Fianna (Irish) A warrior huntress
Fiannah, Fiana, Fianne, Fiane, Fiann, Fian

Fielda (English) From the field
Fieldah, Felda, Feldah

Fife (American) Having dancing eyes
Fyfe, Fifer, Fify, Fifey, Fifee, Fifea, Fifi, Fifie

Fifia (African) Born on a Friday
Fifiah, Fifea, Fifeah, Fifeea, Fifeeah

Filipa (Spanish) Feminine form of Phillip; a friend of horses
Filipah, Filipina, Filipeena, Filipyna, Filippa, Fillipa, Fillippa

Fina (English) Feminine form of Joseph; God will add
Finah, Feena, Fyna, Fifine, Fifna, Fifne, Fini, Feana

^**Finley** (Gaelic) A fair-haired hero
Finlay, Finly, Finlee, Finli, Finlie, Finnley, Finnlee, Finnli, Finn, Fin

Finnea (Gaelic) From the stream of the wood
Finneah, Finnia, Fynnea, Finniah, Fynnia

Fiona (Gaelic) One who is fair; a white-shouldered woman
Fionna, Fione, Fionn, Finna, Fionavar, Fionnghuala, Fionnuala, Fynballa

Firdaus (Arabic) From the garden in paradise

Flair (English) An elegant woman of natural talent
Flaire, Flare, Flayr, Flayre, Flaer, Flaere

Flame (American) A passionate and fiery woman
Flaym, Flayme, Flaime, Flaim, Flaem, Flaeme

Flannery (Gaelic) From the flatlands
Flanery, Flanneri, Flannerie, Flannerey, Flannaree, Flannerea

Fleming (English) Woman from Belgium
Flemyng, Flemming, Flemmyng

Fleta (English) One who is swift
Fletah, Flete, Fleda, Flita, Flyta

Florence (Latin) A flourishing woman; a blooming flower
Florencia, Florentina, Florenza, Florentine, Florentyna, Florenteena, Florenteene, Florentyne

Florizel (English) A young woman in bloom
Florizell, Florizelle, Florizele, Florizel, Florizella, Florizela, Florazel, Florazell

Fola (African) Woman of honor
Folah, Folla, Follah

Fontenot (French) One who is special

Forest (English) A woodland dweller
Forrest

Forever (American) Everlasting

Francesca (Italian) Form of Frances, meaning "one who is free"
Francia, Francina, Francisca, Franchesca, Francie, Frances

Frederica (German) Peaceful ruler
Freda, Freida, Freddie, Rica

Freira (Spanish) A sister
Freirah, Freyira, Freyirah

^**Freya** (Norse) A lady
Freyah, Freyja, Freja

Freydis (Norse) Woman born into the nobility
Freydiss, Freydisse, Freydys, Fredyss, Fraidis, Fradis, Fraydis, Fraedis

^**Frida** (German) Peaceful
Frieda, Fryda

Fuchsia (Latin) Resembling the flower
Fusha, Fushia, Fushea, Fewsha, Fewshia, Fewshea

Fury (Greek) An enraged woman; in mythology, a winged goddess who punished wrongdoers
Furey, Furi, Furie, Furee

G

*****Gabriella** (Italian / Spanish) Feminine form of Gabriel; heroine of God
Gabriela, Gabriellia, Gabrila, Gabryela, Gabryella

Gabrielle (Hebrew) Feminine form of Gabriel; heroine of God
Gabriel, Gabriela, Gabriele, Gabriell, Gabriellen, Gabriellia, Gabrila

Galena (Greek) Feminine form of Galen; one who is calm and peaceful
Galene, Galenah, Galenia, Galenea

Galiana (Arabic) The name of a Moorish princess
Galianah, Galianna, Galianne, Galiane, Galian, Galyana, Galyanna, Galyann

Galila (Hebrew) From the rolling hills
Galilah, Gelila, Gelilah, Gelilia, Gelilya, Glila, Glilah, Galyla

Galilee (Hebrew) From the sacred sea
Galileigh, Galilea, Galiley, Galily, Galili, Galilie

Galina (Russian) Form of Helen, meaning "the shining light"
Galinah, Galyna, Galynah, Galeena, Galeenah, Galine, Galyne, Galeene

Garbi (Basque) One who is pure; clean
Garbie, Garby, Garbey, Garbee, Garbea, Garbeah

Gardenia (English) Resembling the sweet-smelling flower
Gardeniah, Gardenea, Gardyna

Garima (Indian) A woman of importance
Garimah, Garyma, Gareema

Garnet (English) Resembling the dark-red gem
Garnette, Granata, Grenata, Grenatta

Gasha (Russian) One who is well-behaved
Gashah, Gashia, Gashea, Gashiah, Gasheah

Gavina (Latin) Feminine form of Gavin; resembling the white falcon; woman from Gabio

Gaza (Hebrew) Having great strength
Gazah, Gazza, Gazzah

Geila (Hebrew) One who brings joy to others
Geela, Geelah, Geelan, Geilah, Geiliya, Geiliyah, Gelisa, Gellah

^**Gemma** (Latin) As precious as a jewel
Gemmalyn, Gemmalynn, Gem, Gema, Gemmaline, Jemma

⋆**Genesis** (Hebrew) Of the beginning; the first book of the Bible
Genesies, Genesiss, Genessa, Genisis

Genevieve (French) White wave; fair-skinned
Genavieve, Geneve, Genevie, Genivee, Genivieve, Genoveva, Gennie, Genny

Georgia (Greek) Feminine form of George; one who works the earth; a farmer; from the state of Georgia
Georgeann, Georgeanne, Georgina, Georgena, Georgene, Georgetta, Georgette, Georgiana, Jeorjia

Gerardine (English) Feminine form of Gerard; one who is mighty with a spear
Gerarda, Gerardina, Gerardyne, Gererdina, Gerardyna, Gerrardene, Gerhardina, Gerhardine

Gertrude (German) Adored warrior
Geertruide, Geltruda, Geltrudis, Gert, Gerta, Gerte, Gertie, Gertina, Trudy

^**Gia** (Italian) Form of Gianna, meaning "God is Gracious"
Giah

Giada (Italian) Jade
Giadda

⋆**Gianna** (Italian) Feminine form of John, meaning "God is gracious"
Gia, Giana, Giovana

Gillian (Latin) One who is youthful
Gilian, Giliana, Gillianne, Ghilian

Gina (Japanese / English) A silvery woman / form of Eugenia, meaning "a well-born woman"; form of Jean, meaning "God is gracious"
Geana, Geanndra, Geena, Geina, Gena, Genalyn, Geneene, Genelle

Ginger (English) A lively woman; resembling the spice
Gingee, Gingie, Ginjer, Gingea, Gingy, Gingey, Gingi

Ginny (English) Form of Virginia, meaning "one who is chaste; virginal"
Ginnee, Ginnelle, Ginnette, Ginnie, Ginnilee, Ginna, Ginney, Ginni

Giona (Italian) Resembling the bird of peace
Gionah, Gionna, Gyona, Gyonna, Gionnah, Gyonah, Gyonnah

Giovanna (Italian) Feminine form of Giovanni; God is gracious
Geovana, Geovanna, Giavanna, Giovana, Giovani, Giovanni, Giovanie, Giovanee

Giselle (French) One who offers her pledge
Gisel, Gisela, Gisella, Jiselle

Gita (Hindi / Hebrew) A beautiful song / a good woman
Gitah, Geeta, Geetah, Gitika, Gatha, Gayatri, Gitel, Gittel

Gitana (Spanish) A gypsy woman
Gitanah, Gitanna, Gitannah, Gitane

Githa (Anglo-Saxon) A gift from God
Githah, Gytha

^**Giulia** (Italian) Form of Julia, meaning "one who is youthful, daughter of the sky"
***Giuliana**, Giulie, Giulietta, Giuliette*

Gladys (Welsh) Form of Claudia, meaning "one who is lame"
Gladdis, Gladdys, Gladi, Gladis, Gladyss, Gwladys, Gwyladyss, Gleda

Glenna (Gaelic) From the valley between the hills
Gleana, Gleneen, Glenene, Glenine, Glen, Glenn, Glenne, Glennene

Glenys (Welsh) A holy woman
Glenice, Glenis, Glennice, Glennis, Glennys, Glynis

Gloria (Latin) A renowned and highly praised woman
Gloriana, Glorianna, Glorya, Glorie, Gloree, Gloriane

Golda (English) Resembling the precious metal
Goldarina, Goldarine, Goldee, Goldi, Goldie, Goldina, Goldy, Goldia

Gordana (Serbian / Scottish) A proud woman / one who is heroic
Gordanah, Gordanna, Gordania, Gordaniya, Gordanea, Gordannah, Gordaniah, Gordaniyah

*__Grace__ (Latin) Having God's favor; in mythology, the Graces were the personification of beauty, charm, and grace
Gracee, Gracella, Gracelynn, Gracelynne, Gracey, Gracia, Graciana, Gracie, Gracelyn

Gracie (Latin) Form of Grace, meaning "having God's favor"
Gracee, Gracey, Graci

Granada (Spanish) From the Moorish kingdom
Granadda, Grenada, Grenadda

Greer (Scottish) Feminine form of Gregory; one who is alert and watchful
Grear, Grier, Gryer

Gregoria (Latin) Feminine form of Gregory; one who is alert and watchful
Gregoriana, Gregorijana, Gregorina, Gregorine, Gregorya, Gregoryna, Gregorea, Gregoriya

Greta (German) Resembling a pearl
Greeta, Gretal, Grete, Gretel, Gretha, Grethe, Grethel, Gretna, Gretchen

Guadalupe (Spanish) From the valley of wolves
Guadelupe, Lupe, Lupita

Gudny (Swedish) One who is unspoiled
Gudney, Gudni, Gudnie, Gudne, Gudnee, Gudnea, Gudneah

Guinevere (Welsh) One who is fair; of the white wave; in mythology, King Arthur's queen
Guenever, Guenevere, Gueniver, Guenna, Guennola, Guinever, Guinna, Gwen

Guiseppina (Italian) Feminine form of Guiseppe; the Lord will add
Giuseppyna, Giuseppa, Giuseppia, Giuseppea, Guiseppie, Guiseppia, Guiseppa, Giuseppina

Gulielma (German) Feminine form of Wilhelm; determined protector
Guglielma, Guillelmina, Guillielma, Gulielmina, Guillermina

Gulinar (Arabic) Resembling the pomegranate
Gulinare, Gulinear, Gulineir, Gulinara, Gulinaria, Gulinarea

Gwendolyn (Welsh) One who is fair; of the white ring
Guendolen, Guendolin, Guendolinn, Guendolynn, Guenna, Gwen, Gwenda, Gwendaline, Wendy

Gwyneth (Welsh) One who is blessed with happiness
Gweneth, Gwenith, Gwenyth, Gwineth, Gwinneth, Gwinyth, Gwynith, Gwynna

Gytha (English) One who is treasured
Gythah

Habbai (Arabic) One who is much loved
Habbae, Habbay, Habbaye

Habiba (Arabic) Feminine form of Habib; one who is dearly loved; sweetheart
Habibah, Habeeba, Habyba

Hachi (Native American / Japanese) From the river / having good fortune
Hachie, Hachee, Hachiko, Hachiyo, Hachy, Hachey, Hachikka

Hadara (Hebrew) A spectacular ornament; adorned with beauty
Hadarah, Hadarit, Haduraq, Hadarra, Hadarrah

Hadassah (Hebrew) From the myrtle tree
Hadassa, Hadasah, Hadasa

Hadiya (Arabic) A gift from God; a righteous woman
Hadiyah, Hadiyyah, Haadiyah, Haadiya, Hadeeya, Hadeeyah, Hadieya, Hadieyah

Hadlai (Hebrew) In a resting state; one who hinders
Hadlae, Hadlay, Hadlaye

^***Hadley** (English) From the field of heather
Hadlea, Hadleigh, Hadly, Hedlea, Hedleigh, Hedley, Hedlie, Hadlee

Hadria (Latin) From the town in northern Italy
Hadrea, Hadriana, Hadriane, Hadrianna, Hadrien, Hadrienne, Hadriah, Hadreah

Hafthah (Arabic) One who is protected by God
Haftha

Hagab (Hebrew) Resembling a grasshopper
Hagabah, Hagaba, Hagabe

Hagai (Hebrew) One who has been abandoned
Hagae, Hagay, Hagaye, Haggai, Haggae, Hagie, Haggie, Hagi

Hagen (Irish) A youthful woman
Hagan, Haggen, Haggan

Haggith (Hebrew) One who rejoices; the dancer
Haggithe, Haggyth, Haggythe, Hagith, Hagithe, Hagyth, Hagythe

Haidee (Greek) A modest woman; one who is well-behaved
Hadee, Haydee, Haydy, Haidi, Haidie, Haydi, Haydie, Haidy

***Hailey** (English) from the field of hay
Haley, Hayle, Hailee, ***Haylee****, Haylie, Haleigh, Hayley, Haeleigh*

Haimati (Indian) A queen of the snow-covered mountains
Haimatie, Haimaty, Haimatey, Haimatee, Haymati, Haymatie, Haymatee, Haimatea

Haimi (Hawaiian) One who searches for the truth
Haimie, Haimy, Haimey, Haimee, Haymi, Haymie, Haymee, Haimea

Hakana (Turkish) Feminine form of Hakan; ruler of the people; an empress
Hakanah, Hakanna, Hakane, Hakann, Hakanne

Hakkoz (Hebrew) One who has the qualities of a thorn
Hakoz, Hakkoze, Hakoze, Hakkoza, Hakoza

Halak (Hebrew) One who is bald; smooth

Haleigha (Hawaiian) Born with the rising sun
Haleea, Haleya, Halya

Hall (American) One who is distinguished
Haul

Hallie (Scandinavian / Greek / English) From the hall / woman of the sea / from the field of hay
Halley, Hallie, Halle, Hallee, Hally, Halleigh, Hallea, Halleah

Halo (Latin) Having a blessed aura
Haylo, Haelo, Hailo

Halsey (American) A playful woman
Halsy, Halsee, Halsea, Halsi, Halsie, Halcie, Halcy, Halcey

Halyn (American) A unique young woman
Halynn, Halynne, Halin, Halinn, Halinne

Hammon (Hebrew) Of the warm springs

Hamula (Hebrew) Feminine form of Hamul; spared by God
Hamulah, Hamulla, Hamullah

Hana (Japanese / Arabic) Resembling a flower blossom / a blissful woman
Hanah, Hanako

Hanan (Arabic) One who shows mercy and compassion

Hang (Vietnamese) Of the moon

Hanika (Hebrew) A graceful woman
Hanikah, Haneeka, Haneekah, Hanyka, Hanykah, Haneika, Haneikah, Hanieka

Hanita (Indian) Favored with divine grace
Hanitah, Hanyta, Haneeta, Hanytah, Haneetah, Haneita, Haneitah, Hanieta

Haniyah (Arabic) One who is pleased; happy
Haniya, Haniyyah, Haniyya, Hani, Hanie, Hanee, Hany, Haney

***Hannah** (Hebrew) Having favor and grace; in the Bible, mother of Samuel
Hanalee, Hanalise, Hanna, Hanne, Hannele, Hannelore, Hannie, Hanny, Chana

Hanya (Aboriginal) As solid as a stone

Happy (American) A joyful woman
Happey, Happi, Happie, Happee, Happea

Hara (Hebrew) From the mountainous land
Harah, Harra, Harrah

Haradah (Hebrew) One who is filled with fear
Harada

Harika (Turkish) A superior woman
Harikah, Haryka, Hareeka, Harykah, Hareekah, Hareaka, Hareakah

Hariti (Indian) In mythology, the goddess for the protection of children
Haritie, Haryti, Harytie, Haritee, Harytee, Haritea, Harytea

Harley (English) From the meadow of the hares
Harlea, Harlee, Harleen, Harleigh, Harlene, Harlie, Harli, Harly

Harlow (American) An impetuous woman

Harmony (English / Latin) Unity / musically in tune
Harmonie, Harmoni, Harmonee

***Harper** (English) One who plays or makes harps

Harriet (German) Feminine form of Henry; ruler of the house
Harriett, Hanriette, Hanrietta, Harriette, Harrietta, Harrette

Harva (English) A warrior of the army

Hasibah (Arabic) Feminine form of Hasib; one who is noble and respected
Hasiba, Hasyba, Hasybah, Haseeba, Haseebah

Hasina (African) One who is good and beautiful
Hasinah, Hasyna, Hasynah

Haurana (Hebrew) Feminine form of Hauran; woman from the caves
Hauranna, Hauranah, Haurann, Hauranne

Haven (English) One who provides a safe haven
Hayven, Havan, Hayvan, Havon, Hayvon, Havin, Hayvin, Havyn, Hayvyn, Haeven, Haevin, Haevan

Havva (Turkish) A giver of the breath of life
Havvah, Havvia, Havviah

Hayden (English) From the hedged valley
Haden, Haydan, Haydn, Haydon, Haeden, Haedyn, Hadyn

Hayud (Arabic) From the mountain
Hayuda, Hayudah, Hayood, Hayooda

Hazel (English) From the hazel tree
Hazell, Hazelle, Haesel, Hazle, Hazal, Hayzel, Haezel, Haizel

Heartha (Teutonic) A gift from Mother Earth

Heather (English) Resembling the evergreen flowering plant
Hether, Heatha, Heath, Heathe

Heaven (American) From paradise; from the sky
Heavely, Heavenly, Hevean, Hevan, Heavynne, Heavenli, Heavenlie, Heavenleigh, Heavenlee, Heavenley, Heavenlea, Heavyn

Hecate (Greek) In mythology, a goddess of fertility and witchcraft
Hekate

Heidi (German) Of the nobility, serene
Heidy, Heide, Hydie

Heirnine (Greek) Form of Helen, meaning "the shining light"
Heirnyne, Heirneine, Heirniene, Heirneene, Heirneane

Helen (Greek) The shining light; in mythology, Helen was the most beautiful woman in the world
Helene, Halina, Helaine, Helana, Heleena, Helena, Helenna, Hellen, Aleen, Elaine, Eleanor, Elena, Ellen, Galina, Heirnine, Helice, Leanna, Yalena

Helia (Greek) Daughter of the sun
Heliah, Helea, Heleah, Heliya, Heliyah, Heller, Hellar

Helice (Greek) Form of Helen, meaning "the shining light"
Helyce, Heleece, Heliece, Heleace

Helike (Greek) In mythology, a willow nymph who nurtured Zeus
Helica, Helyke, Helika, Helyka, Helyca

Helle (Greek) In mythology, the daughter of Athamas who escaped sacrifice on the back of a golden ram

Helma (German) Form of Wilhelmina, meaning "determined protector"
Helmah, Helmia, Helmea, Helmina, Helmyna, Helmeena, Helmine, Helmyne

Heloise (French) One who is famous in battle
Helois, Heloisa, Helewidis

Hen (English) Resembling the mothering bird

Henrietta (German) Feminine form of Henry; ruler of the house
Henretta, Henrieta, Henriette, Henrika, Henryetta, Hetta, Hette, Hettie

Hephzibah (Hebrew) She is my delight
Hepsiba, Hepzibeth, Hepsey

Herdis (Scandinavian) A battle maiden
Herdiss, Herdisse, Herdys

Hermelinda (Spanish) Bearing a powerful shield
Hermelynda, Hermalinda, Hermalynda, Hermelenda

Hermia (Greek) Feminine form of Hermes; a messenger of the gods
Hermiah, Hermea, Hermila

Hermona (Hebrew) From the mountain peak
Hermonah, Hermonna

Hernanda (Spanish) One who is daring
Hernandia, Hernandea, Hernandiya

Herra (Greek) Daughter of the earth
Herrah

Hersala (Spanish) A lovely woman
Hersalah, Hersalla, Hersallah, Hersalia, Hersaliah, Hersalea, Hersaleah

Hesiena (African) The first-born of twins
Hesienna, Hesienah, Heseina

Hesione (Greek) In mythology, a Trojan princess saved by Hercules from a sea monster

Hester (Greek) A starlike woman
Hestere, Hesther, Hesta, Hestar

Heven (American) A pretty young woman
Hevin, Hevon, Hevun, Hevven, Hevvin, Hevvon, Hevvun

Hezer (Hebrew) A woman of great strength
Hezir, Hezyr, Hezire, Hezyre, Hezere

Hiah (Korean) A bright woman
Heija, Heijah, Hia

Hibiscus (Latin) Resembling the showy flower
Hibiskus, Hibyscus, Hibyskus, Hybiscus, Hybiskus, Hybyscus, Hybyskus

Hikmah (Arabic) Having great wisdom
Hikmat, Hikma

Hilan (Greek) Filled with happines
Hylan, Hilane, Hilann, Hilanne, Hylane, Hylann, Hylanne

Hilary (Latin) A cheerful woman
Hillary, Hillery, Ellery

Hina (Polynesian) In mythology, a dual goddess symbolizing day and night
Hinna, Henna, Hinaa, Hinah, Heena, Hena

Hind (Arabic) Owning a group of camels; a wife of Muhammed
Hynd, Hinde, Hynde

Hinda (Hebrew) Resembling a doe
Hindah, Hindy, Hindey, Hindee, Hindi, Hindie, Hynda, Hyndy

Hiriwa (Polynesian) A silvery woman

Hitomi (Japanese) One who has beautiful eyes
Hitomie, Hitomee, Hitomea, Hitomy, Hitomey

Holda (German) A secretive woman; one who is hidden
Holde

Hollander (Dutch) A woman from Holland
Hollynder, Hollender, Holander, Holynder, Holender, Hollande, Hollanda

Holly (English) Of the holly tree
Holli, Hollie, Hollee, Holley, Hollye, Hollyanne, Holle, Hollea

Holton (American) One who is whimsical
Holten, Holtan, Holtin, Holtyn, Holtun

Holy (American) One who is pious or sacred
Holey, Holee, Holeigh, Holi, Holie, Holye, Holea, Holeah

Hope (English) One who has high expectations through faith

Hortensia (Latin) Woman of the garden
Hartencia, Hartinsia, Hortencia, Hortense, Hortenspa, Hortenxia, Hortinzia, Hortendana

Hova (African) Born into the middle class

Hoyden (American) A spirited woman
Hoiden, Hoydan, Hoidan, Hoydyn, Hoidyn, Hoydin, Hoidin

Hudson (English) One who is adventurous; an explorer
Hudsen, Hudsan, Hudsun, Hudsyn, Hudsin

Hueline (German) An intelligent woman
Huelene, Huelyne, Hueleine, Hueliene, Hueleene, Huleane

Huhana (Maori) Form of Susannah, meaning "white lily"
Huhanah, Huhanna, Huhanne, Huhann, Huhane

Humita (Native American) One who shells corn
Humitah, Humyta, Humeeta, Humieta, Humeita, Humeata, Humytah, Humeetah

Hutena (Hurrian) In mythology, the goddess of fate
Hutenah, Hutenna, Hutyna, Hutina

Huwaidah (Arabic) One who is gentle
Huwaydah, Huwaida

Huyen (Vietnamese) A woman with jet-black hair

Hypatia (Greek) An intellectually superior woman
Hypasia, Hypacia, Hypate

Hypermnestra (Greek) In mythology, the mother of Amphiareos

I

Ianthe (Greek) Resembling the violet flower; in mythology, a sea nymph, a daughter of Oceanus
Iantha, Ianthia, Ianthina

Ibtesam (Arabic) One who smiles often
Ibtisam, Ibtysam

Ibtihaj (Arabic) A delight; bringer of joy
Ibtehaj, Ibtyhaj

Ida (Greek) One who is diligent; hardworking; in mythology, the nymph who cared for Zeus on Mount Ida
Idania, Idaea, Idalee, Idaia, Idania, Idalia, Idalie, Idana

Idil (Latin) A pleasant woman
Idyl, Idill, Idyll

Idoia (Spanish) Refers to the Virgin Mary
Idoea, Idurre, Iratze, Izazkun

Idona (Scandinavian) A fresh-faced woman
Idonah, Idonna, Idonnah

Ife (African) One who loves and is loved
Ifeh, Iffe

Ignatia (Latin) A fiery woman; burning brightly
Igantiah, Ignacia, Ignazia

Iheoma (Hawaiian) Lifted up by God

Ikeida (American) A spontaneous woman
Ikeidah, Ikeyda, Ikeydah

Ilamay (French) From the island
Ilamaye, Ilamai, Ilamae

Ilandere (American) Moon woman
Ilander, Ilanderre, Ilandera, Ilanderra

Ilia (Greek) From the ancient city
Iliah, Ilea, Ileah, Iliya, Iliyah, Ilya, Ilyah

Iliana (English) Form of Aileen, meaning, "the light-bearer"
Ilianna, Ilyana, Ilyanna, Ilene, Iline, Ilyne

Ilithyia (Greek) In mythology, goddess of childbirth
Ilithya, Ilithiya, Ilithyiah

Ilma (German) Form of Wilhelmina, meaning "determined protector"
Ilmah, Illma, Illmah

Ilori (African) A special child; one who is treasured
Illori, Ilorie, Illorie, Ilory, Illory, Ilorey, Illorey, Iloree

Ilta (Finnish) Born at night
Iltah, Illta

Ilyse (German / Greek) Born into the nobility / form of Elyse, meaning "blissful"
Ilysea, Ilysia, Ilysse, Ilysea

Imala (Native American) One who disciplines others
Imalah, Imalla, Imallah, Immala, Immalla

Iman (Arabic) Having great faith
Imani, Imanie, Imania, Imaan, Imany, Imaney, Imanee, Imanea, Imain, Imaine, Imayn

Imanuela (Spanish) A faithful woman
Imanuella, Imanuel, Imanuele, Imanuell

Imari (Japanese) Daughter of today
Imarie, Imaree, Imarea, Imary, Imarey

Imelda (Italian) Warrior in the universal battle
Imeldah, Imalda, Imaldah

Imperia (Latin) A majestic woman
Imperiah, Imperea, Impereah, Imperial, Imperiel, Imperielle, Imperialle

Ina (Polynesian) In mythology, a moon goddess
Inah, Inna, Innah

Inaki (Asian) Having a generous nature
Inakie, Inaky, Inakey, Inakea, Inakee

Inanna (Sumerian) A lady of the sky; in mythology, goddess of love, fertility, war, and the earth
Inannah, Inana, Inanah, Inann, Inanne, Inane

Inara (Arabic) A heaven-sent daughter; one who shines with light
Inarah, Innara, Inarra, Innarra

Inari (Finnish / Japanese) Woman from the lake / one who is successful
Inarie, Inaree, Inary, Inarey, Inarea, Inareah

Inaya (Arabic) One who cares for the well-being of others
Inayah, Inayat

Inca (Indian) An adventurer
Incah, Inka, Inkah, Incka, Inckah

India (English) From the river; woman from India
Indea, Indiah, Indeah, Indya, Indiya, Indee, Inda, Indy

Indiana (English) From the land of the Indians; from the state of Indiana
Indianna, Indyana, Indyanna

Indiece (American) A capable woman
Indeice, Indeace, Indeece, Indiese, Indeise, Indeese, Indease

Indigo (English) Resembling the plant; a purplish-blue dye
Indygo, Indeego

Ineesha (American) A sparkling woman
Ineeshah, Ineisha, Ineishah, Iniesha, Inieshah, Ineasha, Ineashah, Ineysha

Ingalls (American) A peaceful woman

Ingelise (Danish) Having the grace of the god Ing
Ingelisse, Ingeliss, Ingelyse, Ingelisa, Ingelissa, Ingelysa, Ingelyssa

Inghean (Scottish) Her father's daughter
Ingheane, Inghinn, Ingheene, Ingheen, Inghynn

Ingrid (Scandinavian) Having the beauty of the God Ing
Ingred, Ingrad, Inga, Inge, Inger, Ingmar, Ingrida, Ingria, Ingrit, Inkeri

Inis (Irish) Woman from Ennis
Iniss, Inisse, Innis, Inys, Innys, Inyss, Inysse

Intisar (Arabic) One who is victorious; triumphant
Intisara, Intisarah, Intizar, Intizara, Intizarah, Intisarr, Intysarr, Intysar

Iolanthe (Greek) Resembling a violet flower
Iolanda, Iolanta, Iolantha, Iolante, Iolande, Iolanthia, Iolanthea

Iona (Greek) Woman from the island
Ionna, Ioane, Ioann, Ioanne

Ionanna (Hebrew) Filled with grace
Ionannah, Ionana, Ionann, Ionane, Ionanne

Ionia (Greek) Of the sea and islands
Ionya, Ionija, Ioniah, Ionea, Ionessa, Ioneah, Ioniya

Iosepine (Hawaiian) Form of Josephine, meaning "God will add"
Iosephine, Iosefa, Iosefena, Iosefene, Iosefina, Iosefine, Iosepha, Iosephe

Iowa (Native American) Of the Iowa tribe; from the state of Iowa

Iphedeiah (Hebrew) One who is saved by the Lord

Iphigenia (Greek) One who is born strong; in mythology, daughter of Agamemnon
Iphigeneia, Iphigenie

Ipsa (Indian) One who is desired
Ipsita, Ipsyta, Ipseeta, Ipseata, Ipsah

Iratze (Basque) Refers to the Virgin Mary
Iratza, Iratzia, Iratzea, Iratzi, Iratzie, Iratzy, Iratzey, Iratzee

Ireland (Celtic) The country of the Irish
Irelan, Irelann

Irem (Turkish) From the heavenly gardens
Irema, Ireme, Iremia, Iremea

Irene (Greek) A peaceful woman; in mythology, the goddess of peace
Ira, Irayna, Ireen, Iren, Irena, Irenea, Irenee, Irenka, Eirene

Ireta (Greek) One who is serene
Iretah, Iretta, Irettah, Irete, Iret, Irett, Ireta

Iris (Greek) Of the rainbow; a flower; a messenger goddess
Irida, Iridiana, Iridianny, Irisa, Irisha, Irita, Iria, Irea, Iridian, Iriss, Irys, Iryss

Irma (German) A universal woman

Irta (Greek) Resembling a pearl
Irtah

Irune (Basque) Refers to the Holy Trinity
Iroon, Iroone, Iroun, Iroune

***Isabel** (Spanish) Form of Elizabeth, meaning "my God is bountiful; God's promise"
Isabeau, Isabela, Isabele, Isabelita, Isabell, Isabelle, Ishbel, Ysabel

***Isabella** (Italian / Spanish) Form of Isabel, meaning consecrated to God
Isabela, Isabelita, Isobella, Izabella, Isibella, Isibela

Isadore (Greek) A gift from the goddess Isis
Isadora, Isador, Isadoria, Isidor, Isidoro, Isidorus, Isidro, Isidora

Isana (German) A strong-willed woman
Isanah, Isanna, Isane, Isann

Isela (American) A giving woman
Iselah, Isella, Isellah

Isis (Egyptian) In mythology, the most powerful of all goddesses

Isla (Gaelic) From the island
Islae, Islai, Isleta

Isleen (Gaelic) Form of Aisling, meaning "a dream or vision; an inspiration"
Isleene, Islyne, Islyn, Isline, Isleine, Isliene, Islene, Isleyne

Isolde (Celtic) A woman known for her beauty; in mythology, the lover of Tristan
Iseult, Iseut, Isold, Isolda, Isolt, Isolte, Isota, Isotta

Isra (Arabic) One who travels in the evening
Israh, Isria, Isrea, Israt

Itiah (Hebrew) One who is comforted by God
Itia, Iteah, Itea, Itiyah, Itiya, Ityah, Itya

Itidal (Arabic) One who is cautious
Itidalle, Itidall, Itidale

Itsaso (Basque) Woman of the ocean
Itasasso, Itassaso, Itassasso

Iudita (Hawaiian) An affectionate woman
Iuditah, Iudyta, Iudytah, Iudeta, Iudetah

Iuginia (Hawaiian) A high-born woman
Iuginiah, Iuginea, Iugineah, Iugynia

Ivana (Slavic) Feminine form of Ivan; God is gracious
Iva, Ivah, Ivania, Ivanka, Ivanna, Ivanya, Ivanea, Ivane, Ivanne

Ivory (English) Having a creamy-white complexion; as precious as elephant tusks
Ivorie, Ivorine, Ivoreen, Ivorey, Ivoree, Ivori, Ivoryne, Ivorea

Ivy (English) Resembling the evergreen vining plant
Ivie, Ivi, Ivea

Iwilla (American) She shall rise
Iwillah, Iwilah, Iwila, Iwylla, Iwyllah, Iwyla, Iwylah

Ixchel (Mayan) The rainbow lady; in mythology, the goddess of the earth, moon, and healing
Ixchell, Ixchelle, Ixchela, Ixchella, Ixchal, Ixchall, Ixchalle, Ixchala

Iyabo (African) The mother is home

Izanne (American) One who calms others
Izann, Izane, Izana, Izan, Izanna

Izolde (Greek) One who is philosophical
Izold, Izolda

J

Jacey (American) Form of Jacinda, meaning "resembling the hyacinth"
Jacee, Jacelyn, Jaci, Jacine, Jacy, Jaicee, Jaycee, Jacie

Jacinda (Spanish) Resembling the hyacinth
Jacenda, Jacenia, Jacenta, Jacindia, Jacinna, Jacinta, Jacinth, Jacintha, Jacinthe, Jacinthia, Jacynth, Jacyntha, Jacynthe, Jacynthia, Jakinda, Jakinta, Jaikinda, Jaekinda

Jacqueline (French) Feminine form of Jacques; the supplanter
Jackie, Xaquelina, Jacalin, Jacalyn, Jacalynn, Jackalin, Jackalinne, Jackelyn, Jacquelyn

Jade (Spanish) Resembling the green gemstone
Jadeana, Jadee, Jadine, Jadira, Jadrian, Jadrienne, Jady

Jaden (Hebrew / English) One who is thankful to God / form of Jade, meaning "resembling the green gemstone"
Jadine, Jadyn, Jadon, Jayden, Jadyne, Jaydyn, Jaydon, Jaidyn

Jadzia (Polish) A princess; born into royalty
Jadziah, Jadzea, Jadzeah

Jae (English) Feminine form of Jay; resembling a jaybird
Jai, Jaelana, Jaeleah, Jaelyn, Jaenelle, Jaya

Jael (Hebrew) Resembling a mountain goat
Jaella, Jaelle, Jayel, Jaele, Jayil

Jaen (Hebrew) Resembling an ostrich
Jaena, Jaenia, Jaenea, Jaenne

Jaffa (Hebrew) A beautiful woman
Jaffah, Jafit, Jafita

Jalila (Arabic) An important woman; one who is exalted
Jalilah, Jalyla, Jalylah, Jaleela

Jamaica (American) From the island of springs
Jamaeca, Jamaika, Jemaica, Jamika, Jamieka

Jamie (Hebrew) Feminine form of James; she who supplants
Jaima, Jaime, Jaimee, Jaimelynn, Jaimey, Jaimi, Jaimie, Jaimy

Janan (Arabic) Of the heart and soul

Jane (Hebrew) Feminine form of John; God is gracious
Jaina, Jaine, Jainee, Janey, Jana, Janae, Janaye, Jandy, Sine, Janel, Janelle

Janet (Scottish) Feminine form of John, meaning "God is gracious"
Janetta, Jenetta, Janeta, Janette, Janit

Janis (English) Feminine form of John; God is gracious
Janice, Janeece, Janess, Janessa, Janesse, Janessia, Janicia, Janiece

Janiyah (American) Form of Jana, meaning gracious, merciful
Janiya, Janiah

Jarah (Hebrew) A sweet and kind woman

Jasher (Hebrew) One who is righteous; upright
Jashiere, Jasheria, Jasherea

Jaslene (American) Form of Jocelyn, meaning joy
Jaslin, Jaslyn, Jazlyn, Jazlynn

*****Jasmine** (Persian) Resembling the climbing plant with fragrant flowers
Jaslyn, Jaslynn, Jasmin, Jasmyn, Jazmin, Jazmine, Jazmyn

Javiera (Spanish) Feminine form of Xavier; one who is bright; the owner of a new home
Javierah, Javyera, Javyerah, Javeira, Javeirah

Jayda (English) Resembling the green gemstone
***Jada**, Jaydah, Jaida, Jaidah*

^**Jayla** (Arabic) One who is charitable
Jaela, Jaila, Jaylah, Jaylee, Jaylen, Jaylene, ***Jayleen****, Jaylin, Jaylyn, Jaylynn*

Jean (Hebrew) Feminine form of John; God is gracious
Jeanae, Jeanay, Jeane, Jeanee, Jeanelle, Jeanetta, Jeanette, Jeanice, Gina

Jemima (Hebrew) Our little dove; in the Bible, the eldest of Job's daughters
Jemimah, Jamina, Jeminah, Jemmimah, Jemmie, Jemmy, Jem, Jemmi, Jemmey, Jemmee, Jemmea

Jemma (English) Form of Gemma, meaning "as precious as a jewel"
Jemmah, Jema, Jemah, Jemmalyn, Jemalyn

Jena (Arabic) Our little bird
Jenna, Jenah

Jendayi (Egyptian) One who is thankful
Jendayie, Jendayey, Jendayee

Jennifer (Welsh) One who is fair; a beautiful girl
Jenefer, Jeni, Jenifer, Jeniffer, Jenn, Jennee, Jenni, Jen, ***Jenna****, Jenny*

Jeorjia (American) Form of Georgia, meaning "one who works the earth; a farmer"
Jeorgia, Jeorja, Jorja, Jorjette, Jorgette, Jorjeta, Jorjetta, Jorgete

Jereni (Slavic) One who is peaceful
Jerenie, Jereny, Jereney, Jerenee

Jermaine (French) Woman from Germany
Jermainaa, Jermane, Jermayne, Jermina, Jermana, Jermayna

^**Jessica** (Hebrew) The Lord sees all
Jess, Jessa, Jessaca, Jessaka, Jessalin, Jessalyn, Jesse, Jesseca, Yessica, Jessie

Jetta (Danish) Resembling the jet-black lustrous gemstone
Jette, Jett, Jeta, Jete, Jettie, Jetty, Jetti, Jettey

Jewel (French) One who is playful; resembling a precious gem
Jewell, Jewelle, Jewelyn, Jewelene, Jewelisa, Jule, Jewella, Juelline

Jezebel (Hebrew) One who is not exalted; in the Bible, the queen of Israel punished by God
Jessabell, Jetzabel, Jezabel, Jezabella, Jezebelle, Jezibel, Jezibelle, Jezybell

Jie (Chinese) One who is pure; chaste

Jiera (Lithuanian) A lively woman
Jierah, Jyera, Jyerah, Jierra, Jyerra

Jillian (English) Form of Gillian, meaning "one who is youthful"
Jilian, Jiliana, Jillaine, Jillan, Jillana, Jillane, Jillanne, Jillayne, Jillene, Jillesa, Jilliana, Jilliane, Jilliann, Jillianna, Jill

Jimena (Spanish) One who is heard

Jinelle (Welsh) Form of Genevieve, meaning "white wave; fair-skinned"
Jinell, Jinele, Jinel, Jynelle, Jynell, Jynele, Jynel

Jiselle (American) Form of Giselle, meaning "one who offers her pledge"
Jisell, Jisele, Jisela, Jizelle, Joselle, Jisella, Jizella, Jozelle

Jo (English) Feminine form of Joseph; God will add
Jobelle, Jobeth, Jodean, Jodelle, Joetta, Joette, Jolinda, Jolisa

Joanna (French) Feminine form of John, meaning "God is Gracious"
Joana

Jocelyn (German / Latin) From the tribe of Gauts / one who is cheerful, happy
Jocelin, Jocelina, Jocelinda, Joceline, Jocelyne, Jocelynn, Jocelynne, Josalind, Joslyn, Joslynn, Joselyn

Joda (Hebrew) An ancestor of Christ

Jolan (Greek) Resembling a violet flower
Jola, Jolaine, Jolande, Jolanne, Jolanta, Jolantha, Jolandi, Jolanka

^**Jolene** (English) Feminine form of Joseph; God will add
Joeline, Joeleen, Joeline, Jolaine, Jolean, Joleen, Jolena, Jolina

Jolie (French) A pretty young woman
Joly, Joely, Jolee, Joleigh, Joley, Joli

Jonina (Israeli) Resembling a little dove
Joninah, Jonyna, Jonynah, Joneena, Joneenah, Jonine, Jonyne, Joneene

Jorah (Hebrew) Resembling an autumn rose
Jora

Jord (Norse) In mythology, goddess of the earth
Jorde

Jordan (Hebrew) Of the down-flowing river; in the Bible, the river where Jesus was baptized
Jardena, Johrdan, Jordain, Jordaine, Jordana, Jordane, Jordanka, Jordyn, Jordin

Josephine (French) Feminine form of Joseph; God will add
Josefina, Josephene, Jo, Josie, Iosepine

Journey (American) One who likes to travel
Journy, Journi, Journie, Journee

Jovana (Spanish) Feminine form of Jovian; daughter of the sky
Jeovana, Jeovanna, Jovanna, Jovena, Jovianne, Jovina, Jovita, Joviana

Joy (Latin) A delight; one who brings pleasure to others
Jioia, Jioya, Joi, Joia, Joie, Joya, Joyann, Joyanna

Joyce (English) One who brings joy to others
Joice, Joyceanne, Joycelyn, Joycelynn, Joyse, Joyceta

Judith (Hebrew) Woman from Judea
Judithe, Juditha, Judeena, Judeana, Judyth, Judit, Judytha, Judita, Hudes

^***Julia** (Latin) One who is youthful; daughter of the sky
Jiulia, Joleta, Joletta, Jolette, Julaine, Julayna, Julee, Juleen, Julie, Julianne, ***Julieta***

Juliana (Spanish) Form of Julia, meaning "one who is youthful"
Julianna

Juliet (French) Form of Julia, meaning one who is youthful
Juliette, Julitta, Julissa

July (Latin) Form of Julia, meaning "one who is youthful; daughter of the sky"; born during the month of July
Julye

^**June** (Latin) One who is youthful; born during the month of June
Junae, Junel, Junelle, Junette, Junita, Junia

Justice (English) One who upholds moral rightness and fairness
Justyce, Justiss, Justyss, Justis, Justus, Justise

K

Kachina (Native American) A spiritual dancer
Kachine, Kachinah, Kachineh, Kachyna, Kacheena, Kachynah, Kacheenah, Kacheana

Kadin (Arabic) A beloved companion
Kadyn, Kadan, Kaden, Kadon, Kadun, Kaedin, Kaeden, Kaydin

Kaelyn (English) A beautiful girl from the meadow
Kaelynn, Kaelynne, Kaelin, Kailyn, Kaylyn, Kaelinn, Kaelinne

Kagami (Japanese) Displaying one's true image
Kagamie, Kagamy, Kagamey, Kagamee, Kagamea

Kailasa (Indian) From the silver mountain
Kailasah, Kailassa, Kaylasa, Kaelasa, Kailas, Kailase

*****Kaitlyn** (Greek) Form of Katherine, meaning "one who is pure, virginal"
Kaitlin, Kaitlan, Kaitleen, Kaitlynn, Katalin, Katalina, Katalyn, Katelin, Kateline, Katelinn, ***Katelyn****, Katelynn, Katilyn, Katlin*

Kakra (Egyptian) The younger of twins
Kakrah

Kala (Arabic / Hawaiian) A moment in time / form of Sarah, meaning "a princess; lady"
Kalah, Kalla, Kallah

Kalifa (Somali) A chaste and holy woman
Kalifah, Kalyfa, Kalyfah, Kaleefa, Kaleefah, Kalipha, Kalypha, Kaleepha, Kaleafa, Kaleafah, Kaleapha

Kalinda (Indian) Of the sun
Kalindah, Kalynda, Kalinde, Kalindeh, Kalindi, Kalindie, Kalyndi, Kalyndie

Kallie (English) Form of Callie, meaning "a beautiful girl"
Kalli, Kallita, Kally, Kalley, Kallee, Kalleigh, Kallea, Kalleah

Kalma (Finnish) In mythology, goddess of the dead

Kalyan (Indian) A beautiful and auspicious woman
Kalyane, Kalyanne, Kalyann, Kaylana, Kaylanna, Kalliyan, Kaliyan, Kaliyane

Kama (Indian) One who loves and is loved
Kamah, Kamma, Kammah

Kamala (Arabic) A woman of perfection
Kamalah, Kammala, Kamalla

Kamaria (African) Of the moon
Kamariah, Kamarea, Kamareah, Kamariya, Kamariyah

Kambiri (African) Newest addition to the family
Kambirie, Kambiry, Kambyry

Kamea (Hawaiian) The one and only; precious one
Kameo

^**Kamila** (Spanish) Form of Camilla, meaning ceremonial attendant
Kamilah

Kamyra (American) Surrounded by light
Kamira, Kamera, Kamiera, Kameira, Kameera, Kameara

Kanda (Native American) A magical woman
Kandah

Kanika (African) A dark, beautiful woman
Kanikah, Kanyka, Kanicka

Kantha (Indian) A delicate woman
Kanthah, Kanthe, Kantheh

Kanya (Thai) A young girl; a virgin

Kaoru (Japanese) A fragrant girl
Kaori

Kara (Greek / Italian / Gaelic) One who is pure / dearly loved / a good friend
Karah, Karalee, Karalie, Karalyn, Karalynn, Karrah, Karra, Khara

Karcsi (French) A joyful singer
Karcsie, Karcsy, Karcsey, Karcsee, Karcsea

Karen (Greek) Form of Katherine, meaning "one who is pure; virginal"
Karan, Karena, Kariana, Kariann, Karianna, Karianne, Karin, Karina

Karina (Scandinavian / Russian) One who is dear and pure
Karinah, Kareena, Karyna

Karisma (English) Form of Charisma, meaning "blessed with charm"
Kharisma, Karizma, Kharizma

Karissa (Greek) Filled with grace and kindness; very dear
Karisa, Karyssa, Karysa, Karessa, Karesa, Karis, Karise

Karla (German) Feminine form of Karl; a small strong, woman
Karly, Karli, Karlie, Karleigh, Karlee, Karley, Karlin, Karlyn, Karlina, Karleen

Karmel (Latin) Form of Carmel, meaning "of the fruitful orchard"
Karmelle, Karmell, Karmele, Karmela, Karmella

Karoline (English) A small and strong woman
Karolina, Karolinah, Karolyne, Karrie, Karie, Karri, Kari, Karry

Karsen (American) Variation of the Scottish Carson, meaning "from the swamp"
Karsyn, Karsin

Karsten (Greek) The anointed one
Karstin, Karstine, Karstyn, Karston, Karstan, Kiersten, Keirsten

Kasey (Irish) Form of Casey, meaning "a vigilant woman"
Kacie, Kaci, Kacy, KC, Kacee, Kacey, Kasie, Kasi

Kasi (Indian) From the holy city; shining

Kasmira (Slavic) A peacemaker
Kasmirah, Kasmeera

Kate (English) Form of Katherine, meaning "one who is pure, virginal"
Katie, Katey, Kati

*__Katherine__ (Greek) Form of Catherine, meaning "one who is pure; virginal"
Katharine, Katharyn, Kathy, Kathleen, Katheryn, Kathie, Kathrine, Kathryn, Karen, Kay

Katniss (American) From the young adult novel series *The Hunger Games*

Katriel (Hebrew) Crowned by God
Katriele, Katrielle, Katriell

Kaveri (Indian) From the sacred river
Kaverie, Kauveri, Kauverie, Kavery, Kaverey, Kaveree, Kaverea, Kauvery

Kay (English / Greek) The keeper of the keys / form of Katherine, meaning "one who is pure; virginal"
Kaye, Kae, Kai, Kaie, Kaya, Kayana, Kayane, Kayanna

Kayden (American) Form of Kaden, meaning "a beloved companion"

Kayla (Arabic / Hebrew) Crowned with laurel
Kaylah, Kalan, Kalen, Kalin, Kalyn, Kalynn, Kaylan, Kaylana, Kaylin, Kaylen, Kaylynn, Kaylyn, Kayle

*__Kaylee__ (American) Form of Kayla, meaning "crowned with laurel"
Kaleigh, Kaley, Kaelee, Kaeley, Kaeli, Kailee, Kailey, Kalee, Kayleigh, Kayley, Kayli, Kaylie

Kearney (Irish) The winner
Kearny, Kearni, Kearnie, Kearnee, Kearnea

Keaton (English) From a shed town
Keatan, Keatyn, Keatin, Keatun

Keavy (Irish) A lovely and graceful girl
Keavey, Keavi, Keavie, Keavee, Keavea

Keeya (African) Resembling a flower
Keeyah, Kieya, Keiya, Keyya

Kefira (Hebrew) Resembling a young lioness
Kefirah, Kefiera, Kefeira

Keira (Irish) Form of Kiera, meaning "little dark-haired one"
Kierra, Kyera, Kyerra, Keiranne, Kyra, Kyrie, Kira, Kiran

Keisha (American) The favorite child; form of Kezia, meaning "of the spice tree"
Keishla, Keishah, Kecia, Kesha, Keysha, Keesha, Kiesha, Keshia

Kelly (Irish) A lively and bright-headed woman
Kelley, Kelli, Kellie, Kellee, Kelliegh, Kellye, Keely, Keelie, Keeley, Keelyn

Kelsey (English) From the island of ships
Kelsie, Kelcey, Kelcie, Kelcy, Kellsie, Kelsa, Kelsea, Kelsee, Kelsi, Kelsy, Kellsey

Kendall (Welsh) From the royal valley
Kendal, Kendyl, Kendahl, Kindall, Kyndal, Kenley

Kendra (English) Feminine form of Kendrick; having royal power; from the high hill
Kendrah, Kendria, Kendrea, Kindra, Kindria

^**Kenley** (American) Variation of Kinley and McKinley

*__Kennedy__ (Gaelic) A helmeted chief
Kennedi, *Kennedie, Kennedey, Kennedee, Kenadia, Kenadie, Kenadi, Kenady, Kenadey*

Kensington (English) A brash lady
Kensyngton, Kensingtyn, Kinsington, Kinsyngton, Kinsingtyn

^**Kenzie** (American) Diminutive of McKenzie

Kerensa (Cornish) One who loves and is loved
Kerinsa, Keransa, Kerensia, Kerensea, Kerensya, Kerenz, Kerenza, Keranz

Kerr (Scottish) From the marshland

Keshon (American) Filled with happiness
Keyshon, Keshawn, Keyshawn, Kesean, Keysean, Keshaun, Keyshaun, Keshonna

Kevina (Gaelic) Feminine form of Kevin; a beautiful and beloved child
Kevinah, Keva, Kevia, Kevinne, Kevyn, Kevynn

Keyla (English) A wise daughter

Kezia (Hebrew) Of the spice tree
Keziah, Kesia, Kesiah, Kesi, Kessie, Ketzia, Keisha

Khai (American) Unlike the others; unusual
Khae, Khay, Khaye

Khalida (Arabic) Feminine form of Khalid; an immortal woman
Khalidah, Khaleeda, Khalyda

Khaliqa (Arabic) Feminine form of Khaliq; a creator; one who is well-behaved
Khaliqah, Khalyqa, Khaleeqa

Khayriyyah (Arabic) A charitable woman
Khayriyah, Khariyyah, Khariya, Khareeya

Khepri (Egyptian) Born of the morning sun
Kheprie, Kepri, Keprie, Khepry, Kepry, Khepree, Kepree, Kheprea

Khiana (American) One who is different
Khianna, Khiane, Khianne, Khian, Khyana, Khyanna, Kheana, Kheanna

*__Khloe__ (Greek) Form of Chloe, meaning "a flourishing woman, blooming"

Kiara (American) Form of Chiara, meaning "daughter of the light"

Kichi (Japanese) The fortunate one

Kidre (American) A loyal woman
Kidrea, Kidreah, Kidria, Kidriah, Kidri, Kidrie, Kidry, Kidrey

Kiele (Hawaiian) Resembling the gardenia
Kielle, Kiel, Kiell, Kiela, Kiella

Kikka (German) The mistress of all
Kika, Kykka, Kyka

Kiley (American) Form of Kylie, meaning "a boomerang"
Kylie

Kimana (American) Girl from the meadow
Kimanah, Kimanna

Kimball (English) Chief of the warriors; possessing royal boldness
Kimbal, Kimbell, Kimbel, Kymball, Kymbal

Kimberly (English) Of the royal fortress
Kimberley, Kimberli, Kimberlee, Kimberleigh, Kimberlin, Kimberlyn, Kymberlie, Kymberly

Kimeo (American) Filled with happiness
Kimeyo

Kimetha (American) Filled with joy
Kimethah, Kymetha

Kimiko (Japanese) A noble child; without equal

Kimora (American) Form of Kimberly, meaning "royal"

Kina (Hawaiian) Woman of China

Kinley (American) Variation of McKinley, Scottish, meaning offspring of the fair hero

Kinsey (English) The king's victory
Kinnsee, Kinnsey, Kinnsie, Kinsee, Kinsie, Kinzee, Kinzie, Kinzey

^**Kinsley** (English) From the king's meadow
Kinsly, Kinslee, Kinsleigh, Kinsli, Kinslie, Kingsley, Kingslee, Kingslie

Kioko (Japanese) A daughter born with happiness

Kirima (Eskimo) From the hill
Kirimah, Kiryma, Kirymah, Kirema, Kiremah, Kireema, Kireemah, Kireama

Kismet (English) One's destiny; fate

Kiss (American) A caring and compassionate woman
Kyss, Kissi, Kyssi, Kissie, Kyssie, Kissy, Kyssy, Kissey

Kobi (American) Woman from California
Kobie, Koby, Kobee, Kobey, Kobea

Kolette (English) Form of Colette, meaning "victory of the people"
Kolete, Kolett, Koleta, Koletta, Kolet

Komala (Indian) A delicate and tender woman
Komalah, Komalla, Komal, Komali, Komalie, Komalee

Kona (Hawaiian) A girly woman
Konah, Konia, Koniah, Konea, Koneah, Koni, Konie, Koney

Konane (Hawaiian) Daughter of the moonlight

Kreeli (American) A charming and kind girl
Kreelie, Krieli, Krielie, Kryli, Krylie, Kreely, Kriely, Kryly

Krenie (American) A capable woman
Kreni, Kreny, Kreney, Krenee

Kristina (English) Form of Christina, meaning "follower of Christ"
Kristena, Kristine, Kristyne, Kristyna, Krystina, Krystine

Kumi (Japanese) An everlasting beauty
Kumie, Kumy, Kumey, Kumee

Kyla (English) Feminine form of Kyle; from the narrow channel
Kylah, Kylar, Kyle

*__Kylie__ (Australian) A boomerang
Kylee, *Kyleigh, Kyley, Kyli, Kyleen, Kyleen, Kyler, Kily,Kileigh, Kilee, Kilie, Kili, Kilea, Kylea*

Kyra (Greek) Form of Cyrus, meaning "noble"
Kyrah, Kyria, Kyriah, Kyrra, Kyrrah

L

Lacey (French) Woman from Normandy; as delicate as lace
Lace, Lacee, Lacene, Laci, Laciann, Lacie, Lacina, Lacy

Lael (Hebrew) One who belongs to God
Laele, Laelle

*__Laila__ (Arabic) A beauty of the night, born at nightfall
Layla, *Laylah*

Lainil (American) A softhearted woman
Lainill, Lainyl, Lainyll, Laenil, Laenill, Laenyl, Laenyll, Laynil

Lais (Greek) A legendary courtesan
Laise, Lays, Layse, Laisa, Laes, Laese

Lajita (Indian) A truthful woman
Lajyta, Lajeeta, Lajeata

Lake (American) From the still waters
Laken, Laiken, Layken, Layk, Layke, Laik, Laike, Laeken

Lala (Slavic) Resembling a tulip
Lalah, Lalla, Lallah, Laleh

Lalaine (American) A hard-working woman
Lalain, Lalaina, Lalayn, Lalayne, Lalayna, Lalaen, Lalaene, Lalaena

Lalia (Greek) One who is well-spoken
Lali, Lallia, Lalya, Lalea, Lalie, Lalee, Laly, Laley

Lalita (Indian) A playful and charming woman
Lalitah, Laleeta, Laleetah, Lalyta, Lalytah, Laleita, Laleitah, Lalieta

Lamia (Greek) In mythology, a female vampire
Lamiah, Lamiya, Lamiyah, Lamea, Lameah

Lamya (Arabic) Having lovely dark lips
Lamyah, Lamyia, Lama

Lanassa (Russian) A light-hearted woman; cheerful
Lanasa, Lanassia, Lanasia, Lanassiya, Lanasiya

Landon (English) From the long hill
Landyn, Landen

Lang (Scandinavian) Woman of great height

Lani (Hawaiian) From the sky; one who is heavenly
Lanikai

Lanza (Italian) One who is noble and willing
Lanzah, Lanzia, Lanziah, Lanzea, Lanzeah

Lapis (Egyptian) Resembling the dark-blue gemstone
Lapiss, Lapisse, Lapys, Lapyss, Lapysse

Laquinta (American) The fifth-born child

Laramie (French) Shedding tears of love
Larami, Laramy, Laramey, Laramee, Laramea

Larby (American) Form of Darby, meaning “of the deer park”
Larbey, Larbi, Larbie, Larbee, Larbea

Larch (American) One who is full of life
Larche

Lark (English) Resembling the songbird
Larke

Larue (American) Form of Rue, meaning "a medicinal herb"
LaRue, Laroo, Larou

Lashawna (American) Filled with happiness
Lashauna, Laseana, Lashona, Lashawn, Lasean, Lashone, Lashaun

Lata (Indian) Of the lovely vine
Latah

Latanya (American) Daughter of the fairy queen
Latanyah, Latonya, Latania, Latanja, Latonia, Latanea

LaTeasa (Spanish) A flirtatious woman
Lateasa, Lateaza

Latona (Latin) In mythology, the Roman equivalent of Leto, the mother of Artemis and Apollo
Latonah, Latonia, Latonea, Lantoniah, Latoneah

Latrelle (American) One who laughs a lot
Latrell, Latrel, Latrele, Latrella, Latrela

Laudonia (Italian) Praises the house
Laudonea, Laudoniya, Laudomia, Laudomea, Laudomiya

Laura (Latin) Crowned with laurel; from the laurel tree
Lauraine, Lauralee, Laralyn, Laranca, Larea, Lari, Lauralee, Lauren, Loretta

*__Lauren__ (French) Form of Laura, meaning "crowned with laurel; from the laurel tree"
Laren, Larentia, Larentina, Larenzina, Larren, Laryn, Larryn, Larrynn

*__Leah__ (Hebrew) One who is weary; in the Bible, Jacob's first wife
Leia, Leigha, Lia, Liah, Leeya

Leanna (Gaelic) Form of Helen, meaning "the shining light"
Leana, Leann, Leanne, Lee-Ann, Leeann, Leeanne, Leianne, Leyanne

Lecia (English) Form of Alice, meaning "woman of the nobility; truthful; having high moral character"
Licia, Lecea, Licea, Lisha, Lysha, Lesha

Ledell (Greek) One who is queenly
Ledelle, Ledele, Ledella, Ledela, Ledel

^**Legend** (American) One who is memorable
Legende, Legund, Legunde

Legia (Spanish) A bright woman
Legiah, Legea, Legeah, Legiya, Legiyah, Legya, Legyah

Leila (Persian) Night, dark beauty
Leela, Lela

Lenis (Latin) One who has soft and silky skin
Lene, Leneta, Lenice, Lenita, Lennice, Lenos, Lenys, Lenisse

Leona (Latin) Feminine form of Leon; having the strength of a lion
Leeona, Leeowna, Leoine, Leola, Leone, Leonelle, Leonia, Leonie

Lequoia (Native American) Form of Sequoia, meaning "of the giant redwood tree"
Lequoya, Lequoiya, Lekoya

Lerola (Latin) Resembling a blackbird
Lerolla, Lerolah, Lerolia, Lerolea

Leslie (Gaelic) From the holly garden; of the gray fortress
Leslea, Leslee, Lesleigh, Lesley, Lesli, Lesly, Lezlee, Lezley

Leucippe (Greek) In mythology, a nymph
Lucippe, Leucipe, Lucipe

Leucothea (Greek) In mythology, a sea nymph
Leucothia, Leucothiah, Leucotheah

Levora (American) A homebody
Levorah, Levorra, Levorrah, Levoria, Levoriah, Levorea, Levoreah, Levorya

Lewa (African) A very beautiful woman
Lewah

Lewana (Hebrew) Of the white moon
Lewanah, Lewanna, Lewannah

Lia (Italian) Form of Leah, meaning "one who is weary"

Libby (English) Form of Elizabeth, meaning "my God is bountiful; God's promise"
Libba, Libbee, Libbey, Libbie, Libet, Liby, Lilibet, Lilibeth

Liberty (English) An independent woman; having freedom
Libertey, Libertee, Libertea, Liberti, Libertie, Libertas, Libera, Liber

Libra (Latin) One who is balanced; the seventh sign of the zodiac
Leebra, Leibra, Liebra, Leabra, Leighbra, Lybra

Librada (Spanish) One who is free
Libradah, Lybrada, Lybradah

Lieu (Vietnamese) Of the willow tree

Ligia (Greek) One who is musically talented
Ligiah, Ligya, Ligiya, Lygia, Ligea, Lygea, Lygya, Lygiya

^**Lila** (Arabic / Greek) Born at night / resembling a lily
***Lilah**, Lyla, Lylah*

Lilac (Latin) Resembling the bluish-purple flower
Lilack, Lilak, Lylac, Lylack, Lylak, Lilach

Lilette (Latin) Resembling a budding lily
Lilett, Lilete, Lilet, Lileta, Liletta, Lylette, Lylett, Lylete

Liliana (Italian, Spanish) Form of Lillian, meaning "resembling the lily"
Lilliana, Lillianna, Liliannia, Lilyana, Lilia

^**Lilith** (Babylonian) Woman of the night
Lilyth, Lillith, Lillyth, Lylith, Lyllith, Lylyth, Lyllyth, Lilithe

*****Lillian** (Latin) Resembling the lily
Lilian, Liliane, Lilianne, Lilias, Lilas, Lillas, Lillias

Lilo (Hawaiian) One who is generous
Lylo, Leelo, Lealo, Leylo, Lielo, Leilo

*****Lily** (English) Resembling the flower; one who is innocent and beautiful
Leelee, Lil, Lili, Lilie, Lilla, Lilley, Lilli, Lillie, Lilly

Limor (Hebrew) Refers to myrrh
Limora, Limoria, Limorea, Leemor, Leemora, Leemoria, Leemorea

Lin (Chinese) Resembling jade; from the woodland

Linda (Spanish) One who is soft and beautiful
Lindalee, Lindee, Lindey, Lindi, Lindie, Lindira, Lindka, Lindy, Lynn

Linden (English) From the hill of lime trees
Lindenn, Lindon, Lindynn, Lynden, Lyndon, Lyndyn, Lyndin, Lindin

Lindley (English) From the pastureland
Lindly, Lindlee, Lindleigh, Lindli, Lindlie, Leland, Lindlea

Lindsay (English) From the island of linden trees; from Lincoln's wetland
Lind, Lindsea, Lindsee, Lindseigh, Lindsey, Lindsy, Linsay, Linsey

Lisa (English) Form of Elizabeth, meaning "my God is bountiful; God's promise"
Leesa, Liesa, Lisebet, Lise, Liseta, Lisette, Liszka, Lisebeth

Lishan (African) One who is awarded a medal
Lishana, Lishanna, Lyshan, Lyshana, Lyshanna

Lissie (American) Resembling a flower
Lissi, Lissy, Lissey, Lissee, Lissea

Liv (Scandinavian / Latin) One who protects others / from the olive tree
Livia, Livea, Liviya, Livija, Livvy, Livy, Livya, Lyvia

Liya (Hebrew) The Lord's daughter
Liyah, Leeya, Leeyah, Leaya, Leayah

Lo (American) A fiesty woman
Loe, Low, Lowe

Loicy (American) A delightful woman
Loicey, Loicee, Loicea, Loici, Loicie, Loyce, Loice, Loyci

Lokelani (Hawaiian) Resembling a small red rose
Lokelanie, Lokelany, Lokelaney, Lokelanee, Lokelanea

Loki (Norse) In mythology, a trickster god
Lokie, Lokee, Lokey, Loky, Lokea, Lokeah, Lokia, Lokiah

Lola (Spanish) Form of Dolores, meaning "woman of sorrow"
Lolah, Loe, Lolo

^***London** (English) From the capital of England
Londyn

Lorelei (German) From the rocky cliff; in mythology, a siren who lured sailors to their deaths
Laurelei, Laurelie, Loralee, Loralei, Loralie, Loralyn

Loretta (Italian) Form of Laura, meaning "crowned with laurel; from the laurel tree"
Laretta, Larretta, Lauretta, Laurette, Leretta, Loreta, Lorette, Lorretta

Lorraine (French) From the kingdom of Lothair
Laraine, Larayne, Laurraine, Leraine, Lerayne, Lorain, Loraina, Loraine

Love (English) One who is full of affection
Lovey, Loveday, Lovette, Lovi, Lovie, Lov, Luv, Luvey

Lovely (American) An attractive and pleasant woman
Loveli, Loveley, Lovelie, Lovelee, Loveleigh, Lovelea

Luana (Hawaiian) One who is content and enjoys life
Lewanna, Lou-Ann, Louann, Louanna, Louanne, Luanda, Luane, Luann

Lucretia (Latin) A bringer of light; a successful woman; in mythology, a maiden who was raped by the prince of Rome
Lacretia, Loucrecia, Loucrezia, Loucresha, Loucretia, Lucrece, Lucrecia, Lucreecia

^*****Lucy** (Latin) Feminine form of Lucius; one who is illuminated
Luce, Lucetta, Lucette, Luci, Lucia, Luciana, Lucianna, Lucida, ***Lucille***

Lucylynn (American) A lighthearted woman
Lucylyn, Lucylynne, Lucilynn, Lucilyn, Lucilynne

^**Luna** (Latin) Of the moon
Lunah

Lunet (English) Of the crescent moon
Lunett, Lunette, Luneta, Lunete, Lunetta

Lupita (Spanish) Form of Guadalupe, meaning "from the valley of wolves"
Lupe, Lupyta, Lupelina, Lupeeta, Lupieta, Lupeita, Lupeata

Lurissa (American) A beguiling woman
Lurisa, Luryssa, Lurysa, Luressa, Luresa

Luyu (Native American) Resembling the dove

***Lydia** (Greek) A beautiful woman from Lydia
Lidia, Lidie, Lidija, Lyda, Lydie, Lydea, Liddy, Lidiy

Lyla (Arabic) Form of Lila, meaning "born at night, resembling a lily"
Lylah

Lynn (English) Woman of the lake; form of Linda, meaning "one who is soft and beautiful"
Linell, Linnell, Lyn, Lynae, Lyndel, Lyndell, Lynell, Lynelle

^**Lyric** (French) Of the lyre; the words of a song
Lyrica, Lyricia, Lyrik, Lyrick, Lyrika, Lyricka

Lytanisha (American) A scintillating woman
Lytanesha, Lytaniesha, Lytaneisha, Lytanysha, Lytaneesha, Lytaneasha

Macanta (Gaelic) A kind and gentle woman
Macan, Macantia, Macantea, Macantah

Machi (Taiwanese) A good friend
Machie, Machy, Machey, Machee, Machea

Mackenna (Gaelic) Daughter of the handsome man
Mackendra, Mackennah, McKenna, McKendra, Makenna, Makennah

*__Mackenzie__ (Gaelic) Daughter of a wise leader; a fiery woman; one who is fair
***Mckenzie**, Mackenzey, Makensie, **Makenzie**, M'Kenzie, **McKenzie**, Meckenzie, Mackenzee, Mackenzy*

^**McKinley** (English) Offspring of the fair hero

^**Macy** (French) One who wields a weapon
*Macee, Macey, **Maci**, Macie, Maicey, Maicy, Macea, Maicea*

Madana (Ethiopian) One who heals others
Madayna, Madaina, Madania, Madaynia, Madainia

Maddox (English) Born into wealth and prosperity
Madox, Madoxx, Maddoxx

*__Madeline__ (Hebrew) Woman from Magdala
*Mada, Madalaina, Madaleine, Madalena, Madalene, **Madelyn**, Madalyn, Madelynn, Madilyn*

Madhavi (Indian) Feminine form of Madhav; born in the springtime
Madhavie, Madhavee, Madhavey, Madhavy, Madhavea

Madini (Swahili) As precious as a gemstone
Madinie, Madiny, Madiney, Madinee, Madyny, Madyni, Madinea, Madynie

***Madison** (English) Daughter of a mighty warrior
Maddison, Madisen, Madisson, Madisyn, Madyson

Madonna (Italian) My lady; refers to the Virgin Mary
Madonnah, Madona, Madonah

Maeve (Irish) An intoxicating woman
Mave, Meave, Medb, Meabh

Maggie (English) Form of Margaret, meaning "resembling a pearl"
Maggi

Magnolia (French) Resembling the flower
Magnoliya, Magnoliah, Magnolea, Magnoleah, Magnoliyah, Magnolya, Magnolyah

Mahal (Native American) A tender and loving woman
Mahall, Mahale, Mahalle

Mahari (African) One who offers forgiveness
Maharie, Mahary, Maharey

Mahesa (Indian) A powerful and great lady
Maheshvari

Mahira (Arabic) A clever and adroit woman
Mahirah, Mahir, Mahire

Maia (Latin / Maori) The great one; in mythology, the goddess of spring / a brave warrior
Maiah, Mya, Maja

Maida (English) A maiden; a virgin
Maidel, Maidie, Mayda, Maydena, Maydey, Mady, Maegth, Magd

Maiki (Japanese) Resembling the dancing flower
Maikie, Maikei, Maikki, Maikee

Maimun (Arabic) One who is lucky; fortunate
Maimoon, Maimoun

Maine (French) From the mainland; from the state of Maine

Maiolaine (French) As delicate as a flower
Maiolainie, Maiolani

Maisha (African) Giver of life
Maysha, Maishah, Mayshah, Maesha, Maeshah

^**Maisie** (Scottish) Form of Margaret, meaning "resembling a pearl"
Maisee, Maisey, Maisy, Maizie, Mazey, Mazie, Maisi, Maizi

Majaya (Indian) A victorious woman
Majayah

Makala (Hawaiian) Resembling myrtle
Makalah, Makalla, Makallah

Makayla (Celtic / Hebrew / English) Form of Michaela, meaning "who is like God?"
Macaela, MacKayla, Mak, Mechaela, Meeskaela, Mekea, Mekelle

Makani (Hawaiian) Of the wind
Makanie, Makaney, Makany, Makanee

Makareta (Maori) Form of Margaret, meaning "resembling a pearl / the child of light"
Makaretah, Makarita

Makea (Finnish) One who is sweet
Makeah, Makia, Makiah

Makelina (Hawaiian) Form of Madeline, meaning "woman from Magdala"
Makelinah, Makeleena, Makelyna, Makeleana

Makena (African) One who is filled with happiness
Makenah, Makeena, Makeenah, Makeana, Makeanah, Makyna, Makynah, Mackena

Makenna (Irish) Form of McKenna, meaning "of the Irish one"
Makennah

Malak (Arabic) A heavenly messenger; an angel
Malaka, Malaika, Malayka, Malaeka, Malake, Malayk, Malaek, Malakia

Malati (Indian) Resembling a fragrant flower
Malatie, Malaty, Malatey, Malatee, Malatea

Mali (Thai / Welsh) Resembling a flower / form of Molly, meaning "star of the sea / from the sea of bitterness"
Malie, Malee, Maleigh, Maly, Maley

Malia (Hawaiian) Form of Mary, meaning "star of the sea / from the sea of bitterness"
Maliah, Maliyah, Maleah

Malika (Arabic) Destined to be queen
Malikah, Malyka, Maleeka, Maleika, Malieka, Maliika, Maleaka

Malina (Hawaiian) A peaceful woman
Malinah, Maleena, Maleenah, Malyna, Malynah, Maleina, Maliena, Maleana

Malinka (Russian) As sweet as a little berry
Malinkah, Malynka, Maleenka, Malienka, Maleinka, Maleanka

Mana (Polynesian) A charismatic and prestigious woman
Manah

Manal (Arabic) An accomplished woman
Manala, Manall, Manalle, Manalla, Manali

Mandoline (English) One who is accomplished with the stringed instrument
Mandalin, Mandalyn, Mandalynn, Mandelin, Mandellin, Mandellyn, Mandolin, Mandolyn

Mangena (Hebrew) As sweet as a melody
Mangenah, Mangenna, Mangennah

Manyara (African) A humble woman
Manyarah

Maola (Irish) A handmaiden
Maoli, Maole, Maolie, Maolia, Maoly, Maoley, Maolee, Maolea

Mapenzi (African) One who is dearly loved
Mpenzi, Mapenzie, Mapenze, Mapenzy, Mapenzee, Mapenzea

Maram (Arabic) One who is wished for
Marame, Marama, Marami, Maramie, Maramee, Maramy, Maramey, Maramea

Marcella (Latin) Dedicated to Mars, the God of war
Marcela, Marsela, Marsella, Maricela, Maricel

Marcia (Latin) Feminine form of Marcus; dedicated to Mars, the god of war
Marcena, Marcene, Marchita, Marciana, Marciane, Marcianne, Marcilyn, Marcilynn

Marely (American) form of Marley, "meaning of the marshy meadow"

^**Margaret** (Greek / Persian) Resembling a pearl / the child of light
Maighread, Mairead, Mag, Maggi, Maggie, Maggy, Maiga, Malgorzata, Megan, Marwarid, Marjorie, Marged, Makareta

^**Margot** (French) Form of Margaret, meaning "resembling a pearl / the child of light"
Margo, Margeaux, Margaux

*****Maria** (Spanish) Form of Mary, meaning "star of the sea / from the sea of bitterness"
Mariah, Marialena, Marialinda, Marialisa, Maaria, Mayria, Maeria, Mariabella

*****Mariah** (Latin) Form of Mary, meaning "star of the sea"

Mariana (Italian / Spanish) Form of Mary, meaning "star of the sea"
Marianna

Mariane (French) Blend of Mary, meaning "star of the sea / from the sea of bitterness," and Ann, meaning "a woman graced with God's favor"
Mariam, Mariana, Marian, Marion, Maryann, Maryanne, Maryanna, Maryane

Marietta (French) Form of Mary, meaning "star of the sea / from the sea of bitterness"
Mariette, Maretta, Mariet, Maryetta, Maryette, Marieta

Marika (Danish) Form of Mary, meaning "star of the sea / from the sea of bitterness"

Mariko (Japanese) Daughter of Mari; a ball or sphere
Maryko, Mareeko, Marieko, Mareiko

Marilyn (English) Form of Mary, meaning "star of the sea / from the sea of bitterness"
Maralin, Maralyn, Maralynn, Marelyn, Marilee, Marilin

Marissa (Latin) Woman of the sea
Maressa, Maricia, Marisabel, Marisha, Marisse, Maritza, Mariza, Marrissa

Marjam (Slavic) One who is merry
Marjama, Marjamah, Marjami, Marjamie, Marjamy, Marjamey, Marjamee, Marjamea

Marjani (African) Of the coral reef
Marjanie, Marjany, Marjaney, Marjanee, Marjean, Marjeani, Marjeanie, Marijani

Marjorie (English) Form of Margaret, meaning "resembling a pearl / the child of light"
Marcharie, Marge, Margeree, Margerie, Margery, Margey, Margi

Marlene (German) Blend of Mary, meaning "star of the sea / from the sea of bitterness," and Magdalene, meaning "woman from Magdala"
Marlaina, Marlana, Marlane, Marlayna

Marley (English) Of the marshy meadow
Marlee, Marleigh, Marli, Marlie, Marly

Marlis (German) Form of Mary, meaning "star of the sea / from the sea of bitterness"
Marlisa, Marliss, Marlise, Marlisse, Marlissa, Marlys, Marlyss, Marlysa

Marlo (English) One who resembles driftwood
Marloe, Marlow, Marlowe, Marlon

Marsala (Italian) From the place of sweet wine
Marsalah, Marsalla, Marsallah

Martha (Aramaic) Mistress of the house; in the Bible, the sister of Lazarus and Mary
Maarva, Marfa, Marhta, Mariet, Marit, Mart, Marta, Marte

Mary (Latin / Hebrew) Star of the sea / from the sea of bitterness
Mair, Mal, Mallie, Manette, Manon, Manya, Mare, Maren, Maria, Marietta, Marika, Marilyn, Marlis, Maureen, May, Mindel, Miriam, Molly, Mia

Masami (African / Japanese) A commanding woman / one who is truthful
Masamie, Masamee, Masamy, Masamey, Masamea

Mashaka (African) A troublemaker; a mischievous woman
Mashakah, Mashakia

Massachusetts (Native American) From the big hill; from the state of Massachusetts
Massachusets, Massachusette, Massachusetta, Massa, Massachute, Massachusta

Matana (Hebrew) A gift from God
Matanah, Matanna, Matannah, Matai

Matangi (Hindi) In Hinduism, the patron of inner thought
Matangy, Matangie, Matangee, Matangey, Matangea

Matsuko (Japanese) Child of the pine tree

Maureen (Irish) Form of Mary, meaning "star of the sea / from the sea of bitterness"
Maura, Maurene, Maurianne, Maurine, Maurya, Mavra, Maure, Mo

Mauve (French) Of the mallow plant
Mawve

Maven (English) Having great knowledge
Mavin, Mavyn

Maverick (American) One who is wild and free
Maverik, Maveryck, Maveryk, Mavarick, Mavarik

Mavis (French) Resembling a songbird
Mavise, Maviss, Mavisse, Mavys, Mavyss, Mavysse

May (Latin) Born during the month of May; form of Mary, meaning "star of the sea / from the sea of bitterness"
Mae, Mai, Maelynn, Maelee, Maj, Mala, Mayana, Maye

*__Maya__ (Indian / Hebrew) An illusion, a dream / woman of the water
Mya

Mayumi (Japanese) One who embodies truth, wisdom, and beauty

Mazarine (French) Having deep-blue eyes
Mazareen, Mazareene, Mazaryn, Mazaryne, Mazine, Mazyne, Mazeene

McKayla (Gaelic) A fiery woman
McKale, McKaylee, McKaleigh, McKay, McKaye, McKaela

^**Meadow** (American) From the beautiful field
Meadow, Meado, Meadoe, Medow, Medowe, Medoe

Meara (Gaelic) One who is filled with happiness
Mearah

Medea (Greek) A cunning ruler; in mythology, a sorceress
Madora, Medeia, Media, Medeah, Mediah, Mediya

Medini (Indian) Daughter of the earth
Medinie, Mediny, Mediney, Medinee, Medinea

Meditrina (Latin) The healer; in mythology, goddess of health and wine
Meditreena, Meditryna, Meditriena

Medora (Greek) A wise ruler
Medoria, Medorah, Medorra, Medorea

Medusa (Greek) In mythology, a Gorgon with snakes for hair
Medoosa, Medusah, Medoosah, Medousa, Medousah

Meenakshi (Indian) Having beautiful eyes

Megan (Welsh) Form of Margaret, meaning "resembling a pearl / the child of light"
Maegan, Meg, Magan, Magen, Megin, Maygan, Meagan, Meaghan, Meghan

Mehalia (Hebrew) An affectionate woman
Mehaliah, Mehalea, Mehaleah, Mehaliya, Mehaliyah

Melangell (Welsh) A sweet messenger from heaven
Melangelle, Melangela, Melangella, Melangele, Melangel

*__Melanie__ (Greek) A dark-skinned beauty
Malaney, Malanie, Mel, Mela, Melaina, Melaine, Melainey, Melany

Meli (Native American) One who is bitter
Melie, Melee, Melea, Meleigh, Mely, Meley

Melia (Hawaiian / Greek) Resembling the plumeria / of the ash tree; in mythology, a nymph
Melidice, Melitine, Meliah, Meelia, Melya

Melika (Turkish) A great beauty
Melikah, Melicka, Melicca, Melyka, Melycka, Meleeka, Meleaka

Melinda (Latin) One who is sweet and gentle
Melynda, Malinda, Malinde, Mallie, Mally, Malynda, Melinde, Mellinda, Mindy

Melisande (French) Having the strength of an animal
Malisande, Malissande, Malyssandre, Melesande, Melisandra, Melisandre

Melissa (Greek) Resembling a honeybee; in mythology, a nymph
Malissa, Mallissa, Mel, Melesa, Melessa, Melisa, Melise, Melisse

Melita (Greek) As sweet as honey
Malita, Malitta, Melida, Melitta, Melyta, Malyta, Meleeta, Meleata

Melody (Greek) A beautiful song
Melodee, Melodey, Melodi, Melodia, Melodie, Melodea

Merana (American) Woman of the waters
Meranah, Meranna, Merannah

Mercer (English) A prosperous merchant

Meredith (Welsh) A great ruler; protector of the sea
Maredud, Meridel, Meredithe, Meredyth, Meridith, Merridie, Meradith, Meredydd

Meribah (Hebrew) A quarrelsome woman
Meriba

Meroz (Hebrew) From the cursed plains
Meroza, Merozia, Meroze

Merry (English) One who is lighthearted and joyful
Merree, Merri, Merrie, Merrielle, Merrile, Merrilee, Merrili, Merrily

Mertice (English) A well-known lady

Merton (English) From the village near the pond
Mertan, Mertin, Mertun

Metea (Greek) A gentle woman
Meteah, Metia, Metiah

Metin (Greek) A wise counselor
Metine, Metyn, Metyne

Metis (Greek) One who is industrious
Metiss, Metisse, Metys, Metyss, Metysse

Mettalise (Danish) As graceful as a pearl
Metalise, Mettalisse, Mettalisa, Mettalissa

*__Mia__ (Israeli / Latin) Who is like God? / form of Mary, meaning "star of the sea / from the sea of bitterness"
Miah, Mea, Meah, Meya

^**Michaela** (Celtic, Gaelic, Hebrew, English, Irish) Feminine form of Michael; who is like God?
Macaela, MacKayla, Mak, Mechaela, Meeskaela, Mekea, Micaela, ***Mikaela***

Michelle (French) Feminine form of Michael; who is like God?
Machelle, Mashelle, M'chelle, Mechelle, Meechelle, Me'Shell, Meshella, Mischa

Michewa (Tibetan) Sent from heaven
Michewah

Mide (Irish) One who is thirsty
Meeda, Mida

Midori (Japanese) Having green eyes
Midorie, Midory, Midorey, Midoree, Midorea

Mignon (French) One who is cute and petite

Mikayla (English) Feminine form of Michael, meaning "who is like God?"

^***Mila** (Slavic) One who is industrious and hardworking
Milaia, Milaka, Milla, Milia

Milan (Latin) From the city in Italy; one who is gracious
Milaana

Milena (Slavic) The favored one
Mileena, Milana, Miladena, Milanka, Mlada, Mladena

Miley (American) Form of Mili, meaning "a virtuous woman"
Milee, Mylee, Mareli

Miliana (Latin) Feminine of Emeliano; one who is eager and willing
Milianah, Milianna, Miliane, Miliann, Milianne

Milima (Swahili) Woman from the mountains
Milimah, Mileema, Milyma

Millo (Hebrew) Defender of the sacred city
Milloh, Millowe, Milloe

Mima (Hebrew) Form of Jemima, meaning "our little dove"
Mimah, Mymah, Myma

Minda (Native American / Hindi) Having great knowledge
Mindah, Mynda, Myndah, Menda, Mendah

Mindel (Hebrew) Form of Mary, meaning "star of the sea / from the sea of bitterness"
Mindell, Mindelle, Mindele, Mindela, Mindella

Mindy (English) Form of Melinda, meaning "one who is sweet and gentle"
Minda, Mindee, Mindi, Mindie, Mindey, Mindea

Ming Yue (Chinese) Born beneath the bright moon

Minka (Teutonic) One who is resolute; having great strength
Minkah, Mynka, Mynkah, Minna, Minne

Minowa (Native American) One who has a moving voice
Minowah, Mynowa, Mynowah

Minuit (French) Born at midnight
Minueet

Miracle (American) An act of God's hand
Mirakle, Mirakel, Myracle, Myrakle

Mirai (Basque / Japanese) A miracle child / future
Miraya, Mirari, Mirarie, Miraree, Mirae

Miranda (Latin) Worthy of admiration
Maranda, Myranda, Randi

Miremba (Ugandan) A promoter of peace
Mirembe, Mirem, Mirembah, Mirembeh, Mirema

Miriam (Hebrew) Form of Mary, meaning "star of the sea / from the sea of bitterness"
Mariam, Maryam, Meriam, Meryam, Mirham, Mirjam, Mirjana, Mirriam

Mirinesse (English) Filled with joy
Miriness, Mirinese, Mirines, Mirinessa, Mirinesa

Mirit (Hebrew) One who is strong-willed

Mischa (Russian) Form of Michelle, meaning "who is like God?"
Misha

Mistico (Italian) A mystical woman
Mistica, Mystico, Mystica, Mistiko, Mystiko

Mitali (Indian) A friendly and sweet woman
Mitalie, Mitalee, Mitaleigh, Mitaly, Mitaley, Meeta, Mitalea

Miya (Japanese) From the sacred temple
Miyah

Miyo (Japanese) A beautiful daughter
Miyoko

Mizar (Hebrew) A little woman; petite
Mizarr, Mizarre, Mizare, Mizara, Mizaria, Mizarra

Mliss (Cambodian) Resembling a flower
Mlissa, Mlisse, Mlyss, Mlysse, Mlyssa

Mocha (Arabic) As sweet as chocolate
Mochah

Modesty (Latin) One who is without conceit
Modesti, Modestie, Modestee, Modestus, Modestey, Modesta, Modestia, Modestina

Moesha (American) Drawn from the water
Moisha, Moysha, Moeesha, Moeasha, Moeysha

Mohini (Indian) The most beautiful
Mohinie, Mohinee, Mohiny

Moladah (Hebrew) A giver of life
Molada

Molly (Irish) Form of Mary, meaning "star of the sea / from the sea of bitterness"
Moll, Mollee, Molley, Molli, Mollie, Molle, Mollea, Mali

Mona (Gaelic) One who is born into the nobility
Moina, Monah, Monalisa, Monalissa, Monna, Moyna, Monalysa, Monalyssa

Moncha (Irish) A solitary woman
Monchah

Monica (Greek / Latin) A solitary woman / one who advises others
Monnica, Monca, Monicka, Monika, Monike

Monique (French) One who provides wise counsel
Moniqua, Moneeque, Moneequa, Moneeke, Moeneek, Moneaque, Moneaqua, Moneake

Monisha (Hindi) Having great intelligence
Monishah, Monesha, Moneisha, Moniesha, Moneysha, Moneasha

Monroe (Gaelic) Woman from the river
Monrow, Monrowe, Monro

^**Monserrat** (Latin) From the jagged mountain
Montserrat

Montana (Latin) Woman of the mountains; from the state of Montana
Montanna, Montina, Monteene, Montese

Morcan (Welsh) Of the bright sea
Morcane, Morcana, Morcania, Morcanea

Moreh (Hebrew) A great archer; a teacher

Morgan (Welsh) Circling the bright sea; a sea dweller
Morgaine, Morgana, Morgance, Morgane, Morganica, Morgann, Morganne, Morgayne

Morguase (English) In Arthurian legend, the mother of Gawain
Marguase, Margawse, Morgawse, Morgause, Margause

Morina (Japanese) From the woodland town
Morinah, Moreena, Moryna, Moriena, Moreina, Moreana

Mubarika (Arabic) One who is blessed
Mubaarika, Mubaricka, Mubaryka, Mubaricca, Mubarycca

Mubina (Arabic) One who displays her true image
Mubeena, Mubinah, Mubyna, Mubeana, Mubiena

Mudan (Mandarin) Daughter of a harmonious family
Mudane, Mudana, Mudann, Mudaen, Mudaena

Mufidah (Arabic) One who is helpful to others
Mufeeda, Mufeyda, Mufyda, Mufeida, Mufieda, Mufeada

Mugain (Irish) In mythology, the wife of the king of Ulster
Mugayne, Mugaine, Mugane

Muirne (Irish) One who is dearly loved
Muirna

Munay (African) One who loves and is loved
Manay, Munaye, Munae, Munai

Munazza (Arabic) An independent woman; one who is free
Munazzah, Munaza, Munazah

Muriel (Irish) Of the shining sea
Merial, Meriel, Merrill

Murphy (Celtic) Daughter of a great sea warrior
Murphi, Murphie, Murphey

Musoke (African) Having the beauty of a rainbow

Mya (American) Form of Maya, meaning "an illusion, woman of the water"
Myah

Myisha (Arabic) Form of Aisha, meaning "lively; womanly"
Myesha, Myeisha, Myeshia, Myiesha, Myeasha

Myka (Hebrew) Feminine of Micah, meaning "who is like God?"
Micah, Mika

Myrina (Latin) In mythology, an Amazon
Myrinah, Myreena, Myreina, Myriena, Myreana

Myrrh (Egyptian) Resembling the fragrant oil

N

Naama (Hebrew) Feminine form of Noam; an attractive woman; good-looking
Naamah

Naava (Hebrew) A lovely and pleasant woman
Naavah, Nava, Navah, Navit

Nabila (Arabic) Daughter born into nobility; a highborn daughter
Nabilah, Nabeela, Nabyla, Nabeelah, Nabylah, Nabeala, Nabealah

Nadda (Arabic) A very generous woman
Naddah, Nada, Nadah

Nadia (Slavic) One who is full of hope
Nadja, Nadya, Naadiya, Nadine, Nadie, Nadiyah, Nadea, Nadija

Nadirah (Arabic) One who is precious; rare
Nadira, Nadyra, Nadyrah, Nadeera, Nadeerah, Nadra

Naeva (French) Born in the evening
Naevah, Naevia, Naevea, Nayva, Nayvah

Nagge (Hebrew) A radiant woman

Nailah (Arabic) Feminine form of Nail; a successful woman; the acquirer
Na'ila, Na'ilah, Naa'ilah, Naila, Nayla, Naylah, Naela, Naelah

Najia (Arabic) An independent woman; one who is free
Naajia

Najja (African) The second-born child
Najjah

Namid (Native American) A star dancer
Namide, Namyd, Namyde

Namita (Papuan) In mythology, a mother goddess
Namitah, Nameeta, Namyta

Nana (Hawaiian / English) Born during the spring; a star / a grandmother or one who watches over children

Nancy (English) Form of Anna, meaning "a woman graced with God's favor"
Nainsey, Nainsi, Nance, Nancee, Nancey, Nanci, Nancie, Nancsi

Nandalia (Australian) A fiery woman
Nandaliah, Nandalea, Nandaleah, Nandali, Nandalie, Nandalei, Nandalee, Nandaleigh

Nandita (Indian) A delightful daughter
Nanditah, Nanditia, Nanditea

*__Naomi__ (Hebrew / Japanese) One who is pleasant / a beauty above all others
Namoie, Nayomi, Naomee

Narella (Greek) A bright woman; intelligent
Narellah, Narela, Narelah, Narelle, Narell, Narele

Nascio (Latin) In mythology, goddess of childbirth

Natalia (Spanish / Latin) form of Natalie; born on Christmas day
Natalya, Natalja

*__Natalie__ (Latin) Refers to Christ's birthday; born on Christmas Day
Natala, Natalee, Nathalie, Nataline, Nataly, Natasha

Natane (Native American) Her father's daughter
Natanne

Natasha (Russian) Form of Natalie, meaning "born on Christmas Day"
Nastaliya, Nastalya, Natacha, Natascha, Natashenka, Natashia, Natasia, Natosha

Navida (Iranian) Feminine form of Navid; bringer of good news
Navyda, Navidah, Navyda, Naveeda, Naveedah, Naveada, Naveadah

Navya (Indian) One who is youthful
Navyah, Naviya, Naviyah

Nawal (Arabic) A gift of God
Nawall, Nawalle, Nawala, Nawalla

Nawar (Arabic) Resembling a flower
Nawaar

Nazahah (Arabic) One who is pure and honest
Nazaha, Nazihah, Naziha

Nechama (Hebrew) One who provides comfort
Nehama, Nehamah, Nachmanit, Nachuma, Nechamah, Nechamit

Neda (Slavic) Born on a Sunday
Nedda, Nedah, Nedi, Nedie, Neddi, Neddie, Nedaa

Neena (Hindi) A woman who has beautiful eyes
Neenah, Neanah, Neana, Neyna, Neynah

Nefertiti (Egyptian) A queenly woman
Nefertari, Nefertyty, Nefertity, Nefertitie, Nefertitee, Nefertytie, Nefertitea

Neith (Egyptian) In mythology, goddess of war and hunting
Neitha, Neytha, Neyth, Neit, Neita, Neitia, Neitea, Neithe, Neythe

Nekana (Spanish) Woman of sorrow
Nekane, Nekania, Nekanea

Neo (African) A gift from God

Nerissa (Italian / Greek) A black-haired beauty / sea nymph
Narissa, Naryssa, Nericcia, Neryssa, Narice, Nerice, Neris

Nessa (Hebrew / Greek) A miracle child / form of Agnes, meaning "one who is pure; chaste"
Nesha, Nessah, Nessia, Nessya, Nesta, Neta, Netia, Nessie

Netis (Native American) One who is trustworthy
Netiss, Netisse, Netys, Netyss, Netysse

⋆**Nevaeh** (American) Child from heaven

Nevina (Scottish) Feminine form of Nevin; daughter of a saint
Nevinah, Neveena, Nevyna, Nevinne, Nevynne, Neveene, Neveana, Neveane

Newlyn (Gaelic) Born during the spring
Newlynn, Newlynne, Newlin, Newlinn, Newlinne, Newlen, Newlenn, Newlenne

Neziah (Hebrew) One who is pure; a victorious woman
Nezia, Nezea, Nezeah, Neza, Nezah, Neziya, Neziyah

Niabi (Native American) Resembling a fawn
Niabie, Niabee, Niabey, Niaby

Niagara (English) From the famous waterfall
Niagarah, Niagarra, Niagarrah, Nyagara, Nyagarra

Nicole (Greek) Feminine form of Nicholas; of the victorious people
Necole, Niccole, Nichol, Nichole, Nicholle, Nickol, Nickole, Nicol

Nicosia (English) Woman from the capital of Cyprus
Nicosiah, Nicosea, Nicoseah, Nicotia, Nicotea

Nidia (Spanish) One who is gracious
Nydia, Nidiah, Nydiah, Nidea, Nideah, Nibia, Nibiah, Nibea

Nike (Greek) One who brings victory; in mythology, goddess of victory
Nikee, Nikey, Nykee, Nyke

Nilam (Arabic) Resembling a precious blue stone
Neelam, Nylam, Nilima, Nilyma, Nylyma, Nylima, Nealam, Nealama

Nilsine (Scandinavian) Feminine form of Neil; a champion

Nimeesha (African) A princess; daughter born to royalty
Nimeeshah, Nimiesha

Nini (African) As solid as a stone
Ninie, Niny, Niney, Ninee, Ninea

Nishan (African) One who wins awards
Nishann, Nishanne, Nishana, Nishanna, Nyshan, Nyshana

Nitya (Indian) An eternal beauty
Nithya, Nithyah, Nityah

Nixie (German) A beautiful water sprite
Nixi, Nixy, Nixey, Nixee, Nixea

Noelle (French) Born at Christmastime
***Noel**, Noela, Noele, Noe*

Nolcha (Native American) Of the sun
Nolchia, Nolchea

Nomusa (African) One who is merciful
Nomusah, Nomusha, Nomusia, Nomusea, Nomushia, Nomushea

***Nora** (English) Form of Eleanor, meaning "the shining light"
***Norah**, Noora, Norella, Norelle, Norissa, Norri, Norrie, Norry*

Nordica (German) Woman from the north
Nordika, Nordicka, Nordyca, Nordyka, Nordycka, Norda, Norell, Norelle

Nosiwe (African) Mother of the homeland

Noura (Arabic) Having an inner light
Nureh, Nourah, Nure

Nyala (African) Resembling an antelope
Nyalah, Nyalla, Nyallah

^**Nylah** (Gaelic) Cloud or champion

Nyneve (English) In Arthurian legend, another name for the lady of the lake
Nineve, Niniane, Ninyane, Nyniane, Ninieve, Niniveve

Oaisara (Arabic) A great ruler; an empress
Oaisarah, Oaisarra, Oaisarrah

Oamra (Arabic) Daughter of the moon
Oamrah, Oamira, Oamyra, Oameera

Oba (African) In mythology, the goddess of rivers
Obah, Obba, Obbah

Octavia (Latin) Feminine form of Octavius; the eighth-born child
Octaviana, Octavianne, Octavie, Octiana, Octoviana, Ottavia, Octavi, Octavy

Ode (Egyptian / Greek) Traveler of the road / a lyric poem
Odea

Odessa (Greek) Feminine form of Odysseus; one who wanders; an angry woman
Odissa, Odyssa, Odessia, Odissia, Odyssia, Odysseia

Odina (Latin / Scandinavian) From the mountain / feminine form of Odin, the highest of the gods
Odinah, Odeena, Odeene, Odeen, Odyna, Odyne, Odynn, Odeana

Ogin (Native American) Resembling the wild rose

Oheo (Native American) A beautiful woman

Oira (Latin) One who prays to God
Oyra, Oirah, Oyrah

Okalani (Hawaiian) Form of Kalani, meaning "from the heavens"
Okalanie, Okalany, Okalaney, Okalanee, Okaloni, Okalonie, Okalonee, Okalony, Okaloney, Okeilana, Okelani, Okelani, Okelanie, Okelany, Okelaney, Okelanee, Okalanea, Okalonea, Okelanea

Okei (Japanese) Woman of the ocean

Oksana (Russian) Hospitality
Oksanah, Oksie, Aksana

Ola (Nigerian / Hawaiian / Norse) One who is precious / giver of life; well-being / a relic of one's ancestors
Olah, Olla, Ollah

Olaide (American) A thoughtful woman
Olaid, Olaida, Olayd, Olayde, Olayda, Olaed, Olaede, Olaeda

Olathe (Native American) A lovely young woman

Olayinka (Yoruban) Surrounded by wealth and honor
Olayenka, Olayanka

Oleda (English) Resembling a winged creature
Oldedah, Oleta, Olita, Olida, Oletah, Olitah, Olidah

Olethea (Latin) Form of Alethea, meaning "one who is truthful"
Oletheia, Olethia, Oletha, Oletea, Olthaia, Olithea, Olathea, Oletia

Olina (Hawaiian) One who is joyous
Oline, Oleen, Oleene, Olyne, Oleena, Olyna, Olin

^*****Olivia** (Latin) Feminine form of Oliver; of the olive tree; one who is peaceful
Oliviah, Oliva, ***Olive****, Oliveea, Olivet, Olivetta, Olivette, Olivija*

Olwen (Welsh) One who leaves a white footprint
Olwynn, Olvyen, Olvyin

Olympia (Greek) From Mount Olympus; a goddess
Olympiah, Olimpe, Olimpia, Olimpiada, Olimpiana, Olypme, Olympie, Olympi

Omri (Arabic) A red-haired woman
Omrie, Omree, Omrea, Omry, Omrey

Ona (Hebrew) Filled with grace
Onit, Onat, Onah

Ondrea (Slavic) Form of Andrea, meaning "courageous and strong / womanly"
Ondria, Ondrianna, Ondreia, Ondreina, Ondreya, Ondriana, Ondreana, Ondera

Oneida (Native American) Our long-awaited daughter
Onieda, Oneyda, Onida, Onyda

Onida (Native American) The one who has been expected
Onidah, Onyda, Onydah

Ontina (American) An open-minded woman
Ontinah, Onteena, Onteenah, Onteana, Onteanah, Ontiena, Ontienah, Onteina

Oona (Gaelic) Form of Agnes, meaning "one who is pure; chaste"

Opal (Sanskrit) A treasured jewel; resembling the iridescent gemstone
Opall, Opalle, Opale, Opalla, Opala, Opalina, Opaline, Opaleena

Ophelia (Greek) One who offers help to others
Ofelia, Ofilia, OphÈlie, Ophelya, Ophilia, Ovalia, Ovelia, Opheliah

Ophrah (Hebrew) Resembling a fawn; from the place of dust
Ofra, Ofrit, Ophra, Oprah, Orpa, Orpah, Ofrat, Ofrah

Orange (Latin) Resembling the sweet fruit
Orangetta, Orangia, Orangina, Orangea

Orbelina (American) One who brings excitement
Orbelinah, Orbeleena

Orea (Greek) From the mountains
Oreah

Orenda (Iroquois) A woman with magical powers

Oriana (Latin) Born at sunrise
Oreana, Orianna, Oriane, Oriann, Orianne

Oribel (Latin) A beautiful golden child
Orabel, Orabelle, Orabell, Orabela, Orabella, Oribell, Oribelle, Oribele

Orin (Irish) A dark-haired beauty
Orine, Orina, Oryna, Oryn, Oryne

Orinthia (Hebrew / Gaelic) Of the pine tree / a fair lady
Orrinthia, Orenthia, Orna, Ornina, Orinthea, Orenthea, Orynthia, Orynthea

Oriole (Latin) Resembling the gold-speckled bird
Oreolle, Oriolle, Oreole, Oriola, Oriolla, Oriol, Oreola, Oreolla

Orion (Greek) The huntress; a constellation

Orithna (Greek) One who is natural
Orithne, Orythna, Orythne, Orithnia, Orythnia, Orithnea, Orythnea

Orla (Gaelic) The golden queen
Orlah, Orrla, Orrlah, Orlagh, Orlaith, Orlaithe, Orghlaith, Orghlaithe

Orna (Irish / Hebrew) One who is pale-skinned / of the cedar tree
Ornah, Ornette, Ornetta, Ornete, Orneta, Obharnait, Ornat

Ornella (Italian) Of the flowering ash tree

Ornice (Irish) A pale-skinned woman
Ornyce, Ornise, Orynse, Orneice, Orneise, Orniece, Orniese, Orneece

Orva (Anglo-Saxon / French) A courageous friend / as precious as gold

Orynko (Ukrainian) A peaceful woman
Orinko, Orynka, Orinka

Osaka (Japanese) From the city of industry
Osaki, Osakie, Osakee, Osaky, Osakey, Osakea

Osma (English) Feminine form of Osmond; protected by God
Osmah, Ozma, Ozmah

Otina (American) A fortunate woman
Otinah, Otyna, Otynah, Oteena, Oteenah, Oteana, Oteanah, Otiena

Overton (English) From the upper side of town
Overtown

Owena (Welsh) A high-born woman
Owenah, Owenna, Owennah, Owenia, Owenea

Ozora (Hebrew) One who is wealthy
Ozorah, Ozorra, Ozorrah

P

Pace (American) A charismatic young woman
Paice, Payce, Paece, Pase, Paise, Payse, Paese

Pacifica (Spanish) A peaceful woman
Pacifika, Pacyfyca, Pacyfyka, Pacifyca, Pacifyka, Pacyfica, Pacyfika

Pageant (American) A dramatic woman
Pagent, Padgeant, Padgent

Paige (English) A young assistant
Page, Payge, Paege

^***Paisley** (English) Woman of the church
Paislee

Paki (African) A witness of God
Pakki, Packi, Pacci, Pakie, Pakkie, Paky, Pakky, Pakey

Palba (Spanish) A fair-haired woman

Palemon (Spanish) A kind-hearted woman
Palemond, Palemona, Palemonda

Palesa (African) Resembling a flower
Palessa, Palesah, Palysa, Palisa, Paleesa

Paloma (Spanish) Dove-like
Palloma, Palomita, Palometa, Peloma, Aloma

Pamela (English) A woman who is as sweet as honey
Pamelah, Pamella, Pammeli, Pammelie, Pameli, Pamelie, Pamelia, Pamelea

Panagiota (Greek) Feminine form of Panagiotis; a holy woman

Panchali (Indian) A princess; a high-born woman
Panchalie, Panchaly, Panchalli

Panda (English) Resembling the bamboo-eating animal
Pandah

Pandara (Indian) A good wife
Pandarah, Pandarra, Pandaria, Pandarea

Pandora (Greek) A gifted, talented woman; in mythology, the first mortal woman, who unleashed evil upon the world
Pandorah, Pandorra, Pandoria, Pandorea, Pandoriya

Pantxike (Latin) A woman who is free
Pantxikey, Pantxikye, Pantxeke, Pantxyke

Paras (Indian) A woman against whom others are measured

^**Paris** (English) Woman of the city in France
Pariss, Parisse, Parys, Paryss, Parysse

^**Parker** (English) The keeper of the park
Parkyr

Parry (Welsh) Daughter of Harry
Parri, Parrie, Parrey, Parree, Parrea

Parvani (Indian) Born during a full moon
Parvanie, Parvany, Parvaney, Parvanee, Parvanea

Parvati (Hindi) Daughter of the mountain; in Hinduism, a name for the wife of Shiva
Parvatie, Parvaty, Parvatey, Parvatee, Pauravi, Parvatea, Pauravie, Pauravy

Paterekia (Hawaiian) An upper-class woman
Paterekea, Pakelekia, Pakelekea

Patience (English) One who is patient; an enduring woman
Patiencia, Paciencia, Pacencia, Pacyncia, Pacincia, Pacienca

Patricia (English) Feminine form of Patrick; of noble descent
Patrisha, Patrycia, Patrisia, Patsy, Patti, Patty, Patrizia, Pattie, Trisha

Patrina (American) Born into the nobility
Patreena, Patriena, Patreina, Patryna, Patreana

Paula (English) Feminine form of Paul; a petite woman
Paulina, Pauline, Paulette, Paola, Pauleta, Pauletta, Pauli, Paulete

Pausha (Hindi) Resembling the moon
Paushah

Pax (Latin) One who is peaceful; in mythology, the goddess of peace
Paxi, Paxie, Paxton, Paxten, Paxtan, Paxy, Paxey, Paxee

^*__Payton__ (English) From the warrior's village
Paton, Paeton, Paiton, Payten, Paiten

Pearl (Latin) A precious gem of the sea
Pearla, Pearle, Pearlie, Pearly, Pearline, Pearlina, Pearli, Pearley

Pelopia (Greek) In mythology, the wife of Thyestes and mother of Aegisthus
Pelopiah, Pelopea, Pelopeah, Pelopiya

Pembroke (English) From the broken hill
Pembrook, Pembrok, Pembrooke

Pendant (French) A decorated woman
Pendent, Pendante, Pendente

*__Penelope__ (Greek) Resembling a duck; in mythology, the faithful wife of Odysseus
Peneloppe, Penelopy, Penelopey, Penelopi, Penelopie, Penelopee, Penella, Penelia, Penny

Penia (Greek) In mythology, the personification of poverty
Peniah, Penea, Peniya, Peneah, Peniyah

Penthesilea (Greek) In mythology, a queen of the Amazons

Peony (Greek) Resembling the flower
Peoney, Peoni, Peonie, Peonee, Peonea

Pepin (French) An awe-inspiring woman
Peppin, Pepine, Peppine, Pipin, Pippin, Pepen, Pepan, Peppen

Pepita (Spanish) Feminine form of Joseph; God will add
Pepitah, Pepitta, Pepitia, Pepitina

Perdita (Latin) A lost woman
Perditah, Perditta, Perdy, Perdie, Perdi, Perdee, Perdea, Perdeeta

Perdix (Latin) Resembling a partridge
Perdixx, Perdyx, Perdyxx

Peri (Persian / English) In mythology, a fairy / from the pear tree
Perry, Perri, Perie, Perrie, Pery, Perrey, Perey, Peree

Perpetua (Latin) One who is constant; steadfast

Persephone (Greek) In mythology, the daughter of Demeter and Zeus who was abducted to the underworld
Persephoni, Persephonie, Persephony, Persephoney, Persephonee, Persefone, Persefoni, Persefonie

Persis (Greek) Woman of Persia
Persiss, Persisse, Persys, Persyss, Persysse

Pesha (Hebrew) A flourishing woman
Peshah, Peshia, Peshiah, Peshea, Pesheah, Peshe

Petronela (Latin) Feminine form of Peter, as solid and strong as a rock
Petronella, Petronelle, Petronia, Petronilla, Petronille, Petrona, Petronia, Petronel

Petunia (English) Resembling the flower
Petuniah, Petuniya, Petunea, Petoonia, Petounia

*__Peyton__ (English) From the warrior's village
Peyten

Phaedra (Greek) A bright woman; in mythology, the wife of Theseus
Phadra, Phaidra, Phedra, Phaydra, Phedre, Phaedre

Phailin (Thai) Resembling a sapphire
Phaylin, Phaelin, Phalin

Phashestha (American) One who is decorated
Phashesthea, Phashesthia, Phashesthiya

Pheakkley (Vietnamese) A faithful woman
Pheakkly, Pheakkli, Pheakklie, Pheakklee, Pheakkleigh, Pheakklea

Pheodora (Greek) A supreme gift
Pheodorah, Phedora, Phedorah

Phernita (American) A well-spoken woman
Pherneeta, Phernyta, Phernieta, Pherneita, Pherneata

Phia (Italian) A saintly woman
Phiah, Phea, Pheah

Philippa (English) Feminine form of Phillip; a friend of horses
Phillippa, Philipa, Phillipa, Philipinna, Philippine, Phillipina, Phillipine, Pilis

Philomena (Greek) A friend of strength
Filomena, Philomina, Mena

Phoebe (Greek) A bright, shining woman; in mythology, another name for the goddess of the moon
Phebe, Phoebi, Phebi, Phoebie, Phebie, Pheobe, Phoebee, Phoebea

Phoena (Greek) Resembling a mystical bird
Phoenah, Phoenna, Phena, Phenna

Phoenix (Greek) A dark-red color; in mythology, an immortal bird
Phuong, Phoenyx

Phyllis (Greek) Of the foliage; in mythology, a girl who was turned into an almond tree
Phylis, Phillis, Philis, Phylys, Phyllida, Phylida, Phillida, Philida

Pili (Egyptian) The second-born child
Pilie, Pily, Piley, Pilee, Pilea, Pileigh

Pililani (Hawaiian) Having great strength
Pililanie, Pililany, Pililaney, Pililanee, Pililanea

Piluki (Hawaiian) Resembling a small leaf
Pilukie, Piluky, Pilukey, Pilukee, Pilukea

Pineki (Hawaiian) Resembling a peanut
Pinekie, Pineky, Pinekey, Pinekee, Pinekea

Ping (Chinese) One who is peaceful
Pyng

Pinga (Inuit) In mythology, goddess of the hunt, fertility, and healing
Pingah, Pyngah, Pyngah

Pinquana (Native American) Having a pleasant fragrance
Pinquan, Pinquann, Pinquanne, Pinquanna, Pinquane

Piper (English) One who plays the flute
Pipere, Piperel, Piperell, Piperele, Piperelle, Piperela, Piperella, Pyper

Pippi (French / English) A friend of horses / a blushing young woman
Pippie, Pippy, Pippey, Pippee, Pippea

Pirouette (French) A ballet dancer
Piroette, Pirouett, Piroett, Piroueta, Piroeta, Pirouetta, Piroetta, Pirouet

Pisces (Latin) The twelfth sign of the zodiac; the fishes
Pysces, Piscees, Pyscees, Piscez, Pisceez

Pithasthana (Hindi) In Hinduism, a name for the wife of Shiva

Platinum (English) As precious as the metal
Platynum, Platnum, Platie, Plati, Platee, Platy, Platey, Platea

Platt (French) From the plains
Platte

Pleshette (American) An extravagent woman
Pleshett, Pleshet, Pleshete, Plesheta, Pleshetta

Pleun (American) One who is good with words
Pleune

Po (Italian) A lively woman

Podarge (Greek) In mythology, one of the Harpies

Poetry (American) A romantic woman
Poetrey, Poetri, Poetrie, Poetree, Poetrea

Polete (Hawaiian) A kind young woman
Polet, Polett, Polette, Poleta, Poletta

Polina (Russian) A small woman
Polinah, Poleena, Poleenah, Poleana, Poleanah, Poliena, Polienah, Poleina

Polyxena (Greek) In mythology, a daughter of Priam and loved by Achilles
Polyxenah, Polyxenia, Polyxenna, Polyxene, Polyxenea

Pomona (Latin) In mythology, goddess of fruit trees
Pomonah, Pomonia, Pomonea, Pamona, Pamonia, Pamonea

Poni (African) The second-born daughter
Ponni, Ponie, Ponnie, Pony, Ponny, Poney, Ponney, Ponee

Poodle (American) Resembling the dog; one with curly hair
Poudle, Poodel, Poudel

Poonam (Hindi) A kind and caring woman
Pounam

Porter (Latin) The doorkeeper

Posala (Native American) Born at the end of spring
Posalah, Posalla, Posallah

Posh (American) A fancy young woman
Poshe, Posha

Potina (Latin) In mythology, goddess of children's food and drink
Potinah, Potyna, Potena, Poteena, Potiena, Poteina, Poteana

Powder (American) A light-hearted woman
Powdar, Powdir, Powdur, Powdor, Powdi, Powdie, Powdy, Powdey

Praise (Latin) One who expresses admiration
Prayse, Praize, Prayze, Praze, Praese, Praeze

Pramada (Indian) One who is indifferent

Pramlocha (Hindi) In Hinduism, a celestial nymph

Precious (American) One who is treasured
Preshis, Preshys

Presley (English) Of the priest's town
Presly, Preslie, Presli, Preslee

Primola (Latin) Resembling a primrose
Primolah, Primolia, Primoliah, Primolea, Primoleah

Princess (English) A high-born daughter; born to royalty
Princessa, Princesa, Princie, Princi, Princy, Princee, Princey, Princea

Prisca (Latin) From an ancient family
Priscilla, Priscella, Precilla, Presilla, Prescilla, Prisilla, Prisella, Prissy, Prissi

Promise (American) A faithful woman
Promice, Promyse, Promyce, Promis, Promiss, Promys, Promyss

Prudence (English) One who is cautious and exercises good judgment
Prudencia, Prudensa, Prudensia, Prudentia, Predencia, Predentia, Prue, Pru

Pryce (American / Welsh) One who is very dear / an enthusiastic child
Price, Prise, Pryse

Pulcheria (Italian) A chubby baby
Pulcheriah, Pulcherea, Pulchereah, Pulcherya, Pulcheryah, Pulcheriya

Pulika (African) An obedient and well-behaved girl
Pulikah, Pulicca, Pulicka, Pulyka, Puleeka, Puleaka

Pyrena (Greek) A fiery woman
Pyrenah, Pyrina, Pyrinah, Pyryna, Pyrynah, Pyreena, Pyreenah, Pyriena

Pyria (American) One who is cherished
Pyriah, Pyrea, Pyreah, Pyriya, Pyriyah, Pyra

Q

Qadesh (Syrian) In mythology, goddess of love and sensuality
Quedesh, Qadesha, Quedesha, Qadeshia, Quedeshia, Quedeshiya

Qamra (Arabic) Of the moon
Qamrah, Qamar, Qamara, Qamrra, Qamaria, Qamrea, Qamria

Qimat (Indian) A valuable woman
Qimate, Qimatte, Qimata, Qimatta

Qitarah (Arabic) Having a nice fragrance
Qitara, Qytarah, Qytara, Qitaria, Qitarra, Qitarria, Qytarra, Qytarria

Qoqa (Chechen) Resembling a dove

Quana (Native American) One who is aromatic; sweet-smelling
Quanah, Quanna, Quannah, Quania, Quaniya, Quanniya, Quannia, Quanea

Querida (Spanish) One who is dearly loved; beloved
Queridah, Queryda, Querydah, Querrida, Queridda, Querridda, Quereeda, Quereada

Queta (Spanish) Head of the household
Quetah, Quetta, Quettah

Quiana (American) Living with grace; heavenly
Quianah, Quianna, Quiane, Quian, Quianne, Quianda, Quiani, Quianita

Quincy (English) The fifth-born child
Quincey, Quinci, Quincie, Quincee, Quincia, Quinncy, Quinnci, Quyncy

^**Quinn** (English / Irish) Woman who is queenly
Quin, Quinne

Quintana (Latin / English) The fifth girl / queen's lawn
Quintanah, Quinella, Quinta, Quintina, Quintanna, Quintann, Quintara, Quintona

Quintessa (Latin) Of the essence
Quintessah, Quintesa, Quintesha, Quintisha, Quintessia, Quyntessa, Quintosha, Quinticia

Quinyette (American) The fifth-born child
Quinyett, Quinyet, Quinyeta, Quinyette, Quinyete

Quirina (Latin) One who is contentious
Quirinah, Quiryna, Quirynah, Quireena, Quireenah, Quireina, Quireinah, Quiriena

Quiritis (Latin) In mythology, goddess of motherhood
Quiritiss, Quiritisse, Quirytis, Quirytys, Quiritys, Quirityss

R

Rabiah (Egyptian / Arabic) Born in the springtime / of the gentle wind
Rabia, Raabia, Rabi'ah, Rabi

Rachana (Hindi) Born of the creation
Rachanna, Rashana, Rashanda, Rachna

Rachel (Hebrew) The innocent lamb; in the Bible, Jacob's wife
Rachael, Racheal, Rachelanne, Rachelce, Rachele, Racheli, Rachell, Rachelle, Raquel

Radcliffe (English) Of the red cliffs
Radcleff, Radclef, Radclif, Radclife, Radclyffe, Radclyf, Radcliphe, Radclyphe

Radella (English) An elfin counselor
Radell, Radel, Radele, Radela, Raedself, Radself, Raidself

Radmilla (Slavic) Hard-working for the people
Radilla, Radinka, Radmila, Redmilla, Radilu

Rafi'a (Arabic) An exalted woman
Rafia, Rafi'ah, Rafee'a, Rafeea, Rafeeah, Rafiya, Rafiyah

Ragnara (Swedish) Feminine form of Ragnar; one who provides counsel to the army
Ragnarah, Ragnarra, Ragnaria, Ragnarea, Ragnari, Ragnarie, Ragnary, Ragnarey

Rahi (Arabic) Born during the springtime
Rahii, Rahy, Rahey, Rahee, Rahea, Rahie

Rahimah (Arabic) A compassionate woman; one who is merciful
Rahima, Raheema, Raheemah, Raheima, Rahiema, Rahyma, Rahymah, Raheama

Raina (Polish) Form of Regina, meaning "a queenly woman"
Raenah, Raene, Rainah, Raine, Rainee, Rainey, Rainelle, Rainy

Raja (Arabic) One who is filled with hope
Rajah

Raleigh (English) From the clearing of roe deer
Raileigh, Railey, Raley, Rawleigh, Rawley, Raly, Rali, Ralie

Ramona (Spanish) Feminine form of Ramon; a wise protector
Ramee, Ramie, Ramoena, Ramohna, Ramonda, Ramonde, Ramonita, Ramonna

Randi (English) Feminine form of Randall; shielded by wolves; form of Miranda, meaning "worthy of admiration"
Randa, Randee, Randelle, Randene, Randie, Randy, Randey, Randilyn

Raquel (Spanish) Form of Rachel, meaning "the innocent lamb"
Racquel, Racquell, Raquela, Raquelle, Roquel, Roquela, Rakel, Rakell

Rasha (Arabic) Resembling a young gazelle
Rashah, Raisha, Raysha, Rashia, Raesha

Ratana (Thai) Resembling a crystal
Ratanah, Ratanna, Ratannah, Rathana, Rathanna

Rati (Hindi) In Hinduism, goddess of passion and lust
Ratie, Ratea, Ratee, Raty, Ratey

Ratri (Indian) Born in the evening
Ratrie, Ratry, Ratrey, Ratree, Ratrea

Rawiyah (Arabic) One who recites ancient poetry
Rawiya, Rawiyya, Rawiyyah

Rawnie (English) An elegant lady
Rawni, Rawny, Rawney, Rawnee, Rawnea

Raya (Israeli) A beloved friend
Rayah

Raymonde (German) Feminine form of Raymond; one who offers wise protection
Raymondi, Raymondie, Raymondee, Raymondea, Raymonda, Raymunde, Raymunda

Rayna (Hebrew / Scandinavian) One who is pure / one who provides wise counsel
Raynah, Raynee, Rayni, Rayne, Raynea, Raynie

Reba (Hebrew) Form of Rebecca, meaning "one who is bound to God"
Rebah, Reeba, Rheba, Rebba, Ree, Reyba, Reaba

Rebecca (Hebrew) One who is bound to God; in the Bible, the wife of Isaac
Rebakah, Rebbeca, Rebbecca, Rebbecka, Rebeca, Rebeccah, Rebeccea, Becky, Reba

Reese (American) Form of Rhys, meaning "having great enthusiasm for life"
Rhyss, Rhysse, Reece, Reice, Reise, Reace, Rease, Riece

Reagan (Gaelic) Born into royalty; the little ruler
Raegan, Ragan, Raygan, Reganne, Regann, Regane, Reghan, Regan

Regina (Latin) A queenly woman
Regeena, Regena, Reggi, Reggie, Régine, Regine, Reginette, Reginia, Raina

Rehan (Armenian) Resembling a flower
Rehane, Rehann, Rehanne, Rehana, Rehanna, Rehanan, Rehannan, Rehania

Rehoboth (Hebrew) From the city by the river
Rehobothe, Rehobotha, Rehobothia

Rekha (Indian) One who walks a straight line
Rekhah, Reka, Rekah

^**Remy** (French) Woman from the town of Rheims
Remi, Remie, Remmy, Remmi, Remmie, Remmey, Remey

Ren (Japanese) Resembling a water lily

Renée (French) One who has been reborn
Ranae, Ranay, Ranée, Renae, Renata, Renay, Renaye, René

Reseda (Latin) Resembling the mignonette flower
Resedah, Reselda, Resedia, Reseldia

Resen (Hebrew) From the head of the stream; refers to a bridle

Reshma (Arabic) Having silky skin
Reshmah, Reshman, Reshmane, Reshmann, Reshmanne, Reshmana, Reshmanna, Reshmaan

Reya (Spanish) A queenly woman
Reyah, Reyeh, Reye, Reyia, Reyiah, Reyea, Reyeah

Reza (Hungarian) Form of Theresa, meaning "a harvester"
Rezah, Rezia, Reziah, Rezi, Rezie, Rezy, Rezee, Resi

Rezeph (Hebrew) As solid as a stone
Rezepha, Rezephe, Rezephia, Rezephah, Rezephiah

Rhea (Greek) Of the flowing stream; in mythology, the wife of Cronus and mother of gods and goddesses
Rea, Rhae, Rhaya, Rhia, Rhiah, Rhiya, Rheya

Rheda (Anglo-Saxon) A divine woman; a goddess
Rhedah

Rhiannon (Welsh) The great and sacred queen
Rheanna, Rheanne, Rhiana, Rhiann, Rhianna, Rhiannan, Rhianon, Rhyan

Rhonda (Welsh) Wielding a good spear
Rhondelle, Rhondene, Rhondiesha, Rhonette, Rhonnda, Ronda, Rondel, Rondelle

Rhys (Welsh) Having great enthusiasm for life
Rhyss, Rhysse, Reece, Reese, Reice, Reise, Reace, Rease

Ria (Spanish) From the river's mouth
Riah

Riane (Gaelic) Feminine form of Ryan; little ruler
Riana, Rianna, Rianne, Ryann, Ryanne, Ryana, Ryanna, Riann

Rica (English) Form of Frederica, meaning "peaceful ruler"; form of Erica, meaning "ever the ruler / resembling heather"
Rhica, Ricca, Ricah, Rieca, Riecka, Rieka, Riqua, Ryca

Riddhi (Indian) A prosperous woman
Riddhie, Riddhy, Riddhey, Riddhee, Riddhea

Rihanna (Arabic) Resembling sweet basil
Rihana

*__Riley__ (Gaelic) From the rye clearing; a courageous woman
Reilley, Reilly, Rilee, Rileigh, Ryley, Rylee, Ryleigh, Rylie

Rini (Japanese) Resembling a young rabbit
Rinie, Rinee, Rinea, Riny, Riney

Rio (Spanish) Woman of the river
Rhio

Risa (Latin) One who laughs often
Risah, Reesa, Riesa, Rise, Rysa, Rysah, Riseh, Risako

Rita (Greek) Precious pearl
Ritta, Reeta, Reita, Rheeta, Riet, Rieta, Ritah, Reta

Roberta (English) Feminine form of Robert; one who is bright with fame
Robertah, Robbie, Robin

Rochelle (French) From the little rock
Rochel, Rochele, Rochell, Rochella, Rochette, Roschella, Roschelle, Roshelle

Roja (Spanish) A red-haired lady
Rojah

Rolanda (German) Feminine form of Roland; well-known throughout the land
Rolandah, Rolandia, Roldandea, Rolande, Rolando, Rollanda, Rollande

Romhilda (German) A glorious battle maiden
Romhilde, Romhild, Romeld, Romelde, Romelda, Romilda, Romild, Romilde

Ronli (Hebrew) My joy is the Lord
Ronlie, Ronlee, Ronleigh, Ronly, Ronley, Ronlea, Ronia, Roniya

Ronni (English) Form of Veronica, meaning "displaying her true image"
Ronnie, Ronae, Ronay, Ronee, Ronelle, Ronette, Roni, Ronica, Ronika

Rosalind (German / English) Resembling a gentle horse / form of Rose, meaning "resembling the beautiful and meaningful flower"
Ros, Rosaleen, Rosalen, Rosalin, Rosalina, Rosalinda, Rosalinde, Rosaline, Chalina

^**Rose** (Latin) Resembling the beautiful and meaningful flower
Rosa, Rosie, Rosalind, ***Rosalyn***

Roseanne (English) Resembling the graceful rose
Ranna, Rosana, Rosanagh, Rosanna, Rosannah, Rosanne, Roseann, Roseanna

Rosemary (Latin / English) The dew of the sea / resembling a bitter rose
Rosemaree, Rosemarey, Rosemaria, Rosemarie, Rosmarie, Rozmary, Rosamaria, Rosamarie

Rowan (Gaelic) Of the red-berry tree
Rowann, Rowane, Rowanne, Rowana, Rowanna

Rowena (Welsh / German) One who is fair and slender / having much fame and happiness
Rhowena, Roweena, Roweina, Rowenna, Rowina, Rowinna, Rhonwen, Rhonwyn

Ruana (Indian) One who is musically inclined
Ruanah, Ruanna, Ruannah, Ruane, Ruann, Ruanne

*__Ruby__ (English) As precious as the red gemstone
Rubee, Rubi, Rubie, Rubyna, Rubea

Rudella (German) A well-known woman
Rudela, Rudelah, Rudell, Rudelle, Rudel, Rudele, Rudy, Rudie

Rue (English, German) A medicinal herb
Ru, Larue

Rufina (Latin) A red-haired woman
Rufeena, Rufeine, Ruffina, Rufine, Ruffine, Rufyna, Ruffyna, Rufyne

Ruhi (Arabic) A spiritual woman
Roohee, Ruhee, Ruhie, Ruhy, Ruhey, Roohi, Roohie, Ruhea

Rukmini (Hindi) Adorned with gold; in Hinduism, the first wife of Krishna
Rukminie, Rukminy, Rukminey, Rukminee, Rukminea, Rukminni, Rukminii

Rumah (Hebrew) One who has been exalted
Ruma, Rumia, Rumea, Rumiah, Rumeah, Rumma, Rummah

Rumina (Latin) In mythology, a protector goddess of mothers and babies
Ruminah, Rumeena, Rumeenah, Rumeina, Rumiena, Rumyna, Rumeinah, Rumienah

Rupali (Indian) A beautiful woman
Rupalli, Rupalie, Rupalee, Rupallee, Rupal, Rupa, Rupaly, Rupaley

Ruqayyah (Arabic) A gentle woman; a daughter of Muhammad
Ruqayya, Ruqayah, Ruqaya

Ruth (Hebrew) A beloved companion
Ruthe, Ruthelle, Ruthellen, Ruthetta, Ruthi, Ruthie, Ruthina, Ruthine

Ryba (Slavic) Resembling a fish
Rybah, Rybba, Rybbah

Ryder (American) An accomplished horsewoman
Rider

Rylee (American) Form of Riley, meaning "from the rye clearing / a courageous woman"

S

Saba (Greek / Arabic) Woman from Sheba / born in the morning
Sabah, Sabaa, Sabba, Sabbah, Sabaah

Sabana (Spanish) From the open plain
Sabanah, Sabanna, Sabann, Sabanne, Sabane, Saban

Sabi (Arabic) A lovely young lady
Sabie, Saby, Sabey, Sabee, Sabbi, Sabbee, Sabea

Sabirah (Arabic) Having great patience
Sabira, Saabira, Sabeera, Sabiera, Sabeira, Sabyra, Sabirra, Sabyrra

Sabra (Hebrew) Resembling the cactus fruit; to rest
Sabrah, Sebra, Sebrah, Sabrette, Sabbra, Sabraa, Sabarah, Sabarra

Sabrina (English) A legendary princess
Sabrinah, Sabrinna, Sabreena, Sabriena, Sabreina, Sabryna, Sabrine, Sabryne, Cabrina, Zabrina

Sachet (Hindi) Having consciousness
Sachett, Sachette

Sada (Japanese) The pure one
Sadda, Sadaa, Sadako, Saddaa

Sadella (American) A beautiful fairylike princess
Sadel, Sadela, Sadelah, Sadele, Sadell, Sadellah, Sadelle, Sydel

Sadhana (Hindi) A devoted woman
Sadhanah, Sadhanna, Sadhannah, Sadhane, Sadhanne, Sadhann, Sadhan

Sadhbba (Irish) A wise woman
Sadhbh, Sadhba

***Sadie** (English) Form of Sarah, meaning "a princess; lady"
Sadi, Sady, Sadey, Sadee, Saddi, Saddee, Sadiey, Sadye

Sadiya (Arabic) One who is fortunate; lucky
Sadiyah, Sadiyyah, Sadya, Sadyah

Sadzi (American) Having a sunny disposition
Sadzee, Sadzey, Sadzia, Sadziah, Sadzie, Sadzya, Sadzyah, Sadzy

Safa (Arabic) One who is innocent and pure
Safah, Saffa, Sapha, Saffah, Saphah

Saffron (English) Resembling the yellow flower
Saffrone, Saffronn, Saffronne, Safron, Safronn, Safronne, Saffronah, Safrona

Saheli (Indian) A beloved friend
Sahelie, Sahely, Saheley, Sahelee, Saheleigh, Sahyli, Sahelea

Sahila (Indian) One who provides guidance
Sahilah, Saheela, Sahyla, Sahiela, Saheila, Sahela, Sahilla, Sahylla

Sahkyo (Native American) Resembling the mink
Sakyo

Saida (Arabic) Fortunate one; one who is happy
Saidah, Sa'ida, Sayida, Saeida, Saedah, Said, Sayide, Sayidea

Saihah (Arabic) One who is useful; good
Saiha, Sayiha

Sailor (American) One who sails the seas
Sailer, Sailar, Saylor, Sayler, Saylar, Saelor, Saeler, Saelar

Saima (Arabic) A fasting woman
Saimah, Saimma, Sayima

Sajni (Indian) One who is dearly loved
Sajnie, Sajny, Sajney, Sajnee, Sajnea

Sakae (Japanese) One who is prosperous
Sakai, Sakaie, Sakay, Sakaye

Sakari (Native American) A sweet girl
Sakarie, Sakary, Sakarri, Sakarey, Sakaree, Sakarree, Sakarah, Sakarrie

Sakina (Indian / Arabic) A beloved friend / having God-inspired peace of mind
Sakinah, Sakeena, Sakiena, Sakeina, Sakyna, Sakeyna, Sakinna, Sakeana

Sakti (Hindi) In Hinduism, the divine energy
Saktie, Sakty, Sakkti, Sackti, Saktee, Saktey, Saktia, Saktiah

Saku (Japanese) Remembrance of the Lord
Sakuko

Sakura (Japanese) Resembling a cherry blossom
Sakurah, Sakurako, Sakurra

Sala (Hindi) From the sacred sala tree
Salah, Salla, Sallah

Salal (English) An evergreen shrub with flowers and berries
Sallal, Salall, Sallall, Salalle, Salale, Sallale

Salamasina (Samoan) A princess; born to royalty
Salamaseena, Salamasyna, Salamaseana, Salamaseina, Salamasiena

Salina (French) One of a solemn, dignified character
Salin, Salinah, Salinda, Salinee, Sallin, Sallina, Sallinah, Salline

Saloma (Hebrew) One who offers peace and tranquility
Salomah, Salome, Salomia, Salomiah, Schlomit, Shulamit, Salomeaexl, Salomma

Salus (Latin) In mythology, goddess of health and prosperity; salvation
Saluus, Salusse, Saluss

Salwa (Arabic) One who provides comfort; solace
Salwah

Samah (Arabic) A generous, forgiving woman
Sama, Samma, Sammah

***Samantha** (Aramaic) One who listens well
Samanthah, Samanthia, Samanthea, Samantheya, Samanath, Samanatha, Samana, Samanitha

Sameh (Arabic) One who forgives
Sammeh, Samaya, Samaiya

Samina (Arabic) A healthy woman
Saminah, Samine, Sameena, Samyna, Sameana, Sameina, Samynah

Samone (Hebrew) Form of Simone, meaning "one who listens well"
Samoan, Samoane, Samon, Samona, Samonia

Samuela (Hebrew) Feminine form of Samuel; asked of God
Samuelah, Samuella, Samuell, Samuelle, Sammila, Sammile, Samella, Samielle

Sana (Persian / Arabic) One who emanates light / brilliance; splendor
Sanah, Sanna, Sanako, Sanaah, Sane, Saneh

Sanaa (Swahili) Beautiful work of art
Sanae, Sannaa

Sandeep (Punjabi) One who is enlightened
Sandeepe, Sandip, Sandipp, Sandippe, Sandeyp, Sandeype

Sandhya (Hindi) Born at twilight; name of the daughter of the god Brahma
Sandhiya, Sandhyah, Sandya, Sandyah

Sandra (Greek) Form of Alexandra, meaning "a helper and defender of mankind"
Sandrah, Sandrine, Sandy, Sandi, Sandie, Sandey, Sandee, Sanda, Sandrica

Sandrica (Greek) Form of Alexandra, meaning "a helper and defender of mankind"
Sandricca, Sandricah, Sandricka, Sandrickah, Sandrika, Sandrikah, Sandryca, Sandrycah

Sandrine (Greek) Form of Alexandra, meaning "a helper and defender of mankind"
Sandrin, Sandreana, Sandreanah, Sandreane, Sandreen, Sandreena, Sandreenah, Sandreene

Sangita (Indian) One who is musical
Sangitah, Sangeeta, Sangeita, Sangyta, Sangieta, Sangeata

Saniya (Indian) A moment in time preserved
Saniyah, Sanya, Sanea, Sania

Sanjna (Indian) A conscientious woman

Santana (Spanish) A saintly woman
Santa, Santah, Santania, Santaniah, Santaniata, Santena, Santenah, Santenna

Saoirse (Gaelic) An independent woman; having freedom
Saoyrse

Sapna (Hindi) A dream come true
Sapnah, Sapnia, Sapniah, Sapnea, Sapneah, Sapniya, Sapniyah

*** Sarah** (Hebrew) A princess; lady; in the Bible, wife of Abraham
Sara, Sari, Sariah, Sarika, Saaraa, Sarita, Sarina, Sarra, Kala, Sadie

Saraid (Irish) One who is excellent; superior
Saraide, Saraed, Saraede, Sarayd, Sarayde

Sarama (African / Hindi) A kind woman / in Hinduism, Indra's dog
Saramah, Saramma, Sarrama, Sarramma

Saran (African) One who brings joy to others
Sarane, Sarran, Saranne, Saranna, Sarana, Sarann

Sarasvati (Hindi) In Hinduism, goddess of learning and the arts
Sarasvatti, Sarasvatie, Sarasvaty, Sarasvatey, Sarasvatee, Sarasvatea

Saraswati (Hindi) Owning water; in Hinduism, a river goddess
Saraswatti, Saraswatie, Saraswaty, Saraswatey, Saraswatee, Saraswatea

Sardinia (Italian) Woman from a mountainous island
Sardiniah, Sardinea, Sardineah, Sardynia, Sardyniah, Sardynea, Sardyneah

Sasa (Japanese) One who is helpful; gives aid
Sasah

Sasha (Russian) Form of Alexandra, meaning "a helper and defender of mankind"
Sascha, Sashenka, Saskia

Sauda (Swahili) A dark beauty
Saudaa, Sawda, Saudda

*****Savannah** (English) From the open grassy plain
Savanna, Savana, Savanne, Savann, Savane, Savanneh

Savarna (Hindi) Daughter of the ocean
Savarnia, Savarnea, Savarniya, Savarneia

Savitri (Hindi) In Hinduism, the daughter of the god of the sun
Savitari, Savitrie, Savitry, Savitarri, Savitarie, Savitree, Savitrea, Savitrey

Savvy (American) Smart and perceptive woman
Savy, Savvi, Savvie, Savvey, Savee, Savvee, Savvea, Savea

Sayyida (Arabic) A mistress
Sayyidah, Sayida, Sayyda, Seyyada, Seyyida, Seyada, Seyida

^***Scarlett** (English) Vibrant red color; a vivacious woman
Scarlet, Scarlette, Skarlet

Scota (Irish) Woman of Scotland
Scotta, Scotah, Skota, Skotta, Skotah

Sea'iqa (Arabic) Thunder and lightning
Seaqa, Seaqua

Season (Latin) A fertile woman; one who embraces change
Seazon, Seeson, Seezon, Seizon, Seasen, Seasan, Seizen, Seizan

Sebille (English) In Arthurian legend, a fairy
Sebylle, Sebill, Sebile, Sebyle, Sebyl

Secunda (Latin) The second-born child
Secundah, Secuba, Secundus, Segunda, Sekunda

Seda (Armenian) Voices of the forest
Sedda, Sedah, Seddah

Sedona (American) Woman from a city in Arizona
Sedonah, Sedonna, Sedonnah, Sedonia, Sedonea

Seema (Greek) A symbol; a sign
Seyma, Syma, Seama, Seima, Siema

Sefarina (Greek) Of a gentle wind
Sefarinah, Sefareena, Sefareenah, Sefaryna, Sefarynah, Sefareana, Sefareanah

Seiko (Japanese) The force of truth

Selene (Greek) Of the moon
Sela, Selena, Selina, Celina, Zalina

Sema (Arabic) A divine omen; a known symbol
Semah

Senalda (Spanish) A sign; a symbol
Senaldah, Senaldia, Senaldiya, Senaldea, Senaldya

September (American) Born in the month of September
Septimber, Septymber, Septemberia, Septemberea

Sequoia (Native American) Of the giant redwood tree
Sekwoya, Lequoia

Serafina (Latin) A seraph; a heavenly winged angel
Serafinah, Serafine, Seraphina, Serefina, Seraphine, Sera

Serena (Latin) Having a peaceful disposition
Serenah, Serene, Sereena, Seryna, Serenity, Serenitie, Serenitee, Serepta, Cerina, Xerena

Serendipity (American) A fateful meeting; having good fortune
Serendipitey, Serendipitee, Serendipiti, Serendipitie, Serendypyty

⋆**Serenity** (Latin) Peaceful

Sevati (Indian) Resembling the white rose
Sevatie, Sevatti, Sevate, Sevatee, Sevatea, Sevaty, Sevatey, Sevti

Shabana (Arabic) A maiden belonging to the night
Shabanah, Shabanna, Shabaana, Shabanne, Shabane

Shabnan (Persian) A falling raindrop
Shabnane, Shabnann, Shabnanne

Shadha (Arabic) An aromatic fragrance
Shadhah

Shafiqa (Arabic) A compassionate woman
Shafiqah, Shafiqua, Shafeeqa, Shafeequa

Shai (Gaelic) A gift of God
Shay, Shae, Shayla, Shea, Shaye

Sha'ista (Arabic) One who is polite and well-behaved
Shaistah, Shaista, Shaa'ista, Shayista, Shaysta

Shakila (Arabic) Feminine form of Shakil; beautiful one
Shakilah, Shakela, Shakeela, Shakeyla, Shakyla, Shakeila, Shakiela, Shakina

Shakira (Arabic) Feminine form of Shakir; grateful; thankful
Shakirah, Shakiera, Shaakira, Shakeira, Shakyra, Shakeyra, Shakura, Shakirra

Shakti (Indian) A divine woman; having power
Shaktie, Shakty, Shaktey, Shaktee, Shaktye, Shaktea

Shaliqa (Arabic) One who is sisterly
Shaliqah, Shaliqua, Shaleeqa, Shaleequa, Shalyqa, Shalyqua

Shamima (Arabic) A woman full of flavor
Shamimah, Shameema, Shamiema, Shameima, Shamyma, Shameama

Shandy (English) One who is rambunctious; boisterous
Shandey, Shandee, Shandi, Shandie, Shandye, Shandea

Shani (African) A marvelous woman
Shanie, Shany, Shaney, Shanee, Shanni, Shanea, Shannie, Shanny

Shanley (Gaelic) Small and ancient woman
Shanleigh, Shanlee, Shanly, Shanli, Shanlie, Shanlea

Shannon (Gaelic) Having ancient wisdom; river name
Shanon, Shannen, Shannan, Shannin, Shanna, Shannae, Shannun, Shannyn

Shaquana (American) Truth in life
Shaqana, Shaquanah, Shaquanna, Shaqanna, Shaqania

Sharifah (Arabic) Feminine form of Sharif; noble; respected; virtuous
Sharifa, Shareefa, Sharufa, Sharufah, Sharyfa, Sharefa, Shareafa, Shariefa

Sharik (African) One who is a child of God
Shareek, Shareake, Sharicke, Sharick, Sharike, Shareak, Sharique, Sharyk

Sharikah (Arabic) One who is a good companion
Sharika, Shareeka, Sharyka, Shareka, Shariqua, Shareaka

Sharlene (French) Feminine form of Charles; petite and womanly
Sharleene, Sharleen, Sharla, Sharlyne, Sharline, Sharlyn, Sharlean, Sharleane

Sharon (Hebrew) From the plains; a flowering shrub
Sharron, Sharone, Sharona, Shari, Sharis, Sharne, Sherine, Sharun

Shasta (Native American) From the triple-peaked mountain
Shastah, Shastia, Shastiya, Shastea, Shasteya

Shawnee (Native American) A tribal name
Shawni, Shawnie, Shawnea, Shawny, Shawney, Shawnea

Shayla (Irish) Of the fairy palace; form of Shai, meaning "a gift of God"
Shaylah, Shaylagh, Shaylain, Shaylan, Shaylea, Shayleah, Shaylla, Sheyla

Shaylee (Gaelic) From the fairy palace; a fairy princess
Shalee, Shayleigh, Shailee, Shaileigh, Shaelee, Shaeleigh, Shayli, Shaylie

Sheehan (Celtic) Little peaceful one; peacemaker
Shehan, Sheyhan, Shihan, Shiehan, Shyhan, Sheahan

Sheela (Indian) One of cool conduct and character
Sheelah, Sheetal

Sheena (Gaelic) God's gracious gift
Sheenah, Shena, Shiena, Sheyna, Shyna, Sheana, Sheina

Sheherezade (Arabic) One who is a city dweller

Sheila (Irish) Form of Cecilia, meaning "one who is blind"
Sheilah, Sheelagh, Shelagh, Shiela, Shyla, Selia, Sighle, Sheiletta

Shelby (English) From the willow farm
Shelbi, Shelbey, Shelbie, Shelbee, Shelbye, Shelbea

Sheridan (Gaelic) One who is wild and untamed; a searcher
Sheridann, Sheridanne, Sherydan, Sherridan, Sheriden, Sheridon, Sherrerd, Sherida

Sheshebens (Native American) Resembling a small duck

Shifra (Hebrew) A beautiful midwife
Shifrah, Shiphrah, Shiphra, Shifria, Shifriya, Shifrea

Shikha (Indian) Flame burning brightly
Shikhah, Shikkha, Shekha, Shykha

Shima (Native American) Little mother
Shimah, Shimma, Shyma, Shymah

Shina (Japanese) A virtuous woman; having goodness
Shinah, Shinna, Shyna, Shynna

Shobha (Indian) An attractive woman
Shobhah, Shobbha, Shoba, Shobhan, Shobhane

Shoshana (Arabic) Form of Susannah, meaning "white lily"
Shosha, Shoshan, Shoshanah, Shoshane, Shoshanha, Shoshann, Shoshanna, Shoshannah

Shradhdha (Indian) One who is faithful; trusting
Shraddha, Shradha, Shradhan, Shradhane

Shruti (Indian) Having good hearing
Shrutie, Shruty, Shrutey, Shrutee, Shrutye, Shrutea

Shunnareh (Arabic) Pleasing in manner and behavior
Shunnaraya, Shunareh, Shunarreh

Shyann (English) Form of Cheyenne, meaning "unintelligible speaker"
Shyanne, Shyane, Sheyann, Sheyanne, Sheyenne, Sheyene

Shysie (Native American) A quiet child
Shysi, Shysy, Shysey, Shysee, Shycie, Shyci, Shysea, Shycy

Sibyl (English) A prophetess; a seer
Sybil, Sibyla, Sybella, Sibil, Sibella, Sibilla, Sibley, Sibylla

Siddhi (Hindi) Having spiritual power
Sidhi, Syddhi, Sydhi

Sidero (Greek) In mythology, stepmother of Pelias and Neleus
Siderro, Sydero, Sideriyo

Sieglinde (German) Winning a gentle victory

Sienna (Italian) Woman with reddish-brown hair
Siena, Siennya, Sienya, Syenna, Syinna

Sierra (Spanish) From the jagged mountain range
Siera, Syerra, Syera, Seyera, Seeara

Sigfreda (German) A woman who is victorious
Sigfreeda, Sigfrida, Sigfryda, Sigfreyda, Sigfrieda, Sigfriede, Sigfrede

Sigismonda (Teutonic) A victorious defender
Sigismunda

Signia (Latin) A distinguishing sign
Signiya, Signea, Signeia, Signeya, Signa

Sigyn (Norse) In mythology, the wife of Loki

Sihu (Native American) As delicate as a flower

Silka (Latin) Form of Cecelia, meaning "one who is blind"
Silke, Silkia, Silkea, Silkie, Silky, Silkee, Sylka, Sylke

Sima (Arabic) One who is treasured; a prize
Simma, Syma, Simah, Simia, Simiya

Simone (French) One who listens well
Sim, Simonie, Symone, Samone

Sine (Scottish) Form of Jane, meaning "God is gracious"
Sinead, Sineidin, Sioned, Sionet, Sion, Siubhan, Siwan, Sineh

Sinobia (Greek) Form of Zenobia, meaning "child of Zeus"
Sinobiah, Sinobya, Sinobe, Sinobie, Sinovia, Senobia, Senobya, Senobe

Sinopa (Native American) Resembling a fox

Sinope (Greek) In mythology, one of the daughters of Asopus

Siran (Armenian) An alluring and lovely woman

Siren (Greek) In mythology, a sea nymph whose beautiful singing lured sailors to their deaths; refers to a seductive and beautiful woman
Sirene, Sirena, Siryne, Siryn, Syren, Syrena, Sirine, Sirina

Siria (Spanish / Persian) Bright like the sun / a glowing woman
Siriah, Sirea, Sireah, Siriya, Siriyah, Sirya, Siryah

Siroun (Armenian) A lovely woman
Sirune

Sirpuhi (Armenian) One who is holy; pious
Sirpuhie, Sirpuhy, Sirpuhey, Sirpuhea, Sirpuhee

Sissy (English) Form of Cecilia, meaning "one who is blind"
Sissey, Sissie, Sisley, Sisli, Sislee, Sissel, Sissle, Syssy

Sita (Hindi) In Hinduism, goddess of the harvest and wife of Rama

Sive (Irish) A good and sweet girl
Sivney, Sivny, Sivni, Sivnie, Sivnee, Sivnea

Skylar (English) One who is learned, a scholar
Skylare, Skylarr, Skyler, Skylor, Skylir

Sloane (Irish) A strong protector; a woman warrior
Sloan, Slone

Smita (Indian) One who smiles a lot

Snow (American) Frozen rain
Snowy, Snowie, Snowi, Snowey, Snowee, Snowea, Sno

Snowdrop (English) Resembling a small white flower

Solana (Latin / Spanish) Wind from the east / of the sunshine
Solanah, Solanna, Solann, Solanne

Solange (French) One who is religious and dignified

Solaris (Greek) Of the sun
Solarise, Solariss, Solarisse, Solarys, Solaryss, Solarysse, Sol, Soleil

Solita (Latin) One who is solitary
Solitah, Solida, Soledad, Soledada, Soledade

Somatra (Indian) Of the excellent moon

Sona (Arabic) The golden one
Sonika, Sonna

Sonora (Spanish) A pleasant-sounding woman
Sonorah, Sonoria, Sonorya, Sonoriya

Soo (Korean) Having an excellent long life

*Sophia** (Greek) Form of Sophie, meaning great wisdom and foresight
***Sofia**, Sofiya*

*Sophie** (Greek) Wisdom
***Sophia**, Sofiya, Sofie, **Sofia**, Sofi, Sofiyko, Sofronia, Sophronia, Zofia*

Sorina (Romanian) Feminine form of Sorin; of the sun
Sorinah, Sorinna, Sorinia, Soriniya, Sorinya, Soryna, Sorynia, Sorine

Sorrel (French) From the surele plant
Sorrell, Sorrelle, Sorrele, Sorrela, Sorrella

Sparrow (English) Resembling a small songbird
Sparro, Sparroe, Sparo, Sparow, Sparowe, Sparoe

Sslama (Egyptian) One who is peaceful

Stacey (English) Form of Anastasia, meaning "one who shall rise again"
Stacy, Staci, Stacie, Stacee, Stacia, Stasia, Stasy, Stasey

*Stella** (English) Star of the sea
Stela, Stelle, Stele, Stellah, Stelah

Stephanie (Greek) Feminine form of Stephen; crowned in victory
Stephani, Stephany, Stephaney, Stephanee, Stephene, Stephana, Stefanie, Stefani

Stevonna (Greek) A crowned lady
Stevonnah, Stevona, Stevonah, Stevonia, Stevonea, Stevoniya

Styx (Greek) In mythology, the river of the underworld
Stixx, Styxx, Stix

Suave (American) A smooth and courteous woman
Swave

Subhadra (Hindi) In Hinduism, the sister of Krishna

Subhaga (Indian) A fortunate person

Subhuja (Hindi) An auspicious celestial damsel

Subira (African) One who is patient
Subirah, Subirra, Subyra, Subyrra, Subeera, Subeara, Subeira, Subiera

Suhaila (Arabic) Feminine form of Suhail; the second brightest star
Suhayla, Suhaela, Suhala, Suhailah, Suhaylah, Suhaelah, Suhalah

Sulwyn (Welsh) One who shines as bright as the sun
Sulwynne, Sulwynn, Sulwinne, Sulwin, Sulwen, Sulwenn, Sulwenne

Sumana (Indian) A good-natured woman
Sumanah, Sumanna, Sumane, Sumanne, Sumann

Sumi (Japanese) One who is elegant and refined
Sumie

Sumitra (Indian) A beloved friend
Sumitrah, Sumita, Sumytra, Sumyta, Sumeetra, Sumeitra, Sumietra, Sumeatra

Summer (American) Refers to the season; born in summer
Sommer, Sumer, Somer, Somers

Suna (Turkish) A swan-like woman

Sunanda (Indian) Having a sweet character
Sunandah, Sunandia, Sunandiya, Sunandea, Sunandya

Sunila (Indian) Feminine form of Sunil; very blue
Sunilah, Sunilla, Sunilya, Suniliya

Sunniva (English) Gift of the sun
Synnove, Synne, Synnove, Sunn

Surabhi (Indian) Having a lovely fragrance
Surbhii, Surabhie, Surabhy, Surabhey, Surabhee, Surabhea

Susannah (Hebrew) White lily
Susanna, Susanne, Susana, Susane, Susan, Suzanna, Suzannah, Suzanne, Shoshana, Huhana

Sushanti (Indian) A peaceful woman; tranquil
Sushantie, Sushanty, Sushantey, Sushantee, Sushantea

Suzu (Japanese) One who is long-lived
Suzue, Suzuko

Swanhilda (Norse) A woman warrior; in mythology, the daughter of Sigurd
Swanhild, Swanhilde, Svanhilde, Svanhild, Svenhilde, Svenhilda

Swarupa (Indian) One who is devoted to the truth

Sydney (English) Of the wide meadow
Sydny, Sydni, Sydnie, Sydnea, Sydnee, Sidney, Sidne, Sidnee

T

Taariq (Swahili) Resembling the morning star
Tariq, Taarique, Tarique

Tabia (African / Egyptian) One who makes incantations / a talented woman
Tabiah, Tabya, Tabea, Tabeah, Tabiya

Tabita (African) A graceful woman
Tabitah, Tabyta, Tabytah, Tabeeta, Tabeata, Tabieta, Tabeita

Tabitha (Greek) Resembling a gazelle; known for beauty and grace
Tabithah, Tabbitha, Tabetha, Tabbetha, Tabatha, Tabbatha, Tabotha, Tabbotha

Tabora (Spanish) One who plays a small drum
Taborah, Taborra, Taboria, Taborya

Tacincala (Native American) Resembling a deer
Tacincalah, Tacyncala, Tacyncalah, Tacincalla, Tacyncalla

Tahsin (Arabic) Beautification; one who is praised
Tahseen, Tahsene, Tahsyne, Tasine, Tahseene, Tahsean, Tahseane

Tahzib (Arabic) One who is educated and cultured
Tahzeeb, Tahzebe, Tahzybe, Tazib, Tazyb, Tazeeb, Tahzeab, Tazeab

Taithleach (Gaelic) A quiet and calm young lady

Takako (Japanese) A lofty child

Takoda (Native American) Friend to everyone
Takodah, Takodia, Takodya, Takota

Tala (Native American) A stalking wolf
Talah, Talla

Talia (Hebrew / Greek) Morning dew from heaven / blooming
Taliah, Talea, Taleah, Taleya, Tallia, Talieya, Taleea, Taleia

Talihah (Arabic) One who seeks knowledge
Taliha, Talibah, Taliba, Talyha, Taleehah, Taleahah

Taline (Armenian) Of the monestary
Talene, Taleen, Taleene, Talyne, Talinia, Talinya, Taliniya

Talisa (American) Consecrated to God
Talisah, Talysa, Taleesa, Talissa, Talise, Taleese, Talisia, Talisya

Talisha (American) A damsel; an innocent
Talesha, Taleisha, Talysha, Taleesha, Tylesha, Taleysha, Taleshia, Talishia

Talitha (Arabic) A maiden; young girl
Talithah, Taletha, Taleetha, Talytha, Talithia, Talethia, Tiletha, Talith

Tamanna (Indian) One who is desired
Tamannah, Tamana, Tamanah, Tammana, Tammanna

Tamasha (African) Pageant winner
Tamasha, Tomosha, Tomasha, Tamashia, Tamashya

Tamesis (Celtic) In mythology, the goddess of water; source of the name for the river Thames
Tamesiss, Tamesys, Tamesyss

Tangia (American) The angel
Tangiah, Tangya, Tangiya, Tangeah

Tani (Japanese / Melanesian / Tonkinese) From the valley / a sweetheart / a young woman
Tanie, Tany, Taney, Tanee, Tanni, Tanye, Tannie, Tanny

Tania (Russian) Queen of the fairies
Tanya, Tannie, Tanny, Tanika

Tanner (English) One who tans hides
Taner, Tannar, Tannor, Tannis

Tansy (English / Greek) An aromatic yellow flower / having immortality
Tansey, Tansi, Tansie, Tansee, Tansye, Tansea, Tancy, Tanzy

Tanushri (Indian) One who is beautiful; attractive
Tanushrie, Tanushry, Tanushrey, Tanushree, Tanushrea

Tanvi (Indian) Slender and beautiful woman
Tanvie, Tanvy, Tanvey, Tanvee, Tanvye, Tannvi, Tanvea

Tapati (Indian) In mythology, the daughter of the sun god
Tapatie, Tapaty, Tapatey, Tapatee, Tapatye, Tapatea

Taphath (Hebrew) In the Bible, Solomon's daughter
Tafath, Taphathe, Tafathe

Tara (Gaelic / Indian) Of the tower; rocky hill / star; in mythology, an astral goddess
Tarah, Tarra, Tayra, Taraea, Tarai, Taralee, Tarali, Taraya

Tarachand (Indian) Silver star
Tarachande, Tarachanda, Tarachandia, Tarachandea, Tarachandiya, Tarachandya

Taree (Japanese) A bending branch
Tarea, Tareya

Taregan (Native American) Resembling a crane
Tareganne, Taregann

Tareva-chine(shanay) (Native American) One with beautiful eyes

Tariana (American) From the holy hillside
Tarianna, Taryana, Taryanna

Tarika (Indian) A starlet
Tarikah, Taryka, Tarykah, Taricka, Tarickah

Tarisai (African) One to behold; to look at
Tarysai

Tasanee (Thai) A beautiful view
Tasane, Tasani, Tasanie, Tasany, Tasaney, Tasanye, Tasanea

Taskin (Arabic) One who provides peace; satisfaction
Taskine, Taskeen, Taskeene, Taskyne, Takseen, Taksin, Taksyn

Tasnim (Arabic) From the fountain of paradise
Tasnime, Tasneem, Tasneeme, Tasnyme, Tasnym, Tasneam, Tasneame

Tatum (English) Bringer of joy; spirited
Tatom, Tatim, Tatem, Tatam, Tatym

Tavi (Aramaic) One who is well-behaved
Tavie, Tavee, Tavy, Tavey, Tavea

*****Taylor** (English) Cutter of cloth; one who alters garments
Tailor, Taylore, Taylar, Tayler, Talour, Taylre, Tailore, Tailar

Teagan (Gaelic) One who is attractive
Teegan

Tehya (Native American) One who is precious
Tehyah, Tehiya, Tehiyah

Teigra (Greek) Resembling a tiger
Teigre

Telephassa (Latin) In mythology, the queen of Tyre
Telephasa, Telefassa, Telefasa

Temperance (English) Having self-restraint
Temperence, Temperince, Temperancia, Temperanse, Temperense, Temperinse

Tendai (African) Thankful to God
Tenday, Tendae, Tendaa, Tendaye

Tender (American) One who is sensitive; young and vulnerable
Tendere, Tendera, Tenderia, Tenderre, Tenderiya

Teranika (Gaelic) Victory of the earth
Teranikah, Teranieka, Teraneika, Teraneeka, Teranica, Teranicka, Teranicca, Teraneaka

Teresa (Greek) A harvester
Theresa, Theresah, Theresia, Therese, Thera, Tresa, Tressa, Tressam, Reese, Reza

Terpsichore (Greek) In mythology, the muse of dancing and singing
Terpsichora, Terpsichoria, Terpsichoriya

Terra (Latin) From the earth; in mythology, an earth goddess
Terrah, Terah, Teralyn, Terran, Terena, Terenah, Terenna, Terrena

Terrian (Greek) One who is innocent
Terriane, Terrianne, Terriana, Terianna, Terian, Terianne

Tessa (Greek) Form of Teresa, meaning "a harvester"

Tetsu (Japanese) A strong woman
Tetsue

Tetty (English) Form of Elizabeth, meaning "my God is bountiful; God's promise"
Tettey, Tetti, Tettie, Tettee, Tettea

Thandiwe (African) The loving one
Thandywe, Thandiewe, Thandeewe, Thandie, Thandi, Thandee, Thandy, Thandey

Thara (Arabic) One who is wealthy; prosperous
Tharah, Tharra, Tharrah, Tharwat

^**Thea** (Greek) A goddess; in mythology, the mother of the sun, moon, and dawn
Thia, Thya, Theia

Thelma (Greek) One who is ambitious and willful
Thelmah, Telma, Thelmai, Thelmia, Thelmalina

Thelred (English) One who is well-advised
Thelrede, Thelread, Thelredia, Thelredina, Thelreid, Thelreed, Thelryd

Thema (African) A queen
Themah, Theema, Thyma, Theyma, Theama

Theora (Greek) A watcher
Theorra, Theoria, Theoriya, Theorya

Theta (Greek) Eighth letter of the Greek alphabet
Thetta

Thistle (English) Resembling the prickly, flowered plant
Thistel, Thissle, Thissel

Thomasina (Hebrew) Feminine form of Thomas; a twin
Thomasine, Thomsina, Thomasin, Tomasina, Tomasine, Thomasa, Thomaseena, Thomaseana

Thoosa (Greek) In mythology, a sea nymph
Thoosah, Thoosia, Thoosiah, Thusa, Thusah, Thusia, Thusiah, Thousa

Thorberta (Norse) Brilliance of Thor
Thorbiartr, Thorbertha

Thordia (Norse) Spirit of Thor
Thordiah, Thordis, Tordis, Thordissa, Tordissa, Thoridyss

Thuy (Vietnamese) One who is gentle and pure
Thuye, Thuyy, Thuyye

Thy (Vietnamese / Greek) A poet / one who is untamed
Thye

^**Tia** (Spanish / Greek) An aunt / daughter born to royalty
Tiah, Tea, Teah, ***Tiana****, Teea, Tya, Teeya, Tiia*

Tiberia (Italian) Of the Tiber river
Tiberiah, Tiberiya, Tiberya, Tibeeria, Tibearia, Tibieria, Tibeiria

Tiegan (Aztec) A little princess in a big valley
Tiegann, Tieganne

Tierney (Gaelic) One who is regal; lordly
Tiernie, Tierni, Tiernee, Tierny, Tiernea

Tiffany (Greek) Lasting love
Tiffaney, Tiffani, Tiffanie, Tiffanee, Tifany, Tifaney, Tifanee, Tifani

Timothea (English) Feminine form of Timothy; honoring God
Timotheah, Timothia, Timothya, Timothiya

Tina (English) From the river; also shortened form of names ending in -tina
Tinah, Teena, Tena, Teyna, Tyna, Tinna, Teana

Ting (Chinese) Graceful and slim woman

Tirza (Hebrew) One who is pleasant; a delight
Tirzah

Tisa (African) The ninth-born child
Tisah, Tiza

Tita (Latin) Holding a title of honor
Titah, Teeta, Tyta, Teata

Tivona (Hebrew) Lover of nature
Tivonna, Tivone, Tivonia, Tivoniya

Toan (Vietnamese) Form of An-toan, meaning "safe and secure"
Toane, Toanne

Toinette (French) Form of Antoinette, meaning "praiseworthy"
Toinett, Toinete, Toinet, Toineta, Toinetta, Tola

Toki (Japanese / Korean) One who grasps opportunity; hopeful / resembling a rabbit
Tokie, Toky, Tokey, Tokye, Tokiko, Tokee, Tokea

Tola (Polish / Cambodian) Form of Toinette, meaning "praiseworthy" / born during October
Tolah, Tolla, Tollah

Topanga (Native American) From above or a high place
Topangah

Topaz (Latin) Resembling a yellow gemstone
Topazz, Topaza, Topazia, Topaziya, Topazya, Topazea

Tordis (Norse) A goddess
Tordiss, Tordisse, Tordys, Tordyss, Tordysse

Torny (Norse) New; just discovered
Torney, Tornie, Torni, Torne, Torn, Tornee, Tornea

Torunn (Norse) Thor's love
Torun, Torrun, Torrunn

Tory (American) Form of Victoria, meaning "victorious woman; winner; conqueror"
Torry, Torey, Tori, Torie, Torree, Tauri, Torye, Toya

Tosca (Latin) From the Tuscany region
Toscah, Toscka, Toska, Tosckah, Toskah

Tosha (English) Form of Natasha, meaning "born on Christmas"
Toshah, Toshiana, Tasha, Tashia, Tashi, Tassa

Tourmaline (Singhalese) A stone of mixed colors
Tourmalyne, Tourmalina, Tourmalinia

Tova (Hebrew) One who is well-behaved
Tovah, Tove, Tovi, Toba, Toibe, Tovva

Treasa (Irish) Having great strength
Treasah, Treesa, Treisa, Triesa, Treise, Treese, Toirease

Trinity (Latin) The holy three
Trinitey, Triniti, Trinitie, Trinitee, Trynity, Trynitey, Tryniti, Trynitie

Trisha (Latin) Form of Patricia, meaning "of noble descent"
Trishah, Trishia, Tricia, Trish, Trissa, Trisa

Trishna (Polish) In mythology, the goddess of the deceased, protector of graves
Trishnah, Trishnia, Trishniah, Trishnea, Trishneah, Trishniya, Trishniyah, Trishnya

Trisna (Indian) The one desired
Trisnah, Trisnia, Trisniah, Trisnea, Trisneah, Trisniya, Trisniyah, Trisnya

Trudy (German) Form of Gertrude, meaning "adored warrior"
Trudey, Trudi, Trudie, Trude, Trudye, Trudee, Truda, Trudia

Trupti (Indian) State of being satisfied
Truptie, Trupty, Truptey, Truptee, Trupte, Truptea

Tryamon (English) In Arthurian legend, a fairy princess
Tryamonn, Tryamonne, Tryamona, Tryamonna

Tryna (Greek) The third-born child
Trynah

Tsifira (Hebrew) One who is crowned
Tsifirah, Tsifyra, Tsiphyra, Tsiphira, Tsipheera, Tsifeera

Tuccia (Latin) A vestal virgin

Tula (Hindi) Balance; a sign of the zodiac
Tulah, Tulla, Tullah

Tullia (Irish) One who is peaceful
Tulliah, Tullea, Tulleah, Tullya, Tulia, Tulea, Tuleah, Tulya

Tusti (Hindi) One who brings happiness and peace
Tustie, Tusty, Tustey, Tustee, Tuste, Tustea

Tutilina (Latin) In mythology, the protector goddess of stored grain
Tutilinah, Tutileena, Tutileana, Tutilyna, Tutileina, Tutiliena, Tutilena, Tutylina

Tuuli (Finnish) Of the wind
Tuulie, Tuulee, Tuula, Tuuly, Tuuley, Tuulea

Tuyet (Vietnamese) Snow white woman
Tuyett, Tuyete, Tuyette, Tuyeta, Tuyetta

Tyler (English) Tiler of roofs

Tyme (English) The aromatic herb thyme
Time, Thyme, Thime

Tyne (English) Of the river
Tyna

Tyro (Greek) In mythology, a woman who bore twin sons to Poseidon

Tzidkiya (Hebrew) Righteousness of the Lord
Tzidkiyah, Tzidkiyahu

Tzigane (Hungarian) A gypsy
Tzigan, Tzigain, Tzigaine, Tzigayne

U

Uadjit (Egyptian) In mythology, a snake goddess
Ujadet, Uajit, Udjit, Ujadit

Ualani (Hawaiian) Of the heavenly rain
Ualanie, Ualany, Ualaney, Ualanee, Ualanea, Ualania, Ualana

Udavine (American) A thriving woman
Udavyne, Udavina, Udavyna, Udevine, Udevyne, Udevina, Udevyna

Udele (English) One who is wealthy; prosperous
Udelle, Udela, Udella, Udelah, Udellah, Uda, Udah

Uela (American) One who is devoted to God
Uelah, Uella, Uellah

Uganda (African) From the country in Africa
Ugandah, Ugaunda, Ugaundah, Ugawnda, Ugawndah, Ugonda, Ugondah

Ugolina (German) Having a bright spirit; bright mind
Ugolinah, Ugoleena, Ugoliana, Ugolyna, Ugoline, Ugolyn, Ugolyne

Ulalia (Greek) Form of Eulalia, meaning "well-spoken"
Ulaliah, Ulalya, Ulalyah

Ulan (African) Firstborn of twins
Ulann, Ulanne

Ulima (Arabic) One who is wise and astute
Ulimah, Ullima, Ulimma, Uleema, Uleama, Ulyma, Uleima, Uliema

Ulla (German) A willful woman
Ullah, Ullaa, Ullai, Ullae

Uma (Hindi) Mother; in mythology, the goddess of beauty and sunlight
Umah, Umma

Umberla (French) Feminine form of Umber; providing shade; of an earth color
Umberlah, Umberly, Umberley, Umberlee, Umberleigh, Umberli, Umberlea, Umberlie

Ummi (African) Born of my mother
Ummie, Ummy, Ummey, Ummee, Umi

Unity (American) Woman who upholds oneness; togetherness
Unitey, Unitie, Uniti, Unitee, Unitea, Unyty, Unytey, Unytie

Ura (Indian) Loved from the heart
Urah, Urra

Ural (Slavic) From the mountains
Urall, Urale, Uralle

Urbai (American) One who is gentle
Urbae, Urbay, Urbaye

Urbana (Latin) From the city; city dweller
Urbanah, Urbanna, Urbane, Urbania, Urbanya, Urbanne

Uriela (Hebrew) The angel of light
Uriella, Urielle, Uriel, Uriele, Uriell

Urta (Latin) Resembling the spiny plant
Urtah

Utah (Native American) People of the mountains; from the state of Utah

Uzoma (African) One who takes the right path
Uzomah, Uzomma, Uzommah

Uzzi (Hebrew / Arabic) God is my strength / a strong woman
Uzzie, Uzzy, Uzzey, Uzzee, Uzi, Uzie, Uzy, Uzey

V

Vala (German) The chosen one; singled out
Valah, Valla

Valda (Teutonic / German) Spirited in battle / famous ruler
Valdah, Valida, Velda, Vada, Vaida, Vayda, Vaeda

Valdis (Norse) In mythology, the goddess of the dead
Valdiss, Valdys, Valdyss

Valencia (Spanish) One who is powerful; strong; from the city of Valencia
Valenciah, Valyncia, Valencya, Valenzia, Valancia, Valenica, Valanca, Valecia

Valentina (Latin) One who is vigorous and healthy
Valentinah, Valentine, Valenteena, Valenteana, Valentena, Valentyna, Valantina, Valentyne

Valeria (Latin) Form of Valerie, meaning "strong and valiant"
Valara, Valera, Valaria, Valeriana, Veleria, Valora

Valerie (Latin) Feminine form of Valerius; strong and valiant
Valeri, Valeree, Valerey, Valery, Valarie, Valari, Vallery

Vandani (Hindi) One who is honorable and worthy
Vandany, Vandaney, Vandanie, Vandanee, Vandania, Vandanya

Vanessa (Greek) Resembling a butterfly
Vanessah, Vanesa, Vannesa, Vannessa, Vanassa, Vanasa, Vanessia, Vanysa, Yanessa

Vanity (English) Having excessive pride
Vanitey, Vanitee, Vaniti, Vanitie, Vanitty, Vanyti, Vanyty, Vanytie

Vanmra (Russian) A stranger; from a foreign place
Vanmrah

Varda (Hebrew) Resembling a rose
Vardah, Vardia, Vardina, Vardissa, Vardita, Vardysa, Vardyta, Vardit

Varuna (Hindi) Wife of the sea
Varunah, Varuna, Varun, Varunani, Varuni

Vashti (Persian) A lovely woman
Vashtie, Vashty, Vashtey, Vashtee

Vasta (Persian) One who is pretty
Vastah

Vasteen (American) A capable woman
Vasteene, Vastiene, Vastien, Vastein, Vasteine, Vastean, Vasteane

Vasuda (Hindi) Of the earth
Vasudah, Vasudhara, Vasundhara, Vasudhra, Vasundhra

Vayu (Hindi) A vital life force; the air
Vayyu

Vedette (French) From the guard tower
Vedete, Vedett, Vedet, Vedetta, Vedeta

Vedi (Sanskrit) Filled with wisdom
Vedie, Vedy, Vedey, Vedee, Vedea, Vedeah

Vega (Latin) A falling star
Vegah

Vellamo (Finnish) In mythology, the goddess of the sea
Velamo, Vellammo

Ventana (Spanish) As transparent as a window
Ventanah, Ventanna, Ventane, Ventanne

Venus (Greek) In mythology, the goddess of love and beauty
Venis, Venys, Vynys, Venusa, Venusina, Venusia

Veradis (Latin) One who is genuine; truthful
Veradise, Veradys, Veradisa, Verdissa, Veradysa, Veradyssa, Veradisia, Veraditia

Verda (Latin) Springlike; one who is young and fresh
Verdah, Verdea, Virida, Verdy, Verdey, Verde, Verdi, Verdie

Verenase (Swedish) One who is flourishing
Verenese, Verennase, Vyrenase, Vyrennase, Vyrenese, Verenace, Vyrenace

Veronica (Latin) Displaying her true image
Veronicah, Veronic, Veronicca, Veronicka, Veronika, Veronicha, Veronique, Veranique, Ronni

Vesna (Slavic) Messenger; in mythology, the goddess of spring
Vesnah, Vezna, Vesnia, Vesnaa

Vespera (Latin) Evening star; born in the evening
Vesperah, Vespira, Vespeera, Vesperia, Vesper

Vevila (Gaelic) Woman with a melodious voice
Vevilah, Veveela, Vevyla, Vevilla, Vevylla, Vevylle, Vevyle, Vevillia

Vibeke (Danish) A small woman
Vibekeh, Vibeek, Vibeeke, Vybeke, Viheke

Vibhuti (Hindi) Of the sacred ash; a symbol
Vibuti, Vibhutie, Vibhutee

*__Victoria__ (Latin) Victorious woman; winner; conqueror
Victoriah, Victorea, Victoreah, Victorya, Victorria, Victoriya, Vyctoria, Victorine, Tory

Vidya (Indian) Having great wisdom
Vidyah

Viet (Vietnamese) A woman from Vietnam
Vyet, Viett, Vyett, Viette, Vyette

Vigilia (Latin) Wakefulness; watchfulness
Vigiliah, Vygilia, Vygylia, Vijilia, Vyjilia

Vignette (French) From the little vine
Vignete, Vignet, Vignetta, Vignett, Vigneta, Vygnette, Vygnete, Vygnet

Vilina (Hindi) One who is dedicated
Vilinah, Vileena, Vileana, Vylina, Vyleena, Vyleana, Vylyna, Vilinia

Villette (French) From the small village
Vilette, Villete, Vilete, Vilet, Vilett, Villet, Villett, Vylet

Vimala (Indian) Feminine form of Vamal; clean and pure
Vimalah, Vimalia, Vimalla

Vincentia (Latin) Feminine form of Vincent; conquerer; triumphant
Vincentiah, Vincenta, Vincensia, Vincenzia, Vyncentia, Vyncyntia, Vyncenzia, Vycenzya

Violet (French) Resembling the purplish-blue flower
Violett, Violette, Violete, Vyolet, Vyolett, Vyolette, Vyolete, Violeta

Virginia (Latin) One who is chaste; virginal; from the state of Virginia
Virginiah, Virginnia, Virgenya, Virgenia, Virgeenia, Virgeena, Virgena, Ginny

Virtue (Latin) Having moral excellence, chastity, and goodness
Virtu, Vyrtue, Vyrtu, Vertue, Vertu

Viveka (German) Little woman of the strong fortress
Vivekah, Vivecka, Vyveka, Viveca, Vyveca, Vivecca, Vivika, Vivieka

^*__Vivian__ (Latin) Lively woman
Viv, Vivi, ***Vivienne****, Bibiana*

Vixen (American) A flirtatious woman
Vixin, Vixi, Vixie, Vixee, Vixea, Vixeah, Vixy, Vixey

Vlasta (Slavic) A friendly and likable woman
Vlastah, Vlastia, Vlastea, Vlastiah, Vlasteah

Voleta (Greek) The veiled one
Voletah, Voletta, Volita, Volitta, Volyta, Volytta, Volet, Volett

Volva (Scandinavian) In mythology, a female shaman
Volvah, Volvya, Volvaa, Volvae, Volvai, Volvay, Volvia

Vondila (African) Woman who lost a child
Vondilah, Vondilla, Vondilya, Vondilia, Vondyla, Vondylya

Vonna (French) Form of Yvonne, meaning "young archer"
Vonnah, Vona, Vonah, Vonnia, Vonnya, Vonia, Vonya, Vonny

Vonshae (American) One who is confident
Vonshay, Vonshaye, Vonshai

Vor (Norse) In mythology, an omniscient goddess
Vore, Vorr, Vorre

Vulpine (English) A cunning woman; like a fox
Vulpyne, Vulpina, Vulpyna

Vyomini (Indian) A gift of the divine
Vyominie, Vyominy, Vyominey, Vyominee, Vyomyni, Vyomyny, Viomini, Viomyni

W

Wafa (Arabic) One who is faithful; devoted
Wafah, Wafaa, Waffa, Wapha, Waffah, Waphah

Wagaye (African) My sense of value; my price
Wagay, Wagai, Wagae

Wainani (Hawaiian) Of the beautiful waters
Wainanie, Wainany, Wainaney, Wainanee, Wainanea, Wainaneah

Wajihah (Arabic) One who is distinguished; eminent
Wajiha, Wajeeha, Wajyha, Wajeehah, Wajyhah, Wajieha, Wajiehah, Wajeiha

Wakanda (Native American) One who possesses magical powers
Wakandah, Wakenda, Wakinda, Wakynda

Wakeishah (American) Filled with happiness
Wakeisha, Wakieshah, Wakiesha, Wakesha

Walda (German) One who has fame and power
Waldah, Wallda, Walida, Waldine, Waldina, Waldyne, Waldyna, Welda

Walker (English) Walker of the forests
Wallker, Walkher

Walta (African) One who acts as a shield
Waltah

Wanetta (English) A pale-skinned woman
Wanettah, Wanette, Wannette, Wannetta, Wonetta, Wonette, Wonitta, Wonitte

Wangari (African) Resembling the leopard
Wangarie, Wangarri, Wangary, Wangarey, Wangaria, Wangaree

Wanyika (African) Of the bush
Wanyikka, Wanyicka, Wanyicca, Wanyica

Waqi (Arabic) Falling; swooping
Waqqi

Warma (American) A caring woman
Warm, Warme, Warmia, Warmiah, Warmea, Warmeah

Warna (German) One who defends her loved ones
Warnah

Washi (Japanese) Resembling an eagle
Washie, Washy, Washey, Washee, Washea, Washeah

Waynette (English) One who makes wagons
Waynett, Waynet, Waynete, Wayneta, Waynetta

Wednesday (American) Born on a Wednesday
Wensday, Winsday, Windnesday, Wednesdae, Wensdae, Winsdae, Windnesdae, Wednesdai

Welcome (English) A welcome guest
Welcom, Welcomme

Wendy (Welsh) Form of Gwendolyn, meaning "one who is fair; of the white ring"
Wendi, Wendie, Wendee, Wendey, Wenda, Wendia, Wendea, Wendya

Wesley (English) From the western meadow
Wesly, Weslie, Wesli, Weslee, Weslia, Wesleigh, Weslea, Weslei

Whisper (English) One who is soft-spoken
Whysper, Wisper, Wysper

Whitley (English) From the white meadow
Whitly, Whitlie, Whitli, Whitlee, Whitleigh, Whitlea, Whitlia, Whitlya

Whitney (English) From the white island
Whitny, Whitnie, Whitni, Whitnee, Whittney, Whitneigh, Whytny, Whytney

Wicapi (Native American) A holy star

Wijida (Arabic) An excited seeker
Wijidah, Weejida, Weejidah, Wijeeda, Wijeedah, Wijyda, Wijydah, Wijieda

Wileen (Teutonic) A firm defender
Wiline, Wilean, Wileane, Wilyn, Wileene, Wilene, Wyleen, Wyline

Wilhelmina (German) Feminine form of Wilhelm; determined protector
Wilhelminah, Wylhelmina, Wylhelmyna, Willemina, Wilhelmine, Wilhemina, Wilhemine, Helma, Ilma

Willa (English) Feminine version of William, meaning "protector"
Willah, Wylla

Willow (English) One who is hoped for; desired
Willo, Willough

Winetta (American) One who is peaceful
Wineta, Wynetta, Wyneta, Winet, Winett, Winette, Wynet, Wynett

Winnielle (African) A victorious woman
Winniell, Winniele, Winniel, Winniella

Winola (German) Gracious and charming friend
Winolah, Wynola, Winolla, Wynolla, Wynolah, Winollah, Wynollah

Winta (African) One who is desired
Wintah, Whinta, Wynta, Whynta, Whintah, Wyntah, Whyntah

Wisconsin (French) Gathering of waters; from the state of Wisconsin
Wisconsyn, Wisconsen

Woody (American) A woman of the forest
Woodey, Woodi, Woodie, Woodee, Woodea, Woodeah, Woods

Wren (English) Resembling a small songbird
Wrenn, Wrene, Wrena, Wrenie, Wrenee, Wreney, Wrenny, Wrenna

Wynda (Scottish) From the narrow passage
Wyndah, Winda, Windah

Xalvadora (Spanish) A savior
Xalvadorah, Xalbadora, Xalbadorah, Xalvadoria, Xalbadoria

Xanadu (African) From the exotic paradise

Xantara (American) Protector of the Earth
Xantarah, Xanterra, Xantera, Xantarra, Xantarrah, Xanterah, Xanterrah

Xaquelina (Galician) Form of Jacqueline, meaning "the supplanter"
Xaqueline, Xaqueleena, Xaquelyna, Xaquelayna, Xaqueleana

Xerena (Latin) Form of Serena, meaning "having a peaceful disposition"
Xerenah, Xerene, Xeren, Xereena, Xeryna, Xereene, Xerenna

Xhosa (African) Leader of a nation
Xosa, Xhose, Xhosia, Xhosah, Xosah

Xiang (Chinese) Having a nice fragrance
Xyang, Xeang, Xhiang, Xhyang, Xheang

Xiao Hong (Chinese) Of the morning rainbow

Xin Qian (Chinese) Happy and beautiful woman

Xinavane (African) A mother; to propagate
Xinavana, Xinavania, Xinavain, Xinavaine, Xinavaen, Xinavaene

Xirena (Greek) Form of Sirena, meaning "enchantress"
Xirenah, Xireena, Xirina, Xirene, Xyrena, Xyreena, Xyrina, Xyryna

Xi-Wang (Chinese) One with hope

Xochiquetzal (Aztec) Resembling a flowery feather; in mythology, the goddess of love, flowers, and the earth

Xola (African) Stay in peace
Xolah, Xolia, Xolla, Xollah

Xue (Chinese) Woman of snow

Yachne (Hebrew) One who is gracious and hospitable
Yachnee, Yachney, Yachnie, Yachni, Yachnea, Yachneah

Yadra (Spanish) Form of Madre, meaning "mother"
Yadre, Yadrah

Yaffa (Hebrew) A beautiful woman
Yaffah, Yaffit, Yafit, Yafeal

Yakini (African) An honest woman
Yakinie, Yakiney, Yakiny, Yackini, Yackinie, Yackiney, Yackiny, Yakinee

Yalena (Greek) Form of Helen, meaning "the shining light"
Yalenah, Yalina, Yaleena, Yalyna, Yalana, Yaleana, Yalane, Yaleene

Yama (Japanese) From the mountain
Yamma, Yamah, Yammah

Yamin (Hebrew) Right hand
Yamine, Yamyn, Yamyne, Yameen, Yameene, Yamein, Yameine, Yamien

Yana (Hebrew) He answers
Yanna, Yaan, Yanah, Yannah

Yanessa (American) Form of Vanessa, meaning "resembling a butterfly"
Yanessah, Yanesa, Yannesa, Yannessa, Yanassa, Yanasa, Yanessia, Yanysa

Yanka (Slavic) God is good
Yancka, Yancca, Yankka

Yara (Brazilian) In mythology, the goddess of the river; a mermaid
Yarah, Yarrah, Yarra

Yareli (American) The Lord is my light
Yarelie, Yareley, Yarelee, Yarely, Yaresly, Yarelea, Yareleah

Yaretzi (Spanish) Always beloved
Yaretzie, Yaretza, Yarezita

Yashira (Japanese) Blessed with God's grace
Yashirah, Yasheera, Yashyra, Yashara, Yashiera, Yashierah, Yasheira, Yasheirah

Yashona (Hindi) A wealthy woman
Yashonah, Yashawna, Yashauna, Yaseana, Yashawnah, Yashaunah, Yaseanah

Yasmine (Persian) Resembling the jasmine flower
Yasmin, Yasmene, Yasmeen, Yasmeene, Yasmen, Yasemin, Yasemeen, Yasmyn

Yatima (African) An orphan
Yatimah, Yateema, Yatyma, Yateemah, Yatymah, Yatiema, Yatiemah, Yateima

Yedidah (Hebrew) A beloved friend
Yedida, Yedyda, Yedydah, Yedeeda, Yedeedah

Yeira (Hebrew) One who is illuminated
Yeirah, Yaira, Yeyra, Yairah, Yeyrah

Yenge (African) A hardworking woman
Yenga, Yengeh, Yengah

Yeshi (African) For a thousand
Yeshie, Yeshey, Yeshy, Yeshee, Yeshea, Yesheah

Yessica (Hebrew) Form of Jessica, meaning "the Lord sees all"
Yesica, Yessika, Yesika, Yesicka, Yessicka, Yesyka, Yesiko

Yetta (English) Form of Henrietta, meaning "ruler of the house"
Yettah, Yeta, Yette, Yitta, Yettie, Yetty

Yi Min (Chinese) An intelligent woman

Yi Ze (Chinese) Happy and shiny as a pearl

Yihana (African) One deserving congratulations
Yihanah, Yhana, Yihanna, Yihannah, Yhanah, Yhanna, Yhannah

Yinah (Spanish) A victorious woman
Yina, Yinna, Yinnah

Yitta (Hebrew) One who emanates light
Yittah, Yita, Yitah

Ynes (French) Form of Agnes, meaning "pure; chaste"
Ynez, Ynesita

Yogi (Hindi) One who practices yoga
Yogini, Yoginie, Yogie, Yogy, Yogey, Yogee, Yogea, Yogeah

Yohance (African) A gift from God
Yohanse

Yoki (Native American) Of the rain
Yokie, Yokee, Yoky, Yokey, Yokea, Yokeah

Yolanda (Greek) Resembling the violet flower
Yola, Yolana, Yolandah, Colanda

Yomaris (Spanish) I am the sun
Yomariss, Yomarise, Yomarris

Yon (Korean) Resembling a lotus blossom

Yoruba (African) Woman from Nigeria
Yorubah, Yorubba, Yorubbah

Yoshi (Japanese) One who is respectful and good
Yoshie, Yoshy, Yoshey, Yoshee, Yoshiyo, Yoshiko, Yoshino, Yoshea

Ysabel (Spanish) Form of Isabel, meaning "my God is bountiful; God's promise"
Ysabelle, Ysabela, Ysabele, Ysabell, Ysabella, Ysbel, Ysibel, Ysibela

Ysbail (Welsh) A spoiled girl
Ysbale, Ysbayle, Ysbaile, Ysbayl, Ysbael, Ysbaele

Yue (Chinese) Of the moonlight

Yuette (American) A capable woman
Yuett, Yuete, Yuet, Yueta, Yuetta

Yulan (Spanish) A splendid woman
Yulann

Yuna (African) A gorgeous woman
Yunah, Yunna, Yunnah

Yuta (Hebrew / Japanese) One who is awarded praise / one who is superior
Yutah, Yoota, Yootah

Yvonne (French) Young archer
Yvone, Vonne, Vonna

Z

Zabrina (American) Form of Sabrina, meaning "a legendary princess"
Zabreena, Zabrinah, Zabrinna, Zabryna, Zabryne, Zabrynya, Zabreana, Zabreane

Zachah (Hebrew) Feminine form of Zachary; God is remembered
Zacha, Zachie, Zachi, Zachee, Zachea, Zacheah

Zafara (Hebrew) One who sings
Zaphara, Zafarra, Zapharra, Zafarah, Zafarrah, Zapharah, Zapharrah

Zagir (Armenian) Resembling a flower
Zagiri, Zagirie, Zagiree, Zagirea, Zagireah, Zagiry, Zagirey, Zagira

Zahiya (Arabic) A brilliant woman; radiant
Zahiyah, Zehiya, Zehiyah, Zeheeya, Zaheeya, Zeheeyah, Zaheeyah, Zaheiya

Zahra (Arabic / Swahili) White-skinned / flowerlike
Zahrah, Zahraa, Zahre, Zahreh, Zahara, Zaharra, Zahera, Zahira

Zainab (Arabic) A fragrant flowering plant
Zaynab, Zaenab

Zainabu (Swahili) One who is known for her beauty
Zaynabu, Zaenabu

Zalina (French) Form of Selene, meaning "of the moon"; in mythology Selene was the Greek goddess of the moon
Zalinah, Zaleana, Zaleena, Zalena, Zalyna, Zaleen, Zaleene, Zalene

Zama (Latin) One from the town of Zama
Zamah, Zamma, Zammah

Zambda (Hebrew) One who meditates
Zambdah

Zamella (Zulu) One who strives to succeed
Zamellah, Zamy, Zamie, Zami, Zamey, Zamee, Zamea, Zameah

Zamilla (Greek) Having the strength of the sea
Zamillah, Zamila, Zamilah, Zamylla, Zamyllah, Zamyla, Zamylah

Zamora (Spanish) From the city of Zamora
Zamorah, Zamorrah, Zamorra

Zana (Romanian / Hebrew) In mythology, the three graces / shortened form of Susanna, meaning "lily"
Zanna, Zanah, Zannah

Zane (Scandinavian) One who is bold
Zain, Zaine, Zayn, Zayne, Zaen, Zaene

Zanta (Swahili) A beautiful young woman
Zantah

Zarahlinda (Hebrew) Of the beautiful dawn
Zaralinda, Zaralynda, Zarahlindah, Zaralyndah, Zarahlynda, Zarahlyndah, Zaralenda, Zarahlenda

Zariah (Russian / Slavic) Born at sunrise
Zarya, Zariah, Zaryah

Zarifa (Arabic) One who is successful; moves with grace
Zarifah, Zaryfa, Zaryfah, Zareefa, Zareefah, Zariefa, Zariefah, Zareifa

Zarna (Hindi) Resembling a spring of water
Zarnah, Zarnia, Zarniah

Zarqa (Arabic) Having bluish-green eyes; from the city of Zarqa
Zarqaa

Zaylee (English) A heavenly woman
Zayleigh, Zayli, Zaylie, Zaylea, Zayleah, Zayley, Zayly, Zalee

Zaypana (Tibetan) A beautiful woman
Zaypanah, Zaypo, Zaypanna, Zaypannah

Zaza (Hebrew / Arabic) Belonging to all / one who is flowery
Zazah, Zazu, Zazza, Zazzah, Zazzu

Zdenka (Slovene) Feminine form of Zdenek, meaning "from Sidon"
Zdena, Zdenuska, Zdenicka, Zdenika, Zdenyka, Zdeninka, Zdenynka

Zebba (Persian) A known beauty
Zebbah, Zebara, Zebarah, Zebarra, Zebarrah

Zelia (Greek / Spanish) Having great zeal / of the sunshine
Zeliah, Zelya, Zelie, Zele, Zelina, Zelinia

Zenaida (Greek) White-winged dove; in mythology, a daughter of Zeus
Zenaidah, Zenayda, Zenaide, Zenayde, Zinaida, Zenina, Zenna, Zenaydah

Zenechka (Russian) Form of Eugenia, meaning "a well-born woman"

Zenobia (Greek) Child of Zeus
Sinobia

Zephyr (Greek) Of the west wind
Zephyra, Zephira, Zephria, Zephra, Zephyer, Zefiryn, Zefiryna, Zefyrin

Zera (Hebrew) A sower of seeds
Zerah, Zeria, Zeriah, Zera'im, Zerra, Zerrah

Zeraldina (Polish) One who rules with the spear
Zeraldinah, Zeraldeena, Zeraldeenah, Zeraldiena, Zeraldienah, Zeraldeina, Zeraldeinah, Zeraldyna

Zerdali (Turkish) Resembling the wild apricot
Zerdalie, Zerdaly, Zerdaley, Zerdalya, Zerdalia, Zerdalee, Zerdalea

Zesta (American) One with energy and gusto
Zestah, Zestie, Zestee, Zesti, Zesty, Zestey, Zestea, Zesteah

Zetta (Portuguese) Resembling the rose
Zettah

Zhen (Chinese) One who is precious and chaste
Zen, Zhena, Zenn, Zhenni

Zhi (Chinese) A woman of high moral character

Zhong (Chinese) An honorable woman

Zi (Chinese) A flourishing young woman

Zia (Arabic) One who emanates light; splendor
Ziah, Zea, Zeah, Zya, Zyah

Zilias (Hebrew) A shady woman; a shadow
Zilyas, Zylias, Zylyas

Zillah (Hebrew) The shadowed one
Zilla, Zila, Zyla, Zylla, Zilah, Zylah, Zyllah

Zilpah (Hebrew) One who is frail but dignified; in the Bible, a concubine of Jacob
Zilpa, Zylpa, Zilpha, Zylpha, Zylpah, Zilphah, Zylphah

Zimbab (African) Woman from Zimbabwe
Zymbab, Zimbob, Zymbob

Zinat (Arabic) A decoration; graceful beauty
Zeenat, Zynat, Zienat, Zeinat, Zeanat

Zinchita (Incan) One who is dearly loved
Zinchitah, Zinchyta, Zinchytah, Zincheeta, Zincheetah, Zinchieta, Zinchietah, Zincheita

Zintkala Kinyan (Native American) Resembling a flying bird
Zintkalah Kinyan

Ziona (Hebrew) One who symbolizes goodness
Zionah, Zyona, Zyonah

Zipporah (Hebrew) A beauty; little bird; in the Bible, the wife of Moses
Zippora, Ziporah, Zipora, Zypora, Zyppora, Ziproh, Zipporia

Zira (African) The pathway
Zirah, Zirra, Zirrah, Zyra, Zyrah, Zyrra, Zyrrah

Zisel (Hebrew) One who is sweet
Zissel, Zisal, Zysel, Zysal, Zyssel, Zissal, Zyssal

Zita (Latin / Spanish) Patron of housewives and servants / little rose
Zitah, Zeeta, Zyta, Zeetah

Ziwa (Swahili) Woman of the lake
Ziwah, Zywa, Zywah

Zizi (Hungarian) Dedicated to God
Zeezee, Zyzy, Ziezie, Zeazea, Zeyzey

Zoa (Greek) One who is full of life; vibrant

*__Zoe__ (Greek) A life-giving woman; alive
Zoee, Zowey, Zowie, Zowe, Zoelie, Zoeline, Zoelle, ***Zoey***

Zofia (Slavic) Form of Sophia, meaning "wisdom"
Zofiah, Zophia, Zophiah, Zophya, Zofie, Zofee, Zofey

Zora (Slavic) Born at dawn; aurora
Zorah, Zorna, Zorra, Zorya, Zorane, Zory, Zorrah, Zorey

Zoria (Basque) One who is lucky
Zoriah

Zoriona (Basque) One who is happy

Zubeda (Swahili) The best one
Zubedah

Zudora (Arabic) A laborer; hardworking woman
Zudorah, Zudorra

Zula (African) One who is brilliant; from the town of Zula
Zul, Zulay, Zulae, Zulai, Zulah, Zulla, Zullah

Zuni (Native American) One who is creative
Zunie, Zuny, Zuney, Zunee, Zunea, Zuneah

Zurafa (Arabic) A lovely woman
Zurafah, Zirafa, Zirafah, Ziraf, Zurufa, Zurufah

Zuri (Swahili / French) A beauty / lovely and white
Zurie, Zurey, Zuria, Zuriaa, Zury, Zuree, Zurya, Zurisha

Zuwena (African) One who is pleasant and good
Zuwenah, Zwena, Zwenah, Zuwenna, Zuwennah, Zuwyna, Zuwynah

Zuyana (Sioux) One who has a brave heart
Zuyanah, Zuyanna

Zuzena (Basque) One who is correct
Zuzenah, Zuzenna

Zwi (Scandinavian) Resembling a gazelle
Zui, Zwie, Zwee, Zwey

* — *All names with a * in the text denote Top 100 Names of 2015.*

^ — *All names with a ^ in the text denote hot names rising in popularity in 2015.*

Aabha (Indian) One who shines
Abha, Abbha

Aabharan (Hindu) One who is treasured; jewel
Abharan, Abharen, Aabharen, Aabharon

Aaden (Irish) Form of Aidan, meaning "a fiery young man"
Adan, Aden

Aage (Norse) Representative of ancestors
Age, Ake, Aake

Aarif (Arabic) A learned man
Arif, Aareef, Areef, Aareaf, Areaf, Aareif, Areif, Aarief

***Aaron** (Hebrew) One who is exalted; from the mountain of strength
Aaran, Aaren, Aarin, Aaro, Aaronas, Aaronn, Aarron, Aaryn, Eron, Aron, Eran

Abdi (Hebrew) My servant
Abdie, Abdy, Abdey, Abdee

Abdul (Arabic) A servant of God
Abdal, Abdall, Abdalla, Abdallah, Abdel, Abdell, Abdella, Abdellah

Abedi (African) One who worships God
Abedie, Abedy, Abedey, Abedee, Abedea

Abednago (Aramaic) Servant of the god of wisdom, Nabu
Abednego

Abejundio (Spanish) Resembling a bee
Abejundo, Abejundeo, Abedjundiyo, Abedjundeyo

^**Abel** (Hebrew) The life force, breath
Abele, Abell, Abelson, Able, Avel, Avele

Abraham (Hebrew) Father of a multitude; father of nations
Abarran, Avraham, Aberham, Abrahamo, Abrahan, Abrahim, Abram, Abrami, Ibrahim

Abram (Hebrew) Form of Abraham, meaning "father of nations"

Absalom (Hebrew) The father of peace
Absalon, Abshalom, Absolem, Absolom, Absolon, Avshalom, Avsholom

Abu (African) A father
Abue, Aboo, Abou

Abundio (Spanish) A man of plenty
Abbondio, Abondio, Aboundio, Abundo, Abundeo, Aboundeo

Adael (Hebrew) God witnesses
Adaele, Adayel, Adayele

*__Adam__ (Hebrew) Of the earth
Ad, Adamo, Adams, Adan, Adao, Addam, Addams, Addem

Adamson (English) The son of Adam
Adamsson, Addamson, Adamsun, Adamssun

Addy (Teutonic) One who is awe-inspiring
Addey, Addi, Addie, Addee, Addea, Adi, Ady, Adie

Adelpho (Greek) A brotherly man
Aldelfo, Adelfus, Adelfio, Adelphe

Adil (Arabic) A righteous man; one who is fair and just
Adyl, Adiel, Adeil, Adeel, Adeal, Adyeel

Aditya (Hindi) Of the sun
Adithya, Adithyan, Adityah, Aditeya, Aditeyah

Adonis (Greek) In mythology, a handsome young man loved by Aphrodite
Addonia, Adohnes, Adonys

*__Adrian__ (Latin) A man from Hadria
Adrien, Adrain, Adrean, Adreean, Adreyan, Adreeyan, Adriaan

^**Adriel** (Hebrew) From God's flock
Adriell, Adriele, Adryel, Adryell, Adryele

Afif (Arabic) One who is chaste; pure
Afeef, Afief, Afeif, Affeef, Affif, Afyf, Afeaf

Agamemnon (Greek) One who works slowly; in mythology, the leader of the Greeks at Troy
Agamemno, Agamenon

^**Ahmad** (Arabic) One who always thanks God; a name of Muhammed
Ahmed

*__Aidan__ (Irish) A fiery young man
***Aiden**, Aedan, Aeden, Aidano, Aidyn,* ***Ayden**, Aydin, Aydan*

Aiken (English) Constructed of oak; sturdy
Aikin, Aicken, Aickin, Ayken, Aykin, Aycken, Ayckin

Ainsworth (English) From Ann's estate
Answorth, Annsworth, Ainsworthe, Answorthe, Annsworthe

Ajax (Greek) In mythology, a hero of the Trojan war
Aias, Aiastes, Ajaxx, Ajaxe

Ajit (Indian) One who is invincible
Ajeet, Ajeat, Ajeit, Ajiet, Ajyt

Akiko (Japanese) Surrounded by bright light
Akyko

Akin (African) A brave man; a hero
Akeen, Akean, Akein, Akien, Akyn

Akiva (Hebrew) One who protects or provides shelter
Akyva, Akeeva, Akeava, Akieva, Akeiva, Akeyva

Akmal (Arabic) A perfect man
Aqmal, Akmall, Aqmall, Acmal, Acmall, Ackmal, Ackmall

Alaire (French) Filled with joy
Alair, Alaer, Alaere, Alare, Alayr, Alayre

Alamar (Arabic) Covered with gold
Alamarr, Alemar, Alemarr, Alomar, Alomarr

Alan (German / Gaelic) One who is precious / resembling a little rock
Alain, Alann, Allan, Alson, Allin, Allen, Allyn

Alard (German) Of noble strength
Aliard, Allard, Alliard

Albert (German) One who is noble and bright
Alberto, Albertus, Alburt, Albirt, Aubert, Albyrt, Albertos, Albertino

Alden (English) An old friend
Aldan, Aldin, Aldyn, Aldon, Aldun

Aldo (German) Old or wise one; elder
Aldous, Aldis, Aldus, Alldo, Aldys

Aldred (English) An old advisor
Alldred, Aldraed, Alldraed, Aldread, Alldread

Alejandro (Spanish) Form of Alexander, meaning "a helper and defender of mankind"
Alejandrino, Alejo

Alex (English) Form of Alexander, meaning "a helper and defender of mankind"
Aleks, Alecks, Alecs, Allex, Alleks, Allecks, ***Alexis***

***Alexander** (Greek) A helper and defender of mankind
Alex, Alec, Alejandro, Alaxander, Aleksandar, Aleksander, Aleksandr, Alessandro, Alexzander, Zander

Alfonso (Italian) Prepared for battle; eager and ready
Alphonso, Alphonse, Affonso, Alfons, Alfonse, Alfonsin, Alfonsino, Alfonz, Alfonzo

Ali (Arabic) The great one; one who is exalted
Alie, Aly, Aley, Alee

Alijah (American) Form of Elijah, meaning "Jehovah is my god"

Alon (Hebrew) Of the oak tree
Allona, Allon, Alonn

Alonzo (Spanish) Form of Alfonso, meaning "prepared for battle; eager and ready"
Alonso, Alanso, Alanzo, Allonso, Allonzo, Allohnso, Allohnzo, Alohnso

Aloysius (German) A famous warrior
Ahlois, Aloess, Alois, Aloisio, Aloisius, Aloisio, Aloj, Alojzy

Alpha (Greek) The first-born child; the first letter of the Greek alphabet
Alphah, Alfa, Alfah

Alter (Hebrew) One who is old
Allter, Altar, Alltar

Alton (English) From the old town
Aldon, Aldun, Altun, Alten, Allton, Alltun, Allten

Alvin (English) Friend of the elves
Alven, Alvan, Alvyn

Amani (African / Arabic) One who is peaceful / one with wishes and dreams
Amanie, Amany, Amaney, Amanee, Amanye, Amanea, Amaneah

^**Amari** (African) Having great strength; a builder
Amare*, Amarie, Amaree, Amarea, Amary, Amarey*

Amil (Hindi) One who is invaluable
Ameel, Ameal, Ameil, Amiel, Amyl

Amit (Hindi) Without limit; endless
Ameet, Ameat, Ameit, Amiet, Amyt

Amory (German) Ruler and lover of one's home
Aimory, Amery, Amorey, Amry, Amori, Amorie, Amoree, Amorea

Amos (Hebrew) To carry; hardworking
Amoss, Aymoss, Aymos

Andino (Italian) Form of Andrew, meaning "one who is manly; a warrior"
Andyno, Andeeno, Andeano, Andieno, Andeino

Andre (French) Form of Andrew, meaning "manly, a warrior"
Andreas, Andrei, Andrej, Andres, Andrey

*****Andrew** (Greek) One who is manly; a warrior
Andy, Aindrea, Andreas, Andie, Andonia, Andor, Andresj, Anderson, Anders

Andrik (Slavic) Form of Andrew, meaning "one who is manly; a warrior"
Andric, Andrick, Andryk, Andryck, Andryc

*****Angel** (Greek) A messenger of God
Andjelko, Ange, Angelino, Angell, Angelmo, Angelo, Angie, Angy

Angus (Scottish) One force; one strength; one choice
Aengus, Anngus, Aonghus

Anicho (German) An ancestor
Anico, Anecho, Aneco, Anycho, Anyco

Ankur (Indian) One who is blossoming; a sapling

Annan (Celtic) From the brook
Anan

Ansley (English) From the noble's pastureland
Ansly, Anslie, Ansli, Anslee, Ansleigh, Anslea, Ansleah, Anslye

Antenor (Spanish) One who antagonizes
Antener, Antenar, Antenir, Antenyr, Antenur

*****Anthony** (Latin) A flourishing man; of an ancient Roman family
Antal, Antony, Anthoney, Anntoin, Antin, Anton, Antone, Antonello, ***Antonio***

Antoine (French) Form of Anthony, meaning "a flourishing man; of an ancient Roman family"
Antione, Antjuan, Antuan, Antuwain, Antuwaine, Antuwayne, Antuwon, Antwahn

Antonio (Italian) Form of Anthony, meaning "a flourishing man, from an ancient Roman family"
Antonin, Antonino, Antonius, Antonyo

^**Apollo** (Greek) In mythology, the god of archery, music, and poetry

Ara (Armenian / Latin) A legendary king / of the altar; the name of a constellation
Araa, Aira, Arah, Arae, Ahraya

Arcadio (Greek) From an ideal country paradise
Alcadio, Alcado, Alcedio, Arcadios, Arcadius, Arkadi, Arkadios, Arkadius

Arcelio (Spanish) From the altar of heaven
Arcelios, Arcelius, Aricelio, Aricelios, Aricelius

Archard (German) A powerful holy man
Archerd, Archird, Archyrd

Archelaus (Greek) The ruler of the people
Archelaios, Arkelaos, Arkelaus, Arkelaios, Archelaos

^**Archer** (Latin) A skilled bowman

Ardell (Latin) One who is eager
Ardel, Ardelle, Ardele

Arden (Latin / English) One who is passionate and enthusiastic / from the valley of the eagles
Ardan, Arrden, Arrdan, Ardin, Arrdin, Ard, Ardyn, Arrdyn

Arduino (German) A valued friend
Ardwino, Arrduino, Ardueno

Ari (Hebrew) Resembling a lion or an eagle
Aree, Arie, Aristide, Aristides, Arri, Ary, Arye, Arrie

Ariel (Hebrew) A lion of God
Arielle, Ariele, Ariell, Arriel, Ahriel, Airial, Arieal, Arial

Aries (Latin) Resembling a ram; the first sign of the zodiac; a constellation
Arese, Ariese

Arion (Greek) A poet or musician
Arian, Arien, Aryon

Aristotle (Greek) Of high quality
Aristotelis, Aristotellis

Arius (Greek) Enduring life; everlasting; immortal
Areos, Areus, Arios

Arley (English) From the hare's meadow
Arlea, Arleigh, Arlie, Arly, Arleah, Arli, Arlee

^**Armani** (Persian) One who is desired

Arnold (German) The eagle ruler
Arnaldo, Arnaud, Arnauld, Arnault, Arnd, Arndt, Arnel, Arnell

^**Arthur** (Celtic) As strong as a bear; a hero
Aart, Arrt, Art, Artair, Arte, Arther, Arthor, Arthuro

Arvad (Hebrew) A wanderer; voyager
Arpad

Arvin (English) A friend to everyone
Arvinn, Arvinne, Arven, Arvenn, Arvenne, Arvyn, Arvynn, Arvynne

Asa (Hebrew) One who heals others
Asah

Asaph (Hebrew) One who gathers or collects
Asaf, Asaphe, Asafe, Asiph, Asiphe, Asif, Asife

Ash (English) From the ash tree
Ashe

*****Asher** (Hebrew) Filled with happiness
Ashar, Ashor, Ashir, Ashyr, Ashur

Ashley (English) From the meadow of ash trees
Ashely, Asheley, Ashelie, Ashlan, Ashleigh, Ashlen, Ashli, Ashlie

Ashton (English) From the ash-tree town
Asheton, Ashtun, Ashetun, Ashtin, Ashetin, Ashtyn, Ashetyn, Aston

Aslan (Turkish) Resembling a lion
Aslen, Azlan, Azlen

Athens (Greek) From the capital of Greece
Athenios, Athenius, Atheneos, Atheneus

^**Atticus** (Latin) A man from Athens
Attikus, Attickus, Aticus, Atickus, Atikus

Atwell (English) One who lives at the spring
Attwell, Atwel, Attwel

Aubrey (English) One who rules with elf-wisdom
Aubary, Aube, Aubery, Aubry, Aubury, Aubrian, Aubrien, Aubrion

Auburn (Latin) Having a reddish-brown color
Aubirn, Auburne, Aubyrn, Abern, Abirn, Aburn, Abyrn, Aubern

Audley (English) From the old meadow
Audly, Audleigh, Audlee, Audlea, Audleah, Audli, Audlie

August (Irish) One who is venerable; majestic
Austin, Augustine, Agoston, Aguistin, Agustin, Augustin, Augustyn, Avgustin, Augusteen, Agosteen

***Austin** (English) Form of August, meaning "one who is venerable; majestic"
Austen, Austyn, Austan, Auston, Austun

Avery (English) One who is a wise ruler; of the nobility
Avrie, Averey, Averie, Averi, Averee

Aviram (Hebrew) My Father is mighty
Avyram, Avirem, Avyrem

^**Axel** (German / Latin / Hebrew) Source of life; small oak / ax / peace
Aksel, Ax, Axe, Axell, Axil, Axill, Axl

Aya (Hebrew) Resembling a bird
Ayah

***Ayden** (Irish) Form of Aiden, meaning "a fiery young man"

Ayo (African) Filled with happiness
Ayoe, Ayow, Ayowe

Azamat (Arabic) A proud man; one who is majestic

Azi (African) One who is youthful
Azie, Azy, Azey, Azee, Azea

Azmer (Islamic) Resembling a lion
Azmar, Azmir, Azmyr, Azmor, Azmur

B

Baakir (African) The eldest child
Baakeer, Baakyr, Baakear, Baakier, Baakeir

Bachir (Hebrew) The oldest son
Bacheer, Bachear, Bachier, Bacheir, Bachyr

Baha (Arabic) A glorious and splendid man
Bahah

Bailintin (Irish) A valiant man
Bailinten, Bailentin, Bailenten, Bailintyn, Bailentyn

Bain (Irish) A fair-haired man
Baine, Bayn, Bayne, Baen, Baene, Bane, Baines, Baynes

Bajnok (Hungarian) A victorious man
Bajnock, Bajnoc

Bakari (Swahili) One who is promised
Bakarie, Bakary, Bakarey, Bakaree, Bakarea

Bakhit (Arabic) A lucky man
Bakheet, Bakheat, Bakheit, Bakhiet, Bakhyt, Bakht

Bala (Hindi) One who is youthful
Balu, Balue, Balou

Balark (Hindi) Born with the rising sun

Balasi (Basque) One who is flat-footed
Balasie, Balasy, Balasey, Balasee, Balasea

Balbo (Latin) One who mutters
Balboe, Balbow, Balbowe, Ballbo, Balbino, Balbi, Balbie, Balby

Baldwin (German) A brave friend
Baldwine, Baldwinn, Baldwinne, Baldwen, Baldwenn, Baldwenne, Baldwyn, Baldwynn

Balint (Latin) A healthy and strong man
Balent, Balin, Balen, Balynt, Balyn

Balloch (Scottish) From the grazing land

Bancroft (English) From the bean field
Bancrofte, Banfield, Banfeld, Bankroft, Bankrofte

Bandana (Spanish) A brightly colored headwrap
Bandanah, Bandanna, Bandannah

Bandy (American) A fiesty man
Bandey, Bandi, Bandie, Bandee, Bandea

Bansi (Indian) One who plays the flute
Bansie, Bansy, Bansey, Bansee, Bansea

Bao (Vietnamese / Chinese) To order / one who is prized

Baqir (Arabic) A learned man
Baqeer, Baqear, Baqier, Baqeir, Baqyr, Baqer

Barak (Hebrew) Of the lightning flash
Barrak, Barac, Barrac, Barack, Barrack

Baram (Hebrew) The son of the nation
Barem, Barum, Barom, Barim, Barym

Bard (English) A minstrel; a poet
Barde, Bardo

Barden (English) From the barley valley; from the boar's valley
Bardon, Bardun, Bardin, Bardyn, Bardan, Bardene

Bardol (Basque) A farmer
Bardo, Bartol

Bardrick (Teutonic) An ax ruler
Bardric, Bardrik, Bardryck, Bardryk, Bardryc, Bardarick, Bardaric, Bardarik

Barek (Arabic) One who is noble
Barec, Bareck

Barend (German) The hard bear
Barende, Barind, Barinde, Barynd, Barynde

Barnett (English) Of honorable birth
Barnet, Baronet, Baronett

Baron (English) A title of nobility
Barron

Barr (English) A lawyer
Barre, Bar

Barra (Gaelic) A fair-haired man

^**Barrett** (German / English) Having the strength of a bear / one who argues
Baret, Barrat, Barratt, Barret, Barrette

Barry (Gaelic) A fair-haired man
Barrey, Barri, Barrie, Barree, Barrea, Barrington, Barryngton, Barringtun

Bartholomew (Aramaic) The son of the farmer
Bart, Bartel, Barth, Barthelemy, Bartho, Barthold, Bartholoma, Bartholomaus, Bartlett, Bartol

Bartlett (French) Form of Bartholomew, meaning "the son of the farmer"
Bartlet, Bartlitt, Bartlit, Bartlytt, Bartlyt

Bartley (English) From the meadow of birch trees
Bartly, Bartli, Bartlie, Bartlee, Bartlea, Bartleah, Bartleigh

Bartoli (Spanish) Form of Bartholomew, meaning "the son of the farmer"
Bartolie, Bartoly, Bartoley, Bartolee, Bartoleigh, Bartolea, Bartolo, Bartolio

Barton (English) From the barley town
Bartun, Barten, Bartan, Bartin, Bartyn

Barwolf (English) The ax-wolf
Barrwolf, Barwulf, Barrwulf

Basant (Arabic) One who smiles often
Basante

Bassett (English) A little person
Baset, Basset, Basett

Basy (American) A homebody
Basey, Basi, Basie, Basee, Basea, Basye

Baurice (American) Form of Maurice, meaning "a dark-skinned man; Moorish"
Baurell, Baureo, Bauricio, Baurids, Baurie, Baurin

Bay (Vietnamese / English) The seventh-born child; born during the month of July / from the bay
Baye, Bae, Bai

Beal (French) A handsome man
Beals, Beale, Beall, Bealle

Beamer (English) One who plays the trumpet
Beamor, Beamir, Beamyr, Beamur, Beamar, Beemer, Beemar, Beemir

Beau (French) A handsome man, an admirer
Bo

Becher (Hebrew) The firstborn son

Beckett (English) From the small stream; from the brook
Becket

Bedar (Arabic) One who is attentive
Beder, Bedor, Bedur, Bedyr, Bedir

Beircheart (Anglo-Saxon) Of the intelligent army

Bela (Slavic) A white-skinned man
Belah, Bella, Bellah

Belden (English) From the beautiful valley
Beldan, Beldon, Beldun, Beldin, Beldyn, Bellden, Belldan, Belldon, Belldun, Belldin, Belldyn

Belen (Greek) Of an arrow
Belin, Belyn, Belan, Belon, Belun

Belindo (English) A handsome and tender man
Belyndo, Belindio, Belyndio, Belindeo, Belyndeo, Belindiyo, Belyndiyo, Belindeyo

Bellarmine (Italian) One who is handsomely armed
Bellarmin, Bellarmeen, Bellarmeene, Bellarmean, Bellarmeane, Bellarmyn, Bellarmyne

Belton (English) From the beautiful town
Bellton, Beltun, Belltun, Belten, Bellten

Belvin (American) Form of Melvin, meaning "a friend who offers counsel"
Belven, Belvyn, Belvon, Belvun, Belvan

Bem (African) A peaceful man

Ben (English) Form of Benjamin, meaning "son of the south; son of the right hand"
Benn, Benni, Bennie, Bennee, Benney, Benny, Bennea, Benno

*****Benjamin** (Hebrew) Son of the south; son of the right hand
Ben, Benejamen, Beniamino, Benjaman, Benjamen, Benjamino, Benjamon, Benjiman, Benjimen

Bennett (English) Form of Benedict, meaning "one who is blessed"
Benett, Bennet, Benet

^***Bentley** (English) From the meadow of bent grass
Bently, Bentleigh, Bentlee, Bentlie

Berdy (German) Having a brilliant mind
Berdey, Berdee, Berdea, Berdi, Berdie

Beresford (English) From the barley ford
Beresforde, Beresfurd, Beresfurde, Beresferd, Beresferde, Berford, Berforde, Berfurd

Berkeley (English) From the meadow of birch trees
Berkely, Berkeli, Berkelie, Berkelea, Berkeleah, Berkelee, Berkeleigh, Berkley

Bernard (German) As strong and brave as a bear
Barnard, Barnardo, Barnhard, Barnhardo, Bearnard, Bernardo, Bernarr, Bernd

Berry (English) Resembling a berry fruit
Berrey, Berri, Berrie, Berree, Berrea

Bert (English) One who is illustrious
Berte, Berti, Bertie, Bertee, Bertea, Berty, Bertey

Bethel (Hebrew) The house of God
Bethell, Bethele, Bethelle, Betuel, Betuell, Betuele, Betuelle

Bevis (Teutonic) An archer
Beviss, Bevys, Bevyss, Beavis, Beaviss, Beavys, Beavyss

Biagio (Italian) One who has a stutter
Biaggio

Birney (English) From the island with the brook
Birny, Birnee, Birnea, Birni, Birnie

Black (English) A dark-skinned man
Blak, Blac, Blacke

Blackwell (English) From the dark spring
Blackwel, Blackwelle, Blackwele

Blade (English) One who wields a sword or knife
Blayd, Blayde, Blaid, Blaide, Blaed, Blaede

Blagden (English) From the dark valley
Blagdon, Blagdan, Blagdun, Blagdin, Blagdyn

Blaine (Scottish / Irish) A saint's servant / a thin man
Blayne, Blane, Blain, Blayn, Blaen, Blaene, Blainy, Blainey

Blaise (Latin / American) One with a lisp or a stutter / a fiery man
Blaze, Blaize, Blaiz, Blayze, Blayz, Blaez, Blaeze

*__Blake__ (English) A dark, handsome man
Blayk, Blayke, Blaik, Blaike, Blaek, Blaeke

Bliss (English) Filled with happiness
Blis, Blyss, Blys

Blondell (English) A fair-haired boy
Blondel, Blondele, Blondelle

Boaz (Hebrew) One who is swift
Boaze, Boas, Boase

Bob (English) Form of Robert, meaning "one who is bright with fame"
Bobbi, Bobbie, Bobby, Bobbey, Bobbee, Bobbea

^**Bodhi** (Buddhist) To become aware
Bode, Bodie

Bogart (French) One who is strong with the bow
Bogaard, Bogaart, Bogaerd, Bogey, Bogie, Bogi, Bogy, Bogee

Bonaventure (Latin) One who undertakes a blessed venture
Bonaventura, Buenaventure, Buenaventura, Bueaventure, Bueaventura

Booker (English) One who binds books; a scribe
Bookar, Bookir, Bookyr, Bookur, Bookor

Bosley (English) From the meadow near the forest
Bosly, Boslee, Boslea, Bosleah, Bosleigh, Bosli, Boslie, Bozley

Boston (English) From the town near the forest; from the city of Boston
Bostun, Bostin, Bostyn, Bosten, Bostan

Boyce (French) One who lives near the forest
Boice, Boyse, Boise

Boyd (Celtic) A blond-haired man
Boyde, Boid, Boide, Boyden, Boydan, Boydin, Boydyn, Boydon

Boynton (Irish) From the town near the river Boyne
Boyntun, Boynten, Boyntin, Boyntan, Boyntyn

Bracken (English) Resembling the large fern
Braken, Brackan, Brakan, Brackin, Brakin, Brackyn

Braddock (English) From the broadly spread oak
Bradock, Braddoc, Bradoc, Braddok, Bradok

Braden (Gaelic / English) Resembling salmon / from the wide valley
Bradan, Bradon, Bradin, Bradyn, Braeden, Brayden

Bradford (English) From the wide ford
Bradforde, Bradferd, Bradferde

Bradley (English) From the wide meadow
Bradly, Bradlea, Bradleah, Bradlee, Bradleigh, Bradli

Brady (Irish) The son of a large-chested man
Bradey, Bradee, Bradea, Bradi, Bradie, Braidy, Braidey, Braidee

Bramley (English) From the wild gorse meadow; from the raven's meadow
Bramly, Bramlee, Bramlea

*__Brandon__ (English) From the broom or gorse hill
Brandun, Brandin, Brandyn, Brandan, Branden, Brannon, Brannun, Brannen

Branson (English) The son of Brand or Brandon
Bransun, Bransen, Bransan, Bransin, Bransyn

Brant (English) Steep, tall

^**Brantley** (English) Form of Brant, meaning "steep, tall"
Brantly

Braxton (English) From Brock's town
Braxtun, Braxten, Braxtan, Braxtyn

*__Brayden__ (Gaelic / English) Form of Braden, meaning "resembling salmon / from the wide valley"
Braydon, Braydan, Braydin, Braydyn

^**Braylen** (American) Combination of Brayden and Lynn
Braylon

Brendan (Irish) Born to royalty; a prince
Brendano, Brenden, Brendin, Brendon, Brendyn, Brendun

Brennan (Gaelic) A sorrowful man; a teardrop
Brenan, Brenn, Brennen, Brennin, Brennon, Brenin, Brennun, Brennyn

Brent (English) From the hill
Brendt, Brennt, Brentan, Brenten, Brentin, Brenton, Brentun, Brentyn

Brett (Latin) A man from Britain or Brittany
Bret, Breton, Brette, Bretton, Brit, Briton, Britt, Brittain

Brewster (English) One who brews
Brewer, Brewstere

Brian (Gaelic / Celtic) Of noble birth / having great strength
Briano, Briant, Brien, Brion, Bryan, Bryant, Bryen, Bryent

Briar (English) Resembling a thorny plant
Brier, Bryar, Bryer

Brock (English) Resembling a badger
Broc

Broderick (English) From the wide ridge
Broderik, Broderic, Brodrick, Brodryk, Brodyrc, Brodrik, Broderyc, Brodrig

*__Brody__ (Gaelic / Irish) From the ditch
Brodie, Brodey, Brodi, Brodee

Brogan (Gaelic) One who is sturdy
Broggan, Brogen, Broggen, Brogon, Broggon, Brogun, Broggun, Brogin, Broggin, Brogyn

^**Brooks** (English) From the running stream
Brookes

^**Bruce** (Scottish) A man from Brieuse; one who is well-born; from an influential family
Brouce, Brooce, Bruci, Brucie, Brucey, Brucy

Bruno (German) A brown-haired man
Brunoh, Brunoe, Brunow, Brunowe, Bruin, Bruine, Brunon, Brunun

Bryce (Scottish / Anglo-Saxon) One who is speckled / the son of a nobleman
Brice, Bricio, Brizio, Brycio

^**Bryson** (Welsh) The son of Brice
Brisen, Brysin, Brysun, Brysyn, ***Brycen***

Bud (English) One who is brotherly
Budd, Buddi, Buddie, Buddee, Buddey, Buddy

Budha (Hindi) Another name for the planet Mercury
Budhan, Budhwar

Bulat (Russian) Having great strength
Bulatt

Burbank (English) From the riverbank of burrs
Burrbank, Burhbank

Burgess (German) A free citizen of the town
Burges, Burgiss, Burgis, Burgyss, Burgys, Burgeis

Burne (English) Resembling a bear; from the brook; the brown-haired one
Burn, Beirne, Burnis, Byrn, Byrne, Burns, Byrnes

Burnet (French) Having brown hair
Burnett, Burnete, Burnette, Bernet, Bernett, Bernete, Bernette

Burton (English) From the fortified town
Burtun, Burten, Burtin, Burtyn, Burtan

Butler (English) The keeper of the bottles (wine, liquor)
Buttler, Butlar, Butlor, Butlir, Buttlir, Butlyr

Byron (English) One who lives near the cow sheds
Byrom, Beyren, Beyron, Biren, Biron, Buiron, Byram, Byran

C

Cable (French) One who makes rope
Cabel, Caibel, Caible, Caybel, Cayble, Caebel, Caeble, Cabe

Caddis (English) Resembling a worsted fabric
Caddys, Caddiss, Caddice

Cade (English / French) One who is round / of the cask
Caid, Caide, Cayd, Cayde, Caed, Caede

Cadell (Welsh) Having the spirit of battle
Cadel, Caddell, Caddel

Caden (Welsh) Spirit of Battle
Caiden, Cayden

Cadmus (Greek) A man from the east; in mythology, the man who founded Thebes
Cadmar, Cadmo, Cadmos, Cadmuss

Cadogan (Welsh) Having glory and honor during battle
Cadogawn, Cadwgan, Cadwgawn, Cadogaun

Caesar (Latin) An emperor
Caezar, Casar, Cezar, Chezare, Caesarius, Ceasar, Ceazer

Cain (Hebrew) One who wields a spear; something acquired; in the Bible, Adam and Eve's first son who killed his brother Abel
Cayn, Caen, Cane, Caine, Cayne, Caene

Caird (Scottish) A traveling metal worker
Cairde, Cayrd, Cayrde, Caerd, Caerde

Cairn (Gaelic) From the mound of rocks
Cairne, Cairns, Caern, Caerne, Caernes

Caith (Irish) Of the battlefield
Caithe, Cayth, Caythe, Cathe, Caeth, Caethe

Calbert (English) A cowboy
Calberte, Calburt, Calburte, Calbirt, Calbirte, Calbyrt, Calbyrte

Cale (English) Form of Charles, meaning "one who is manly and strong / a free man"
Cail, Caile, Cayl, Cayle, Cael, Caele

*__Caleb__ (Hebrew) Resembling a dog
Cayleb, Caileb, Caeleb, Calob, Cailob, Caylob, Caelob, Kaleb

Calian (Native American) A warrior of life
Calien, Calyan, Calyen

Callum (Gaelic) Resembling a dove
Calum

Calvin (French) The little bald one
Cal, Calvyn, Calvon, Calven, Calvan, Calvun, Calvino

Camara (African) One who teaches others

*__Camden__ (Gaelic) From the winding valley
Camdene, Camdin, Camdyn, Camdan, Camdon, Camdun

Cameo (English) A small, perfect child
Cammeo

*__Cameron__ (Scottish) Having a crooked nose
Cameren, Cameran, Camerin, Cameryn, Camerun, Camron, Camren, Camran, Tameron

Campbell (Scottish) Having a crooked mouth
Campbel, Cambell, Cambel, Camp, Campe, Cambeul, Cambeull, Campbeul

Candan (Turkish) A sincere man
Canden, Candin, Candyn, Candon, Candun

Cannon (French) An official of the church
Canon, Cannun, Canun, Cannin, Canin

Canyon (Spanish / English) From the footpath / from the deep ravine
Caniyon, Canyun, Caniyun

Capricorn (Latin) The tenth sign of the zodiac; the goat

Cargan (Gaelic) From the small rock
Cargen, Cargon, Cargun, Cargin, Cargyn

Carl (German) Form of Karl, meaning "a free man"
Carel, Carlan, Carle, Carlens, Carlitis, Carlin, Carlo, ***Carlos***

Carlos (Spanish) Form of Karl, meaning "a free man"
Carolos, Carolo, Carlito

Carlsen (Scandinavian) The son of Carl
Carlssen, Carlson, Carlsson, Carlsun, Carllsun, Carlsin, Carllsin, Carlsyn

Carlton (English) From the free man's town
Carltun, Carltown, Carston, Carstun, Carstown, Carleton, Carletun, Carlten

Carmichael (Scottish) A follower of Michael

Carmine (Latin / Aramaic) A beautiful song / the color crimson
Carman, Carmen, Carmin, Carmino, Carmyne, Carmon, Carmun, Carmyn

***Carson** (Scottish) The son of a marsh dweller
Carsen, Carsun, Carsan, Carsin, Carsyn

***Carter** (English) One who transports goods; one who drives a cart
Cartar, Cartir, Cartyr, Cartor, Cartur, Cartere, Cartier, Cartrell

Cartland (English) From Carter's land
Carteland, Cartlan, Cartlend, Cartelend, Cartlen

Cary (Celtic / Welsh / Gaelic) From the river / from the fort on the hill / having dark features
Carey, Cari, Carie, Caree, Carea, Carry, Carrey, Carri

Case (French) Refers to a chest or box
Cace

Cash (Latin) money

^**Cason** (Greek) A seer
Casen, Kaysen

Cassander (Spanish) A brother of heroes
Casander, Casandro, Cassandro, Casandero

Cassius (Latin) One who is empty; hollow; vain
Cassios, Cassio, Cach, Cache, Cashus, Cashos, Cassian, Cassien

Castel (Spanish) From the castle
Castell, Castal, Castall, Castol, Castoll, Castul, Castull, Castil

Castor (Greek) Resembling a beaver; in mythology, one of the Dioscuri
Castur, Caster, Castar, Castir, Castyr, Castorio, Castoreo, Castoro

Cat (American) Resembling the animal
Catt, Chait, Chaite

Cathmore (Irish) A renowned fighter
Cathmor, Cathemore

Cato (Latin) One who is all-knowing
Cayto, Caito, Caeto

Caton (Spanish) One who is knowledgable
Caten, Catun, Catan, Catin, Catyn

Cavell (Teutonic) One who is bold
Cavel, Cavele, Cavelle

Caxton (English) From the lump settlement
Caxtun, Caxten

Celesto (Latin) From heaven
Célestine, Celestino, Celindo, Celestyne, Celestyno

Cephas (Hebrew) As solid as a rock

Cesar (Spanish) Form of Caesar, meaning "emperor"
Cesare, Cesaro, Cesario

Chad (English) One who is warlike
Chaddie, Chadd, Chadric, Chadrick, Chadrik, Chadryck, Chadryc, Chadryk

Chadwick (English) From Chad's dairy farm
Chadwik, Chadwic, Chadwyck, Chadwyk, Chadwyc

Chai (Hebrew) A giver of life
Chaika, Chaim, Cahyim, Cahyyam

Chalkley (English) From the chalk meadow
Chalkly, Chalkleigh, Chalklee, Chalkleah, Chalkli, Chalklie, Chalklea

Champion (English) A warrior; the victor
Champeon, Champiun, Champeun, Champ

Chan (Spanish / Sanskrit) Form of John, meaning "God is gracious" / a shining man
Chayo, Chano, Chawn, Chaun

Chanan (Hebrew) God is compassionate
Chanen, Chanin, Chanyn, Chanun, Chanon

Chance (English) Having good fortune

^**Chandler** (English) One who makes candles
Chandlar, Chandlor

Chaniel (Hebrew) The grace of God
Chanyel, Chaniell, Chanyell

Channing (French / English) An official of the church / resembling a young wolf
Channyng, Canning, Cannyng

Chao (Chinese) The great one

Chappel (English) One who works in the chapel
Capel, Capell, Capello, Cappel, Chappell

*__Charles__ (English / German) One who is manly and strong / a free man
Charls, Chas, Charli, Charlie, Charley, Charly, Charlee, Charleigh, Cale, Chuck, Chick

Charleson (English) The son of Charles
Charlesen, Charlesin, Charlesyn, Charlesan, Charlesun

Charlton (English) From the free man's town
Charleton, Charltun, Charletun, Charleston, Charlestun

Charro (Spanish) A cowboy
Charo

*__Chase__ (English) A huntsman
Chace, Chasen, Chayce, Chayse, Chaise, Chaice, Chaece, Chaese

Chatwin (English) A warring friend
Chatwine, Chatwinn, Chatwinne, Chatwen, Chatwenn, Chatwenne, Chatwyn, Chatwynn

Chaviv (Hebrew) One who is dearly loved
Chaveev, Chaveav, Chaviev, Chaveiv, Chavyv, Chavivi, Chavivie, Chavivy

Chay (Gaelic) From the fairy place
Chaye, Chae

Chelsey (English) From the landing place for chalk
Chelsee, Chelseigh, Chelsea, Chelsi, Chelsie, Chelsy, Chelcey, Chelcy

Cheslav (Russian) From the fortified camp
Cheslaw

Chester (Latin) From the camp of the soldiers
Chet, Chess, Cheston, Chestar, Chestor, Chestur, Chestir, Chestyr

Chico (Spanish) A boy; a lad

Chien (Vietnamese) A combative man

Chiron (Greek) A wise tutor
Chyron, Chirun, Chyrun

Chogan (Native American) Resembling a blackbird
Chogen, Chogon, Chogun, Chogin, Chogyn

Choni (Hebrew) A gracious man
Chonie, Chony, Choney, Chonee, Chonea

***Christian** (Greek) A follower of Christ
Chrestien, Chretien, Chris, Christan, Christer, Christiano, Cristian

***Christopher** (Greek) One who bears Christ inside
Chris, Kit, Christof, Christofer, Christoffer, Christoforo, Christoforus, Christoph, Christophe, Cristopher, Cristofer

Chuchip (Native American) A deer spirit

Chuck (English) Form of Charles, meaning "one who is manly and strong / a free man"
Chucke, Chucki, Chuckie, Chucky, Chuckey, Chuckee, Chuckea

Chul (Korean) One who stands firm

Chun (Chinese) Born during the spring

Cid (Spanish) A lord
Cyd

Cillian (Gaelic) One who suffers strife

Ciqala (Native American) The little one

Cirrus (Latin) A lock of hair; resembling the cloud
Cyrrus

Clair (Latin) One who is bright
Clare, Clayr, Claer, Clairo, Claro, Claero

Clancy (Celtic) Son of the red-haired warrior
Clancey, Clanci, Clancie, Clancee, Clancea, Clansey, Clansy, Clansi

Clark (English) A cleric; a clerk
Clarke, Clerk, Clerke, Clerc

Claude (English) One who is lame
Claud, Claudan, Claudell, Claidianus, Claudicio, Claudien, Claudino, Claudio

Clay (English) Of the earth's clay

Clayton (English) From the town settled on clay
Claytun, Clayten, Claytin, Claytyn, Claytan, Cleyton, Cleytun, Cleytan

Cleon (Greek) A well-known man
Cleone, Clion, Clione, Clyon, Clyone

Clifford (English) From the ford near the cliff
Cliff, Clyfford, Cliford, Clyford

Cliffton (English) From the town near the cliff
Cliff, Cliffe, Clyff, Clyffe, Clifft, Clift, Clyfft, Clyft

Clinton (English) From the town on the hill
Clynton, Clintun, Clyntun, Clint, Clynt, Clinte, Clynte

Clive (English) One who lives near the cliff
Clyve, Cleve

Cluny (Irish) From the meadow
Cluney, Cluni, Clunie, Clunee, Clunea, Cluneah

^**Clyde** (Scottish) From the river Clyde
Clide

Clide Cobden (English) From the cottage in the valley
Cobdenn, Cobdale, Cobdail, Cobdaile, Cobdell, Cobdel, Cobdayl, Cobdayle

Coby (English) Form of Jacob, meaning "he who supplants"
Cobey

Cody (Irish / English) One who is helpful; a wealthy man / acting as a cushion
Codi, Codie, Codey, Codee, Codeah, Codea, Codier, Codyr

Colbert (French) A famous and bright man
Colvert, Culbert, Colburt, Colbirt, Colbyrt, Colbart, Culburt, Culbirt

Colby (English) From the coal town
Colbey, Colbi, Colbie, Colbee, Collby, Coalby, Colbea, Colbeah

***Cole** (English) Having dark features; having coal-black hair
Coley, Coli, Coly, Colie, Colee, Coleigh, Colea, Colson

Coleridge (English) From the dark ridge
Colerige, Colridge, Colrige

Colgate (English) From the dark gate
Colegate, Colgait, Colegait, Colgayt, Colegayt, Colgaet

Colin (Scottish) A young man; a form of Nicholas, meaning "of the victorious people"
Cailean, Colan, Colyn, Colon, Colen, Collin, Collan

Colt (English) A young horse; from the coal town
Colte

Colter (English) A horse herdsman
Coltere, Coltar, Coltor, Coltir, Coltyr, Coulter, Coultar, Coultir

***Colton** (English) From the coal town
Colten, Coltun, Coltan, Coltin, Coltyn, Coltrain

Comanche (Native American) A tribal name
Comanchi, Comanchie, Comanchee, Comanchea, Comanchy, Comanchey

Comus (Latin) In mythology, the god of mirth and revelry
Comas, Comis, Comys

Conan (English / Gaelic) Resembling a wolf / one who is high and mighty
Conant

Condon (Celtic) A dark, wise man
Condun, Condan, Conden, Condin, Condyn

Cong (Chinese) A clever man

Conn (Irish) The chief
Con

Connecticut (Native American) From the place beside the long river / from the state of Connecticut

Connery (Scottish) A daring man
Connary, Connerie, Conneri, Connerey, Connarie, Connari, Connarey, Conary

***Connor** (Gaelic) A wolf lover
Conor, Conner, Coner, Connar, Conar, Connur, Conur, Connir, Conir

Conroy (Irish) A wise adviser
Conroye, Conroi

Constantine (Latin) One who is steadfast; firm
Dinos

Consuelo (Spanish) One who offers consolation
Consuel, Consuelio, Consueleo, Consueliyo, Consueleyo

Conway (Gaelic) The hound of the plain; from the sacred river
Conwaye, Conwai, Conwae, Conwy

Cook (English) One who prepares meals for others
Cooke

Cooney (Irish) A handsome man
Coony, Cooni, Coonie, Coonee, Coonea

***Cooper** (English) One who makes barrels
Coop, Coopar, Coopir, Coopyr, Coopor, Coopur, Coopersmith, Cupere

Corbett (French) Resembling a young raven
Corbet, Corbete, Corbette, Corbit, Corbitt, Corbite, Corbitte

Corcoran (Gaelic) Having a ruddy complexion
Cochran

Cordero (Spanish) Resembling a lamb
Corderio, Corderiyo, Cordereo, Cordereyo

Corey (Irish) From the hollow; of the churning waters
Cory, Cori, Corie, Coree, Corea, Correy, Corry, Corri

Coriander (Greek) A romantic man; resembling the spice
Coryander, Coriender, Coryender

Corlan (Irish) One who wields a spear
Corlen, Corlin, Corlyn, Corlon, Corlun

Corrado (German) A bold counselor
Corrade, Corradeo, Corradio

Corridon (Irish) One who wields a spear
Corridan, Corridun, Corriden, Corridin, Corridyn

Cortez (Spanish) A courteous man
Cortes

Cosmo (Greek) The order of the universe
Cosimo, Cosmé, Cosmos, Cosmas, Cozmo, Cozmos, Cozmas

Cotton (American) Resembling or farmer of the plant
Cottin, Cotten, Cottyn, Cottun, Cottan

Courtney (English) A courteous man; courtly
Cordney, Cordni, Cortenay, Corteney, Cortni, Cortnee, Cortneigh, Cortney

Covert (English) One who provides shelter
Couvert

Covey (English) A brood of birds
Covy, Covi, Covie, Covee, Covea, Covvey, Covvy, Covvi

Covington (English) From the town near the cave
Covyngton, Covingtun, Covyngtun

Cox (English) A coxswain
Coxe, Coxi, Coxie, Coxey, Coxy, Coxee, Coxea

Coyle (Irish) A leader during battle
Coyl, Coil, Coile

Craig (Gaelic) From the rocks; from the crag
Crayg, Craeg, Craige, Crayge, Craege, Crage, Crag

Crandell (English) From the valley of cranes
Crandel, Crandale, Crandail, Crandaile, Crandayl, Crandayle, Crandael, Crandaele

Crawford (English) From the crow's ford
Crawforde, Crawferd, Crawferde, Crawfurd, Crawfurde

Creed (Latin) A guiding principle; a belief
Creede, Cread, Creade, Creedon, Creadon, Creedun, Creadun, Creedin

Creek (English) From the small stream
Creeke, Creak, Creake, Creik, Creike

Creighton (Scottish) From the border town
Creightun, Crayton, Craytun, Craiton, Craitun, Craeton, Craetun, Crichton

Crescent (French) One who creates; increasing; growing
Creissant, Crescence, Cressant, Cressent, Crescant

Cruz (Spanish) Of the cross

Cuarto (Spanish) The fourth-born child
Cuartio, Cuartiyo, Cuarteo

Cullen (Gaelic) A good-looking young man
Cullin, Cullyn, Cullan, Cullon, Cullun

Cunningham (Gaelic) Descendant of the chief
Conyngham, Cuningham, Cunnyngham, Cunyngham

Curcio (French) One who is courteous
Curceo

Cuthbert (English) One who is bright and famous
Cuthbeorht, Cuthburt, Cuthbirt, Cuthbyrt

Cyneley (English) From the royal meadow
Cynely, Cyneli, Cynelie, Cynelee, Cynelea, Cyneleah, Cyneleigh

Czar (Russian) An emperor

D

Dacey (Gaelic / Latin) A man from the south / a man from Dacia
Dacy, Dacee, Dacea, Daci, Dacie, Daicey, Daicy

Dack (English) From the French town of Dax
Dacks, Dax

Daedalus (Greek) A craftsman
Daldalos, Dedalus

Dag (Scandinavian) Born during the daylight
Dagney, Dagny, Dagnee, Dagnea, Dagni, Dagnie, Daeg, Dagget

Daijon (American) A gift of hope
Dayjon, Daejon, Dajon

Dainan (Australian) A kindhearted man
Dainen, Dainon, Dainun, Dainyn, Dainin, Daynan, Daynen, Daynon

Daire (Irish) A wealthy man
Dair, Daere, Daer, Dayr, Dayre, Dare, Dari, Darie

Daivat (Hindi) A powerful man

Dakarai (African) Filled with happiness

Dakota (Native American) A friend to all
Daccota, Dakoda, Dakodah, Dakotah, Dakoeta, Dekota, Dekohta, Dekowta

Dallan (Irish) One who is blind
Dalan, Dallen, Dalen, Dalin, Dallin, Dallyn, Dalyn, Dallon, Dalon, Dallun, Dalun

Dallas (Scottish) From the dales
Dalles, Dallis, Dallys, Dallos

Dalton (English) from the town in the valley
Daltun, Dalten, Daltan, Daltin, Daltyn, Daleten, Dalte, Daulten

Damario (Greek / Spanish) Resembling a calf / one who is gentle
Damarios, Damarius, Damaro, Damero, Damerio, Damereo, Damareo, Damerios

^**Damian** (Greek) One who tames or subdues others
Daemon, Daimen, Daimon, Daman, Damen, Dameon, Damiano, Damianos, ***Damon***

Dane (English) A man from Denmark
Dain, Daine, Dayn, Dayne

Danely (Scandinavian) A man from Denmark
Daneley, Daneli, Danelie, Danelee, Daneleigh, Danelea, Daineley, Dainely

Daniachew (African) A mediator

*****Daniel** (Hebrew) God is my judge
Dan, Danal, Daneal, Danek, Danell, Danial, Daniele, Danil, Danilo

Danso (African) A reliable man
Dansoe, Dansow, Dansowe

Dante (Latin) An enduring man; everlasting
Dantae, Dantay, Dantel, Daunte, Dontae, Dontay, Donte, Dontae

Daoud (Arabian) Form of David, meaning "the beloved one"
Daoude, Dawud, Doud, Daud, Da'ud

Daphnis (Greek) In mythology, the son of Hermes
Daphnys

Dar (Hebrew) Resembling a pearl
Darr

Darcel (French) Having dark features
Darcell, Darcele, Darcelle, Darcio, Darceo

Dardanus (Greek) In mythology, the founder of Troy
Dardanio, Dardanios, Dardanos, Dard, Darde

Darek (English) Form of Derek, meaning "the ruler of the tribe"
Darrek, Darec, Darrec, Darreck, Dareck

Darion (Greek) A gift
Darian, Darien, Dariun, Darrion, Darrian, Darrien, Daryon, Daryan

Darius (Greek) A kingly man; one who is wealthy
Darias, Dariess, Dario, Darious, Darrius, Derrius, Derrious, Derrias

Darlen (American) A sweet man; a darling
Darlon, Darlun, Darlan, Darlin, Darlyn

Darnell (English) From the hidden place
Darnall, Darneil, Darnel, Darnele, Darnelle

Darold (English) Form of Harold, meaning "the ruler of an army"
Darrold, Derald, Derrald, Derold, Derrold

Darren (Gaelic / English) A great man / a gift from God
Darran, Darrin, Darryn, Darron, Darrun, Daren, Darin, Daran

Dash (American) A charming man

Darvell (French) From the eagle town
Darvel, Darvele, Darvelle

Dasras (Indian) A handsome man

Dasya (Indian) A servant

*__David__ (Hebrew) The beloved one
Dave, Davey, Davi, Davidde, Davide, Davie, Daviel, Davin, Daoud

Davis (English) The son of David
Davies, Daviss, Davys, Davyss

Davu (African) Of the beginning
Davue, Davoo, Davou, Davugh

Dawson (English) The son of David
Dawsan, Dawsen, Dawsin, Dawsun

Dax (French) From the French town Dax
Daxton

Dayton (English) From the sunny town

Deacon (Greek) The dusty one; a servant
Deecon, Deakon, Deekon, Deacun, Deecun, Deakun, Deekun, Deacan

Dean (English) From the valley; a church official
Deane, Deen, Deene, Dene, Deans, Deens, Deani, Deanie

DeAndre (American) A manly man
D'André, DeAndrae, DeAndray, Diandray, Diondrae, Diondray

Dearon (American) One who is much loved
Dearan, Dearen, Dearin, Dearyn, Dearun

Decker (German / Hebrew) One who prays / a piercing man
Deker, Decer, Dekker, Deccer, Deck, Decke

^**Declan** (Irish) The name of a saint

Dedrick (English) Form of Dietrich, meaning "the ruler of the tribe"
Dedryck, Dedrik, Dedryk, Dedric, Dedryc

Deegan (Irish) A black-haired man
Deagan, Degan, Deegen, Deagen, Degen, Deegon, Deagon, Degon

Deinorus (American) A lively man
Denorius, Denorus, Denorios, Deinorius, Deinorios

Dejuan (American) A talkative man
Dejuane, Dewon, Dewonn, Dewan, Dewann, Dwon, Dwonn, Dajuan

Delaney (Irish / French) The dark challenger / from the elder-tree grove
Delany, Delanee, Delanea, Delani, Delanie, Delainey, Delainy, Delaini

Delaware (English) From the state of Delaware
Delawair, Delaweir, Delwayr, Delawayre, Delawaire, Delawaer, Delawaere

Delius (Greek) A man from Delos
Delios, Delos, Delus, Delo

Dell (English) From the small valley
Delle, Del

Delmon (English) A man of the mountain
Delmun, Delmen, Delmin, Delmyn, Delmont, Delmonte, Delmond, Delmonde

Delsi (American) An easygoing guy
Delsie, Delsy, Delsey, Delsee, Delsea, Delci, Delcie, Delcee

Delvin (English) A godly friend
Delvinn, Delvinne, Delvyn, Delvynn, Delvynne, Delven, Delvenn, Delvenne

Demarcus (American) The son of Marcus
DeMarcus, DaMarkiss, DeMarco, Demarkess, DeMarko, Demarkus, DeMarques, DeMarquez

Dembe (African) A peaceful man
Dembi, Dembie, Dembee, Dembea, Dembey, Demby

Denali (American) From the national park
Denalie, Denaly, Denaley, Denalee, Denalea, Denaleigh

Denley (English) From the meadow near the valley
Denly, Denlea, Denleah, Denlee, Denleigh, Denli, Denlie

Denman (English) One who lives in the valley
Denmann, Denmin, Denmyn, Denmen, Denmon, Denmun

Dennis (French) A follower of Dionysus
Den, Denies, Denis, Dennes, Dennet, Denney, Dennie, Denys, Dennys

Dennison (English) The son of Dennis
Denison, Dennisun, Denisun, Dennisen, Denisen, Dennisan, Denisan

Deo (Greek) A godly man

Deonte (French) An outgoing man
Deontay, Deontaye, Deontae, Dionte, Diontay, Diontaye, Diontae

Deotis (American) A learned man; a scholar
Deotiss, Deotys, Deotyss, Deotus, Deotuss

Derek (English) The ruler of the tribe
Dereck, Deric, Derick, Derik, Deriq, Derk, Derreck, Derrek, Derrick

Dervin (English) A gifted friend
Dervinn, Dervinne, Dervyn, Dervynn, Dervynne, Dervon, Dervan, Dervun

Deshan (Hindi) Of the nation
Deshal, Deshad

Desiderio (Latin) One who is desired; hoped for
Derito, Desi, Desideratus, Desiderios, Desiderius, Desiderus, Dezi, Diderot

Desmond (Gaelic) A man from South Munster
Desmonde, Desmund, Desmunde, Dezmond, Dezmonde, Dezmund, Dezmunde, Desmee

Desperado (Spanish) A renegade

Destin (French) Recognizing one's certain fortune; fate
Destyn, Deston, Destun, Desten, Destan

Destrey (American) A cowboy
Destry, Destree, Destrea, Destri, Destrie

Deutsch (German) A German

Devanshi (Hindi) A divine messenger
Devanshie, Devanshy, Devanshey, Devanshee

Devante (Spanish) One who fights wrongdoing

Deverell (French) From the riverbank
Deverel, Deveral, Deverall, Devereau, Devereaux, Devere, Deverill, Deveril

Devlin (Gaelic) Having fierce bravery; a misfortunate man
Devlyn, Devlon, Devlen, Devlan, Devlun

Devon (English) From the beautiful farmland; of the divine
Devan, Deven, Devenn, Devin, Devonn, Devone, Deveon, Devonne

Dewitt (Flemish) A blond-haired man
DeWitt, Dewytt, DeWytt, Dewit, DeWit, Dewyt, DeWyt

^**Dexter** (Latin) A right-handed man; one who is skillful
Dextor, Dextar, Dextur, Dextir, Dextyr, Dexton, Dextun, Dexten

Dhyanesh (Indian) One who meditates
Dhianesh, Dhyaneshe, Dhianeshe

Dice (American) A gambling man
Dyce

Dichali (Native American) One who talks a lot
Dichalie, Dichaly, Dichaley, Dichalee, Dichalea, Dichaleigh

*****Diego** (Spanish) Form of James, meaning "he who supplants"
Dyego, Dago

Diesel (American) Having great strength
Deisel, Diezel, Deizel, Dezsel

Dietrich (German) The ruler of the tribe
Dedrick

Digby (Norse) From the town near the ditch
Digbey, Digbee, Digbea, Digbi, Digbie

Diji (African) A farmer
Dijie, Dijee, Dijea, Dijy, Dijey

Dillon (Gaelic) Resembling a lion; a faithful man
Dillun, Dillen, Dillan, Dillin, Dillyn, Dilon, Dilan, Dilin

Dino (Italian) One who wields a little sword
Dyno, Dinoh, Dynoh, Deano, Deanoh, Deeno, Deenoh, Deino

Dinos (Greek) Form of Constantine, meaning "one who is steadfast; firm"
Dynos, Deanos, Deenos, Deinos, Dinose, Dinoz

Dins (American) One who climbs to the top
Dinz, Dyns, Dynz

Dionysus (Greek) The god of wine and revelry
Dion, Deion, Deon, Deonn, Deonys, Deyon, Diandre

Dior (French) The golden one
D'Or, Diorr, Diorre, Dyor, Deor, Dyorre, Deorre

Diron (American) Form of Darren, meaning "a great man / a gift from God"
Dirun, Diren, Diran, Dirin, Diryn, Dyron, Dyren

Dixon (English) The son of Dick
Dixen, Dixin, Dixyn, Dixan, Dixun

Doane (English) From the rolling hills
Doan

Dobber (American) An independent man
Dobbar, Dobbor, Dobbur, Dobbir, Dobbyr

Dobbs (English) A fiery man
Dobbes, Dobes, Dobs

Domevlo (African) One who doesn't judge others
Domivlo, Domyvlo

Domingo (Spanish) Born on a Sunday
Domyngo, Demingo, Demyngo

***Dominic** (Latin) A lord
Demenico, Dom, Domenic, Domenico, Domenique, Domini, Dominick, Dominico

Domnall (Gaelic) A world ruler
Domhnall, Domnull, Domhnull

Don (Scottish) Form of Donald, meaning "ruler of the world"
Donn, Donny, Donney, Donnie, Donni, Donnee, Donnea, Donne

Donald (Scottish) Ruler of the world
Don, Donold, Donuld, Doneld, Donild, Donyld

Donato (Italian) A gift from God

Donovan (Irish) A brown-haired chief
Donavan, Donavon, Donevon, Donovyn

Dor (Hebrew) Of this generation
Doram, Doriel, Dorli, Dorlie, Dorlee, Dorlea, Dorleigh, Dorly

Doran (Irish) A stranger; one who has been exiled
Doren, Dorin, Doryn

Dorsey (Gaelic) From the fortress near the sea
Dorsy, Dorsee, Dorsea, Dorsi, Dorsie

Dost (Arabic) A beloved friend
Doste, Daust, Dauste, Dawst, Dawste

Dotson (English) The son of Dot
Dotsen, Dotsan, Dotsin, Dotsyn, Dotsun, Dottson, Dottsun, Dottsin

Dove (American) A peaceful man
Dovi, Dovie, Dovy, Dovey, Dovee, Dovea

Drade (American) A serious-minded man
Draid, Draide, Drayd, Drayde, Draed, Draede, Dradell, Dradel

Drake (English) Resembling a dragon
Drayce, Drago, Drakie

Drew (Welsh) One who is wise
Drue, Dru

Driscoll (Celtic) A mediator; one who is sorrowful; a messenger
Dryscoll, Driscol, Dryscol, Driskoll, Dryskoll, Driskol, Dryskol, Driskell

Druce (Gaelic / English) A wise man; a druid / the son of Drew
Drews, Drewce, Druece, Druse, Druson, Drusen

Drummond (Scottish) One who lives on the ridge
Drummon, Drumond, Drumon, Drummund, Drumund, Drummun

Duane (Gaelic) A dark or swarthy man
Dewain, Dewayne, Duante, Duayne, Duwain, Duwaine, Duwayne, Dwain

Dublin (Irish) From the capital of Ireland
Dublyn, Dublen, Dublan, Dublon, Dublun

Duc (Vietnamese) One who has upstanding morals

Due (Vietnamese) A virtuous man

Duke (English) A title of nobility; a leader
Dooke, Dook, Duki, Dukie, Dukey, Duky, Dukee, Dukea

Dumi (African) One who inspires others
Dumie, Dumy, Dumey, Dumee, Dumea

Dumont (French) Man of the mountain
Dumonte, Dumount, Dumounte

Duncan (Scottish) A dark warrior
Dunkan, Dunckan, Dunc, Dunk, Dunck

Dundee (Scottish) From the town on the Firth of Tay
Dundea, Dundi, Dundie, Dundy, Dundey

Dung (Vietnamese) A brave man; a heroic man

Dunton (English) From the town on the hill
Duntun, Dunten, Duntan, Duntin, Duntyn

Durin (Norse) In mythology, one of the fathers of the dwarves
Duryn, Duren, Duran, Duron, Durun

Durjaya (Hindi) One who is difficult to defeat

Durrell (English) One who is strong and protective
Durrel, Durell, Durel

Dustin (English / German) From the dusty area / a courageous warrior
Dustyn, Dusten, Dustan, Duston, Dustun, Dusty, Dustey, Dusti

Duvall (French) From the valley
Duval, Duvale

Dwade (English) A dark traveler
Dwaid, Dwaide, Dwayd, Dwayde, Dwaed, Dwaede

Dwight (Flemish) A white- or blond-haired man
Dwite, Dwhite, Dwyght, Dwighte

Dyami (Native American) Resembling an eagle
Dyamie, Dyamy, Dyamey, Dyamee, Dyamea, Dyame

Dyer (English) A creative man
Dier, Dyar, Diar, Dy, Dye, Di, Die

*__Dylan__ (Welsh) Son of the sea
Dyllan, Dylon, Dyllon, Dylen, Dyllen, Dylun, Dyllun, Dylin

Dzigbode (African) One who is patient

Eagan (Irish) A fiery man
Eegan, Eagen, Eegen, Eagon, Eegon, Eagun, Eegun

Eagle (Native American) Resembling the bird
Eegle, Eagel, Eegel

Eamon (Irish) Form of Edmund, meaning "a wealthy protector"
Eaman, Eamen, Eamin, Eamyn, Eamun, Eamonn, Eames, Eemon

Ean (Gaelic) Form of John, meaning "God is gracious"
Eion, Eyan, Eyon, Eian

Earl (English) A nobleman
Earle, Erle, Erl, Eorl

Easey (American) An easy-going man
Easy, Easi, Easie, Easee, Easea, Eazey, Eazy, Eazi

Eastman (English) A man from the east
East, Easte, Eeste

^**Easton** (English) Eastern place
Eastan, Easten, Eastyn

Eckhard (German) Of the brave sword point
Eckard, Eckardt, Eckhardt, Ekkehard, Ekkehardt, Ekhard, Ekhardt

Ed (English) Form of Edward, meaning "a wealthy protector"
Edd, Eddi, Eddie, Eddy, Eddey, Eddee, Eddea, Edi

Edan (Celtic) One who is full of fire
Edon, Edun

Edbert (English) One who is prosperous and bright
Edberte, Edburt, Edburte, Edbirt, Edbirte, Edbyrt, Edbyrte

Edenson (English) Son of Eden
Eadenson, Edensun, Eadensun, Edinson

Edgar (English) A powerful and wealthy spearman
Eadger, Edgardo, Edghur, Edger

Edison (English) Son of Edward
Eddison, Edisun, Eddisun, Edisen, Eddisen, Edisyn, Eddisyn, Edyson

Edlin (Anglo-Saxon) A wealthy friend
Edlinn, Edlinne, Edlyn, Edlynn, Edlynne, Eadlyn, Eadlin, Edlen

Edmund (English) A wealthy protector
Ed, Eddie, Edmond, Eamon

Edom (Hebrew) A red-haired man
Edum, Edam, Edem, Edim, Edym

Edred (Anglo-Saxon) A king
Edread, Edrid, Edryd

Edward (English) A wealthy protector
Ed, Eadward, Edik, Edouard, Eduard, Eduardo, Edvard, Edvardas, Edwardo

Edwardson (English) The son of Edward
Edwardsun, Eadwardsone, Eadwardsun

Edwin (English) A wealthy friend
Edwinn, Edwinne, Edwine, Edwyn, Edwynn, Edwynne, Edwen, Edwenn

Effiom (African) Resembling a crocodile
Efiom, Effyom, Efyom, Effeom, Efeom

Efigenio (Greek) Form of Eugene, meaning "a well-born man"
Ephigenio, Ephigenios, Ephigenius, Efigenios

Efrain (Spanish) Form of Ephraim, meaning "one who is fertile; productive"
Efraine, Efrayn, Efrayne, Efraen, Efraene, Efrane

Efrat (Hebrew) One who is honored
Efratt, Ephrat, Ephratt

Egesa (Anglo-Saxon) One who creates terror
Egessa, Egeslic, Egeslick, Egeslik

Eghert (German) An intelligent man
Egherte, Eghurt, Eghurte, Eghirt, Eghirte, Eghyrt

Egidio (Italian) Resembling a young goat
Egydio, Egideo, Egydeo, Egidiyo, Egydiyo, Egidius

Eilert (Scandinavian) Of the hard point
Elert, Eilart, Elart, Eilort, Elort, Eilurt, Elurt, Eilirt

Eilon (Hebrew) From the oak tree
Eilan, Eilin, Eilyn, Eilen, Eilun

Einar (Scandinavian) A leading warrior
Einer, Ejnar, Einir, Einyr, Einor, Einur, Ejnir, Ejnyr

Einri (Teutonic) An intelligent man
Einrie, Einry, Einrey, Einree, Einrea

Eisig (Hebrew) One who laughs often
Eisyg

Eladio (Spanish) A man from Greece
Eladeo, Eladiyo, Eladeyo

Elbert (English / German) A well-born man / a bright man
Elberte, Elburt, Elburte, Elbirt, Elbirte, Ethelbert, Ethelburt, Ethelbirt

Eldan (English) From the valley of the elves

Eldon (English) From the sacred hill
Eldun

Eldorado (Spanish) The golden man

Eldred (English) An old, wise advisor
Eldrid, Eldryd, Eldrad, Eldrod, Edlrud, Ethelred

Eldrick (English) An old, wise ruler
Eldrik, Eldric, Eldryck, Eldryk, Eldryc, Eldrich

^**Eleazar** (Hebrew) God will help
Elazar, Eleasar, Eliezer, Elazaro, Eleazaro, Elazer

Eli (Hebrew) One who has ascended; my God on High
Ely

Eliachim (Hebrew) God will establish
Eliakim, Elyachim, Elyakim, Eliakym

Elian (Spanish) A spirited man
Elyan, Elien, Elyen, Elion, Elyon, Eliun, Elyun

Elias (Hebrew) Form of Elijah, meaning "Jehovah is my god"
Eliyas

Elihu (Hebrew) My God is He
Elyhu, Elihue, Elyhue

Elijah (Hebrew) Jehovah is my God
Elija, Eliyahu, Eljah, Elja, Elyjah, Elyja, Elijuah, Elyjuah

Elimu (African) Having knowledge of science
Elymu, Elimue, Elymue, Elimoo, Elymoo

Elisha (Hebrew) God is my salvation
Elisee, Eliseo, Elisher, Eliso, Elisio, Elysha, Elysee, Elyseo

Elliott (English) Form of Elijah, meaning "Jehovah is my God"
Eliot, Eliott, Elliot, Elyot

Ellory (Cornish) Resembling a swan
Ellorey, Elloree, Ellorea, Ellori, Ellorie, Elory, Elorey

Ellsworth (English) From the nobleman's estate
Elsworth, Ellswerth, Elswerth, Ellswirth, Elswirth, Elzie

Elman (English) A nobleman
Elmann, Ellman, Ellmann

Elmo (English / Latin) A protector / an amiable man
Elmoe, Elmow, Elmowe

Elmot (American) A lovable man
Elmott, Ellmot, Ellmott

Elof (Swedish) The only heir
Eluf, Eloff, Eluff, Elov, Ellov, Eluv, Elluv

Elois (German) A famous warrior
Eloys, Eloyis, Elouis

Elpidio (Spanish) A fearless man; having heart
Elpydio, Elpideo, Elpydeo, Elpidios, Elpydios, Elpidius

Elroy (Irish / English) A red-haired young man / a king
Elroi, Elroye, Elric, Elryc, Elrik, Elryk, Elrick, Elryck

Elston (English) From the nobleman's town
Ellston, Elstun, Ellstun, Elson, Ellson, Elsun, Ellsun

Elton (English) From the old town
Ellton, Eltun, Elltun, Elten, Ellten, Eltin, Elltin, Eltyn

Eluwilussit (Native American) A holy man

Elvey (English) An elf warrior
Elvy, Elvee, Elvea, Elvi, Elvie

Elvis (Scandinavian) One who is wise
Elviss, Elvys, Elvyss

Elzie (English) Form of Ellsworth, meaning "from the nobleman's estate"
Elzi, Elzy, Elzey, Elzee, Elzea, Ellzi, Ellzie, Ellzee

Emest (German) One who is serious
Emeste, Emesto, Emestio, Emestiyo, Emesteo, Emesteyo, Emo, Emst

Emil (Latin) One who is eager; an industrious man
Emelen, Emelio, Emile, Emilian, Emiliano, Emilianus, Emilio, Emilion

Emiliano (Spanish) Form of Emil, meaning "one who is eager"

Emmanuel (Hebrew) God is with us
Manuel, Manny, Em, Eman, Emmannuel

^**Emmett** (German) A universal man
Emmet, Emmit, Emmitt, Emmot

Emrys (Welsh) An immortal man

Enapay (Native American) A brave man
Enapaye, Enapai, Enapae

Enar (Swedish) A great warrior
Ener, Enir, Enyr, Enor, Enur

Engelbert (German) As bright as an angel
Englebert, Englbert, Engelburt, Engleburt, Englburt, Englebirt, Engelbirt, Englbirt

Enoch (Hebrew) One who is dedicated to God
Enoc, Enok, Enock

Enrique (Spanish) The ruler of the estate
Enrico, Enriko, Enricko, Enriquez, Enrikay, Enreekay, Enrik, Enric

Enyeto (Native American) One who walks like a bear

^**Enzo** (Italian) The ruler of the estate
Enzio, Enzeo, Enziyo, Enzeyo

Eoin Baiste (Irish) Refers to John the Baptist

Ephraim (Hebrew) One who is fertile; productive
Eff, Efraim, Efram, Efrem, Efrain

Eric (Scandinavian) Ever the ruler
Erek, Erich, Erick, Erik, Eriq, Erix, Errick, Eryk

Ernest (English) One who is sincere and determined; serious
Earnest, Ernesto, Ernestus, Ernst, Erno, Ernie, Erni, Erney

Eron (Spanish) Form of Aaron, meaning "one who is exalted"
Erun, Erin, Eran, Eren, Eryn

Errigal (Gaelic) From the small church
Errigel, Errigol, Errigul, Errigil, Errigyl, Erigal, Erigel, Erigol

Erskine (Gaelic) From the high cliff
Erskin, Erskyne, Erskyn, Erskein, Erskeine, Erskien, Erskiene

Esam (Arabic) A safeguard
Essam

Esben (Scandinavian) Of God
Esbin, Esbyn, Esban, Esbon, Esbun

Esmé (French) One who is esteemed
Esmay, Esmaye, Esmai, Esmae, Esmeling, Esmelyng

Esmun (American) A kind man
Esmon, Esman, Esmen, Esmin, Esmyn

Esperanze (Spanish) Filled with hope
Esperance, Esperence, Esperenze, Esperanzo, Esperenzo

Estcott (English) From the eastern cottage
Estcot

Esteban (Spanish) One who is crowned in victory
Estebon, Estevan, Estevon, Estefan, Estefon, Estebe, Estyban, Estyvan

*__Ethan__ (Hebrew) One who is firm and steadfast
Ethen, Ethin, Ethyn, Ethon, Ethun, Eitan, Etan, Eithan

Ethanael (American) God has given me strength
Ethaniel, Ethaneal, Ethanail, Ethanale

Ethel (Hebrew) One who is noble
Ethal, Etheal

Etlelooaat (Native American) One who shouts

Eudocio (Greek) One who is respected
Eudoceo, Eudociyo, Eudoceyo, Eudoco

*__Eugene__ (Greek) A well-born man
Eugean, Eugenie, Ugene, Efigenio, Gene, ***Owen***

Eulogio (Greek) A reasonable man
Eulogiyo, Eulogo, Eulogeo, Eulogeyo

Euodias (Greek) Having good fortune
Euodeas, Euodyas

Euphemios (Greek) One who is well-spoken
Eufemio, Eufemius, Euphemio, Eufemios, Euphemius, Eufemius

Euphrates (Turkish) From the great river
Eufrates, Euphraites, Eufraites, Euphraytes, Eufraytes

Eusebius (Greek) One who is devout
Esabio, Esavio, Esavius, Esebio, Eusabio, Eusaio, Eusebio, Eusebios

Eustace (Greek) Having an abundance of grapes
Eustache, Eustachios, Eustachius, Eustachy, Eustaquio, Eustashe, Eustasius, Eustatius

*__Evan__ (Welsh) Form of John, meaning "God is gracious"
Evann, Evans, Even, Evin, Evon, Evyn, Evian, Evien

Evander (Greek) A benevolent man
Evandor, Evandar, Evandir, Evandur, Evandyr

Everett (English) Form of Everhard, meaning "as strong as a bear"

Evett (American) A bright man
Evet, Evatt, Evat, Evitt, Evit, Evytt, Evyt

Eyal (Hebrew) Having great strength

Eze (African) A king

Ezeji (African) The king of yams
Ezejie, Ezejy, Ezejey, Ezejee, Ezejea

Ezekiel (Hebrew) Strengthened by God
Esequiel, Ezechiel, Eziechiele, Eziequel, Ezequiel, Ezekial, Ezekyel, Esquevelle, Zeke

F

Factor (English) A businessman
Facter, Factur, Factir, Factyr, Factar

Fairbairn (Scottish) A fair-haired boy
Fayrbairn, Faerbairn, Fairbaern, Fayrbaern, Faerbaern, Fairbayrn, Fayrbayrn, Faerbayrn

Fairbanks (English) From the bank along the path
Fayrbanks, Faerbanks, Farebanks

Faisal (Arabic) One who is decisive; resolute
Faysal, Faesal, Fasal, Feisal, Faizal, Fasel, Fayzal, Faezal

Fakhir (Arabic) A proud man
Fakheer, Fakhear, Fakheir, Fakhier, Fakhyr, Faakhir, Faakhyr, Fakhr

Fakih (Arabic) A legal expert
Fakeeh, Fakeah, Fakieh, Fakeih, Fakyh

Falco (Latin) Resembling a falcon; one who works with falcons
Falcon, Falconer, Falconner, Falk, Falke, Falken, Falkner, Faulconer

Fam (American) A family-oriented man

Fang (Scottish) From the sheep pen
Faing, Fayng, Faeng

Faraji (African) One who provides consolation
Farajie, Farajy, Farajey, Farajee, Farajea

Fardoragh (Irish) Having dark features

Fargo (American) One who is jaunty
Fargoh, Fargoe, Fargouh

Farha (Arabic) Filled with happiness
Farhah, Farhad, Farhan, Farhat, Farhani, Farhanie, Farhany, Farhaney

Fariq (Arabic) One who holds rank as lieutenant general
Fareeq, Fareaq, Fareiq, Farieq, Faryq, Farik, Fareek, Fareak

Farnell (English) From the fern hill
Farnel, Farnall, Farnal, Fernauld, Farnauld, Fernald, Farnald

Farold (English) A mighty traveler
Farould, Farald, Farauld, Fareld

Farran (Irish / Arabic / English) Of the land / a baker / one who is adventurous
Fairran, Fayrran, Faerran, Farren, Farrin, Farron, Ferrin, Ferron

Farrar (English) A blacksmith
Farar, Farrer, Farrier, Ferrar, Ferrars, Ferrer, Ferrier, Farer

Farro (Italian) Of the grain
Farroe, Faro, Faroe, Farrow, Farow

Fatik (Indian) Resembling a crystal
Fateek, Fateak, Fatyk, Fatiek, Fateik

Faust (Latin) Having good luck
Fauste, Faustino, Fausto, Faustos, Faustus, Fauston, Faustin, Fausten

Fawcett (American) An audacious man
Fawcet, Fawcette, Fawcete, Fawce, Fawci, Fawcie, Fawcy, Fawcey

Fawwaz (Arabic) A successful man
Fawaz, Fawwad, Fawad

Fay (Irish) Resembling a raven
Faye, Fai, Fae, Feich

Februus (Latin) A pagan god

Fedor (Russian) A gift from God
Faydor, Feodor, Fyodor, Fedyenka, Fyodr, Fydor, Fjodor

Feechi (African) One who worships God
Feechie, Feechy, Feechey, Feechee, Feachi, Feachie

Feivel (Hebrew) The brilliant one
Feival, Feivol, Feivil, Feivyl, Feivul, Feiwel, Feiwal, Feiwol

Felim (Gaelic) One who is always good
Felym, Feidhlim, Felimy, Felimey, Felimee, Felimea, Felimi, Felimie

Felipe (Spanish) Form of Phillip, meaning "one who loves horses"
Felippe, Filip, Filippo, Fillip, Flip, Fulop, Fullop, Fulip

Felix (Latin) One who is happy and prosperous

Felton (English) From the town near the field
Feltun, Felten, Feltan, Feltyn, Feltin

Fenn (English) From the marsh
Fen

Ferdinand (German) A courageous voyager
Ferdie, Ferdinando, Fernando

Fergus (Gaelic) The first and supreme choice
Fearghas, Fearghus, Feargus, Fergie, Ferguson, Fergusson, Furgus, Fergy

Ferrell (Irish) A brave man; a hero
Ferell, Ferel, Ferrel

Fiacre (Celtic) Resembling a raven
Fyacre, Fiacra, Fyacra, Fiachra, Fyachra, Fiachre, Fyachre

Fielding (English) From the field
Fieldyng, Fielder, Field, Fielde, Felding, Feldyng, Fields

Fiero (Spanish) A fiery man
Fyero

Finbar (Irish) A fair-haired man
Finnbar, Finnbarr, Fionn, Fionnbharr, Fionnbar, Fionnbarr, Fynbar, Fynnbar

Finch (English) Resembling the small bird
Fynch, Finche, Fynche, Finchi, Finchie, Finchy, Finchey, Finchee

Fineas (Egyptian) A dark-skinned man
Fyneas, Finius, Fynius

Finian (Irish) A handsome man; fair
Finan, Finnian, Fionan, Finien, Finnien, Finghin, Finneen, Fineen

Finn (Gaelic) A fair-haired man
Fin, Fynn, Fyn, Fingal, Fingall

^**Finnegan** (Irish) A fair-haired man
Finegan, Finnegen, Finegen, Finnigan, Finigan

Finnley (Gaelic) A fair-haired hero
Findlay, Findley, Finly, Finlay, Finlee, Finnly, Finnley

Fiorello (Italian) Resembling a little flower
Fiorelo, Fiorelio, Fioreleo, Fiorellio, Fiorelleo

Fisher (English) A fisherman
Fischer, Fysher

Fitch (English) Resembling an ermine
Fytch, Fich, Fych, Fitche, Fytche

Fitzgerald (English) The son of Gerald
Fytzgerald

Flann (Irish) One who has a ruddy complexion
Flan, Flainn, Flannan, Flannery, Flanneri, Flannerie, Flannerey

Fletcher (English) One who makes arrows
Fletch, Fletche, Flecher

Flynn (Irish) One who has a ruddy complexion
Flyn, Flinn, Flin, Flen, Flenn, Floinn

Fogarty (Irish) One who has been exiled
Fogartey, Fogartee, Fogartea, Fogarti, Fogartie, Fogerty, Fogertey, Fogerti

Foley (English) A creative man
Foly, Folee, Foli, Folie

Folker (German) A guardian of the people
Folkar, Folkor, Folkur, Folkir, Folkyr, Folke, Folko, Folkus

Fonso (German) Form of Alfonso, meaning "prepared for battle; eager and ready"
Fonzo, Fonsie, Fonzell, Fonzie, Fonsi, Fonsy, Fonsey, Fonsee

Fontaine (French) From the water source
Fontayne, Fontaene, Fontane, Fonteyne, Fontana, Fountain

^**Ford** (English) From the river crossing
Forde, Forden, Fordan, Fordon, Fordun, Fordin, Fordyn, Forday

Fouad (Arabic) One who has heart
Fuad

Francisco (Spanish) A man from France
Francesco, Franchesco, Fransisco

Frank (Latin) Form of Francis, meaning "a man from France; one who is free"
Franco, Frankie

Fred (German) Form of Frederick, meaning "a peaceful ruler"
Freddi, Freddie, Freddy, Freddey, Freddee, Freddea, Freddis, Fredis

Frederick (German) A peaceful ruler
Fred, Fredrick, Federico, Federigo, Fredek, Frederic, Frederich, Frederico, Frederik, Fredric

Freeborn (English) One who was born a free man
Freeborne, Freebourn, Freebourne, Freeburn, Freeburne, Free

Fremont (French) The protector of freedom
Freemont, Fremonte

Frigyes (Hungarian) A mighty and peaceful ruler

Frode (Norse) A wise man
Froad, Froade

Froyim (Hebrew) A kind man
Froiim

Fructuoso (Spanish) One who is fruitful
Fructo, Fructoso, Fructuso

Fu (Chinese) A wealthy man

Fudail (Arabic) Of high moral character
Fudaile, Fudayl, Fudayle, Fudale, Fudael, Fudaele

Fulbright (English) A brilliant man
Fullbright, Fulbrite, Fullbrite, Fulbryte, Fullbryte, Fulbert, Fullbert

Fulki (Indian) A spark
Fulkie, Fulkey, Fulky, Fulkee, Fulkea

Fullerton (English) From Fuller's town
Fullertun, Fullertin, Fullertyn, Fullertan, Fullerten

Fursey (Gaelic) The name of a missionary saint
Fursy, Fursi, Fursie, Fursee, Fursea

Fyfe (Scottish) A man from Fifeshire
Fife, Fyffe, Fiffe, Fibh

Fyren (Anglo-Saxon) A wicked man
Fyrin, Fyryn, Fyran, Fyron, Fyrun

G

Gabai (Hebrew) A delightful man

Gabbana (Italian) A creative man
Gabbanah, Gabana, Gabanah, Gabbanna, Gabanna

Gabbo (English) To joke or scoff
Gabboe, Gabbow, Gabbowe

Gabor (Hebrew) God is my strength
Gabur, Gabar, Gaber, Gabir, Gabyr

Gabra (African) An offering
Gabre

*__Gabriel__ (Hebrew) A hero of God
Gabrian, Gabriele, Gabrielli, Gabriello, Gaby, Gab, Gabbi, Gabbie

Gad (Hebrew / Native American) Having good fortune / from the juniper tree
Gadi, Gadie, Gady, Gadey, Gadee, Gadea

Gadiel (Arabic) God is my fortune
Gadiell, Gadiele, Gadielle, Gaddiel, Gaddiell, Gadil, Gadeel, Gadeal

Gaffney (Irish) Resembling a calf
Gaffny, Gaffni, Gaffnie, Gaffnee, Gaffnea

Gage (French) Of the pledge
Gaige, Gaege, Gauge

Gahuj (African) A hunter

Gair (Gaelic) A man of short stature
Gayr, Gaer, Gaire, Gayre, Gaere, Gare

Gaius (Latin) One who rejoices
Gaeus

Galal (Arabic) A majestic man
Galall, Gallal, Gallall

Galbraith (Irish) A foreigner; a Scot
Galbrait, Galbreath, Gallbraith, Gallbreath, Galbraithe, Gallbraithe, Galbreathe, Gallbreathe

Gale (Irish / English) A foreigner / one who is cheerful
Gail, Gaill, Gaille, Gaile, Gayl, Gayle, Gaylle, Gayll

Galen (Greek) A healer; one who is calm
Gaelan, Gaillen, Galan, Galin, Galyn, Gaylen, Gaylin, Gaylinn

Gali (Hebrew) From the fountain
Galie, Galy, Galey, Galee, Galea, Galeigh

Galip (Turkish) A victorious man
Galyp, Galup, Galep, Galap, Galop

Gallagher (Gaelic) An eager helper
Gallaghor, Gallaghar, Gallaghur, Gallaghir, Gallaghyr, Gallager, Gallagar, Gallagor

Galt (English) From the high, wooded land
Galte, Gallt, Gallte

Galtero (Spanish) Form of Walter, meaning "the commander of the army"
Galterio, Galteriyo, Galtereo, Galtereyo, Galter, Galteros, Galterus, Gualterio

Gamaliel (Hebrew) God's reward
Gamliel, Gamalyel, Gamlyel, Gamli, Gamlie, Gamly, Gamley, Gamlee

Gameel (Arabic) A handsome man
Gameal, Gamil, Gamiel, Gameil, Gamyl

Gamon (American) One who enjoys playing games
Gamun, Gamen, Gaman, Gamin, Gamyn, Gammon, Gammun, Gamman

Gan (Chinese) A wanderer

Gandy (American) An adventurer
Gandey, Gandi, Gandie, Gandee, Gandea

Gann (English) One who defends with a spear
Gan

^**Gannon** (Gaelic) A fair-skinned man
Gannun, Gannen, Gannan, Gannin, Gannyn, Ganon, Ganun, Ganin

Garcia (Spanish) One who is brave in battle
Garce, Garcy, Garcey, Garci, Garcie, Garcee, Garcea

Gared (English) Form of Gerard, meaning "one who is mighty with a spear"
Garad, Garid, Garyd, Garod, Garud

Garman (English) A spearman
Garmann, Garmen, Garmin, Garmon, Garmun, Garmyn, Gar, Garr

Garrett (English) Form of Gerard, meaning "one who is mighty with a spear"
Garett, Garret, Garretson, Garritt, Garrot, Garrott, Gerrit, Gerritt

Garrison (French) Prepared
Garris, Garrish, Garry, Gary

Garson (English) The son of Gar (Garrett, Garrison, etc.)
Garrson, Garsen, Garrsen, Garsun, Garrsun, Garsone, Garrsone

Garth (Scandinavian) The keeper of the garden
Garthe, Gart, Garte

Garvey (Gaelic) A rough but peaceful man
Garvy, Garvee, Garvea, Garvi, Garvie, Garrvey, Garrvy, Garrvee

Garvin (English) A friend with a spear
Garvyn, Garven, Garvan, Garvon, Garvun

Gary (English) One who wields a spear
Garey, Gari, Garie, Garea, Garee, Garry, Garrey, Garree

Gassur (Arabic) A courageous man
Gassor, Gassir, Gassyr, Gassar, Gasser

Gaston (French) A man from Gascony
Gastun, Gastan, Gasten, Gascon, Gascone, Gasconey, Gasconi, Gasconie

Gate (American) One who is close-minded
Gates, Gait, Gaite, Gaits

⋆**Gavin** (Welsh) A little white falcon
Gavan, Gaven, Gavino, Gavyn, Gavynn, Gavon, Gavun, Gavyno

Gazali (African) A mystic
Gazalie, Gazaly, Gazaley, Gazalee, Gazalea, Gazaleigh

Geirleif (Norse) A descendant of the spear
Geirleaf, Geerleif, Geerleaf

Geirstein (Norse) One who wields a rock-hard spear
Geerstein, Gerstein

Gellert (Hungarian) A mighty soldier
Gellart, Gellirt, Gellyrt, Gellort, Gellurt

Genaro (Latin) A dedicated man
Genaroh, Genaroe, Genarow, Genarowe

Gene (English) Form of Eugene, meaning "a well-born man"
Genio, Geno, Geneo, Gino, Ginio, Gineo

Genet (African) From Eden
Genat, Genit, Genyt, Genot, Genut

Genoah (Italian) From the city of Genoa
Genoa, Genovise, Genovize

Geoffrey (English) Form of Jeffrey, meaning "a man of peace"
Geffrey, Geoff, Geoffery, Geoffroy, Geoffry, Geofrey, Geofferi, Geofferie

George (Greek) One who works the earth; a farmer
Georas, Geordi, Geordie, Georg, Georges, Georgi, Georgie, Georgio, Yegor, Jurgen, Joren

Gerald (German) One who rules with the spear
Jerald, Garald, Garold, Gearalt, Geralde, Geraldo, Geraud, Gere, Gerek

Gerard (French) One who is mighty with a spear
Gerord, Gerrard, Gared, Garrett

Geremia (Italian) Form of Jeremiah, meaning "one who is exalted by the Lord"
Geremiah, Geremias, Geremija, Geremiya, Geremyah, Geramiah, Geramia

Germain (French / Latin) A man from Germany / one who is brotherly
Germaine, German, Germane, Germanicus, Germano, Germanus, Germayn, Germayne

Gerry (German) Short form of names beginning with Ger-, such as Gerald or Gerard
Gerrey, Gerri, Gerrie, Gerrea, Gerree

Gershom (Hebrew) One who has been exiled
Gersham, Gershon, Gershoom, Gershem, Gershim, Gershym, Gershum, Gersh

Getachew (African) Their master

Ghazi (Arabic) An invader; a conqueror
Ghazie, Ghazy, Ghazey, Ghazee, Ghazea

Ghoukas (Armenian) Form of Lucas, meaning "a man from Lucania"
Ghukas

Giancarlo (Italian) One who is gracious and mighty
Gyancarlo

^**Gideon** (Hebrew) A mighty warrior; one who fells trees
Gideone, Gidi, Gidon, Gidion, Gid, Gidie, Gidy, Gidey

Gilam (Hebrew) The joy of the people
Gylam, Gilem, Gylem, Gilim, Gylim, Gilym, Gylym, Gilom

Gilbert (French / English) Of the bright promise / one who is trustworthy
Gib, Gibb, Gil, Gilberto, Gilburt, Giselbert, Giselberto, Giselbertus

Gildas (Irish / English) One who serves God / the golden one
Gyldas, Gilda, Gylda, Gilde, Gylde, Gildea, Gyldea, Gildes

Giles (Greek) Resembling a young goat
Gyles, Gile, Gil, Gilles, Gillis, Gilliss, Gyle, Gyl

Gill (Gaelic) A servant
Gyll, Gilly, Gilley, Gillee, Gillea, Gilli, Gillie, Ghill

Gillivray (Scottish) A servant of God
Gillivraye, Gillivrae, Gillivrai

Gilmat (Scottish) One who wields a sword
Gylmat, Gilmet, Gylmet

Gilmer (English) A famous hostage
Gilmar, Gilmor, Gilmur, Gilmir, Gilmyr, Gillmer, Gillmar, Gillmor

Gilon (Hebrew) Filled with joy
Gilun, Gilen, Gilan, Gilin, Gilyn, Gilo

Ginton (Arabic) From the garden
Gintun, Gintan, Ginten, Gintin, Gintyn

Giovanni (Italian) Form of John, meaning "God is gracious"
Geovani, Geovanney, Geovanni, Geovanny, Geovany, Giannino, Giovan, Giovani, Yovanny

Giri (Indian) From the mountain
Girie, Giry, Girey, Giree, Girea

Girvan (Gaelic) The small rough one
Gyrvan, Girven, Gyrven, Girvin, Gyrvin, Girvyn, Gyrvyn, Girvon

Giulio (Italian) One who is youthful
Giuliano, Giuleo

Giuseppe (Italian) Form of Joseph, meaning "God will add"
Giuseppi, Giuseppie, Giuseppy, Giuseppee, Giuseppea, Giuseppey, Guiseppe, Guiseppi

Gizmo (American) One who is playful
Gismo, Gyzmo, Gysmo, Gizmoe, Gismoe, Gyzmoe, Gysmoe

Glade (English) From the clearing in the woods
Glayd, Glayde, Glaid, Glaide, Glaed, Glaede

Glaisne (Irish) One who is calm; serene
Glaisny, Glaisney, Glaisni, Glaisnie, Glaisnee, Glasny, Glasney, Glasni

Glasgow (Scottish) From the city in Scotland
Glasgo

Glen (Gaelic) From the secluded narrow valley
Glenn, Glennard, Glennie, Glennon, Glenny, Glin, Glinn, Glyn

Glover (English) One who makes gloves
Glovar, Glovir, Glovyr, Glovur, Glovor

Gobind (Sanskrit) The cow finder
Gobinde, Gobinda, Govind, Govinda, Govinde

Goby (American) An audacious man
Gobi, Gobie, Gobey, Gobee, Gobea

Godfrey (German) God is peace
Giotto, Godefroi, Godfry, Godofredo, Goffredo, Gottfrid, Gottfried, Godfried

Godfried (German) God is peace
Godfreed, Gjord

Gogo (African) A grandfatherly man

Goldwin (English) A golden friend
Goldwine, Goldwinn, Goldwinne, Goldwen, Goldwenn, Goldwenne, Goldwyn, Goldwynn

Goode (English) An upstanding man
Good, Goodi, Goodie, Goody, Goodey, Goodee, Goodea

Gordon (Gaelic) From the great hill; a hero
Gorden, Gordin, Gordyn, Gordun, Gordan, Gordi, Gordie, Gordee

Gormley (Irish) The blue spearman
Gormly, Gormlee, Gormlea, Gormleah, Gormleigh, Gormli, Gormlie, Gormaly

Goro (Japanese) The fifth-born child

Gotzon (Basque) A heavenly messenger; an angel

Gower (Welsh) One who is pure; chaste
Gwyr, Gowyr, Gowir, Gowar, Gowor, Gowur

Gozal (Hebrew) Resembling a baby bird
Gozall, Gozel, Gozell, Gozale, Gozele

Grady (Gaelic) One who is famous; noble
Gradey, Gradee, Gradea, Gradi, Gradie, Graidy, Graidey, Graidee

Graham (English) From the graveled area; from the gray home
Graem

Grand (English) A superior man
Grande, Grandy, Grandey, Grandi, Grandie, Grandee, Grandea, Grander

Granger (English) A farmer
Grainger, Graynger, Graenger, Grange, Graynge, Graenge, Grainge, Grangere

Grant (English) A tall man; a great man
Grante, Graent

Granville (French) From the large village
Granvylle, Granvil, Granvyl, Granvill, Granvyll, Granvile, Granvyle, Grenvill

Gray (English) A gray-haired man
Graye, Grai, Grae, Greye, Grey, Graylon, Graylen, Graylin

^***Grayson** (English) The son of a gray-haired man
Graysen, Graysun, Graysin, ***Greyson****, Graysan, Graison, Graisun, Graisen*

Greenwood (English) From the green forest
Greenwode

Gregory (Greek) One who is vigilant; watchful
Greg, Greggory, Greggy, Gregori, Gregorie, Gregry, Grigori

Gremian (Anglo-Saxon) One who enrages others
Gremien, Gremean, Gremyan

Gridley (English) From the flat meadow
Gridly, Gridlee, Gridlea, Gridleah, Gridleigh, Gridli, Gridlie

Griffin (Latin) Having a hooked nose
Griff, Griffen, Griffon, Gryffen, Gryffin, Gryphen

Griffith (Welsh) A mighty chief
Griffyth, Gryffith, Gryffyth

Grimsley (English) From the dark meadow
Grimsly, Grimslee, Grimslea, Grimsleah, Grimsleigh, Grimsli, Grimslie

Griswold (German) From the gray forest
Griswald, Gryswold, Gryswald, Greswold, Greswald

Guban (African) One who has been burnt
Guben, Gubin, Gubyn, Gubon, Gubun

Guedado (African) One who is unwanted

Guerdon (English) A warring man
Guerdun, Guerdan, Guerden, Guerdin, Guerdyn

Guido (Italian) One who acts as a guide
Guidoh, Gwedo, Gwido, Gwydo, Gweedo

Guillaume (French) Form of William, meaning "the determined protector"
Gillermo, Guglielmo, Guilherme, Guillermo, Gwillyn, Gwilym, Guglilmo

Gulshan (Hindi) From the gardens

Gunner (Scandinavian) A bold warrior
Gunnar, Gunnor, Gunnur, Gunnir, Gunnyr

Gunnolf (Norse) A warrior wolf
Gunolf, Gunnulf, Gunulf

Gur (Hebrew) Resembling a lion cub
Guryon, Gurion, Guriel, Guriell, Guryel, Guryell, Guri, Gurie

Gurpreet (Indian) A devoted follower
Gurpreat, Gurpriet, Gurpreit, Gurprit, Gurpryt

Guru (Indian) A teacher; a religious head

Gurutz (Basque) Of the holy cross
Guruts

Gus (German) A respected man; one who is exalted
Guss

Gustav (Scandinavian) Of the staff of the gods
Gus, Gustave, Gussie, Gustaf, Gustof, Tavin

Gusty (American) Of the wind; a revered man
Gustey, Gustee, Gustea, Gusti, Gustie, Gusto

Guwayne (American) Form of Wayne, meaning "one who builds wagons"
Guwayn, Guwain, Guwaine, Guwaen, Guwaene, Guwane

Gwalchmai (Welsh) A battle hawk

Gwandoya (African) Suffering a miserable fate

Gwydion (Welsh) In mythology, a magician
Gwydeon, Gwydionne, Gwydeonne

Gylfi (Scandinavian) A king
Gylfie, Gylfee, Gylfea, Gylfi, Gylfie, Gylphi, Gylphie, Gylphey

Gypsy (English) A wanderer; a nomad
Gipsee, Gipsey, Gipsy, Gypsi, Gypsie, Gypsey, Gypsee, Gipsi

Habimama (African) One who believes in God
Habymama

Hadden (English) From the heather-covered hill
Haddan, Haddon, Haddin, Haddyn, Haddun

Hadriel (Hebrew) The splendor of God
Hadryel, Hadriell, Hadryell

Hadwin (English) A friend in war
Hadwinn, Hadwinne, Hadwen, Hadwenn, Hadwenne, Hadwyn, Hadwynn, Hadwynne

Hafiz (Arabic) A protector
Haafiz, Hafeez, Hafeaz, Hafiez, Hafeiz, Hafyz, Haphiz, Haaphiz

Hagar (Hebrew) A wanderer

Hagen (Gaelic) One who is youthful
Haggen, Hagan, Haggan, Hagin, Haggin, Hagyn, Haggyn, Hagon

Hagop (Armenian) Form of James, meaning "he who supplants"
Hagup, Hagap, Hagep, Hagip, Hagyp

Hagos (African) Filled with happiness

Hahnee (Native American) A beggar
Hahnea, Hahni, Hahnie, Hahny, Hahney

Haim (Hebrew) A giver of life
Hayim, Hayyim

Haines (English) From the vined cottage; from the hedged enclosure
Haynes, Haenes, Hanes, Haine, Hayne, Haene, Hane

Hajari (African) One who takes flight
Hajarie, Hajary, Hajarey, Hajaree, Hajarea

Haji (African) Born during the hajj
Hajie, Hajy, Hajey, Hajee, Hajea

Hakan (Norse / Native American) One who is noble / a fiery man

Hakim (Arabic) One who is wise; intelligent
Hakeem, Hakeam, Hakeim, Hakiem, Hakym

Hal (English) A form of Henry, meaning "the ruler of the house"; a form of Harold, meaning "the ruler of an army"

Halford (English) From the hall by the ford
Hallford, Halfurd, Hallfurd, Halferd, Hallferd

Halil (Turkish) A beloved friend
Haleel, Haleal, Haleil, Haliel, Halyl

Halla (African) An unexpected gift
Hallah, Hala, Halah

Hallberg (Norse) From the rocky mountain
Halberg, Hallburg, Halburg

Halle (Norse) As solid as a rock

Halley (English) From the hall near the meadow
Hally, Halli, Hallie, Halleigh, Hallee, Halleah, Hallea

Halliwell (English) From the holy spring
Haligwell

Hallward (English) The guardian of the hall
Halward, Hallwerd, Halwerd, Hallwarden, Halwarden, Hawarden, Haward, Hawerd

Hamid (Arabic / Indian) A praiseworthy man / a beloved friend
Hameed, Hamead, Hameid, Hamied, Hamyd, Haamid

Hamidi (Swahili) One who is commendable
Hamidie, Hamidy, Hamidey, Hamidee, Hamidea, Hamydi, Hamydie, Hamydee

Hamilton (English) From the flat-topped hill
Hamylton, Hamiltun, Hamyltun, Hamilten, Hamylten, Hamelton, Hameltun, Hamelten

Hamlet (German) From the little home
Hamlett, Hammet, Hammett, Hamnet, Hamnett, Hamlit, Hamlitt, Hamoelet

Hammer (German) One who makes hammers; a carpenter
Hammar, Hammor, Hammur, Hammir, Hammyr

Hampden (English) From the home in the valley
Hampdon, Hampdan, Hampdun, Hampdyn, Hampdin

Hancock (English) One who owns a farm
Hancok, Hancoc

Hanford (English) From the high ford
Hanferd, Hanfurd, Hanforde, Hanferde, Hanfurde

Hanisi (Swahili) Born on a Thursday
Hanisie, Hanisy, Hanisey, Hanisee, Hanisea, Hanysi, Hanysie, Hanysy

Hank (English) Form of Henry, meaning "the ruler of the house"
Hanke, Hanks, Hanki, Hankie, Hankee, Hankea, Hanky, Hankey

Hanley (English) From the high meadow
Hanly, Hanleigh, Hanleah, Hanlea, Hanlie, Hanli

Hanoch (Hebrew) One who is dedicated
Hanock, Hanok, Hanoc

Hanraoi (Irish) Form of Henry, meaning "the ruler of the house"

Hansraj (Hindi) The swan king

Hardik (Indian) One who has heart
Hardyk, Hardick, Hardyck, Hardic, Hardyc

Hare (English) Resembling a rabbit

Harence (English) One who is swift
Harince, Harense, Harinse

Hari (Indian) Resembling a lion
Harie, Hary, Harey, Haree, Harea

Harim (Arabic) A superior man
Hareem, Haream, Hariem, Hareim, Harym

Harkin (Irish) Having dark red hair
Harkyn, Harken, Harkan, Harkon, Harkun

Harlemm (American) A soulful man
Harlam, Harlom, Harlim, Harlym, Harlem

Harlow (English) From the army on the hill
Harlowe, Harlo, Harloe

Harold (Scandinavian) The ruler of an army
Hal, Harald, Hareld, Harry, Darold

Harper (English) One who plays or makes harps
Harpur, Harpar, Harpir, Harpyr, Harpor, Hearpere

Harrington (English) From Harry's town; from the herring town
Harringtun, Harryngton, Harryngtun, Harington, Haringtun, Haryngton, Haryntun

Harrison (English) The son of Harry
Harrisson, Harris, Harriss, Harryson

Harshad (Indian) A bringer of joy
Harsh, Harshe, Harsho, Harshil, Harshyl, Harshit, Harshyt

Hartford (English) From the stag's ford
Harteford, Hartferd, Harteferd, Hartfurd, Hartefurd, Hartforde, Harteforde, Hartferde

Haru (Japanese) Born during the spring

Harvey (English / French) One who is ready for battle / a strong man
Harvy, Harvi, Harvie, Harvee, Harvea, Harv, Harve, Hervey

Hasim (Arabic) One who is decisive
Haseem, Haseam, Hasiem, Haseim, Hasym

Haskel (Hebrew) An intelligent man
Haskle, Haskell, Haskil, Haskill, Haske, Hask

Hasso (German) Of the sun
Hassoe, Hassow, Hassowe

Hassun (Native American) As solid as a stone

Hastiin (Native American) A man

Hastin (Hindi) Resembling an elephant
Hasteen, Hastean, Hastien, Hastein, Hastyn

Hawes (English) From the hedged place
Haws, Hayes, Hays, Hazin, Hazen, Hazyn, Hazon, Hazan

Hawiovi (Native American) One who descends on a ladder
Hawiovie, Hawiovy, Hawiovey, Hawiovee, Hawiovea

Hawkins (English) Resembling a small hawk
Haukins, Hawkyns, Haukyn

Hawthorne (English) From the hawthorn tree
Hawthorn

*__Hayden__ (English) From the hedged valley
Haydan, Haydon, Haydun, Haydin, Haydyn, Haden, Hadan, Hadon

Haye (Scottish) From the stockade
Hay, Hae, Hai

Hazaiah (Hebrew) God will decide
Hazaia, Haziah, Hazia

Hazleton (English) From the hazel-tree town
Hazelton, Hazletun, Hazelton, Hazleten, Hazelten

Heath (English) From the untended land of flowering shrubs
Heathe, Heeth, Heethe

Heaton (English) From the town on high ground
Heatun, Heeton, Heetun, Heaten, Heeten

Heber (Hebrew) A partner or companion
Heeber, Hebar, Heebar, Hebor, Heebor, Hebur, Heebur, Hebir

Hector (Greek) One who is steadfast; in mythology, the prince of Troy
Hecter, Hekter, Heckter

Helio (Greek) Son of the sun
Heleo, Helios, Heleos

Hem (Indian) The golden son

Hemendu (Indian) Born beneath the golden moon
Hemendue, Hemendoo

Hemi (Maori) Form of James, meaning "he who supplants"
Hemie, Hemy, Hemee, Hemea, Hemey

Henderson (Scottish) The son of Henry
Hendrie, Hendries, Hendron, Hendri, Hendry, Hendrey, Hendree, Hendrea

^**Hendrick** (English) Form of Henry, meaning "the ruler of the house"
Hendryck, Hendrik, Hendryk, Hendric, Hendryc, Hendrix

^**Henley** (English) From the high meadow
Henly, Henleigh, Henlea, Henleah, Henlee, Henli, Henlie

^*__Henry__ (German) The ruler of the house
Hal, Hank, Harry, Henny, Henree, Henri, Hanraoi, Hendrick, Henrik

Heraldo (Spanish) Of the divine

Hercules (Greek) In mythology, a son of Zeus who possessed superhuman strength
Herakles, Hercule, Herculi, Herculie, Herculy, Herculey, Herculee

Herman (German) A soldier
Hermon, Hermen, Hermun, Hermin, Hermyn, Hermann, Hermie

Herne (English) Resembling a heron
Hern, Hearn, Hearne

Hero (Greek) The brave defender
Heroe, Herow, Herowe

Hershel (Hebrew) Resembling a deer
Hersch, Herschel, Herschell, Hersh, Hertzel, Herzel, Herzl, Heschel

Herwin (Teutonic) A friend of war
Herwinn, Herwinne, Herwen, Herwenn, Herwenne, Herwyn, Herwynn, Herwynne

Hesed (Hebrew) A kind man

Hesutu (Native American) A rising yellow-jacket nest
Hesutou, Hesoutou

Hewson (English) The son of Hugh
Hewsun

Hiawatha (Native American) He who makes rivers
Hiawathah, Hyawatha, Hiwatha, Hywatha

Hickok (American) A famous frontier marshal
Hickock, Hickoc, Hikock, Hikoc, Hikok, Hyckok, Hyckock, Hyckoc

Hidalgo (Spanish) The noble one
Hydalgo

Hideaki (Japanese) A clever man; having wisdom
Hideakie, Hideaky, Hideakey, Hideakee, Hideakea

Hieronim (Polish) Form of Jerome, meaning "of the sacred name"
Hieronym, Hieronymos, Hieronimos, Heronim, Heronym, Heronymos, Heronimos

Hietamaki (Finnish) From the sand hill
Hietamakie, Hietamaky, Hietamakey, Hietamakee, Hietamakea

Hieu (Vietnamese) A pious man

Hikmat (Islamic) Filled with wisdom
Hykmat

Hildefuns (German) One who is ready for battle
Hildfuns, Hyldefuns, Hyldfuns

Hillel (Hebrew) One who is praised
Hyllel, Hillell, Hyllell, Hilel, Hylel, Hilell, Hylell

Hiranmay (Indian) The golden one
Hiranmaye, Hiranmai, Hiranmae, Hyranmay, Hyranmaye, Hyranmai, Hyranmae

Hiroshi (Japanese) A generous man
Hiroshie, Hiroshy, Hiroshey, Hiroshee, Hiroshea, Hyroshi, Hyroshie, Hyroshey

Hirsi (African) An amulet
Hirsie, Hirsy, Hirsey, Hirsee, Hirsea

Hisoka (Japanese) One who is secretive
Hysoka, Hisokie, Hysokie, Hisoki, Hysoki, Hisokey, Hysokey, Hisoky

Hitakar (Indian) One who wishes others well
Hitakarin, Hitakrit

Hobart (American) Form of Hubert, meaning "having a shining intellect"
Hobarte, Hoebart, Hoebarte, Hobert, Hoberte, Hoburt, Hoburte, Hobirt

Hohberht (German) One who is high and bright
Hohbert, Hohburt, Hohbirt, Hohbyrt, Hoh

Holcomb (English) From the deep valley
Holcom, Holcombe

Holden (English) From a hollow in the valley
Holdan, Holdyn, Holdon

^**Holland** (American) From the Netherlands
Hollend, Hollind, Hollynd, Hollande, Hollende, Hollinde, Hollynde

Hollis (English) From the holly tree
Hollys, Holliss, Hollyss, Hollace, Hollice, Holli, Hollie, Holly

Holman (English) A man from the valley
Holmann, Holmen, Holmin, Holmyn, Holmon, Holmun

Holt (English) From the forest
Holte, Holyt, Holyte, Holter, Holtar, Holtor, Holtur, Holtir

Honaw (Native American) Resembling a bear
Honawe, Honau

Hondo (African) A warring man
Hondoh, Honda, Hondah

Honesto (Spanish) One who is honest
Honestio, Honestiyo, Honesteo, Honesteyo, Honestoh

Honon (Native American) Resembling a bear
Honun, Honen, Honan, Honin, Honyn

Honovi (Native American) Having great strength
Honovie, Honovy, Honovey, Honovee, Honovea

Honza (Czech) A gift from God

Horsley (English) From the horse meadow
Horsly, Horslea, Horsleah, Horslee, Horsleigh, Horsli, Horslie

Horst (German) From the thicket
Horste, Horsten, Horstan, Horstin, Horstyn, Horston, Horstun, Horstman

Hoshi (Japanese) Resembling a star
Hoshiko, Hoshyko, Hoshie, Hoshee, Hoshea, Hoshy, Hoshey

Hototo (Native American) One who whistles; a warrior spirit that sings

Houston (Gaelic / English) From Hugh's town / from the town on the hill
Huston, Houstyn, Hustin, Husten, Hustin, Houstun

Howard (English) The guardian of the home
Howerd, Howord, Howurd, Howird, Howyrd, Howi, Howie, Howy

Howi (Native American) Resembling a turtle dove

Hrothgar (Anglo-Saxon) A king
Hrothgarr, Hrothegar, Hrothegarr, Hrothgare, Hrothegare

Hubert (German) Having a shining intellect
Hobart, Huberte, Huburt, Huburte, Hubirt, Hubirte, Hubyrt, Hubyrte, Hubie, Uberto

Hudson (English) The son of Hugh; from the river
Hudsun, Hudsen, Hudsan, Hudsin, Hudsyn

Hugin (Norse) A thoughtful man
Hugyn, Hugen, Hugan, Hugon, Hugun

Humam (Arabic) A generous and brave man

Hungan (Haitian) A spirit master or priest
Hungen, Hungon, Hungun, Hungin, Hungyn

Hungas (Irish) A vigorous man

***Hunter** (English) A great huntsman and provider
Huntar, Huntor, Huntur, Huntir, Huntyr, Hunte, Hunt, Hunting

Husky (American) A big man; a manly man
Huski, Huskie, Huskey, Huskee, Huskea, Husk, Huske

Huslu (Native American) Resembling a hairy bear
Huslue, Huslou

Husto (Spanish) A righteous man
Hustio, Husteo, Hustiyo, Husteyo

Huynh (Vietnamese) An older brother

I

Iakovos (Hebrew) Form of Jacob, meaning "he who supplants"
Iakovus, Iakoves, Iakovas, Iakovis, Iakovys

***Ian** (Gaelic) Form of John, meaning "God is gracious"
Iain, Iaine, Iayn, Iayne, Iaen, Iaene, Iahn

Iavor (Bulgarian) From the sycamore tree
Iaver, Iavur, Iavar, Iavir, Iavyr

^**Ibrahim** (Arabic) Form of Abraham, meaning "father of a multitude; father of nations"
Ibraheem, Ibraheim, Ibrahiem, Ibraheam, Ibrahym

Ichabod (Hebrew) The glory has gone
Ikabod, Ickabod, Icabod, Ichavod, Ikavod, Icavod, Ickavod, Icha

Ichtaca (Nahuatl) A secretive man
Ichtaka, Ichtacka

Ida (Anglo-Saxon) A king
Idah

Idi (African) Born during the holiday of Idd
Idie, Idy, Idey, Idee, Idea

Ido (Arabic / Hebrew) A mighty man / to evaporate
Iddo, Idoh, Iddoh

Idris (Welsh) An eager lord
Idrys, Idriss, Idrisse, Idryss, Idrysse

Iefan (Welsh) Form of John, meaning "God is gracious"
Iefon, Iefen, Iefin, Iefyn, Iefun, Ifan, Ifon, Ifen

Ifor (Welsh) An archer
Ifore, Ifour, Ifoure

Igasho (Native American) A wanderer
Igashoe, Igashow, Igashowe

Ignatius (Latin) A fiery man; one who is ardent
Ignac, Ignace, Ignacio, Ignacius, Ignatious, Ignatz, Ignaz, Ignazio

Igor (Scandinavian / Russian) A hero / Ing's soldier
Igoryok

Ihit (Indian) One who is honored
Ihyt, Ihitt, Ihytt

Ihsan (Arabic) A charitable man
Ihsann, Ihsen, Ihsin, Ihsyn, Ihson, Ihsun

Ike (Hebrew) Form of Isaac, meaning "full of laughter"
Iki, Ikie, Iky, Ikey, Ikee, Ikea

^**Iker** (Basque) A visitor
Ikar, Ikir, Ikyr, Ikor, Ikur

Ilario (Italian) A cheerful man
Ilareo, Ilariyo, Ilareyo, Ilar, Ilarr, Ilari, Ilarie, Ilary

Ilhuitl (Nahuatl) Born during the daytime

Illanipi (Native American) An amazing man
Illanipie, Illanipy, Illanipey, Illanipee, Illanipea

Iluminado (Spanish) One who shines brightly
Illuminado, Iluminato, Illuminato, Iluminados, Iluminatos, Illuminados, Illuminatos

Imaran (Indian) Having great strength
Imaren, Imaron, Imarun, Imarin, Imaryn

Inaki (Basque) An ardent man
Inakie, Inaky, Inakey, Inakee, Inakea, Inacki, Inackie, Inackee

Ince (Hungarian) One who is innocent
Inse

Indiana (English) From the land of the Indians; from the state of Indiana
Indianna, Indyana, Indyanna

Ingemar (Scandinavian) The son of Ing
Ingamar, Ingemur, Ingmar, Ingmur, Ingar, Ingemer, Ingmer

Inger (Scandinavian) One who is fertile
Inghar, Ingher

Ingo (Scandinavian / Danish) A lord / from the meadow
Ingoe, Ingow, Ingowe

Ingram (Scandinavian) A raven of peace
Ingra, Ingrem, Ingrim, Ingrym, Ingrum, Ingrom, Ingraham, Ingrahame, Ingrams

Iniko (African) Born during troubled times
Inicko, Inico, Inyko, Inycko, Inyco

Iranga (Sri Lankan) One who is special

Irenbend (Anglo-Saxon) From the iron bend
Ironbend

Irwin (English) A friend of the wild boar
Irwinn, Irwinne, Irwyn, Irwynne, Irwine, Irwen, Irwenn, Irwenne

***Isaac** (Hebrew) Full of laughter
Ike, Isaack, Isaak, Isac, Isacco, Isak, Issac, Itzak

***Isaiah** (Hebrew) God is my salvation
Isa, Isaia, Isais, Isia, Isiah, Issiah, Izaiah, Iziah

Iseabail (Hebrew) One who is devoted to God
Iseabaile, Iseabayl, Iseabyle, Iseabael, Iseabaele

Isham (English) From the iron one's estate
Ishem, Ishom, Ishum, Ishim, Ishym, Isenham

Isidore (Greek) A gift of Isis
Isador, Isadore, Isidor, Isidoro, Isidorus, Isidro

Iskander (Arabic) Form of Alexander, meaning "a helper and defender of mankind"
Iskinder, Iskandar, Iskindar, Iskynder, Iskyndar, Iskender, Iskendar

Israel (Hebrew) God perseveres
Israeli, Israelie, Isreal, Izrael

Istvan (Hungarian) One who is crowned
Istven, Istvin, Istvyn, Istvon, Istvun

Iulian (Romanian) A youthful man
Iulien, Iulio, Iuleo

Ivan (Slavic) Form of John, meaning "God is gracious"
Ivann, Ivanhoe, Ivano, Iwan, Iban, Ibano, Ivanti, Ivantie

Ives (Scandinavian) The archer's bow; of the yew wood
Ivair, Ivar, Iven, Iver, Ivo, Ivon, Ivor, Ivaire

Ivy (English) Resembling the evergreen vining plant
Ivee, Ivey, Ivie, Ivi, Ivea

Iyar (Hebrew) Surrounded by light
Iyyar, Iyer, Iyyer

J

Ja (Korean / African) A handsome man / one who is magnetic

Jabari (African) A valiant man
Jabarie, Jabary, Jabarey, Jabaree, Jabarea

Jabbar (Indian) One who consoles others
Jabar

Jabin (Hebrew) God has built; one who is perceptive

Jabon (American) A fiesty man
Jabun, Jabin, Jabyn, Jaben, Jaban

^**Jace** (Hebrew) God is my salvation
Jacen, Jacey, Jacian, Jacy, Jaice, Jayce, Jaece, ***Jase***

Jacinto (Spanish) Resembling a hyacinth
Jacynto, Jacindo, Jacyndo, Jacento, Jacendo, Jacenty, Jacentey, Jacentee

*****Jack** (English) Form of John, meaning "God is gracious"
Jackie, Jackman, Jacko, Jacky, Jacq, Jacqin, Jak, Jaq

*****Jackson** (English) The son of Jack or John
Jacksen, Jacksun, Jacson, Jakson, Jaxen, Jaxon, Jaxun, ***Jaxson***

*****Jacob** (Hebrew) He who supplants
Jake, James, Kuba, Iakovos, Yakiv, Yankel, Yaqub, Jaco, Jacobo, Jacobi, Jacoby, Jacobie, Jacobey, Jacobo

Jacoby (Hebrew) Form of Jacob, meaning "he who supplants"

Jadal (American) One who is punctual
Jadall, Jadel, Jadell

Jade (Spanish) Resembling the green gemstone
Jadee, Jadie, Jayde, Jaden

^***Jaden** (Hebrew / English) One who is thankful to God; God has heard / form of Jade, meaning "resembling the green gemstone"
Jaiden, Jadyn, Jaeden, Jaidyn, ***Jayden****, Jaydon*

Jagan (English) One who is self-confident
Jagen, Jagin, Jagyn, Jagon, Jagun, Jago

Jahan (Indian) Man of the world
Jehan, Jihan, Jag, Jagat, Jagath

Jaidayal (Indian) The victory of kindness
Jadayal, Jaydayal, Jaedayal

Jaime (Spanish) Form of James, meaning "he who supplants"
Jamie, Jaimee, Jaimey, Jaimi, Jaimie, Jaimy, Jamee

Jaimin (French) One who is loved
Jaimyn, Jamin, Jamyn, Jaymin, Jaymyn, Jaemin, Jaemyn

Jairdan (American) One who enlightens others
Jardan, Jayrdan, Jaerdan, Jairden, Jarden, Jayrden, Jaerden

Jaja (African) A gift from God

Jajuan (American) One who loves God

Jake (English) Form of Jacob, meaning "he who supplants"
Jaik, Jaike, Jayk, Jayke, Jakey, Jaky

Jakome (Basque) Form of James, meaning "he who supplants"
Jackome, Jakom, Jackom, Jacome

^**Jalen** (American) One who heals others; one who is tranquil
Jaylon, Jaelan, Jalon, Jaylan, ***Jaylen****, Jalan,* ***Jaylin***

Jamal (Arabic) A handsome man
Jamail, Jahmil, Jam, Jamaal, Jamy, Jamar

Jamar (American) Form of Jamal, meaning "a handsome man"
Jamarr, Jemar, Jemarr, Jimar, Jimarr, Jamaar, Jamari, Jamarie

*__James__ (Hebrew) Form of Jacob, meaning "he who supplants"
Jaimes, Jaymes, Jame, Jaym, Jaim, Jaem, Jaemes, Jamese, Jim, Jaime, Diego, Hagop, Hemi, Jakome

^__Jameson__ (English) The son of James
Jaimison, Jamieson, Jaymeson, ***Jamison****, Jaimeson, Jaymison, Jaemeson, Jaemison*

Jamin (Hebrew) The right hand of favor
Jamian, Jamiel, Jamon, Jaymin, Jaemin, Jaymon

Janesh (Hindi) A leader of the people
Janeshe

Japa (Indian) One who chants
Japeth, Japesh, Japendra

Japheth (Hebrew) May he expand; in the Bible, one of Noah's sons
Jaypheth, Jaepheth, Jaipheth, Jafeth, Jayfeth

Jarah (Hebrew) One who is as sweet as honey
Jarrah, Jara, Jarra

Jared (Hebrew) Of the descent; descending
Jarad, Jarod, Jarrad, Jarryd, Jarred, Jarrod, Jaryd, Jerod, Jerrad, Jered

Jarman (German) A man from Germany
Jarmann, Jerman, Jermann

Jaron (Israeli) A song of rejoicing
Jaran, Jaren, Jarin, Jarran, Jarren, Jarrin, Jarron, Jaryn

Jaroslav (Slavic) Born with the beauty of spring
Jaroslaw

Jarrett (English) One who is strong with the spear
Jaret, Jarret, Jarrott, Jerett, Jarritt, Jaret

*__Jason__ (Hebrew / Greek) God is my salvation / a healer; in mythology, the leader of the Argonauts
Jacen, Jaisen, Jaison, Jasen, Jasin, Jasun, Jayson, Jaysen

Jaspar (Persian) One who holds the treasure
Jasper, Jaspir, Jaspyr, Jesper, Jespar, Jespir, Jespyr

Jatan (Indian) One who is nurturing

Javan (Hebrew) Man from Greece; in the Bible, Noah's grandson
Jayvan, Jayven, Jayvon, Javon, Javern, Javen

Javier (Spanish) The owner of a new house
Javiero

Jax (American) Form of Jackson, meaning "son of Jack or John"

Jay (Latin / Sanskrit) Resembling a jaybird / one who is victorious
Jae, Jai, Jaye, Jayron, Jayronn, Jey

^*__Jayce__ (American) Form of Jason, meaning "God is my salvation"
Jayse, Jace, ***Jase***

Jean (French) Form of John, meaning "God is gracious"
Jeanne, Jeane, Jene, Jeannot, Jeanot

Jedidiah (Hebrew) One who is loved by God
Jedadiah, Jedediah, Jed, Jedd, Jedidiya, Jedidiyah, Jedadia, Jedadiya

Jeffrey (English) A man of peace
Jeff, Geoffrey, Jeffery, Jeffree

Jelani (African) One who is mighty; strong
Jelanie, Jelany, Jelaney, Jelanee, Jelanea

Jennett (Hindi) One who is heaven-sent
Jenett, Jennet, Jenet, Jennitt, Jenitt, Jennit, Jenit

Jerald (English) Form of Gerald, meaning "one who rules with the spear"
Jeraldo, Jerold, Jerrald, Jerrold

*__Jeremiah__ (Hebrew) One who is exalted by the Lord
Jeremia, Jeremias, Jeremija, Jeremiya, Jeremyah, Jeramiah, Jeramia, Jerram, Geremia

Jeremy (Hebrew) Form of Jeremiah, meaning "one who is exalted by the Lord"
Jeramey, Jeramie, Jeramy, Jerami, Jereme, Jeromy

Jermaine (French / Latin) A man from Germany / one who is brotherly
Jermain, Jermane, Jermayne, Jermin, Jermyn, Jermayn, Jermaen, Jermaene

Jerome (Greek) Of the sacred name
Jairome, Jeroen, Jeromo, Jeronimo, Jerrome, Jerom, Jerolyn, Jerolin, Hieronim

Jerram (Hebrew) Form of Jeremiah, meaning "one who is exalted by the Lord"
Jeram, Jerrem, Jerem, Jerrym, Jerym

Jesimiel (Hebrew) The Lord establishes
Jessimiel

Jesse (Hebrew) God exists; a gift from God; God sees all
Jess, Jessey, Jesiah, Jessie, Jessy, Jese, Jessi, Jessee

***Jesus** (Hebrew) God is my salvation
Jesous, Jesues, ***Jesús****, Xesus*

Jett (English) Resembling the jet-black lustrous gemstone
Jet, Jette

Jibril (Arabic) Refers to the archangel Gabriel
Jibryl, Jibri, Jibrie, Jibry, Jibrey, Jibree

Jim (English) Form of James, meaning "he who supplants"
Jimi, Jimmee, Jimmey, Jimmie, Jimmy, Jimmi, Jimbo

Jimoh (African) Born on a Friday
Jymoh, Jimo, Jymo

Jivan (Hindi) A giver of life
Jivin, Jiven, Jivyn, Jivon

Joab (Hebrew) The Lord is my father
Joabb, Yoav

Joachim (Hebrew) One who is established by God; God will judge
Jachim, Jakim, Joacheim, Joaquim, Joaquin, Josquin, Joakim, Joakeen

Joe (English) Form of Joseph, meaning "God will add"
Jo, Joemar, Jomar, Joey, Joie, Joee, Joeye

Joel (Hebrew) Jehovah is God; God is willing

Johan (German) Form of John, meaning "God is gracious"

***John** (Hebrew) God is gracious; in the Bible, one of the Apostles
Sean, Jack, Juan*, Ian, Ean,* ***Evan****, Giovanni, Hanna, Hovannes, Iefan, Ivan, Jean, Xoan, Yochanan, Yohan, Johnn, Johnny, Jhonny*

Jonah (Hebrew) Resembling a dove; in the Bible, the man swallowed by a whale

Jonas (Greek) Form of Jonah, meaning "resembling a dove"

*__Jonathan__ (Hebrew) A gift of God
Johnathan, Johnathon, Jonathon, Jonatan, Jonaton, Jonathen, Johnathen, Jonaten, Yonatan

*__Jordan__ (Hebrew) Of the down-flowing river; in the Bible, the river where Jesus was baptized
Johrdan, Jordain, Jordaine, Jordane, Jordanke, Jordann, Jorden, Jordaen

Jorge (Spanish) Form of George, meaning "one who works the earth; a farmer"

*__Jose__ (Spanish) Form of Joseph, meaning "God will add"
José, Joseito, Joselito

*__Joseph__ (Hebrew) God will add
Joe, Guiseppe, Yosyp, Jessop, Jessup, Joop, Joos, ***José****, Jose, Josef, Joseito*

*__Joshua__ (Hebrew) God is salvation
Josh, Joshuah, Josua, Josue, Joushua, Jozua, Joshwa, Joshuwa

*__Josiah__ (Hebrew) God will help
Josia, Josias, Joziah, Jozia, Jozias

Journey (American) One who likes to travel
Journy, Journi, Journie, Journee, Journye, Journea

*__Juan__ (Spanish) Form of John, meaning "God is gracious"
Juanito, Juwan, Jwan

Judah (Hebrew) One who praises God
Juda, Jude, Judas, Judsen, Judson, Judd, Jud

Jude (Latin) Form of Judah, meaning "one who praises God"

*__Julian__ (Greek) The child of Jove; one who is youthful
Juliano, Julianus, Julien, Julyan, Julio, Jolyon, Jullien, Julen

Julius (Greek) One who is youthful
Juleus, Yuliy

Juma (African) Born on a Friday
Jumah

Jumbe (African) Having great strength
Jumbi, Jumbie, Jumby, Jumbey, Jumbee

Jumoke (African) One who is dearly loved
Jumok, Jumoak

Jun (Japanese) One who is obedient

Junaid (Arabic) A warrior
Junaide, Junayd, Junayde

Jung (Korean) A righteous man

Jurgen (German) Form of George, meaning "one who works the earth; a farmer"
Jorgen, Jurgin, Jorgin

Justice (English) One who upholds moral rightness and fairness
Justyce, Justiss, Justyss, Justis, Justus, Justise

*__Justin__ (Latin) One who is just and upright
Joost, Justain, Justan, Just, Juste, Justen, Justino, Justo

Justinian (Latin) An upright ruler
Justinien, Justinious, Justinius, Justinios, Justinas, Justinus

K

Kabir (Indian) A spiritual leader
Kabeer, Kabear, Kabier, Kabeir, Kabyr, Kabar

Kabonesa (African) One who is born during difficult times

Kacancu (African) The first-born child
Kacancue, Kakancu, Kakancue, Kacanku, Kacankue

Kacey (Irish) A vigilant man; one who is alert
Kacy, Kacee, Kacea, Kaci, Kacie, Kasey, Kasy, Kasi

Kachada (Native American) A white-skinned man

Kaden (Arabic) A beloved companion
Kadan, Kadin, Kadon, Kaidan, Kaiden, Kaidon, Kaydan, ***Kayden***

Kadmiel (Hebrew) One who stands before God
Kamiell

Kaemon (Japanese) Full of joy; one who is right-handed
Kamon, Kaymon, Kaimon

Kagen (Irish) A fiery man; a thinker
Kaigen, Kagan, Kaigan, Kaygen, Kaygan, Kaegen, Kaegan

Kahoku (Hawaiian) Resembling a star
Kahokue, Kahokoo, Kahokou

Kai (Hawaiian / Welsh / Greek) Of the sea / the keeper of the keys / of the earth
Kye

Kaimi (Hawaiian) The seeker
Kaimie, Kaimy, Kaimey, Kaimee, Kaimea

Kalama (Hawaiian) A source of light
Kalam, Kalame

Kale (English) Form of Charles, meaning "one who is manly and strong / a free man"

Kaleb (Hebrew) Resembling an aggressive dog
Kaileb, Kaeleb, Kayleb, Kalob, Kailob, Kaelob

Kalidas (Hindi) A poet or musician; a servant of Kali
Kalydas

Kalki (Indian) Resembling a white horse
Kalkie, Kalky, Kalkey, Kalkee, Kalkea

Kalkin (Hindi) The tenth-born child
Kalkyn, Kalken, Kalkan, Kalkon, Kalkun

Kamden (English) From the winding valley
Kamdun, Kamdon, Kamdan, Kamdin, Kamdyn

Kane (Gaelic) The little warrior
Kayn, Kayne, Kaen, Kaene, Kahan, Kahane

Kang (Korean) A healthy man

Kano (Japanese) A powerful man
Kanoe, Kanoh

Kantrava (Indian) Resembling a roaring animal

Kaper (American) One who is capricious
Kahper, Kapar, Kahpar

Kapono (Hawaiian) A righteous man

Karcsi (French) A strong, manly man
Karcsie, Karcsy, Karcsey, Karcsee, Karcsea

Karl (German) A free man
Carl, Karel, Karlan, Karle, Karlens, Karli, Karlin, Karlo, Karlos

Karman (Gaelic) The lord of the manor
Karmen, Karmin, Karmyn, Karmon, Karmun

^**Karson** (Scottish) Form of Carson, meaning son of a marsh dweller
Karsen

^**Karter** (English) Form of Carter, meaning one who drives a cart

Kashvi (Indian) A shining man
Kashvie, Kashvy, Kashvey, Kashvee, Kashvea

Kasib (Arabic) One who is fertile
Kaseeb, Kaseab, Kasieb, Kaseib, Kasyb

Kasim (Arabic) One who is divided
Kassim, Kaseem, Kasseem, Kaseam, Kasseam, Kasym, Kassym

Kasimir (Slavic) One who demands peace
Kasimeer, Kasimear, Kasimier, Kasimeir, Kasimyr, Kaz, Kazimierz

Kason (Basque) Protected by a helmet
Kasin, Kasyn, Kasen, Kasun, Kasan

Katzir (Hebrew) The harvester
Katzyr, Katzeer, Katzear, Katzier, Katzeir

Kaushal (Indian) One who is skilled
Kaushall, Koshal, Koshall

Kazim (Arabic) An even-tempered man
Kazeem, Kazeam, Kaziem, Kazeim, Kazym

Keahi (Hawaiian) Of the flames
Keahie, Keahy, Keahey, Keahee, Keahea

Kealoha (Hawaiian) From the bright path
Keeloha, Kieloha

Kean (Gaelic / English) A warrior / one who is sharp
Keane, Keen, Keene, Kein, Keine, Keyn, Keyne, Kien

Keandre (American) One who is thankful
Kiandre, Keandray, Kiandray, Keandrae, Kiandrae, Keandrai, Kiandrai

Keanu (Hawaiian) Of the mountain breeze
Keanue, Kianu, Kianue, Keanoo, Kianoo, Keanou

Keaton (English) From the town of hawks
Keatun, Keeton, Keetun, Keyton, Keytun

Kedar (Arabic) A powerful man
Keder, Kedir, Kedyr, Kadar, Kader, Kadir, Kadyr

Kefir (Hebrew) Resembling a young lion
Kefyr, Kefeer, Kefear, Kefier, Kefeir

Keegan (Gaelic) A small and fiery man
Kegan, Keigan, Keagan, Keagen, Keegen

Keith (Scottish) Man from the forest
Keithe, Keath, Keathe, Kieth, Kiethe, Keyth, Keythe, Keithen

Kellach (Irish) One who suffers strife during battle
Kelach, Kellagh, Kelagh, Keallach

^**Kellen** (Gaelic / German) One who is slender / from the swamp
Kellan, *Kellon, Kellun, Kellin*

Kelley (Celtic / Gaelic) A warrior / one who defends
Kelly, Kelleigh, Kellee, Kellea, Kelleah, Kelli, Kellie

Kendi (African) One who is much loved
Kendie, Kendy, Kendey, Kendee, Kendea

Kendrick (English / Gaelic) A royal ruler / the champion
Kendric, Kendricks, Kendrik, Kendrix, Kendryck, Kenrick, Kenrik, Kenricks

Kenley (English) From the king's meadow
Kenly, Kenlee, Kenleigh, Kenlea, Kenleah, Kenli, Kenlie

Kenn (Welsh) Of the bright waters

Kennedy (Gaelic) A helmeted chief
Kennedi, Kennedie, Kennedey, Kennedee, Kennedea, Kenadie, Kenadi, Kenady

Kenneth (Irish) Born of the fire; an attractive man
Kennet, Kennett, Kennith, Kennit, Kennitt

Kent (English) From the edge or border
Kentt, Kennt, Kentrell

Kenton (English) From the king's town
Kentun, Kentan, Kentin, Kenten, Kentyn

Kenyon (Gaelic) A blond-haired man
Kenyun, Kenyan, Kenyen, Kenyin

Kepler (German) One who makes hats
Keppler, Kappler, Keppel, Keppeler

Kerbasi (Basque) A warrior
Kerbasie, Kerbasee, Kerbasea, Kerbasy, Kerbasey

Kershet (Hebrew) Of the rainbow

Kesler (American) An energetic man; one who is independent
Keslar, Keslir, Keslyr, Keslor, Keslur

Keung (Chinese) A universal spirit

*__Kevin__ (Gaelic) A beloved and handsome man
Kevyn, Kevan, Keven, Keveon, Kevinn, Kevion, Kevis, Kevon

Khairi (Swahili) A kingly man
Khairie, Khairy, Khairey, Khairee, Khairea

Khalon (American) A strong warrior
Khalun, Khalen, Khalan, Khalin, Khalyn

Khayri (Arabic) One who is charitable
Khayrie, Khayry, Khayrey, Khayree, Khayrea

Khouri (Arabic) A spiritual man; a priest
Khourie, Khoury, Khourey, Khouree, Kouri, Kourie, Koury, Kourey

Khushi (Indian) Filled with happiness
Khushie, Khushey, Khushy, Khushee

Kibbe (Native American) A nocturnal bird
Kybbe

Kibo (African) From the highest mountain peak
Keybo, Keebo, Keabo, Keibo, Kiebo

Kidd (English) Resembling a young goat
Kid, Kydd, Kyd

Kiefer (German) One who makes barrels
Keefer, Keifer, Kieffer, Kiefner, Kieffner, Kiefert, Kuefer, Kueffner

^**Kieran** (Gaelic) Having dark features; the little dark one
Keiran, Keiron, Kernan, Kieren, Kiernan, Kieron, Kierren, Kierrien, Kierron, Keeran, Keeron, Keernan, Keeren, Kearan, Kearen, Kearon, Kearnan

Kim (Vietnamese) As precious as gold
Kym

Kimoni (African) A great man
Kimonie, Kimony, Kimoney, Kimonee, Kymoni, Kymonie, Kymony, Kymoney

Kincaid (Celtic) The leader during battle
Kincade, Kincayd, Kincayde, Kincaide, Kincaed, Kincaede, Kinkaid, Kinkaide

Kindin (Basque) The fifth-born child
Kinden, Kindan, Kindyn, Kindon, Kindun

Kindle (American) To set aflame
Kindel, Kyndle, Kyndel

^**King** (English) The royal ruler
Kyng, Kingsley

Kingston (English) From the king's town
Kingstun, Kinston, Kindon

Kinnard (Irish) From the tall hill
Kinard, Kinnaird, Kinaird, Kynnard, Kynard, Kynnaird, Kynaird

Kinsey (English) The victorious prince
Kynsey, Kinsi, Kynsi, Kinsie, Kynsie, Kinsee, Kynsee, Kinsea

Kione (African) One who has come from nowhere

Kioshi (Japanese) One who is quiet
Kioshe, Kioshie, Kioshy, Kioshey, Kioshee, Kyoshi, Kyoshe, Kyoshie

Kipp (English) From the small pointed hill
Kip, Kipling, Kippling, Kypp, Kyp, Kiplyng, Kipplyng, Kippi

Kiri (Vietnamese) Resembling the mountains
Kirie, Kiry, Kirey, Kiree, Kirea

Kirk (Norse) A man of the church
Kyrk, Kerk, Kirklin, Kirklyn

Kirkland (English) From the church's land
Kirklan, Kirklande, Kyrkland, Kyrklan, Kyrklande

Kirkley (English) From the church's meadow
Kirkly, Kirkleigh, Kirklea, Kirkleah, Kirklee, Kirkli, Kirklie

Kit (English) Form of Christopher, meaning "one who bears Christ inside"
Kitt, Kyt, Kytt

Kitchi (Native American) A brave young man
Kitchie, Kitchy, Kitchey, Kitchee, Kitchea

Kitoko (African) A handsome man
Kytoko

Kivi (Finnish) As solid as stone
Kivie, Kivy, Kivey, Kivee, Kivea

Knight (English) A noble solidier
Knights

^**Knox** (English) From the rounded hill

Knud (Danish) A kind man
Knude

Kobe (African / Hungarian) Tortoise / Form of Jacob, meaning "he who supplants"
Kobi, Koby

Kody (English) One who is helpful
Kodey, Kodee, Kodea, Kodi, Kodie

Koen (German) An honest advisor
Koenz, Kunz, Kuno

Kohana (Native American / Hawaiian) One who is swift / the best

Kohler (German) One who mines coal
Koler

Kojo (African) Born on a Monday
Kojoe, Koejo, Koejoe

Koka (Hawaiian) A man from Scotland

^**Kolton** (American) Form of Colton, meaning from the coal town
Kolten, Koltan

Konane (Hawaiian) Born beneath the bright moon
Konain, Konaine, Konayn, Konayne, Konaen, Konaene

Konnor (English) A wolf lover; one who is strong-willed
Konnur, Konner, Konnar, Konnir, Konnyr

Koofrey (African) Remember me
Koofry, Koofri, Koofrie, Koofree

Kordell (English) One who makes cord
Kordel, Kord, Kordale

Koresh (Hebrew) One who digs in the earth; a farmer
Koreshe

Kory (Irish) From the hollow; of the churning waters
Korey, Kori, Korie, Koree, Korea, Korry, Korrey, Korree

Kozma (Greek) One who is decorated
Kozmah

Kozue (Japanese) Of the tree branches
Kozu, Kozoo, Kozou

Kraig (Gaelic) From the rocky place; as solid as a rock
Kraige, Krayg, Krayge, Kraeg, Kraege, Krage

Kramer (German) A shopkeeper
Kramar, Kramor, Kramir, Kramur, Kramyr, Kraymer, Kraimer, Kraemer

Krany (Czech) A man of short stature
Kraney, Kranee, Kranea, Krani, Kranie

Krikor (Armenian) A vigilant watchman
Krykor, Krikur, Krykur

Kristian (Scandinavian) An annointed Christian
Kristan, Kristien, Krist, Kriste, Krister, Kristar, Khristian, Khrist

Kristopher (Scandinavian) A follower of Christ
Khristopher, Kristof, Kristofer, Kristoff, Kristoffer, Kristofor, Kristophor, Krystof

Kuba (Polish) Form of Jacob, meaning "he who supplants"
Kubas

Kuckunniwi (Native American) Resembling a little wolf
Kukuniwi

Kuleen (Indian) A high-born man
Kulin, Kulein, Kulien, Kulean, Kulyn

Kumar (Indian) A prince; a male child

Kuri (Japanese) Resembling a chestnut
Kurie, Kury, Kurey, Kuree, Kurea

Kuron (African) One who gives thanks
Kurun, Kuren, Kuran, Kurin, Kuryn

Kurt (German) A brave counselor
Kurte

Kushal (Indian) A talented man; adroit
Kushall

Kwaku (African) Born on a Wednesday
Kwakue, Kwakou, Kwako, Kwakoe

Kwan (Korean) Of a bold character
Kwon

Kwintyn (Polish) The fifth-born child
Kwentyn, Kwinton, Kwenton, Kwintun, Kwentun, Kwintan, Kwentan, Kwinten

^**Kyle** (Gaelic) From the narrow channel
Kile, Kiley, Kye, Kylan, Kyrell, Kylen, Kily, Kili

Kylemore (Gaelic) From the great wood
Kylmore, Kylemor, Kylmor

Kyrone (English) Form of Tyrone, meaning "from Owen's land"
Kyron, Keirohn, Keiron, Keirone, Keirown, Kirone

L

Lacey (French) Man from Normandy; as delicate as lace
Lacy, Laci, Lacie, Lacee, Lacea

Lachlan (Gaelic) From the land of lakes
Lachlen, Lachlin, Lachlyn, Locklan, Locklen, Locklin, Locklyn, Loklan

Lachman (Gaelic) A man from the lake
Lachmann, Lockman, Lockmann, Lokman, Lokmann, Lakman, Lakmann

Ladan (Hebrew) One who is alert and aware
Laden, Ladin, Ladyn, Ladon, Ladun

Ladd (English) A servant; a young man
Lad, Laddey, Laddie, Laddy, Laddi, Laddee, Laddea, Ladde

Ladislas (Slavic) A glorious ruler
Lacko, Ladislaus, Laslo, Laszlo, Lazlo, Ladislav, Ladislauv, Ladislao

Lagrand (American) A majestic man
Lagrande

Laibrook (English) One who lives on the road near the brook
Laebrook, Laybrook, Laibroc, Laebroc, Laybroc, Laibrok, Laebrok, Laybrok

Laird (Scottish) The lord of the manor
Layrd, Laerd, Lairde, Layrde, Laerde

Laken (American) Man from the lake
Laike, Laiken, Laikin, Lakin, Lakyn, Lakan, Laikyn, Laeken

Lalam (Indian) The best
Lallam, Lalaam, Lallaam

Lam (Vietnamese) Having a full understanding

Laman (Arabic) A bright and happy man
Lamaan, Lamann, Lamaann

Lamar (German / French) From the renowned land / of the sea
Lamarr, Lamarre, Lemar, Lemarr

Lambert (Scandinavian) The light of the land
Lambart, Lamberto, Lambirt, Landbert, Lambirto, Lambrecht, Lambret, Lambrett

Lambi (Norse) In mythology, the son of Thorbjorn
Lambie, Lamby, Lambey, Lambe, Lambee

Lameh (Arabic) A shining man

Lamorak (English) In Arthurian legend, the brother of Percival
Lamerak, Lamurak, Lamorac, Lamerac, Lamurac, Lamorack, Lamerack, Lamurack

Lance (English) Form of Lancelot, meaning an attendant, a knight of the Round Table

Lander (English) One who owns land
Land, Landers, Landis, Landiss, Landor, Lande, Landry, Landri

***Landon** (English) From the long hill
***Landyn**, Landan, Landen, Landin, Lando, Langdon, Langden, Langdan*

Lane (English) One who takes the narrow path
Laine, Lain, Laen, Laene, Layne, Layn

Langhorn (English) Of the long horn
Langhorne, Lanhorn, Lanhorne

Langilea (Polynesian) Having a booming voice, like thunder
Langileah, Langilia, Langiliah

^Langston (English) From the tall man's town
Langsten, Langstun, Langstown, Langstin, Langstyn, Langstan, Langton, Langtun

Langundo (Native American / Polynesian) A peaceful man / one who is graceful

Langworth (English) One who lives near the long paddock
Langworthe, Lanworth, Lanworthe

Lanier (French) One who works with wool

Lantos (Hungarian) One who plays the lute
Lantus

Lapidos (Hebrew) One who carries a torch
Lapydos, Lapidot, Lapydot, Lapidoth, Lapydoth, Lapidus, Lapydus

Laquinton (American) Form of Quinton, meaning "from the queen's town or settlement"
Laquinntan, Laquinnten, Laquinntin, Laquinnton, Laquintain, Laquintan, Laquintyn, Laquintynn

Lar (Anglo-Saxon) One who teaches others

Larson (Scandinavian) The son of Lawrence
Larsan, Larsen, Larsun, Larsin, Larsyn

Lasalle (French) From the hall
Lasall, Lasal, Lasale

Lashaun (American) An enthusiastic man
Lashawn, Lasean, Lashon, Lashond

Lassit (American) One who is open-minded
Lassyt, Lasset

Lathan (American) Form of Nathan, meaning "a gift from God"
Lathen, Lathun, Lathon, Lathin, Lathyn, Laian, Laten, Latun

Latimer (English) One who serves as an interpreter
Latymer, Latimor, Latymor, Latimore, Latymore, Lattemore, Lattimore

Latty (English) A generous man
Lattey, Latti, Lattie, Lattee, Lattea

Laurian (English) One who lives near the laurel trees
Laurien, Lauriano, Laurieno, Lawrian, Lawrien, Lawriano, Lawrieno

Lave (Italian) Of the burning rock
Lava

Lawford (English) From the ford near the hill
Lawforde, Lawferd, Lawferde, Lawfurd, Lawfurde

Lawler (Gaelic) A soft-spoken man; one who mutters
Lauler, Lawlor, Loller, Lawlar, Lollar, Loller, Laular, Laulor

Lawley (English) From the meadow near the hill
Lawly, Lawli, Lawlie, Lawleigh, Lawlee, Lawlea, Lawleah

Lawrence (Latin) Man from Laurentum; crowned with laurel
Larance, Laranz, Larenz, Larrance, Larrence, Larrens, Larrey, Larry

Laziz (Arabic) One who is pleasant
Lazeez, Lazeaz, Laziez, Lazeiz, Lazyz

Leaman (American) A powerful man
Leeman, Leamon, Leemon, Leamond, Leamand

Lear (Greek) Of the royalty
Leare, Leer, Leere

Leather (American) As tough as hide
Lether

Leavitt (English) A baker
Leavit, Leavytt, Leavyt, Leavett, Leavet

Leben (English) Filled with hope

Lech (Slavic) In mythology, the founder of the Polish people
Leche

Ledyard (Teutonic) The protector of the nation
Ledyarde, Ledyerd, Ledyerde

Lee (English) From the meadow
Leigh, Lea, Leah, Ley

Leeto (African) One who embarks on a journey
Leato, Leito, Lieto

Legend (American) One who is memorable
Legende, Legund, Legunde

^**Leighton** (English) From the town near the meadow
Leightun, Layton, Laytun, Leyton, Leytun

Lekhak (Hindi) An author
Lekhan

Leland (English) From the meadow land

Lema (African) One who is cultivated
Lemah, Lemma, Lemmah

Lemon (American) Resembling the fruit
Lemun, Lemin, Lemyn, Limon, Limun, Limin, Limyn, Limen

Len (Native American) One who plays the flute

Lencho (African) Resembling a lion
Lenchos, Lenchio, Lenchiyo, Lencheo, Lencheyo

^**Lennon** (English) Son of love
Lennan

Lennor (English) A courageous man

Lennox (Scottish) One who owns many elm trees
Lenox, Lenoxe, Lennix, Lenix, Lenixe

Lensar (English) One who stays with his parents
Lenser, Lensor, Lensur

Lenton (American) A pious man
Lentin, Lentyn, Lentun, Lentan, Lenten, Lent, Lente

*__Leo__ (Latin) Having the strength of a lion
Lio, Lyo, Leon

Leon (Greek) Form of Leo, meaning "resembling a lion"

Leonard (German) Having the strength of a lion
Len, Lenard, Lenn, Lennard, Lennart, Lennerd, Leonardo

Leor (Latin) One who listens well
Leore

Lerato (Latin) The song of my soul
Leratio, Lerateo

Leron (French / Arabic) The circle / my song
Lerun, Leran, Leren, Lerin, Leryn

Leroy (French) The king
Leroi, Leeroy, Leeroi, Learoy, Learoi

*__Levi__ (Hebrew) We are united as one; in the Bible, one of Jacob's sons
Levie, Levin, Levyn, Levy, Levey, Levee

Li (Chinese) Having great strength

*__Liam__ (Gaelic) Form of William, meaning "the determined protector"

Lian (Chinese) Of the willow

Liang (Chinese) A good man
Lyang

Lidmann (Anglo-Saxon) A man of the sea; a sailor
Lidman, Lydmann, Lydman

Lif (Scandinavian) An energetic man; lively

Lihau (Hawaiian) A spirited man

Like (Asian) A soft-spoken man
Lyke

Lilo (Hawaiian) One who is generous
Lylo, Leelo, Lealo, Leylo, Lielo, Leilo

***Lincoln** (English) From the village near the lake
Lincon, Lyncon, Linc, Lynk, Lync

Lindford (English) From the linden-tree ford
Linford, Lindforde, Linforde, Lyndford, Lynford, Lyndforde, Lynforde

Lindhurst (English) From the village by the linden trees
Lyndhurst, Lindenhurst, Lyndenhurst, Lindhirst, Lindherst, Lyndhirst, Lyndherst, Lindenhirst

Lindley (English) From the meadow of linden trees
Lindly, Lindleigh, Lindlea, Lindleah, Lindlee, Lindli

Lindman (English) One who lives near the linden trees
Lindmann, Lindmon

Line (English) From the bank

Lipût (Hungarian) A brave young man

Lisimba (African) One who has been attacked by a lion
Lisymba, Lysimba, Lysymba

Liu (Asian) One who is quiet; peaceful

Llewellyn (Welsh) Resembling a lion
Lewellen, Lewellyn, Llewellen, Llewelyn, Llwewellin, Llew, Llewe, Llyweilun

Lochan (Hindi / Irish) The eyes / one who is lively

***Logan** (Gaelic) From the little hollow
Logann, Logen, Login, Logyn, Logenn, Loginn, Logynn

Lolonyo (African) The beauty of love
Lolonyio, Lolonyeo, Lolonio, Lolonea

Loman (Gaelic) One who is small and bare
Lomann, Loeman, Loemann

Lombard (Latin) One who has a long beard
Lombardi, Lombardo, Lombardie, Lombardy, Lombardey, Lombardee

London (English) From the capital of England
Lundon, Londen, Lunden

Lonzo (Spanish) One who is ready for battle
Lonzio, Lonzeo

Lootah (Native American) Refers to the color red
Loota, Loutah, Louta, Lutah, Luta

Lorcan (Irish) The small fierce one
Lorcen, Lorcin, Lorcyn, Lorcon, Lorcun, Lorkan, Lorken, Lorkin

Lord (English) One who has authority and power
Lorde, Lordly, Lordley, Lordlee, Lordlea, Lordleigh, Lordli, Lordlie

Lore (Basque / English) Resembling a flower / form of Lawrence, meaning "man from Laurentum; crowned with laurel"
Lorea

Lorimer (Latin) One who makes harnesses
Lorrimer, Lorimar, Lorrimar, Lorymar, Lorrymar, Lorymer, Lorrymer

Louis (German) A famous warrior
Lew, Lewes, Lewis, Lodewick, Lodovico, Lou, Louie, Lucho, ***Luis***

Luba (Yugoslavian) One who loves and is loved
Lubah

*__Lucas__ (English) A man from Lucania
Lukas, Loucas, Loukas, Luckas, Louckas, Lucus, Lukus, Ghoukas

Lucian (Latin) Surrounded by light
Luciano, Lucianus, Lucien, Lucio, Lucjan, Lukianos, Lukyan, Luce

Lucky (English) A fortunate man
Luckey, Luckee, Luckea, Lucki, Luckie

Ludlow (English) The ruler of the hill
Ludlowe

*__Luis__ (Spanish) Form of Louis, meaning "a famous warrior"
Luiz

*__Luke__ (Greek) A man from Lucania
Luc, Luken

Lunt (Scandinavian) From the grove
Lunte

Luthando (Latin) One who is dearly loved

Luther (German) A soldier of the people
Louther, Luter, Luthero, Lutero, Louthero, Luthus, Luthas, Luthos

Lux (Latin) A man of the light
Luxe, Luxi, Luxie, Luxee, Luxea, Luxy, Luxey

Ly (Vietnamese) A reasonable man

Lynn (English) A man of the lake
Linn, Lyn, Lynne, Linne

M

Maahes (Egyptian) Resembling a lion

Mac (Gaelic) The son of Mac (Macarthur, Mackinley, etc.)
Mack, Mak, Macky, Macki, Mackie, Mackee, Mackea

Macadam (Gaelic) The son of Adam
Macadhamh, MacAdam, McAdam, MacAdhamh

Macallister (Gaelic) The son of Alistair
MacAlister, McAlister, McAllister, Macalister

Macardle (Gaelic) The son of great courage
MacArdle, McCardle, Macardell, MacArdell, McCardell

Macartan (Gaelic) The son of Artan
MacArtan, McArtan, Macarten, MacArten, McArten

Macarthur (Gaelic) The son of Arthur
MacArthur, McArthur, Macarther, MacArther, McArther

Macauslan (Gaelic) The son of Absalon
MacAuslan, McAuslan, Macauslen, MacAuslen, McAuslen

Maccoll (Gaelic) The son of Coll
McColl, Maccoll, MacColl

Maccrea (Gaelic) The son of grace
McCrea, Macrae, MacCrae, MacCray, MacCrea

Macedonio (Greek) A man from Macedonia
Macedoneo, Macedoniyo, Macedoneyo

Macgowan (Gaelic) The son of a blacksmith
MacGowan, Magowan, McGowan, McGowen, McGown, MacCowan, MacCowen

Machau (Hebrew) A gift from God

Machenry (Gaelic) The son of Henry
MacHenry, McHenry

Machk (Native American) Resembling a bear

Macintosh (Gaelic) The son of the thane
MacIntosh, McIntosh, Macintoshe, MacIntoshe, McIntoshe, Mackintosh, MacKintosh

Mackay (Gaelic) The son of fire
MacKay, McKay, Mackaye, MacKaye, McKaye

Mackinley (Gaelic) The son of the white warrior
MacKinley, McKinley, MacKinlay, McKinlay, Mackinlay, Mackinlie, MacKinlie

Macklin (Gaelic) The son of Flann
Macklinn, Macklyn, Macklynn, Macklen, Macklenn

Maclaine (Gaelic) The son of John's servant
MacLaine, Maclain, MacLain, Maclayn, McLaine, McLain, Maclane, MacLane

Macleod (Gaelic) The son of the ugly one
MacLeod, McLeod, McCloud, MacCloud

Macmurray (Gaelic) The son of Murray
MacMurray, McMurray, Macmurra, MacMurra

Macnab (Gaelic) The son of the abbot
MacNab, McNab

Macon (English / French) To make / from the city in France
Macun, Makon, Makun, Maken, Mackon, Mackun

Macqueen (Gaelic) The son of the good man
MacQueen, McQueen

Macrae (Gaelic) The son of Ray
MacRae, McRae, Macray, MacRay, McRay, Macraye, MacRaye, McRaye

Madden (Pakistani) One who is organized; a planner
Maddon, Maddan, Maddin, Maddyn, Maddun, Maden, Madon, Madun

^**Maddox** (Welsh) The son of the benefactor
Madox, Madocks, Maddocks, Maddux

Madhur (Indian) A sweet man

Magee (Gaelic) The son of Hugh
MacGee, McGee, MacGhee, Maghee

Maguire (Gaelic) The son of the beige one
Magwire, MacGuire, McGuire, MacGwire, McGwire

Magus (Latin) A sorcerer
Magis, Magys, Magos, Magas, Mages

Mahan (American) A cowboy
Mahahn, Mahen, Mayhan, Maihan, Maehan, Mayhen, Maihen, Maehen

Mahant (Indian) Having a great soul
Mahante

Mahatma (Hindi) Of great spiritual development

Mahfouz (Arabic) One who is protected
Mafouz, Mahfooz, Mafooz, Mahfuz, Mafuz

Mahkah (Native American) Of the earth
Mahka, Makah, Maka

Mahmud (Arabic) One who is praiseworthy
Mahmood, Mahmoud, Mehmood, Mehmud, Mehmoud

Mailhairer (French) An ill-fated man

Maimon (Arabic) One who is dependable; having good fortune
Maymon, Maemon, Maimun, Maymun, Maemun, Mamon, Mamun

Maitland (English) From the meadow land
Maytland, Maetland, Maitlande, Maytlande, Maetlande

Majdy (Arabic) A glorious man
Majdey, Majdi, Majdie, Majdee, Majdea

Makaio (Hawaiian) A gift from God

Makena (Hawaiian) Man of abundance
Makenah

Makin (Arabic) Having great strength
Makeen, Makean, Makein, Makien, Makyn

Makis (Hebrew) A gift from God
Madys, Makiss, Makyss, Makisse, Madysse

Malachi (Hebrew) A messenger of God
Malachie, Malachy, Malaki, Malakia, Malakie, Malaquias, Malechy, Maleki

Malawa (African) A flourishing man

Malcolm (Gaelic) Follower of St. Columbus
Malcom, Malcolum, Malkolm, Malkom, Malkolum

Mali (Indian) A ruler; the firstborn son
Malie, Maly, Maley, Malee, Malea

Mamoru (Japanese) Of the earth
Mamorou, Mamorue, Mamorew, Mamoroo

Manchester (English) From the city in England
Manchestar, Manchestor, Manchestir, Manchestyr, Manchestur

Mandan (Native American) A tribal name
Manden, Mandon, Mandun, Mandin, Mandyn

Mandhatri (Indian) A prince; born to royalty
Mandhatrie, Mandhatry, Mandhatrey, Mandhatree, Mandhatrea

Mani (African) From the mountain
Manie, Many, Maney, Manee, Manea

Manjit (Indian) A conqueror of the mind; having great knowledge
Manjeet, Manjeat, Manjeit, Manjiet, Manjyt

Manley (English) From the man's meadow; from the hero's meadow
Manly, Manli, Manlie, Manlea, Manleah, Manlee, Manleigh

Manmohan (Indian) A handsome and pleasing man
Manmohen, Manmohin, Manmohyn

Mannheim (German) From the hamlet in the swamp
Manheim

Mano (Hawaiian) Resembling a shark
Manoe, Manow, Manowe

Manohar (Indian) A delightful and captivating man
Manoharr, Manohare

Mansel (English) From the clergyman's house
Mansle, Mansell, Mansele, Manselle, Manshel, Manshele, Manshell, Manshelle

Mansfield (English) From the field near the small river
Mansfeld, Maunfield, Maunfeld

Manton (English) From the man's town; from the hero's town
Mantun, Manten, Mannton, Manntun, Mannten

Manu (African) The second-born child
Manue, Manou, Manoo

Manuel (Spanish) Form of Emmanuel, meaning "God is with us"
Manuelo, Manuello, Manolito, Manolo, Manollo, Manny, Manni

Manya (Indian) A respected man
Manyah

Manzo (Japanese) The third son with ten-thousand-fold strength

Mar (Spanish) Of the sea
Marr, Mare, Marre

Marcel (French) The little warrior
Marceau, Marcelin, Marcellin, Marcellino, Marcell, Marcello, Marcellus, Marcelo

Marcus (Latin) Form of Mark, meaning "dedicated to Mars, the god of war"
Markus, Marcas, Marco, Markos

Mariatu (African) One who is pure; chaste
Mariatue, Mariatou, Mariatoo

Marid (Arabic) A rebellious man
Maryd

Mario (Latin) A manly man
Marius, Marios, Mariano, Marion, Mariun, Mareon

Mark (Latin) Dedicated to Mars, the god of war
Marc, Markey, Marky, Marki, Markie, Markee, Markea, Markov

Marmion (French) Our little one
Marmyon, Marmeon

Marsh (English) From the marshland
Marshe

Marshall (French / English) A caretaker of horses / a steward
Marchall, Marischal, Marischall, Marschal, Marshal, Marshell, Marshel, Marschall

Marston (English) From the town near the marsh
Marstun, Marsten, Marstin, Marstyn, Marstan

Martin (Latin) Dedicated to Mars, the god of war
Martyn, Mart, Martel, Martell, Marten, Martenn, Marti, Martie

Marvin (Welsh) A friend of the sea
Marvinn, Marvinne, Marven, Marvenn, Marvenne, Marvyn, Marvynn, Marvynne, Mervin

Maryland (English) Honoring Queen Mary; from the state of Maryland
Mariland, Maralynd, Marylind, Marilind

Masanao (Japanese) A good man

Masao (Japanese) A righteous man

^*__Mason__ (English) One who works with stone
Masun, Masen, Masan, Masin, Masyn, Masson, Massun, Massen, ***Maison***

Masselin (French) A young Thomas
Masselyn, Masselen, Masselan, Masselon, Masselun, Maselin, Maselyn, Maselon

Masura (Japanese) A good destiny
Masoura

Mataniah (Hebrew) A gift from God
Matania, Matanya, Matanyahu, Mattania, Mattaniah, Matanyah

Matata (African) One who causes trouble

Matin (Arabic) Having great strength
Maten, Matan, Matyn, Maton, Matun

Matisse (French) One who is gifted
Matiss, Matysse, Matyss, Matise, Matyse

Matlock (American) A rancher
Matlok, Matloc

^**Matteo** (Italian) Form of Matthew, meaning "a gift from God"
Mateo

*__Matthew__ (Hebrew) A gift from God
Matt, Mathew, Matvey, Mateas, Mattix, Madteos, Matthias, Mat, Mateo, Matteo, Mateus

Matunde (African) One who is fruitful
Matundi, Matundie

Matvey (Russian) Form of Matthew, meaning "a gift from God"
Matvy, Matvee, Matvea, Matvi, Matvie, Motka, Matviyko

Matwau (Native American) The enemy

Maurice (Latin) A dark-skinned man; Moorish
Maurell, Maureo, Mauricio, Maurids, Maurie, Maurin, Maurio, Maurise, Baurice

^**Maverick** (English) An independent man; a non-conformist
Maveric, Maverik, Mavrick, Mavric, Mavrik

*****Max** (English) Form of Maxwell, meaning from Mack's spring

^**Maximilian** (Latin) The greatest
Max, Macks, Maxi, Maxie, Maxy, Maxey, Maxee, Maxea, ***Maximiliano***

Maxfield (English) From Mack's field
Mackfield, Maxfeld, Macksfeld

Maxwell (English) From Mack's spring
Maxwelle, Mackswell, Maxwel, Mackswel, Mackwelle, Maxwill, Maxwille, Mackswill

Mayer (Latin / German / Hebrew) A large man / a farmer / one who is shining bright
Maier, Mayar, Mayor, Mayir, Mayur, Meyer, Meir, Myer

Mayfield (English) From the strong one's field
Mayfeld, Maifield, Maifeld, Maefield, Maefeld

Mayo (Gaelic) From the yew tree plain
Mayoe, Maiyo, Maeyo, Maiyoe, Maeyoe, Mayoh, Maioh

Mccoy (Gaelic) The son of Coy
McCoy

McKenna (Gaelic) The son of Kenna; to ascend
McKennon, McKennun, McKennen, McKennan

Mckile (Gaelic) The son of Kyle
McKile, Mckyle, McKyle, Mackile, Mackyle, MacKile, MacKyle

Medad (Hebrew) A beloved friend
Meydad

Medgar (German) Having great strength
Medgarr, Medgare, Medgard, Medárd

Medwin (German) A strong friend
Medwine, Medwinn, Medwinne, Medwen, Medwenn, Medwenne, Medwyn, Medwynn

Meged (Hebrew) One who has been blessed with goodness

Mehdi (Arabian) One who is guided
Mehdie, Mehdy, Mehdey, Mehdee, Mehdea

Mehetabel (Hebrew) One who is favored by God
Mehetabell, Mehitabel, Mehitabell, Mehytabel, Mehytabell

Meilyr (Welsh) A regal ruler

Meinrad (German) A strong counselor
Meinred, Meinrod, Meinrud, Meinrid, Meinryd

Meka (Hawaiian) Of the eyes
Mekah

Melancton (Greek) Resembling a black flower
Melankton, Melanctun, Melanktun, Melancten, Melankten, Melanchton, Melanchten, Melanchthon

Mele (Hawaiian) One who is happy

Melesio (Spanish) An attentive man; one who is careful
Melacio, Melasio, Melecio, Melicio, Meliseo, Milesio

Meletius (Greek) A cautious man
Meletios, Meletious, Meletus, Meletos

Meli (Native American) One who is bitter
Melie, Mely, Meley, Melee, Melea, Meleigh

Melker (Swedish) A king
Melkar, Melkor, Melkur, Melkir, Melkyr

Melton (English) From the mill town
Meltun, Meltin, Meltyn, Melten, Meltan

Melville (English) From the mill town
Melvill, Melvil, Melvile, Melvylle, Melvyll, Melvyl, Melvyle

Melvin (English) A friend who offers counsel
Melvinn, Melvinne, Melven, Melvenn, Melvenne, Melvyn, Melvynn, Melvynne, Belvin

Memphis (American) From the city in Tennessee
Memfis, Memphys, Memfys, Memphus, Memfus

Menachem (Hebrew) One who provides comfort
Menaheim, Menahem, Menachim, Menachym, Menahim, Menahym, Machum, Machem

Menassah (Hebrew) A forgetful man
Menassa, Menass, Menas, Menasse, Menasseh

Menefer (Egyptian) Of the beautiful city
Menefar, Menefir, Menefyr, Menefor, Menefur

Menelik (African) The son of a wise man
Menelick, Menelic, Menelyk, Menelyck, Menelyc

Merewood (English) From the forest with the lake
Merwood, Merewode, Merwode

Merlin (Welsh) Of the sea fortress; in Arthurian legend, the wizard and mentor of King Arthur
Merlyn, Merlan, Merlon, Merlun, Merlen, Merlinn, Merlynn, Merlonn

Merrill (English) Of the shining sea
Meril, Merill, Merrel, Merrell, Merril, Meryl, Merryll, Meryll

Merton (English) From the town near the lake
Mertun, Mertan, Merten, Mertin, Mertyn, Murton, Murtun, Murten

Mervin (Welsh) Form of Marvin, meaning "a friend of the sea"
Mervinn, Mervinne, Mervyn, Mervynn, Mervynne, Merven, Mervenn, Mervenne

Meshach (Hebrew) An enduring man
Meshack, Meshac, Meshak, Meeshach, Meeshack, Meeshak, Meeshac

Mhina (African) One who is delightful
Mhinah, Mheena, Mheenah, Mheina, Mheinah, Mhienah, Mhienah, Mhyna

Micah (Hebrew) Form of Michael, meaning "who is like God?"
Mica, Mycah

***Michael** (Hebrew) Who is like God?
Makai, Micael, Mical, Micha, Michaelangelo, Michail, Michal, Micheal, ***Miguel****, Mick*

Mick (English) Form of Michael, meaning "who is like God?"
Micke, Mickey, Micky, Micki, Mickie, Mickee, Mickea, Mickel

Mieko (Japanese) A bright man

Miguel (Portuguese / Spanish) Form of Michael, meaning "who is like God?"
Migel, Myguel

Milan (Latin) An eager and hardworking man
Mylan

Miles (German / Latin) One who is merciful / a soldier
Myles, Miley, Mily, Mili, Milie, Milee

Milford (English) From the mill's ford
Millford, Milfurd, Millfurd, Milferd, Millferd, Milforde, Millforde, Milfurde

Miller (English) One who works at the mill
Millar, Millor, Millur, Millir, Millyr, Myller, Millen, Millan

^**Milo** (German) Form of Miles, meaning "one who is merciful"
Mylo

Milson (English) The son of Miles
Milsun, Milsen, Milsin, Milsyn, Milsan

Mimir (Norse) In mythology, a giant who guarded the well of wisdom
Mymir, Mimeer, Mimyr, Mymeer, Mymyr, Meemir, Meemeer, Meemyr

Miner (Latin / English) One who works in the mines / a youth
Minor, Minar, Minur, Minir, Minyr

Mingan (Native American) Resembling a gray wolf
Mingen, Mingin, Mingon, Mingun, Mingyn

Minh (Vietnamese) A clever man

Minster (English) Of the church
Mynster, Minstar, Mynstar, Minstor, Mynstor, Minstur, Mynstur, Minstir

Miracle (American) An act of God's hand
Mirakle, Mirakel, Myracle, Myrakle

Mirage (French) An illusion
Myrage

Mirumbi (African) Born during a period of rain
Mirumbie, Mirumby, Mirumbey, Mirumbee, Mirumbea

Missouri (Native American) From the town of large canoes; from the state of Missouri
Missourie, Mizouri, Mizourie, Missoury, Mizoury, Missuri, Mizuri, Mizury

Mitchell (English) Form of Michael, meaning "who is like God?"
Mitch, Mitchel, Mytch, Mitchum, Mytchill, Mitcham

Mitsu (Japanese) Of the light
Mytsu, Mitsue, Mytsue

Mochni (Native American) Resembling a talking bird
Mochnie, Mochny, Mochney, Mochnee, Mochnea

Modesty (Latin) One who is without conceit
Modesti, Modestie, Modestee, Modestus, Modestey, Modesto, Modestio, Modestine

Mogens (Dutch) A powerful man
Mogen, Mogins, Mogin, Mogyns, Mogyn, Mogan, Mogans

Mohajit (Indian) A charming man
Mohajeet, Mohajeat, Mohajeit, Mohajiet, Mohajyt

Mohammed (Arabic) One who is greatly praised; the name of the prophet and founder of Islam
Mahomet, Mohamad, Mohamed, Mohamet, Mohammad, Muhammad, Muhammed, Mehmet

Mohave (Native American) A tribal name
Mohav, Mojave

Mojag (Native American) One who is never quiet

Molan (Irish) The servant of the storm
Molen

Momo (American) A warring man

Mona (African) A jealous man
Monah

Mongo (African) A well-known man
Mongoe, Mongow, Mongowe

Mongwau (Native American) Resembling an owl

Monroe (Gaelic) From the mouth of the river Roe
Monro, Monrow, Monrowe, Munro, Munroe, Munrow, Munrowe

Montenegro (Spanish) From the black mountain

Montgomery (French) From Gomeric's mountain
Monty, Montgomerey, Montgomeri, Montgomerie, Montgomeree, Montgomerea

Monty (English) Form of Montgomery, meaning "from Gomeric's mountain"
Montey, Monti, Montie, Montee, Montea, Montes, Montez

Moon (American) Born beneath the moon; a dreamer

Mooney (Irish) A wealthy man
Moony, Mooni, Moonie, Maonaigh, Moonee, Moonea, Moone

Moose (American) Resembling the animal; a big, strong man
Moos, Mooze, Mooz

Moran (Irish) A great man
Morane, Morain, Moraine, Morayn, Morayne, Moraen, Moraene

Morathi (African) A wise man
Morathie, Morathy, Morathey, Morathee, Morathea

Moreland (English) From the moors
Moorland, Morland

Morley (English) From the meadow on the moor
Morly, Morleigh, Morlee, Morlea, Morleah, Morli, Morlie, Moorley

Morpheus (Greek) In mythology, the god of dreams
Morfeus, Morphius, Mofius

Mortimer (French) Of the still water; of the dead sea
Mortymer, Morty, Mortey, Morti, Mortie, Mortee, Mortea, Mort, Morte

Moses (Hebrew) A savior; in the Bible, the leader of the Israelites; drawn from the water
Mioshe, Mioshye, Mohsen, Moke, Moise, Moises, Mose, Moshe

Mostyn (Welsh) From the mossy settlement
Mostin, Mosten, Moston, Mostun, Mostan

Moswen (African) A light-skinned man
Moswenn, Moswenne, Moswin, Moswinn, Moswinne, Moswyn, Moswynn, Moswynne

Moubarak (Arabian) One who is blessed
Mubarak, Moobarak

Mounafes (Arabic) A rival

Muhannad (Arabic) One who wields a sword
Muhanned, Muhanad, Muhaned, Muhunnad, Muhunad, Muhanned, Muhaned

Mukhtar (Arabic) The chosen one
Muktar

Mukisa (Ugandan) Having good fortune
Mukysa

Mulcahy (Irish) A war chief
Mulcahey, Mulcahi, Mulcahie, Mulcahee, Mulcahea

Mundhir (Arabic) One who cautions others
Mundheer, Mundhear, Mundheir, Mundhier, Mundhyr

Murdock (Scottish) From the sea
Murdok, Murdoc, Murdo, Murdoch, Murtagh, Murtaugh, Murtogh, Murtough

Murfain (American) Having a warrior spirit
Murfaine, Murfayn, Murfayne, Murfaen, Murfaene, Murfane

Muriel (Gaelic) Of the shining sea
Muryel, Muriell, Muryell, Murial, Muriall, Muryal, Muryall, Murell

Murphy (Gaelic) A warrior of the sea
Murphey, Murphee, Murphea, Murphi, Murphie, Murfey, Murfy, Murfee

Murray (Gaelic) The lord of the sea
Murrey, Murry, Murri, Murrie, Murree, Murrea, Murry

Murron (Celtic) A bitter man
Murrun, Murren, Murran, Murrin, Murryn

Murtadi (Arabic) One who is content
Murtadie, Murtady, Murtadey, Murtadee, Murtadea

Musad (Arabic) One who is lucky
Musaad, Mus'ad

Mushin (Arabic) A charitable man
Musheen, Mushean, Mushein, Mushien, Mushyn

Muskan (Arabic) One who smiles often
Musken, Muskon, Muskun, Muskin, Muskyn

Muslim (Arabic) An adherent of Islam
Muslym, Muslem, Moslem, Moslim, Moslym

Mustapha (Arabic) The chosen one
Mustafa, Mostapha, Mostafa, Moustapha, Moustafa

Muti (Arabic) One who is obedient
Mutie, Muty, Mutey, Mutee, Mutea, Muta

Myron (Greek) Refers to myrrh, a fragrant oil
Myrun, Myran, Myren, Myrin, Myryn, Miron, Mirun, Miran

Mystique (French) A man with an air of mystery
Mystic, Mistique, Mysteek, Misteek, Mystiek, Mistiek, Mysteeque, Misteeque

N

Nabendu (Indian) Born beneath the new moon
Nabendue, Nabendoo, Nabendou

Nabhi (Indian) The best
Nabhie, Nabhy, Nabhey, Nabhee, Nabhea

Nabhomani (Indian) Of the sun
Nabhomanie, Nabhomany, Nabhomaney, Nabhomanee, Nabhomanea

Nabil (Arabic) A highborn man
Nabeel, Nabeal, Nabeil, Nabiel, Nabyl

Nabu (Babylonian) In mythology, the god of writing and wisdom
Nabue, Naboo, Nabo, Nebo, Nebu, Nebue, Neboo

Nachshon (Hebrew) An adventurous man; one who is daring
Nachson

Nadav (Hebrew) A generous man
Nadaav

Nadif (African) One who is born between seasons
Nadeef, Nadief, Nadeif, Nadyf, Nadeaf

Nadim (Arabic) A beloved friend
Nadeem, Nadeam, Nadiem, Nadeim, Nadym

Naftali (Hebrew) A struggling man; in the Bible, one of Jacob's sons
Naphtali, Naphthali, Neftali, Nefthali, Nephtali, Nephthali, Naftalie, Naphtalie

Nagel (German) One who makes nails
Nagle, Nagler, Naegel, Nageler, Nagelle, Nagele, Nagell

Nahir (Hebrew) A clear-headed and bright man
Naheer, Nahear, Naheir, Nahier, Nahyr, Naher

Nahum (Hebrew) A compassionate man
Nahom, Nahoum, Nahoom, Nahuem

Naji (Arabic) One who is safe
Najea, Naje, Najee, Najie, Najy, Najey, Nanji, Nanjie

Najib (Arabic) Of noble descent; a highborn man
Najeeb, Najeab, Najeib, Najieb, Najyb, Nageeb, Nageab, Nagyb

Nally (Irish) A poor man
Nalley, Nalli, Nallie, Nallee, Nallea, Nalleigh

Namir (Israeli) Resembling a leopard
Nameer, Namear, Namier, Nameir, Namyr

Nandan (Indian) One who is pleasing
Nanden, Nandin, Nandyn, Nandon, Nandun

Naotau (Indian) Our new son
Naotou

Napier (French / English) A mover / one who takes care of the royal linens
Neper

Napoleon (Italian / German) A man from Naples / son of the mists
Napolean, Napolion, Napoleone, Napoleane, Napolione

Narcissus (Greek) Resembling a daffodil; self-love; in mythology, a youth who fell in love with his reflection
Narciso, Narcisse, Narkissos, Narses, Narcisus, Narcis, Narciss

Naresh (Indian) A king
Nareshe, Natesh, Nateshe

Nasih (Arabic) One who advises others
Nasyh

Natal (Spanish) Born at Christmastime
Natale, Natalino, Natalio, Natall, Natalle, Nataleo, Natica

*__Nathan__ (Hebrew) Form of Nathaniel, meaning "a gift from God"
Nat, Natan, Nate, Nathen, Nathon, Nathin, Nathyn, Nathun, Lathan

*__Nathaniel__ (Hebrew) A gift from God
Nathan, Natanael, Nataniel, Nathanael, Nathaneal, Nathanial, Nathanyal, Nathanyel, Nethanel

Nature (American) An outdoorsy man
Natural

Navarro (Spanish) From the plains
Navaro, Navarrio, Navario, Navarre, Navare, Nabaro, Nabarro

Naveed (Persian) Our best wishes
Navead, Navid, Navied, Naveid, Navyd

Nazim (Arabian) Of a soft breeze
Nazeem, Nazeam, Naziem, Nazeim, Nazym

Nebraska (Native American) From the flat water land; from the state of Nebraska

Neckarios (Greek) Of the nectar; one who is immortal
Nectaire, Nectarios, Nectarius, Nektario, Nektarius, Nektarios, Nektaire

Neelotpal (Indian) Resembling the blue lotus
Nealotpal, Nielotpal, Neilotpal, Nilothpal, Neelothpal

Negm (Arabian) Resembling a star

Nehal (Indian) Born during a period of rain
Nehall, Nehale, Nehalle

Nehemiah (Hebrew) God provides comfort
Nehemia, Nechemia, Nechemiah, Nehemya, Nehemyah, Nechemya, Nechemyah

Neil (Gaelic) The champion
Neal, Neale, Neall, Nealle, Nealon, Neel, Neilan, Neile

Neirin (Irish) Surrounded by light
Neiryn, Neiren, Neerin, Neeryn, Neeren

Nelek (Polish) Resembling a horn
Nelec, Neleck

Nelson (English) The son of Neil; the son of a champion
Nealson, Neilson, Neillson, Nelsen, Nilson, Nilsson, Nelli, Nellie

Neptune (Latin) In mythology, god of the sea
Neptun, Neptoon, Neptoone, Neptoun, Neptoune

Neroli (Italian) Resembling an orange blossom
Nerolie, Neroly, Neroley, Neroleigh, Nerolea, Nerolee

Nevan (Irish) The little saint
Naomhan

Neville (French) From the new village
Nev, Nevil, Nevile, Nevill, Nevylle, Nevyl, Nevyle, Nevyll

Newcomb (English) From the new valley
Newcom, Newcome, Newcombe, Neucomb, Neucombe, Neucom, Neucome

Newlin (Welsh) From the new pond
Newlinn, Newlyn, Newlynn, Neulin, Neulinn, Neulyn, Neulynn

Newman (English) A new-comer
Newmann, Neuman, Neumann

Nhat (Vietnamese) Having a long life
Nhatt, Nhate, Nhatte

Niaz (Persian) A gift
Nyaz

Nibaw (Native American) One who stands tall
Nybaw, Nibau, Nybau

^***Nicholas** (Greek) Of the victorious people
Nick, Nicanor, Niccolo, Nichol, Nicholai, Nicholaus, Nikolai, Nicholl, Nichols, Colin, Nicolas, ***Nico***

Nick (English) Form of Nicholas, meaning "of the victorious people"
Nik, Nicki, Nickie, Nickey, Nicky, Nickee, Nickea, Niki

Nickler (American) One who is swift
Nikler, Nicler, Nyckler, Nykler, Nycler

Nicomedes (Greek) One who thinks of victory
Nikomedes, Nicomedo, Nikomedo

Nihal (Indian) One who is content
Neehal, Neihal, Niehal, Neahal, Neyhal, Nyhal

Nihar (Indian) Covered with the morning's dew
Neehar, Niehar, Neihar, Neahar, Nyhar

Nikan (Persian) One who brings good things
Niken, Nikin, Nikyn, Nikon, Nikun

Nikshep (Indian) One who is treasured
Nykshep

Nikunja (Indian) From the grove of trees

Nino (Italian / Spanish) God is gracious / a young boy
Ninoshka

Nirad (Indian) Of the clouds
Nyrad

Niran (Thai) The eternal one
Nyran, Niren, Nirin, Niryn, Niron, Nirun, Nyren, Nyrin

Nirav (Indian) One who is quiet
Nyrav

Nirbheet (Indian) A fearless man
Nirbhit, Nirbhyt, Nirbhay, Nirbhaye, Nirbhai, Nirbhae

Niremaan (Arabic) One who shines as brightly as fire
Nyremaan, Nireman, Nyreman

Nishan (Armenian) A sign or symbol

Nishok (Indian) Filled with happiness
Nyshok, Nishock, Nyshock

Nissan (Hebrew) A miracle child
Nisan

Niyol (Native American) Of the wind

Njord (Scandinavian) A man from the north
Njorde, Njorth, Njorthe

***Noah** (Hebrew) A peaceful wanderer
Noa

Nodin (Native American) Of the wind
Nodyn, Noden, Nodan, Nodon, Nodun

***Nolan** (Gaelic) A famous and noble man; a champion of the people
Nolen, Nolin, Nolon, Nolun, Nolyn, Noland, Nolande

North (English) A man from the north
Northe

Northcliff (English) From the northern cliff
Northcliffe, Northclyf, Northclyff, Northclyffe

Norval (Scottish) From the northern valley
Norvall, Norvale, Norvail, Norvaile, Norvayl, Norvayle, Norvael, Norvaele

Norward (English) A guardian of the north
Norwarde, Norwerd, Norwerde, Norwurd, Norwurde

Noshi (Native American) A fatherly man
Noshie, Noshy, Noshey, Noshee, Noshea, Nosh, Noshe

Notaku (Native American) Resembling a growling bear
Notakou, Notakue, Notakoo

Nuhad (Arabic) A brave young man
Nuehad, Nouhad, Neuhad

Nukpana (Native American) An evil man
Nukpanah, Nukpanna, Nukpannah, Nuckpana, Nucpana

Nulte (Irish) A man from Ulster
Nulti, Nultie, Nulty, Nultey, Nultee, Nultea

Nuncio (Spanish) A messenger
Nunzio

Nuriel (Hebrew) God's light
Nuriell, Nuriele, Nurielle, Nuryel, Nuryell, Nuryele, Nuryelle, Nooriel

Nuru (African) My light
Nurue, Nuroo, Nurou, Nourou, Nooroo

Nyack (African) One who is persistent
Niack, Nyak, Niak, Nyac, Niac

Nye (English) One who lives on the island
Nyle, Nie, Nile

O

Obedience (American) A well-behaved man
Obediance, Obedyence, Obedeynce

Oberon (German) A royal bear; having the heart of a bear
Oberron

Obert (German) A wealthy and bright man
Oberte, Oberth, Oberthe, Odbart, Odbarte, Odbarth, Odbarthe, Odhert

Ochi (African) Filled with laughter
Ochie, Ochee, Ochea, Ochy, Ochey

Odam (English) A son-in-law
Odom, Odem, Odum

Ode (Egyptian / Greek) Traveler of the road / a lyric poem

Oded (Hebrew) One who is supportive and encouraging

Oder (English) From the river
Odar, Odir, Odyr, Odur

Odin (Norse) In mythology, the supreme deity
Odyn, Odon, Oden, Odun

Odinan (Hungarian) One who is wealthy and powerful
Odynan, Odinann, Odynann

Odion (African) The first-born of twins
Odiyon, Odiun, Odiyun

Odissan (African) A wanderer; traveler
Odyssan, Odisan, Odysan, Odissann, Odyssann, Odisann, Odysann

Ofir (Hebrew) The golden son
Ofeer, Ofear, Ofyr, Ofier, Ofeir, Ofer

Ogaleesha (Native American) A man wearing a red shirt
Ogaleasha, Ogaleisha, Ogaleysha, Ogalesha, Ogaliesha, Ogalisha

Oghe (Irish) One who rides horses
Oghi, Oghie, Oghee, Oghea, Oghy, Oghey

Oguz (Hungarian) An arrow
Oguze, Oguzz, Oguzze

Ohanko (Native American) A reckless man
Ohankio, Ohankiyo

Ojaswit (Indian) A powerful and radiant man
Ojaswyt, Ojaswin, Ojaswen, Ojaswyn, Ojas

Okal (African) To cross
Okall

Okan (Turkish) Resembling a horse
Oken, Okin, Okyn

Okapi (African) Resembling an animal with a long neck
Okapie, Okapy, Okapey, Okapee, Okapea, Okape

Okechuku (African) Blessed by God

Oki (Japanese) From the center of the ocean
Okie, Oky, Okey, Okee, Okea

Oklahoma (Native American) Of the red people; from the state of Oklahoma

Oktawian (African) The eighth-born child
Oktawyan, Oktawean, Octawian, Octawyan, Octawean

Olaf (Scandinavian) The remaining of the ancestors
Olay, Ole, Olef, Olev, Oluf, Uolevi

Olafemi (African) A lucky young man
Olafemie, Olafemy, Olafemey, Olafemee, Olafemea

Oleg (Russian) One who is holy
Olezka

***Oliver** (Latin) From the olive tree
Oliviero, Olivero, Olivier, Oliviero, Olivio, Ollie

Olney (English) From the loner's field
Olny, Olnee, Olnea, Olni, Olnie, Ollaneg, Olaneg

Olujimi (African) One who is close to God
Olujimie, Olujimy, Olujimey, Olujimee, Olujimea

Olumide (African) God has arrived
Olumidi, Olumidie, Olumidy, Olumidey, Olumidee, Olumidea, Olumyde, Olumydi

Omar (Arabic) A flourishing man; one who is well-spoken
Omarr, Omer

Omeet (Hebrew) My light
Omeete, Omeit, Omeite, Omeyt, Omeyte, Omit, Omeat, Omeate

Omega (Greek) The last great one; the last letter of the Greek alphabet
Omegah

Onaona (Hawaiian) Having a pleasant scent

Ond (Hungarian) The tenth-born child
Onde

Ondrej (Czech) A manly man
Ondrejek, Ondrejec, Ondrousek, Ondravsek

Onkar (Indian) The purest one
Onckar, Oncar, Onkarr, Onckarr, Oncarr

Onofrio (Italian) A defender of peace
Onofre, Onofrius, Onophrio, Onophre, Onfrio, Onfroi

Onslow (Arabic) From the hill of the enthusiast
Onslowe, Ounslow, Ounslowe

Onyebuchi (African) God is in everything
Onyebuchie, Onyebuchy, Onyebuchey, Onyebuchee, Onyebuchea

Oqwapi (Native American) Resembling a red cloud
Oqwapie, Oqwapy, Oqwapey, Oqwapee, Oqwapea

Oram (English) From the enclosure near the riverbank
Oramm, Oraham, Orahamm, Orham, Orhamm

Ordell (Latin) Of the beginning
Ordel, Ordele, Ordelle, Orde

Ordway (Anglo-Saxon) A fighter armed with a spear
Ordwaye, Ordwai, Ordwae

Oren (Hebrew / Gaelic) From the pine tree / a pale-skinned man
Orenthiel, Orenthiell, Orenthiele, Orenthielle, Orenthiem, Orenthium, Orin

Orion (Greek) A great hunter

Orleans (Latin) The golden child
Orlean, Orleane, Orleens, Orleen, Orleene, Orlins, Olryns, Orlin

Orly (Hebrew) Surrounded by light
Orley, Orli, Orlie, Orlee, Orleigh, Orlea

Ormod (Anglo-Saxon) A sorrowful man

Ormond (English) One who defends with a spear / from the mountain of bears
Ormonde, Ormund, Ormunde, Ormemund, Ormemond, Ordmund, Ordmunde, Ordmond

Ornice (Irish / Hebrew) A pale-skinned man / from the cedar tree
Ornyce, Ornise, Orynse, Orneice, Orneise, Orniece, Orniese, Orneece

Orris (Latin) One who is inventive
Orriss, Orrisse, Orrys, Orryss, Orrysse

Orson (Latin) Resembling a bear; raised by a bear
Orsen, Orsin, Orsini, Orsino, Orsis, Orsonio, Orsinie, Orsiny

Orth (English) An honest man
Orthe

Orton (English) From the settlement by the shore
Ortun, Oraton, Oratun

Orville (French) From the gold town
Orvell, Orvelle, Orvil, Orvill, Orvele, Orvyll, Orvylle, Orvyl

Orwel (Welsh) Of the horizon
Orwell, Orwele, Orwelle

Os (English) The divine

Osborn (Norse) A bear of God
Osborne, Osbourn, Osbourne, Osburn, Osburne

Oscar (English / Gaelic) A spear of the gods / a friend of deer
Oskar, Osker, Oscer, Osckar, Oscker, Oszkar, Oszcar

Osher (Hebrew) A man of good fortune

Osias (Greek) Salvation
Osyas

Osileani (Polynesian) One who talks a lot
Osileanie, Osileany, Osileaney, Osileanee, Osileanea

Oswald (English) The power of God
Oswalde, Osvald, Osvaldo, Oswaldo, Oswell, Osvalde, Oswallt, Osweald

Oswin (English) A friend of God
Oswinn, Oswinne, Oswen, Oswenn, Oswenne, Oswyn, Oswynn, Oswynne

Othniel (Hebrew) God's lion
Othniell, Othnielle, Othniele, Othnyel, Othnyell, Othnyele, Othnyelle

Otmar (Teutonic) A famous warrior
Otmarr, Othmar, Othmarr, Otomar, Ottomar

Otoahhastis (Native American) Resembling a tall bull

Ottokar (German) A spirited warrior
Otokar, Otokarr, Ottokarr, Ottokars, Otokars, Ottocar, Otocar, Ottocars

Ouray (Native American) The arrow
Ouraye, Ourae, Ourai

Ourson (French) Resembling a little bear
Oursun, Oursoun, Oursen, Oursan, Oursin, Oursyn

Ovid (Latin) A shepherd; an egg
Ovyd, Ovidio, Ovido, Ovydio, Ovydo, Ovidiu, Ovydiu, Ofydd

***Owen** (Welsh / Gaelic) Form of Eugene, meaning "a well-born man" / a youthful man
Owenn, Owenne, Owin, Owinn, Owinne, Owyn, Owynn, Owynne

Oxton (English) From the oxen town
Oxtun, Oxtown, Oxnaton, Oxnatun, Oxnatown

Oz (Hebrew) Having great strength
Ozz, Ozzi, Ozzie, Ozzy, Ozzey, Ozzee, Ozzea, Ozi

Ozni (Hebrew) One who knows God
Oznie, Ozny, Ozney, Oznee, Oznea

Ozuru (Japanese) Resembling a stork
Ozurou, Ozourou, Ozuroo, Ozooroo

P

Paavo (Finnish) Form of Paul, meaning "a small or humble man"
Paaveli

Pace (Hebrew / English) Refers to Passover / a peaceful man
Paice, Payce, Paece, Pacey, Pacy, Pacee, Paci, Pacie

Pacho (Spanish) An independent man; one who is free

Pachu'a (Native American) Resembling a water snake

Paco (Spanish) A man from France
Pacorro, Pacoro, Paquito

Padgett (French) One who strives to better himself
Padget, Padgette, Padgete, Padgeta, Padgetta, Padge, Paget, Pagett

Padman (Indian) Resembling the lotus
Padmann

Padruig (Scottish) Of the royal family

Paine (Latin) Man from the country; a peasant
Pain, Payn, Payne, Paen, Paene, Pane, Paien

Palamedes (English) In Arthurian legend, a knight
Palomydes, Palomedes, Palamydes, Palsmedes, Palsmydes, Pslomydes

Palban (Spanish) A blond-haired man
Palben, Palbin, Palbyn, Palbon, Palbun

Paley (English) Form of Paul, meaning "a small or humble man"
Paly, Pali, Palie, Palee, Palea

Palladin (Greek) Filled with wisdom
Palladyn, Palladen, Palladan, Paladin, Paladyn, Paladen, Paladan

Palmer (English) A pilgrim bearing a palm branch
Pallmer, Palmar, Pallmar, Palmerston, Palmiro, Palmeero, Palmeer, Palmire

Pan (Greek) In mythology, god of the shepherds
Pann

Panama (Spanish) From the canal

Pancho (Spanish) A man from France

Pankaj (Indian) Resembling the lotus flower

Panya (African) Resembling a mouse
Panyah

Panyin (African) The first-born of twins
Panyen

Paras (Hindi) A touchstone
Parasmani, Parasmanie, Parasmany, Parasmaney, Parasmanee

***Parker** (English) The keeper of the park
Parkar, Parkes, Parkman, Park

Parley (Scottish) A reluctant man
Parly, Parli, Parlie, Parlee, Parlea, Parle

Parmenio (Spanish) A studious man; one who is intelligent
Parmenios, Parmenius

Parounag (Armenian) One who is thankful

Parrish (Latin) Man of the church
Parish, Parrishe, Parishe, Parrysh, Parysh, Paryshe, Parryshe, Parisch

Parry (Welsh) The son of Harry
Parrey, Parri, Parrie, Parree, Parrea

Parthenios (Greek) One who is pure; chaste
Parthenius

Parthik (Greek) One who is pure; chaste
Parthyk, Parthick, Parthyck, Parthic, Parthyc

Pascal (Latin) Born during Easter
Pascale, Pascalle, Paschal, Paschalis, Pascoe, Pascual, Pascuale, Pasqual

Patamon (Native American) Resembling a tempest
Patamun, Patamen, Pataman, Patamyn, Patamin

Patch (American) Form of Peter, meaning "as solid and strong as a rock"
Pach, Patche, Patchi, Patchie, Patchy, Patchey, Patchee

Patrick (Latin) A nobleman; patrician
Packey, Padric, Pat, Patrece, Patric, Patrice, Patreece, Patricio

Patton (English) From the town of warriors
Paten, Patin, Paton, Patten, Pattin, Paddon, Padden, Paddin

Patwin (Native American) A manly man
Patwinn, Patwinne, Patwyn, Patwynne, Patwynn, Patwen, Patwenn, Patwenne

Paul (Latin) A small or humble man
Pauley, Paulie, Pauly, Paley, Paavo

Paurush (Indian) A courageous man
Paurushe, Paurushi, Paurushie, Paurushy, Paurushey, Paurushee

Pavanjit (Indian) Resembling the wind
Pavanjyt, Pavanjeet, Pavanjeat, Pavanjete

Paxton (English) From the peaceful town
Packston, Paxon, Paxten, Paxtun, Packstun, Packsten

Pazel (Hebrew) God's gold; treasured by God
Pazell, Pazele, Pazelle

Pearroc (English) Man of the forest
Pearoc, Pearrok, Pearok, Pearrock, Pearock

Pecos (American) From the river; a cowboy
Pekos, Peckos

Pedro (Spanish) Form of Peter, meaning "as solid and strong as a rock"
Pedrio, Pepe, Petrolino, Piero, Pietro

Pelham (English) From the house of furs; from Peola's home
Pellham, Pelam, Pellam

Pell (English) A clerk or one who works with skins
Pelle, Pall, Palle

Pelon (Spanish) Filled with joy
Pellon

Pelton (English) From the town by the lake
Pellton, Peltun, Pelltun, Peltan, Pelltan, Pelten, Pellten, Peltin

Penda (African) One who is dearly loved
Pendah, Penha, Penhah

Penley (English) From the enclosed meadow
Penly, Penleigh, Penli, Penlie, Penlee, Penlea, Penleah, Pennley

Penrod (German) A respected commander

Pentele (Hungarian) A merciful man
Pentelle, Pentel, Pentell

Penuel (Hebrew) The face of God
Penuell, Penuele, Penuelle

Percival (French) One who can pierce the vale"
Purcival, Percy, Percey, Perci, Percie, Percee, Percea, Persy, Persey, Persi

Peregrine (Latin) One who travels; a wanderer
Perry, Perree, Perrea, Perri, Perrie, Perregrino

Perez (Hebrew) To break through
Peretz

Pericles (Greek) One who is in excess of glory
Perricles, Perycles, Perrycles, Periclees, Perriclees, Peryclees, Perryclees, Periclez

Perk (American) One who is cheerful and jaunty
Perke, Perky, Perkey, Perki, Perkie, Perkee, Perkea

Perkinson (English) The son of Perkin; the son of Peter
Perkynson

Perseus (Greek) In mythology, son of Zeus who slew Medusa
Persius, Persyus, Persies, Persyes

Perth (Celtic) From the thorny thicket
Perthe, Pert, Perte

Perye (English) From the pear tree

Peter (Greek) As solid and strong as a rock
Peder, Pekka, Per, Petar, Pete, Peterson, Petr, Petre, Pierce, Patch, Pedro

Petuel (Hindi) The Lord's vision
Petuell, Petuele, Petuelle

Peyton (English) From the village of warriors
Payton, Peytun, Paytun, Peyten, Payten, Paiton, Paitun, Paiten

Pharis (Irish) A heroic man
Pharys, Pharris, Pharrys

Phex (American) A kind man
Phexx

Philemon (Hebrew) A loving man
Phylemon, Philimon, Phylimon, Philomon, Phylomon, Philamon, Phylamon

Philetus (Greek) A collector
Phyletus, Philetos, Phyletos

Phillip (Greek) One who loves horses
Phil, Philip, Felipe, Filipp, Phillie, Philly

Philo (Greek) One who loves and is loved

Phoebus (Greek) A radiant man
Phoibos

Phomello (African) A successful man
Phomelo

Phong (Vietnamese) Of the wind

Phuc (Vietnamese) One who is blessed
Phuoc

Picardus (Hispanic) An adventurous man
Pycardus, Picardos, Pycardos, Picardas, Pycardas, Picardis, Pycardis, Picardys

Pickworth (English) From the woodcutter's estate
Pikworth, Picworth, Pickworthe, Pikworthe, Picworthe

Pierce (English) Form of Peter, meaning "as solid and strong as a rock"
Pearce, Pears, Pearson, Pearsson, Peerce, Peirce, Pierson, Piersson

Pin (Vietnamese) Filled with joy
Pyn

Pio (Latin) A pious man
Pyo, Pios, Pius, Pyos, Pyus

Pirro (Greek) A red-haired man
Pyrro

Pitney (English) From the island of the stubborn man
Pitny, Pitni, Pitnie, Pitnee, Pitnea, Pytney, Pytny, Pytni

Pittman (English) A laborer
Pyttman, Pitman, Pytman

Plantagenet (French) Resembling the broom flower

Poetry (American) A romantic man
Poetrey, Poetri, Poetrie, Poetree, Poetrea, Poet, Poete

Pollux (Greek) One who is crowned
Pollock, Pollok, Polloc, Pollack, Polloch

Polo (African) Resembling an alligator
Poloe, Poloh

Ponce (Spanish) The fifth-born child
Ponse

Pongor (Hungarian) A mighty man
Pongorr, Pongoro, Pongorro

Poni (African) The second-born son
Ponni, Ponie, Ponnie, Pony, Ponny, Poney, Ponney, Ponee

Pons (Latin) From the bridge
Pontius, Ponthos, Ponthus

Poornamruth (Indian) Full of sweetness
Pournamruth

Poornayu (Indian) Full of life; blessed with a full life
Pournayu, Poornayou, Pournayou, Poornayue, Pournayue

Porat (Hebrew) A productive man

Porfirio (Greek) Refers to a purple coloring
Porphirios, Prophyrios, Porfiro, Porphyrios

Powhatan (Native American) From the chief's hill

Prabhakar (Hindu) Of the sun

Prabhat (Indian) Born during the morning

Pragun (Indian) One who is straightforward; honest

Pramod (Indian) A delightful young man

Pranit (Indian) One who is humble; modest
Pranyt, Praneet, Praneat

Prasad (Indian) A gift from God

Prashant (Indian) One who is peaceful; calm
Prashante, Prashanth, Prashanthe

Pratap (Hindi) A majestic man

Pravat (Thai) History

Prem (Indian) An affectionate man

Prentice (English) A student; an apprentice
Prentyce, Prentise, Prentyse, Prentiss, Prentis

Prescott (English) From the priest's cottage
Prescot, Prestcot, Prestcott, Preostcot

Preston (English) From the priest's town
Prestin, Prestyn, Prestan, Prestun, Presten, Pfeostun

Prewitt (French) A brave young one
Prewet, Prewett, Prewit, Pruitt, Pruit, Pruet, Pruett

Prine (English) One who surpasses others
Pryne

Prometheus (Greek) In mythology, he stole fire from the heavens and gave it to man
Promitheus, Promethius, Promithius

Prop (American) A fun-loving man
Propp, Proppe

Prosper (Latin) A fortunate man
Prospero, Prosperus

Pryderi (Celtic) Son of the sea
Pryderie, Prydery, Prydereу, Pryderee, Pryderea

Prydwen (Welsh) A handsome man
Prydwenn, Prydwenne, Prydwin, Prydwinne, Prydwinn, Prydwyn, Prydwynn, Prydwynne

Pullman (English) One who works on a train
Pulman, Pullmann, Pulmann

Pyralis (Greek) Born of fire
Pyraliss, Pyralisse, Pyralys, Pyralyss, Pyralysse, Pyre

Qabil (Arabic) An able-bodied man
Qabyl, Qabeel, Qabeal, Qabeil, Qabiel

Qadim (Arabic) From an ancient family
Qadeem, Qadiem, Qadeim, Qadym, Qadeam

Qaiser (Arabic) A king; a ruler
Qeyser

Qamar (Arabic) Born beneath the moon
Qamarr, Quamar, Quamarr

Qimat (Hindi) A highly valued man
Qymat

Qing (Chinese) Of the deep water
Qyng

Quaashie (American) An ambitious man
Quashie, Quashi, Quashy, Quashey, Quashee, Quashea, Quaashi, Quaashy

Quaddus (American) A bright man
Quadus, Quaddos, Quados

Quade (Latin) The fourth-born child
Quadrees, Quadres, Quadrys, Quadries, Quadreis, Quadreys, Quadreas, Quadrhys

Quaid (Irish) Form of Walter, meaning "the commander of the army"
Quaide, Quayd, Quayde, Quaed, Quaede

Quashawn (American) A tenacious man
Quashaun, Quasean, Quashon, Quashi, Quashie, Quashee, Quashea, Quashy

Qued (Native American) Wearing a decorated robe

Quentin (Latin) The fifth-born child
Quent, Quenten, Quenton, Quentun, Quentan, Quentyn, Quente, Qwentin

Quick (American) One who is fast; a witty man
Quik, Quicke, Quic

Quillan (Gaelic) Resembling a cub
Quilan, Quillen, Quilen, Quillon, Quilon

Quilliam (Gaelic) Form of William, meaning "the determined protector"
Quilhelm, Quilhelmus, Quilliams, Quilliamson

Quimby (Norse) From the woman's estate
Quimbey, Quimbee, Quimbea, Quimbi, Quimbie

Quincy (English) The fifth-born child; from the fifth son's estate
Quincey, Quinci, Quincie, Quincee, Quinncy, Quinnci, Quyncy, Quyncey

Quinlan (Gaelic) A strong and healthy man
Quindlan, Quinlen, Quindlen, Quinian, Quinlin, Quindlin, Quinlyn, Quindlyn

Quinn (Gaelic) One who provides counsel; an intelligent man
Quin, Quinne, Qwinn, Quynn, Qwin, Quiyn, Quyn, Qwinne

Quintavius (American) The fifth-born child
Quintavios, Quintavus, Quintavies

Quinto (Spanish) The fifth-born child
Quynto, Quintus, Quintos, Quinty, Quinti, Quintie

Quinton (Latin) From the queen's town or settlement
Laquinton

Quintrell (English) An elegant and dashing man
Quintrel, Quintrelle, Quyntrell, Quyntrelle, Quyntrel, Quyntrele, Quintrele

Quirinus (Latin) One who wields a spear
Quirinos, Quirynus, Quirynos, Quirinius, Quirynius

Quito (Spanish) A lively man
Quyto, Quitos, Quytos

Quoc (Vietnamese) A patriot
Quok, Quock

Qutub (Indian) One who is tall

R

Rabbaanee (African) An easy-going man

Rabbi (Hebrew) The master

Rach (African) Resembling a frog

Radames (Egyptian) A hero
Radamays, Radamayes, Radamais, Radamaise

Radford (English) From the red ford
Radforde, Radferd, Radfurd, Radferde, Radfurde

Rafael (Spanish) Form of Raphael, meaning "one who is healed by God"
Raphael, Raphaello, Rafaello

Rafe (Irish) A tough man
Raffe, Raff, Raf, Raif, Rayfe, Raife, Raef, Raefe

Rafi (Arabic) One who is exalted
Rafie, Rafy, Rafey, Rafea, Rafee, Raffi, Raffie, Raffy

Rafiki (African) A gentle friend
Rafikie, Rafikea, Rafikee, Rafiky, Rafikey

Rafiya (African) A dignified man
Rafeeya, Rafeaya, Rafeiya, Rafieya

Raghib (Arabic) One who is desired
Ragheb, Ragheeb, Ragheab, Raghyb, Ragheib, Raghieb

Ragnar (Norse) A warrior who places judgment
Ragnor, Ragner, Ragnir, Ragnyr, Ragnur, Regnar

Rahim (Arabic) A compassionate man
Rahym, Raheim, Rahiem, Raheem, Raheam

Raiden (Japanese) In mythology, the god of thunder and lightning
Raidon, Rayden, Raydon, Raeden, Raedon, Raden

Raimi (African) A compassionate man
Raimie, Raimy, Raimey, Raimee, Raimea

Rajab (African) A glorified man

Rajan (Indian) A king
Raj, Raja, Rajah

Rajarshi (Indian) The king's sage
Rajarshie, Rajarshy, Rajarshey, Rajarshee, Rajarshea

Rajesh (Hindi) The king's rule

Rajit (Indian) One who is decorated
Rajeet, Rajeit, Rajiet, Rajyt, Rajeat

Rajiv (Hindi) To be striped
Rajyv, Rajeev, Rajeav

Ralph (English) Wolf counsel
Ralf, Ralphe, Ralfe, Ralphi, Ralphie, Ralphee, Ralphea, Ralphy, Raoul

Ram (Hebrew / Sanskrit) A superior man / one who is pleasing
Rahm, Rama, Rahma, Ramos, Rahmos, Ramm

Rambert (German) Having great strength; an intelligent man
Ramberte, Ramberth, Ramberthe, Ramburt

Rami (Arabic) A loving man
Ramee, Ramea, Ramie, Ramy, Ramey

Ramiro (Portuguese) A famous counselor; a great judge
Ramyro, Rameero, Rameyro, Ramirez, Ramyrez, Rameerez

Ramsey (English) From the raven island; from the island of wild garlic
Ramsay, Ramsie, Ramsi, Ramsee, Ramsy, Ramsea, Ramzy, Ramzey

Rand (German) One who shields others
Rande

Randall (German) The wolf shield
Randy, Randal, Randale, Randel, Randell, Randl, Randle, Randon, Rendall

Randolph (German) The wolf shield
Randy, Randolf, Ranolf, Ranolph, Ranulfo, Randulfo, Randwulf, Ranwulf, Randwolf

Randy (English) Form of Randall or Randolph, meaning "the wolf shield"
Randey, Randi, Randie, Randee, Randea

Rang (English) Resembling a raven
Range

Rangey (English) From raven's island
Rangy, Rangi, Rangie, Rangee, Rangea

Rangle (American) A cowboy
Rangel

Ranjan (Indian) A delightful boy

Raoul (French) Form of Ralph, meaning "wolf counsel"
Raoule, Raul, Roul, Rowl, Raule, Roule, Rowle

Raqib (Arabic) A glorified man
Raqyb, Raqeeb, Raqeab, Rakib, Rakeeb, Rakeab, Rakyb

Rashard (American) A good-hearted man
Rasherd, Rashird, Rashurd, Rashyrd

Rashaun (American) Form of Roshan, meaning "born during the daylight"
Rashae, Rashane, Rashawn, Rayshaun, Rayshawn, Raishaun, Raishawn, Raeshaun

Ratul (Indian) A sweet man
Ratule, Ratoul, Ratoule, Ratool, Ratoole

Raulo (Spanish) One who is wise
Rawlo

Ravi (Hindi) From the sun
Ravie, Ravy, Ravey, Ravee, Ravea

Ravid (Hebrew) A wanderer; one who searches
Ravyd, Raveed, Ravead, Raviyd, Ravied, Raveid

Ravindra (Indian) The strength of the sun
Ravyndra

Ravinger (English) One who lives near the ravine
Ravynger

Rawlins (French) From the renowned land
Rawlin, Rawson, Rawlinson, Rawlings, Rawling, Rawls, Rawl, Rawle

Ray (English) Form of Raymond, meaning "a wise protector"
Rae, Rai, Rayce, Rayder, Rayse, Raye, Rayford, Raylen

Rayfield (English) From the field of roe deer
Rayfeld

Rayhurn (English) From the roe deer's stream
Rayhurne, Rayhorn, Rayhorne, Rayhourn, Rayhourne

Raymond (German) A wise protector
Ray, Raemond, Raemondo, Raimond, Raimondo, Raimund, Raimundo, Rajmund, Ramon

Rebel (American) An outlaw
Rebell, Rebele, Rebelle, Rebe, Rebbe, Rebbi, Rebbie, Rebbea

Redwald (English) Strong counsel
Redwalde, Raedwalde, Raedwald

Reeve (English) A bailiff
Reve, Reave, Reeford, Reeves, Reaves, Reves, Reaford

Regal (American) Born into royalty
Regall

Regan (Gaelic) Born into royalty; the little ruler
Raegan, Ragan, Raygan, Reganne, Regann, Regane, Reghan, Reagan

Regenfrithu (English) A peaceful raven

Reggie (Latin) Form of Reginald, meaning "the king's advisor"
Reggi, Reggy, Reggey, Reggea, Reggee, Reg

Reginald (Latin) The king's advisor
Reggie, Reynold, Raghnall, Rainault, Rainhold, Raonull, Raynald, Rayniero, Regin, Reginaldo

Regine (French) One who is artistic
Regeen, Regeene, Regean, Regeane, Regein, Regeine, Regien, Regiene

^**Reid** (English) A red-haired man; one who lives near the reeds
Read, Reade, Reed, Reede, Reide, Raed

Reilly (Gaelic) An outgoing man
Reilley, Reilli, Reillie, Reillee, Reilleigh, Reillea

^**Remington** (English) From the town of the raven's family
Remyngton, Remingtun, Remyngtun

Renweard (Anglo-Saxon) The guardian of the house
Renward, Renwarden, Renwerd

Renzo (Japanese) The third-born son

Reuben (Hebrew) Behold, a son!
Reuban, Reubin, Reuven, Rouvin, Rube, Ruben, Rubin, Rubino

Rev (American) One who is distinct
Revv, Revin, Reven, Revan, Revyn, Revon, Revun

Rex (Latin) A king
Reks, Recks, Rexs

Rexford (English) From the king's ford
Rexforde, Rexferd, Rexferde, Rexfurd, Rexfurde

Reynold (English) Form of Reginald, meaning "the king's advisor"
Reynald, Reynaldo, Reynolds, Reynalde, Reynolde

Rhett (Latin) A well-spoken man
Rett, Rhet

^**Rhys** (Welsh) Having great enthusiasm for life

Richard (English) A powerful ruler
Rick, Rich, Ricard, Ricardo, Riccardo, Richardo, Richart, Richerd, Rickard, Rickert

Richmond (French / German) From the wealthy hill / a powerful protector
Richmonde, Richmund, Richmunde

Rick (English) Form of Richard, meaning "a powerful ruler"
Ric, Ricci, Ricco, Rickie, Ricki, Ricky, Rico, Rik

Rickward (English) A strong protector
Rickwerd, Rickwood, Rikward, Ricward, Rickweard, Rikweard, Ricweard

Riddock (Irish) From the smooth field
Ridock, Riddoc, Ridoc, Ryddock, Rydock, Ryddoc, Rydoc, Ryddok

Ridgeway (English) One who lives on the road near the ridge
Rydgeway, Rigeway, Rygeway

Rigg (English) One who lives near the ridge
Rig, Ridge, Rygg, Ryg, Rydge, Rige, Ryge, Riggs

Riley (English) From the rye clearing
Ryly, Ryli, Rylie, Rylee,Ryleigh, Rylea, Ryleah

Riordain (Irish) A bright man
Riordane, Riordayn, Riordaen, Reardain, Reardane, Reardayn, Reardaen

Riordan (Gaelic) A royal poet; a bard or minstrel
Riorden, Rearden, Reardan, Riordon, Reardon

Ripley (English) From the noisy meadow
Riply, Ripleigh, Ripli, Riplie, Riplea, Ripleah, Riplee, Rip

Rishley (English) From the untamed meadow
Rishly, Rishli, Rishlie, Rishlee, Rishlea, Rishleah, Rishleigh

Rishon (Hebrew) The first-born son
Ryshon, Rishi, Rishie, Rishea, Rishee, Rishy, Rishey

Risley (English) From the brushwood meadow
Risly, Risli, Rislie, Risleigh, Rislea, Risleah, Rislee

Riston (English) From the brushwood settlement
Ryston, Ristun, Rystun

Ritter (German) A knight
Rytter, Ritt, Rytt

River (American) From the river
Ryver, Rivers, Ryvers

Roald (Norse) A famous ruler
Roal

Roam (American) One who wanders, searches
Roami, Roamie, Roamy, Roamey, Roamea, Roamee

Roark (Gaelic) A champion
Roarke, Rorke, Rourke, Rork, Rourk, Ruark, Ruarke

⋆**Robert** (German) One who is bright with fame
Bob, Rupert, Riobard, Roban, Robers, Roberto, Robertson, Robartach

Rochester (English) From the stone fortress

Rockford (English) From the rocky ford
Rockforde, Rokford, Rokforde, Rockferd, Rokferd, Rockfurd, Rokfurd

Roderick (German) A famous ruler
Rod, Rodd, Roddi, Roddie, Roddy, Roddee, Roddea

Rodney (German / English) From the famous one's island / from the island's clearing
Rodny, Rodni, Rodnie

Rogelio (Spanish) A famous soldier
Rogelo, Rogeliyo, Rogeleo, Rogeleyo, Rojelio, Rojeleo

Roland (German) From the renowned land
Roeland, Rolando, Roldan, Roley, Rollan, Rolland, Rollie, Rollin

Roman (Latin) A citizen of Rome
Romain, Romaine, Romeo

Romeo (Italian) Traveler to Rome

Ronald (Norse) The king's advisor
Ranald, Renaldo, Ronal, Ronaldo, Rondale, Roneld, Ronell, Ronello

^**Ronan** (Gaelic) Resembling a little seal
Ronin

Rong (Chinese) Having glory

Rook (English) Resembling a raven
Rooke, Rouk, Rouke, Ruck, Ruk

Rooney (Gaelic) A red-haired man
Roony, Rooni, Roonie, Roonea, Roonee, Roon, Roone

Roosevelt (Danish) From the field of roses
Rosevelt

Roper (English) One who makes rope
Rapere

Rory (Gaelic) A red-haired man
Rori, Rorey, Rorie, Rorea, Roree, Rorry, Rorrey, Rorri

Roshan (Hindi) Born during the daylight
Rashaun

Roslin (Gaelic) A little red-haired boy
Roslyn, Rosselin, Rosslyn, Rozlin, Rozlyn, Rosling, Rozling

Roswald (German) Of the mighty horses
Rosswald, Roswalt, Rosswalt

Roswell (English) A fascinating man
Rosswell, Rozwell, Roswel, Rozwel

Roth (German) A red-haired man
Rothe

Rousseau (French) A little red-haired boy
Roussell, Russo, Rousse, Roussel, Rousset, Rousskin

Rowdy (English) A boisterous man
Rowdey, Rowdi, Rowdie, Rowdee, Rowdea

Roy (Gaelic / French) A red-haired man / a king
Roye, Roi, Royer, Ruy

Royce (German / French) A famous man / son of the king
Roice, Royse, Roise

Ruadhan (Irish) A red-haired man; the name of a saint
Ruadan, Ruadhagan, Ruadagan

Ruarc (Irish) A famous ruler
Ruarck, Ruarcc, Ruark, Ruarkk, Ruaidhri, Ruaidri

Rubio (Spanish) Resembling a ruby

Rudeger (German) A friendly man
Rudegar, Rudger, Rudgar, Rudiger, Rudigar

Rudolph (German) A famous wolf
Rodolfo, Rodolph, Rodolphe, Rodolpho, Rudy, Rudey, Rudi, Rudie

Rudyard (English) From the red paddock

Rufus (Latin) A red-haired man
Ruffus, Rufous, Rufino

Ruiz (Spanish) A good friend

Rujul (Indian) An honest man
Rujool, Rujoole, Rujule, Rujoul, Rujoule

Rumford (English) From the broad ford
Rumforde, Rumferd, Rumferde, Rumfurd

Rupert (English) Form of Robert, meaning "one who is bright with fame"
Ruprecht

Rushford (English) From the ford with rushes
Rusheford, Rushforde, Rusheforde, Ryscford

Russell (French) A little red-haired boy
Russel, Roussell, Russ, Rusel, Rusell

Russom (African) The chief; the boss
Rusom, Russome, Rusome

Rusty (English) One who has red hair or a ruddy complexion
Rustey, Rusti, Rustie, Rustee, Rustea, Rust, Ruste, Rustice

Rutherford (English) From the cattle's ford
Rutherfurd, Rutherferd, Rutherforde, Rutherfurde

*__Ryan__ (Gaelic) The little ruler; little king
Rian, Rien, Rion, Ryen, Ryon, Ryun, Rhyan, Rhyen

*__Ryder__ (English) An accomplished horseman
Rider, Ridder, Ryden, Rydell, Rydder

Ryker (Danish) Form of Richard, meaning "a powerful ruler"
Riker

Rylan (English) Form of Ryland, meaning "from the place where rye is grown"
Ryelan, Ryle

^**Ryland** (English) From the place where Rye is grown

S

Saarik (Hindi) Resembling a small songbird
Saarick, Saaric, Sarik, Sarick, Saric, Saariq, Sareek, Sareeq

Saber (French) Man of the sword
Sabere, Sabr, Sabre

Sabir (Arabic) One who is patient
Sabyr, Sabeer, Sabear, Sabeir, Sabier, Sabri, Sabrie, Sabree

Saddam (Arabic) A powerful ruler; the crusher
Saddum, Saddim, Saddym

Sadiq (Arabic) A beloved friend
Sadeeq, Sadyq, Sadeaq, Sadeek, Sadeak, Sadyk, Sadik

Saga (American) A storyteller
Sago

Sagar (Indian / English) A king / one who is wise
Saagar, Sagarr, Saagarr

Sagaz (Spanish) One who is clever
Sagazz

Sagiv (Hebrew) Having great strength
Sagev, Segiv, Segev

Sahaj (Indian) One who is natural

Saieshwar (Hindi) A well-known saint
Saishwar

Sailor (American) Man who sails the seas
Sailer, Sailar, Saylor, Sayler, Saylar, Saelor

Saith (English) One who is well-spoken
Saithe, Sayth, Saythe, Saeth, Saethe, Sath, Sathe

Sajal (Indian) Resembling a cloud
Sajall, Sajjal, Sajjall

Sajan (Indian) One who is dearly loved
Sajann, Sajjan, Sajjann

Saki (Japanese) One who is cloaked
Sakie, Saky, Sakey, Sakee, Sakea

Salaam (African) Resembling a peach

Salehe (African) A good man
Saleh, Salih

Salim (Arabic) One who is peaceful
Saleem, Salem, Selim

Salute (American) A patriotic man
Saloot, Saloote, Salout

Salvador (Spanish) A savior
Sal, Sally, Salvadore, Xalvador

Samanjas (Indian) One who is proper

Samarth (Indian) A powerful man; one who is efficient
Samarthe

Sameen (Indian) One who is treasured
Samine, Sameene, Samean, Sameane, Samyn, Samyne

Sami (Arabic) One who has been exalted
Samie, Samy, Samey, Samee, Samea

Sammohan (Indian) An attractive man

Sampath (Indian) A wealthy man
Sampathe, Sampat

Samson (Hebrew) As bright as the sun; in the Bible, a man with extraordinary strength
Sampson, Sansom, Sanson, Sansone

*__Samuel__ (Hebrew) God has heard
Sam, Sammie, Sammy, Samuele, Samuello, Samwell, Samuelo, Sammey

Samuru (Japanese) The name of God

Sandburg (English) From the sandy village
Sandbergh, Sandberg, Sandburgh

Sandon (English) From the sandy hill
Sanden, Sandan, Sandun, Sandyn, Sandin

Sanford (English) From the sandy crossing
Sandford, Sanforde, Sandforde, Sanfurd, Sanfurde, Sandfurd, Sandfurde

Sang (Vietnamese) A bright man
Sange

Sanjiro (Japanese) An admirable man
Sanjyro

Sanjiv (Indian) One who lives a long life
Sanjeev, Sanjyv, Sanjeiv, Sanjiev, Sanjeav, Sanjivan

Sanorelle (American) An honest man
Sanorell, Sanorel, Sanorele

Santana (Spanish) A saintly man
Santanna, Santanah, Santannah, Santa

Santiago (Spanish) Refers to St. James

Santo (Italian) A holy man
Sante, Santino, Santos, Santee, Santi, Santie, Santea, Santy

Sapan (Indian) A dream or vision
Sapann

Sar (Anglo-Saxon) One who inflicts pain
Sarlic, Sarlik

Sarbajit (Indian) The conqueror
Sarbajeet, Sarbajyt, Sarbajeat, Sarbajet, Sarvajit, Sarvajeet, Sarvajyt, Sarvajeat

Sarojin (Hindu) Resembling a lotus
Saroj

Sarosh (Persian) One who prays
Saroshe

Satayu (Hindi) In Hinduism, the brother of Amavasu and Vivasu
Satayoo, Satayou, Satayue

Satoshi (Japanese) Born from the ashes
Satoshie, Satoshy, Satoshey, Satoshee, Satoshea

Satparayan (Indian) A good-natured man

Saturn (Latin) In mythology, the god of agriculture
Saturnin, Saturno, Saturnino

Satyankar (Indian) One who speaks the truth
Satyancar, Satyancker

Saville (French) From the willow town
Savil, Savile, Savill, Savyile, Savylle, Savyle, Sauville, Sauvile

Savir (Indian) A great leader
Savire, Saveer, Saveere, Savear, Saveare, Savyr, Savyre

Sawyer (English) One who works with wood
Sayer, Saer

Saxon (English) A swordsman
Saxen, Saxan, Saxton, Saxten, Saxtan

Sayad (Arabic) An accomplished hunter

Scadwielle (English) From the shed near the spring
Scadwyelle, Scadwiell, Scadwyell, Scadwiel, Scadwyel, Scadwiele, Scadwyele

Scand (Anglo-Saxon) One who is disgraced
Scande, Scandi, Scandie, Scandee, Scandea

Sceotend (Anglo-Saxon) An archer

Schaeffer (German) A steward
Schaffer, Shaeffer, Shaffer, Schaeffur, Schaffur, Shaeffur, Shaffur

Schelde (English) From the river
Shelde

Schneider (German) A tailor
Shneider, Sneider, Snider, Snyder

Schubert (German) One who makes shoes
Shubert, Schuberte, Shuberte, Schubirt, Shubirt, Schuburt, Shuburt

Scirocco (Italian) Of the warm wind
Sirocco, Scyrocco, Syrocco

Scott (English) A man from Scotland
Scot, Scottie, Scotto, Scotty, Scotti, Scottey, Scottee, Scottea

Scowyrhta (Anglo-Saxon) One who makes shoes

Seabury (English) From the village by the sea
Seaburry, Sebury, Seburry, Seaberry, Seabery, Seberry

Seaman (English) A mariner

Sean (Irish) Form of John, meaning "God is gracious"
Shaughn, Shawn, Shaun, Shon, Shohn, Shonn, Shaundre, Shawnel

Seanachan (Irish) One who is wise

Seanan (Hebrew / Irish) A gift from God / an old, wise man
Sinon, Senen, Siobhan

***Sebastian** (Greek) The revered one
Sabastian, Seb, Sebastiano, Sebastien, Sebestyen, Sebo, Sebastyn, Sebestyen

Sedgwick (English) From the place of sword grass
Sedgewick, Sedgewyck, Sedgwyck, Sedgewic, Sedgewik, Sedgwic, Sedgwik, Sedgewyc

Seerath (Indian) A great man
Seerathe, Searath, Searathe

Sef (Egyptian) Son of yesterday
Sefe

Seferino (Greek) Of the west wind
Seferio, Sepherino, Sepherio, Seferyno, Sepheryno

Seignour (French) Lord of the house

Selas (African) Refers to the Trinity
Selassi, Selassie, Selassy, Selassey, Selassee, Selassea

Selestino (Spanish) One who is heaven-sent
Selestyno, Selesteeno, Selesteano

Sellers (English) One who dwells in the marshland
Sellars, Sellurs, Sellirs, Sellyrs

Seminole (Native American) A tribal name
Semynole

Seppanen (Finnish) A blacksmith
Sepanen, Seppenen, Sepenen, Seppanan, Sepanan

September (American) Born in the month of September
Septimber, Septymber, Septemberia, Septemberea

Septimus (Latin) The seventh-born child
Septymus

Seraphim (Hebrew) The burning ones; heavenly winged angels
Sarafino, Saraph, Serafin, Serafino, Seraph, Seraphimus, Serafim

Sereno (Latin) One who is calm; tranquil

Serfati (Hebrew) A man from France
Sarfati, Serfatie, Sarfatie, Serfaty, Sarfaty, Serfatey, Sarfatey, Serfatee

Sergio (Latin) An attendant; a servant
Seargeoh, Serge, Sergei, Sergeo, Sergey, Sergi, Sergios, Sergiu

Seth (Hebrew) One who has been appointed
Sethe, Seath, Seathe, Zeth

Seung (Korean) A victorious successor

Seven (American) Refers to the number; the seventh-born child
Sevin, Sevyn

Sewati (Native American) Resembling a bear claw
Sewatie, Sewaty, Sewatey, Sewatee, Sewatea

Sexton (English) The church's custodian
Sextun, Sextan, Sextin, Sextyn

Seymour (French) From the French town of Saint Maur
Seamore, Seamor, Seamour, Seymore

Shaan (Hebrew) A peaceful man

Shade (English) A secretive man
Shaid, Shaide, Shayd, Shayde, Shaed, Shaede

Shadi (Persian / Arabic) One who brings happiness and joy / a singer
Shadie, Shady, Shadey

Shadrach (Hebrew) Under the command of the moon god Aku
Shadrack, Shadrick, Shad

Shah (Persian) The king

Shai (Hebrew) A gift from God

Shail (Indian) A mountain rock
Shaile, Shayl, Shayle, Shael, Shaele, Shale

Shaka (African) A tribal leader
Shakah

Shakir (Arabic) One who is grateful
Shakeer, Shaqueer, Shakier, Shakeir, Shakear, Shakar, Shaker, Shakyr

Shane (English) Form of John, meaning "God is gracious"
Shayn, Shayne, Shaine, Shain

Shannon (Gaelic) Having ancient wisdom
Shanan, Shanen, Shannan, Shannen, Shanon

Shardul (Indian) Resembling a tiger
Shardule, Shardull, Shardulle

Shashi (Indian) Of the moon-beam
Shashie, Shashy, Shashey, Shashee, Shashea, Shashhi

Shavon (American) One who is open-minded
Shavaughn, Shavonne, Shavaun, Shovon, Shovonne, Shovaun

Shaw (English) From the woodland
Shawe

Shaykeen (American) A successful man
Shaykean, Shaykein, Shakeyn, Shakine

Shea (Gaelic) An admirable man / from the fairy fortress
Shae, Shai, Shay, Shaye, Shaylon, Shays

Sheen (English) A shining man
Sheene, Shean, Sheane

Sheffield (English) From the crooked field
Sheffeld

Sheldon (English) From the steep valley
Shelden, Sheldan, Sheldun, Sheldin, Sheldyn, Shel

Shelley (English) From the meadow's ledge
Shelly, Shelli, Shellie, Shellee, Shellea, Shelleigh, Shelleah

Shelton (English) From the farm on the ledge
Shellton, Sheltown, Sheltun, Shelten, Shelny, Shelney, Shelni, Shelnie

Shem (Hebrew) Having a well-known name

Shepherd (English) One who herds sheep
Shepperd, Shep, Shepard, Shephard, Shepp, Sheppard

Sheridan (Gaelic) A seeker
Sheredan, Sheridon, Sherridan, Seireadan, Sheriden, Sheridun, Sherard, Sherrard

Sherlock (English) A fair-haired man
Sherlocke, Shurlock, Shurlocke

Sherman (English) One who cuts wool cloth
Shermon, Scherman, Schermann, Shearman, Shermann, Sherm, Sherme

Sherrerd (English) From the open field
Shererd, Sherrard, Sherard

Shields (Gaelic) A faithful protector
Sheelds, Shealds

Shikha (Indian) A fiery man
Shykha

Shiloh (Hebrew) He who was sent
Shilo, Shyloh, Shylo

Shing (Chinese) A victorious man
Shyng

Shino (Japanese) A bamboo stem
Shyno

Shipton (English) From the ship town; from the sheep town

Shiro (Japanese) The fourth-born son
Shyro

Shorty (American) A man who is small in stature
Shortey, Shorti, Shortie, Shortee, Shortea

Shreshta (Indian) The best; one who is superior

Shubhang (Indian) A handsome man

Shuraqui (Arabic) A man from the east

Siamak (Persian) A bringer of joy
Syamak, Siamack, Syamack, Siamac, Syamac

Sidor (Russian) One who is talented
Sydor

Sierra (Spanish) From the jagged mountain range
Siera, Syerra, Syera, Seyera, Seeara

Sigehere (English) One who is victorious
Sygehere, Sigihere, Sygihere

Sigenert (Anglo-Saxon) A king
Sygenert, Siginert, Syginert

Sigmund (German) The victorious protector
Siegmund, Sigmond, Zsigmond, Zygmunt

Sihtric (Anglo-Saxon) A king
Sihtrik, Sihtrick, Syhtric, Syhtrik, Syhtrick, Sihtryc, Sihtryk, Sihtryck

Sik'is (Native American) A friendly man

Silas (Latin) Form of Silvanus, meaning "a woodland dweller"

Silny (Czech) Having great strength
Silney, Silni, Silnie, Silnee, Silnea

Simbarashe (African) The power of God
Simbarashi, Simbarashie, Simbarashy, Simbarashey, Simbarashee

Simcha (Hebrew) Filled with joy
Symcha, Simha, Symha

Simmons (Hebrew) The son of Simon
Semmes, Simms, Syms, Simmonds, Symonds, Simpson, Symms, Simson

Simon (Hebrew) God has heard
Shimon, Si, Sim, Samien, Semyon, Simen, Simeon, Simone

Sinai (Hebrew) From the clay desert

Sinclair (English) Man from Saint Clair
Sinclaire, Sinclare, Synclair, Synclaire, Synclare

Singer (American) A vocalist
Synger

Sion (Armenian) From the fortified hill
Sionne, Syon, Syonne

Sirius (Greek) Resembling the brightest star
Syrius

Siyavash (Persian) One who owns black horses
Siyavashe

Skerry (Norse) From the rocky island
Skereye, Skerrey, Skerri, Skerrie, Skerree, Skerrea

Slade (English) Son of the valley
Slaid, Slaide, Slaed, Slaede, Slayd, Slayde

Sladkey (Slavic) A glorious man
Sladky, Sladki, Sladkie, Sladkee, Sladkea

Smith (English) A blacksmith
Smyth, Smithe, Smythe, Smedt, Smid, Smitty, Smittee, Smittea

Snell (Anglo-Saxon) One who is bold
Snel, Snelle, Snele

Solange (French) An angel of the sun

Solaris (Greek) Of the sun
Solarise, Solariss, Solarisse, Solarys, Solaryss, Solarysse, Solstice, Soleil

Somer (French) Born during the summer
Somers, Sommer, Sommers, Sommar, Somar

Somerset (English) From the summer settlement
Sommerset, Sumerset, Summerset

Songaa (Native American) Having great strength
Songan

Sophocles (Greek) An ancient playwright
Sofocles

Sorley (Irish) Of the summer vikings
Sorly, Sorlee, Sorlea, Sorli, Sorlie

Soumil (Indian) A beloved friend
Soumyl, Soumille, Soumylle, Soumill, Soumyll

Southern (English) Man from the south
Sothern, Suthern

Sovann (Cambodian) The golden son
Sovan, Sovane

Spark (English / Latin) A gallant man / to scatter
Sparke, Sparki, Sparkie, Sparky, Sparkey, Sparkee, Sparkea

Spencer (English) One who dispenses provisions
Spenser

Squire (English) A knight's companion; the shield-bearer
Squier, Squiers, Squires, Squyre, Squyres

Stanford (English) From the stony ford
Standford, Standforde, Standforde, Stamford

Stanhope (English) From the stony hollow
Stanhop

Stanton (English) From the stone town
Stantown, Stanten, Staunton, Stantan, Stantun

Stark (German) Having great strength
Starke, Starck, Starcke

Stavros (Greek) One who is crowned

Steadman (English) One who lives at the farm
Stedman, Steadmann, Stedmann, Stedeman

Steed (English) Resembling a stallion
Steede, Stead, Steade

Stephen (Greek) Crowned with garland
Staffan, Steba, Steben, Stefan, Stefano, Steffan, Steffen, Steffon, Steven, Steve

Sterling (English) One who is highly valued
Sterlyng, Stirling, Sterlyn

Stian (Norse) A voyager; one who is swift
Stig, Styg, Stygge, Stieran, Steeran, Steeren, Steeryn, Stieren

Stilwell (Anglo-Saxon) From the quiet spring
Stillwell, Stilwel, Stylwell, Styllwell, Stylwel, Stillwel

Stobart (German) A harsh man
Stobarte, Stobarth, Stobarthe

Stockley (English) From the meadow of tree stumps
Stockly, Stockli, Stocklie, Stocklee, Stockleigh

Storm (American) Of the tempest; stormy weather; having an impetuous nature
Storme, Stormy, Stormi, Stormie, Stormey, Stormee, Stormea

Stowe (English) A secretive man
Stow, Stowey, Stowy, Stowee, Stowea, Stowi, Stowie

Stratford (English) From the street near the river ford
Strafford, Stratforde, Straford, Strafforde, Straforde

Stratton (Scottish) A homebody
Straton, Stratten, Straten, Strattan, Stratan, Strattun, Stratun

Strider (English) A great warrior
Stryder

Striker (American) An aggressive man
Strike, Stryker, Stryke

Struthers (Irish) One who lives near the brook
Struther, Sruthair, Strother, Strothers

Stuart (English) A steward; the keeper of the estate
Steward, Stewart, Stewert, Stuert, Stu, Stew

Suave (American) A smooth and sophisticated man
Swave

Subhi (Arabic) Born during the early morning hours
Subhie, Subhy, Subhey, Subhee, Subhea

Suffield (English) From the southern field
Suffeld, Suthfeld, Suthfield

Sullivan (Gaelic) Having dark eyes
Sullavan, Sullevan, Sullyvan

Sully (English) From the southern meadow
Sulley, Sulli, Sullie, Sulleigh, Sullee, Sullea, Sulleah, Suthley

Sultan (African / American) A ruler / one who is bold
Sultane, Sulten, Sultun, Sulton, Sultin, Sultyn

Suman (Hindi) A wise man

Sundiata (African) Resembling a hungry lion
Sundyata, Soundiata, Soundyata, Sunjata

Sundown (American) Born at dusk
Sundowne

Su'ud (Arabic) One who has good luck
Suoud

Swahili (Arabic) Of the coastal people
Swahily, Swahiley, Swahilee, Swahiley, Swaheeli, Swaheelie, Swaheely, Swaheeley

Sylvester (Latin) Man from the forest
Silvester, Silvestre, Silvestro, Sylvestre, Sylvestro, Sly, Sevester, Seveste

Syon (Indian) One who is followed by good fortune

Szemere (Hungarian) A man of small stature
Szemir, Szemeer, Szemear, Szemyr

T

Tabari (Arabic) A famous historian
Tabarie, Tabary, Tabarey, Tabaree, Tabarea

Tabbai (Hebrew) A well-behaved boy
Tabbae, Tabbay, Tabbaye

Tabbart (German) A brilliant man
Tabbert, Tabart, Tabert, Tahbert, Tahberte

Tacari (African) As strong as a warrior
Tacarie, Tacary, Tacarey, Tacaree, Tacarea

Tadao (Japanese) One who is satisfied

Tadeusuz (Polish) One who is worthy of praise
Tadesuz

Tadi (Native American) Of the wind
Tadie, Tady, Tadey, Tadee, Tadea

Tadzi (American / Polish) Resembling the loon / one who is praised
Tadzie, Tadzy, Tadzey, Tadzee, Tadzea

Taft (French / English) From the homestead / from the marshes
Tafte

Taggart (Gaelic) Son of a priest
Taggert, Taggort, Taggirt, Taggyrt

Taghee (Native American) A chief
Taghea, Taghy, Taghey, Taghi, Taghie

Taheton (Native American) Resembling a hawk

Tahoe (Native American) From the big water
Taho

Tahoma (Native American) From the snowy mountain peak
Tehoma, Tacoma, Takoma, Tohoma, Tocoma, Tokoma, Tekoma, Tecoma

Taishi (Japanese) An ambitious man
Taishie, Taishy, Taishey, Taishee, Taishea

Taj (Indian) One who is crowned
Tahj, Tajdar

Tajo (Spanish) Born during the daytime

Taksony (Hungarian) One who is content; well-fed
Taksoney, Taksoni, Taksonie, Taksonee, Taksonea, Tas

Talasi (Native American) Resembling a cornflower
Talasie, Talasy, Talasey, Talasee, Talasea

Talford (English) From the high ford
Talforde, Tallford, Tallforde

Talfryn (Welsh) From the high hill
Talfrynn, Talfrin, Talfrinn, Talfren, Talfrenn, Tallfryn, Tallfrin, Tallfren

Talmai (Hebrew) From the furrows
Talmae, Talmay, Talmaye

Talmon (Hebrew) One who is oppressed
Talman, Talmin, Talmyn, Talmen

Talo (Finnish) From the homestead

Tam (Vietnamese / Hebrew) Having heart / one who is truthful

Taman (Hindi) One who is needed

Tamarius (American) A stubborn man
Tamarias, Tamarios, Tamerius, Tamerias, Tamerios

Tameron (American) Form of Cameron, meaning "having a crooked nose"
Tameren, Tameryn, Tamryn, Tamerin, Tamren, Tamrin, Bamron

Tammany (Native American) A friendly chief
Tammani, Tammanie, Tammaney, Tammanee, Tammanea

Tanafa (Polynesian) A drumbeat

Taneli (Hebrew) He will be judged by God
Tanelie, Tanely, Taneley, Tanelee, Tanelea

Tanish (Indian) An ambitious man
Tanishe, Taneesh, Taneeshe, Taneash, Taneashe, Tanysh, Tanyshe

Tanjiro (Japanese) The prized second-born son
Tanjyro

Tank (American) A man who is big and strong
Tankie, Tanki, Tanky, Tankey, Tankee, Tankea

Tanner (English) One who makes leather
Tannere, Tannor, Tannar, Tannir, Tannyr, Tannur, Tannis

Tannon (German) From the fir tree
Tannan, Tannen, Tannin, Tansen, Tanson, Tannun, Tannyn

Tano (Ghanese) From the river
Tanu

Tao (Chinese) One who will have a long life

Taos (Spanish) From the city in New Mexico

Tapani (Hebrew) A victorious man
Tapanie, Tapany, Tapaney, Tapanee, Tapanea

Tapko (American) Resembling an antelope

Tappen (Welsh) From the top of the cliff
Tappan, Tappon, Tappin, Tappyn, Tappun

Taran (Gaelic) Of the thunder
Taren, Taron, Tarin, Taryn, Tarun

Taranga (Indian) Of the waves

Taregan (Native American) Resembling a crane
Taregen, Taregon, Taregin, Taregyn

Tarit (Indian) Resembling lightning
Tarite, Tareet, Tareete, Tareat, Tareate, Taryt, Taryte

Tarn (Norse) From the mountain pool

Tarquin (Latin) One who is impulsive
Tarquinn, Tarquinne, Tarquen, Tarquenn, Tarquenne, Tarquyn, Tarquynn, Tarquynne

Tarrant (American) One who upholds the law
Tarrent, Tarrint, Tarrynt, Tarront, Tarrunt

Tarun (Indian) A youthful man
Taroun, Taroon, Tarune, Taroune, Taroone

Tashi (Tibetan) One who is prosperous
Tashie, Tashy, Tashey, Tashee, Tashea

^**Tate** (English) A cheerful man; one who brings happiness to others
Tayt, Tayte, Tait, Taite, Taet, Taete

Tausiq (Indian) One who provides strong backing
Tauseeq, Tauseaq, Tausik, Tauseek, Tauseak

Tavaris (American) Of misfortune; a hermit
Tavarius, Tavaress, Tavarious, Tavariss, Tavarous, Tevarus, Tavorian, Tavarian

Tavas (Hebrew) Resembling a peacock

Tavi (Aramaic) A good man
Tavie, Tavy, Tavey, Tavee, Tavea

Tavin (German) Form of Gustav, meaning "of the staff of the gods"
Tavyn, Taven, Tavan, Tavon, Tavun, Tava, Tave

Tawa (Native American) Born beneath the sun
Tawah

Tay (Scottish) From the river
Taye, Tae, Tai

Taylor (English) Cutter of cloth, one who alters garments

Teagan (Gaelic) A handsome man
Teegan, Teygan, Tegan, Teigan

Ted (English) Form of Theodore, meaning "a gift from God"
Tedd, Teddy, Teddi, Teddie, Teddee, Teddea, Teddey, Tedric

Tedmund (English) A protector of the land
Tedmunde, Tedmond, Tedmonde, Tedman, Theomund, Theomond, Theomunde, Theomonde

Teetonka (Native American) One who talks too much
Teitonka, Tietonka, Teatonka, Teytonka

Tegene (African) My protector
Tegeen, Tegeene, Tegean, Tegeane

Teiji (Japanese) One who is righteous
Teijo

Teilo (Welsh) A saintly man

Teka (African) He has replaced

Tekeshi (Japanese) A formidable and brave man
Tekeshie, Tekeshy, Tekeshey, Tekeshee, Tekeshea

Telly (Greek) The wisest man
Telley, Tellee, Tellea, Telli, Tellie

Temman (Anglo-Saxon) One who has been tamed

Temple (Latin) From the sacred place
Tempel, Templar, Templer, Templo

Teneangopte (Native American) Resembling a high-flying bird

Tennant (English) One who rents
Tennent, Tenant, Tenent

Tennessee (Native American) From the state of Tennessee
Tenese, Tenesee, Tenessee, Tennese, Tennesee, Tennesse

Teon (Anglo-Saxon) One who harms others

Teris (Irish) The son of Terence
Terys, Teriss, Teryss, Terris, Terrys, Terriss, Terryss

^**Terrance** (Latin) From an ancient Roman clan
Tarrants, Tarrance, Tarrence, Tarrenz, Terencio, Terance, Terrence, Terrey, Terry

Terrian (American) One who is strong and ambitious
Terrien, Terriun, Terriyn

Terron (English) Form of Terence, meaning "from an ancient Roman clan"
Tarran, Tarren, Tarrin

Teshi (African) One who is full of laughter
Teshie, Teshy, Teshey, Teshee, Teshea

Tessema (African) One to whom people listen

Tet (Vietnamese) Born on New Year's

Teteny (Hungarian) A chieftain

Teva (Hebrew) A natural man
Tevah

Texas (Native American) One of many friends; from the state of Texas
Texus, Texis, Texes, Texos, Texys

Teyrnon (Celtic) A regal man
Teirnon, Tayrnon, Tairnon, Taernon, Tiarchnach, Tiarnach

Thabo (African) Filled with happiness

Thackary (English) Form of Zachary, meaning "the Lord remembers"
Thackery, Thakary, Thakery, Thackari, Thackarie, Thackarey, Thackaree, Thackarea

Thaddeus (Aramaic) Having heart
Tad, Tadd, Taddeo, Taddeusz, Thad, Thadd, Thaddaios, Thaddaos

Thandiwe (African) One who is dearly loved
Thandie, Thandi, Thandy, Thandey, Thandee, Thandea

Thang (Vietnamese) One who is victorious

Thanus (American) One who owns land

Thao (Vietnamese) One who is courteous

Thatcher (English) One who fixes roofs
Thacher, Thatch, Thatche, Thaxter, Thacker, Thaker, Thackere, Thakere

Thayer (Teutonic) Of the nation's army

^**Theodore** (Greek) A gift from God
Ted, Teddy, Teddie, Theo, Theodor

Theron (Greek) A great hunter
Therron, Tharon, Theon, Tharron

Theseus (Greek) In mythology, hero who slew the Minotaur
Thesius, Thesyus

Thinh (Vietnamese) A prosperous man

*****Thomas** (Aramaic) One of twins
Tam, Tamas, Tamhas, Thom, Thomason, Thomson, Thompson, Tomas

Thor (Norse) In mythology, god of thunder
Thorian, Thorin, Thorsson, Thorvald, Tor, Tore, Turo, Thorrin

Thorburn (Norse) Thor's bear
Thorburne, Thorbern, Thorberne, Thorbjorn, Thorbjorne, Torbjorn, Torborg, Torben

Thormond (Norse) Protected by Thor
Thormonde, Thormund, Thormunde, Thurmond, Thurmonde, Thurmund, Thurmunde, Thormun

Thorne (English) From the thorn bush
Thorn

Thornycroft (English) From the field of thorn bushes
Thornicroft, Thorneycroft, Thorniecroft, Thorneecroft, Thorneacroft

Thuong (Vietnamese) One who loves tenderly

Thurston (English) From Thor's town; Thor's stone
Thorston, Thorstan, Thorstein, Thorsten, Thurstain, Thurstan, Thursten, Torsten

Thuy (Vietnamese) One who is kind

Tiassale (African) It has been forgotten

Tiberio (Italian) From the Tiber river
Tibero, Tyberio, Tybero, Tiberius, Tiberios, Tyberius, Tyberios

Tibor (Slavic) From the sacred place

Tiburon (Spanish) Resembling a shark

Tiernan (Gaelic) Lord of the manor
Tiarnan, Tiarney, Tierney, Tierny, Tiernee, Tiernea, Tierni, Tiernie

Tilian (Anglo-Saxon) One who strives to better himself
Tilien, Tiliun, Tilion

Tilon (Hebrew) A generous man
Tilen, Tilan, Tilun, Tilin, Tilyn

Tilton (English) From the fertile estate
Tillton, Tilten, Tillten, Tiltan, Tilltan, Tiltin, Tilltin, Tiltun

Timir (Indian) Born in the darkness
Timirbaran

Timothy (Greek) One who honors God
Tim, Timmo, Timmothy, Timmy, Timo, Timofei, Timofeo

Tin (Vietnamese) A great thinker

Tino (Italian) A man of small stature
Teeno, Tieno, Teino, Teano, Tyno

Tip (American) A form of Thomas, meaning "one of twins"
Tipp, Tipper, Tippy, Tippee, Tippea, Tippey, Tippi, Tippie

Tisa (African) The ninth-born child
Tisah, Tysa, Tysah

^**Titus** (Greek / Latin) Of the giants / a great defender
Tito, Titos, Tytus, Tytos, Titan, Tytan, Tyto

Toa (Polynesian) A brave-hearted woman

Toan (Vietnamese) One who is safe
Toane

Tobias (Hebrew) The Lord is good
Toby

Todd (English) Resembling a fox
Tod

Todor (Bulgarian) A gift from God
Todos, Todros

Tohon (Native American) One who loves the water

Tokala (Native American) Resembling a fox
Tokalo

Tomer (Hebrew) A man of tall stature
Tomar, Tomur, Tomir, Tomor, Tomyr

Tomi (Japanese / African) A wealthy man / of the people
Tomie, Tomee, Tomea, Tomy, Tomey

Tonauac (Aztec) One who possesses the light

Torger (Norse) The power of Thor's spear
Thorger, Torgar, Thorgar, Terje, Therje

Torht (Anglo-Saxon) A bright man
Torhte

Torin (Celtic) One who acts as chief
Toran, Torean, Toren, Torion, Torran, Torrian, Toryn

Tormaigh (Irish) Having the spirit of Thor
Tormey, Tormay, Tormaye, Tormai, Tormae

Torr (English) From the tower
Torre

Torrence (Gaelic) From the little hills
Torence, Torrance, Torrens, Torrans, Toran, Torran, Torrin, Torn, Torry

Torry (Norse / Gaelic) Refers to Thor / form of Torrence, meaning "from the little hills"
Torrey, Torree, Torrea, Torri, Torrie, Tory, Torey, Tori

Toshiro (Japanese) One who is talented and intelligent
Toshihiro

Tostig (English) A well-known earl
Tostyg

Toviel (Hebrew) The Lord is good
Toviell, Toviele, Tovielle, Tovi, Tovie, Tovee, Tovea, Tovy

Toyo (Japanese) A man of plenty

Tracy (Gaelic) One who is warlike
Tracey, Traci, Tracie, Tracee, Tracea, Treacy, Trace, Tracen

Travis (French) To cross over
Travys, Traver, Travers, Traviss, Trevis, Trevys, Travus, Traves

Treffen (German) One who socializes
Treffan, Treffin, Treffon, Treffyn, Treffun

Tremain (Celtic) From the town built of stone
Tramain, Tramaine, Tramayne, Tremaine, Tremayne, Tremaen, Tremaene, Tramaen

Tremont (French) From the three mountains
Tremonte, Tremount, Tremounte

Trenton (English) From the town near the rushing rapids
Trent, Trynt, Trenten, Trentyn

Trevin (English) From the fair town
Trevan, Treven, Trevian, Trevion, Trevon, Trevyn, Trevonn

Trevor (Welsh) From the large village
Trefor, Trevar, Trever, Treabhar, Treveur, Trevir, Trevur

Trey (English) The third-born child
Tre, Trai, Trae, Tray, Traye, Trayton, Treyton, Trayson

Trigg (Norse) One who is truthful
Trygg

Tripp (English) A traveler
Trip, Trypp, Tryp, Tripper, Trypper

Tripsy (American) One who enjoys dancing
Tripsey, Tripsee, Tripsea, Tripsi, Tripsie

Tristan (Celtic) A sorrowful man; in Arthurian legend, a knight of the Round Table
Trystan, Tris, Tristam, Tristen, Tristian, Tristin, Triston, Tristram

Trocky (American) A manly man
Trockey, Trocki, Trockie, Trockee, Trockea

Trong (Vietnamese) One who is respected

Troy (Gaelic) Son of a foot-soldier
Troye, Troi

Trumbald (English) A bold man
Trumbold, Trumbalde, Trumbolde

Trygve (Norse) One who wins with bravery

Tse (Native American) As solid as a rock

Tsidhqiyah (Hebrew) The Lord is just
Tsidqiyah, Tsidhqiya, Tsdqiya

Tsubasa (Japanese) A winged being
Tsubasah, Tsubase, Tsubaseh

Tucker (English) One who makes garments
Tuker, Tuckerman, Tukerman, Tuck, Tuckman, Tukman, Tuckere, Toukere

Tuketu (Native American) Resembling a running bear
Tuketue, Tuketoo, Tuketou, Telutci, Telutcie, Telutcy, Telutcey, Telutcee

Tulsi (Indian) A holy man
Tulsie, Tulsy, Tulsey, Tulsee, Tulsea

Tumaini (African) An optimist
Tumainie, Tumainee, Tumainy, Tumainey, Tumayni, Tumaynie, Tumaynee, Tumayney

Tunde (African) One who returns
Tundi, Tundie, Tundee, Tundea, Tundy, Tundey

Tunleah (English) From the town near the meadow
Tunlea, Tunleigh, Tunly, Tunley, Tunlee, Tunli, Tunlie

Tupac (African) A messenger warrior
Tupack, Tupoc, Tupock

Turfeinar (Norse) In mythology, the son of Rognvald
Turfaynar, Turfaenar, Turfanar, Turfenar, Turfainar

Tushar (Indian) Of the snow
Tusharr, Tushare

Tusita (Chinese) One who is heaven-sent

Twrgadarn (Welsh) From the strong tower

Txanton (Basque) Form of Anthony, meaning "a flourishing man; of an ancient Roman family"
Txantony, Txantoney, Txantonee, Txantoni, Txantonie, Txantonea

Tybalt (Latin) He who sees the truth
Tybault, Tybalte, Tybaulte

Tye (English) From the fenced-in pasture
Tyg, Tyge, Tie, Tigh, Teyen

Tyfiell (English) Follower of the god Tyr
Tyfiel, Tyfielle, Tyfiele

***Tyler** (English) A tiler of roofs
Tilar, Tylar, Tylor, Tiler, Tilor, Ty, Tye, Tylere

Typhoon (Chinese) Of the great wind
Tiphoon, Tyfoon, Tifoon, Typhoun, Tiphoun, Tyfoun, Tifoun

Tyrone (French) From Owen's land
Terone, Tiron, Tirone, Tyron, Ty, Kyrone

Tyson (French) One who is high-spirited; fiery
Thyssen, Tiesen, Tyce, Tycen, Tyeson, Tyssen, Tysen, Tysan

U

U (Korean) A kind and gentle man

Uaithne (Gaelic) One who is innocent; green
Uaithn, Uaythne, Uaythn, Uathne, Uathn, Uaethne, Uaethn

Ualan (Scottish) Form of Valentine, meaning "one who is strong and healthy"
Ualane, Ualayn, Ualayne, Ualen, Ualon

Uba (African) One who is wealthy; lord of the house
Ubah, Ubba, Ubbah

Uberto (Italian) Form of Hubert, meaning "having a shining intellect"
Ulberto, Umberto

Udath (Indian) One who is noble
Udathe

Uddam (Indian) An exceptional man

Uddhar (Indian) One who is free; an independent man
Uddharr, Udhar, Udharr

Udell (English) From the valley of yew trees
Udale, Udel, Udall, Udayle, Udayl, Udail, Udaile, Udele

Udi (Hebrew) One who carries a torch
Udie, Udy, Udey, Udee, Udea

Udup (Indian) Born beneath the moon's light
Udupp, Uddup, Uddupp

Udyan (Indian) Of the garden
Uddyan, Udyann, Uddyann

Ugo (Italian) A great thinker

Uland (English) From the noble country
Ulande, Ulland, Ullande, Ulandus, Ullandus

Ulhas (Indian) Filled with happiness
Ulhass, Ullhas, Ullhass

Ull (Norse) Having glory; in mythology, god of justice and patron of agriculture
Ulle, Ul, Ule

Ulmer (German) Having the fame of the wolf
Ullmer, Ullmar, Ulmarr, Ullmarr, Ulfmer, Ulfmar, Ulfmaer

Ultman (Indian) A godly man
Ultmann, Ultmane

Umrao (Indian) One who is noble

Unai (Basque) A shepherd
Unay, Unaye, Unae

Unathi (African) God is with us
Unathie, Unathy, Unathey, Unathee, Unathea

Uncas (Native American) Resembling a fox
Unkas, Unckas

Ungus (Irish) A vigorous man
Unguss

Unique (American) Unlike others; the only one
Unikue, Unik, Uniqui, Uniqi, Uniqe, Unikque, Unike, Unicke

Uolevi (Finnish) Form of Olaf, meaning "the remaining of the ancestors"
Uolevie, Uolevee, Uolevy, Uolevey, Uolevea

Upchurch (English) From the upper church
Upchurche

Uranus (Greek) In mythology, the father of the Titans
Urainus, Uraynus, Uranas, Uraynas, Urainas, Uranos, Uraynos, Urainos

Uri (Hebrew) Form of Uriah, meaning "the Lord is my light"
Urie, Ury, Urey, Uree, Urea

Uriah (Hebrew) The Lord is my light
Uri, Uria, Urias, Urija, Urijah, Uriyah, Urjasz, Uriya

Urjavaha (Hindu) Of the Nimi dynasty

Urtzi (Basque) From the sky
Urtzie, Urtzy, Urtzey, Urtzee, Urtzea

Usher (Latin) From the mouth of the river
Ushar, Ushir, Ussher, Usshar, Usshir

Ushi (Chinese) As strong as an ox
Ushie, Ushy, Ushey, Ushee, Ushea

Utah (Native American) People of the mountains; from the state of Utah

Utsav (Indian) Born during a celebration
Utsavi, Utsave, Utsava, Utsavie, Utsavy, Utsavey, Utsavee, Utsavea

Utt (Arabic) One who is kind and wise
Utte

Uzi (Hebrew) Having great power
Uzie, Uzy, Uzey, Uzee, Uzea, Uzzi, Uzzie, Uzzy

Uzima (African) One who is full of life
Uzimah, Uzimma, Uzimmah, Uzyma

Uzziah (Hebrew) The Lord is my strength
Uzzia, Uziah, Uzia, Uzzya, Uzzyah, Uzyah, Uzya, Uzziel

V

Vachel (French) Resembling a small cow
Vachele, Vachell

Vachlan (English) One who lives near water

Vadar (Dutch) A fatherly man
Vader, Vadyr

Vadhir (Spanish) Resembling a rose
Vadhyr, Vadheer

Vadim (Russian) A good-looking man
Vadime, Vadym, Vadyme, Vadeem, Vadeeme

Vaijnath (Hindi) Refers to Lord Shiva
Vaejnath, Vaijnathe, Vaejnathe

Valdemar (German) A well-known ruler
Valdemarr, Valdemare, Valto, Valdmar, Valdmarr, Valdimar, Valdimarr

Valentine (Latin) One who is strong and healthy
Val, Valentin, Valentino, Valentyne, Ualan

Valerian (Latin) One who is strong and healthy
Valerien, Valerio, Valerius, Valery, Valeryan, Valere, Valeri, Valerii

Valin (Hindi) The monkey king

Valle (French) From the glen
Vallejo

Valri (French) One who is strong
Valrie, Valry, Valrey, Valree

Vance (English) From the marshland
Vanse

Vanderveer (Dutch) From the ferry
Vandervere, Vandervir, Vandervire, Vandervyr, Vandervyre

Vandy (Dutch) One who travels; a wanderer
Vandey, Vandi, Vandie, Vandee

Vandyke (Danish) From the dike
Vandike

Vanir (Norse) Of the ancient gods

Varante (Arabic) From the river

Vardon (French) From the green hill
Varden, Verdon, Verdun, Verden, Vardun, Vardan, Verddun, Varddun

Varg (Norse) Resembling a wolf

Varick (German) A protective ruler
Varrick, Warick, Warrick

Varius (Latin) A versatile man
Varian, Varinius

Variya (Hindi) The excellent one

Vasava (Hindi) Refers to Indra

Vashon (American) The Lord is gracious
Vashan, Vashawn, Vashaun, Vashone, Vashane, Vashayn, Vashayne

Vasin (Indian) A great ruler
Vasine, Vaseen, Vaseene, Vasyn, Vasyne

Vasuki (Hindi) In Hinduism, a serpent king
Vasukie, Vasuky, Vasukey, Vasukee, Vasukea

Vasuman (Indian) Son born of fire

Vasyl (Slavic) A king
Vasil, Vassil, Wasyl

Vatsa (Indian) Our beloved son
Vathsa

Vatsal (Indian) One who is affectionate

Velimir (Croatian) One who wishes for great peace
Velimeer, Velimyr, Velimire, Velimeere, Velimyre

Velyo (Bulgarian) A great man
Velcho, Veliko, Velin, Velko

Vere (French) From the alder tree

Verge (Anglo-Saxon) One who owns four acres

Vernon (French) From the alder-tree grove
Vern, Vernal, Vernard, Verne, Vernee, Vernen, Verney, Vernin

Verrill (French) One who is faithful
Verill, Verrall, Verrell, Verroll, Veryl, Veryll, Verol, Verall

Vibol (Cambodian) A man of plenty
Viboll, Vibole, Vybol, Vyboll, Vybole

Victor (Latin) One who is victorious; the champion
Vic, Vick, Victoriano

Vidal (Spanish) A giver of life
Videl, Videlio, Videlo, Vidalo, Vidalio, Vidas

Vidar (Norse) Warrior of the forest; in mythology, a son of Odin
Vidarr

Vien (Vietnamese) One who is complete; satisfied

Vincent (Latin) One who prevails; the conqueror
Vicente, Vicenzio, Vicenzo, Vin, Vince, Vincens, Vincente, Vincentius

Viorel (Romanian) Resembling the bluebell
Viorell, Vyorel, Vyorell

Vipin (Indian) From the forest
Vippin, Vypin, Vypyn, Vyppin, Vyppyn, Vipyn, Vippyn

Vipul (Indian) A man of plenty
Vypul, Vipull, Vypull, Vipool, Vypool

Virag (Hungarian) Resembling a flower

Virgil (Latin) The staff-bearer
Verge, Vergil, Vergilio, Virgilio, Vergilo, Virgilo, Virgilijus

Virginius (Latin) One who is pure; chaste
Virginio, Virgino

Vitéz (Hungarian) A courageous warrior

Vito (Latin) One who gives life
Vital, Vitale, Vitalis, Vitaly, Vitas, Vitus, Vitali, Vitaliy, Vid

Vitus (Latin) Giver of life
Wit

Vladimir (Slavic) A famous prince
Vladamir, Vladimeer, Vladimyr, Vladimyre, Vladamyr, Vladamyre, Vladameer, Vladimer

Vladislav (Slavic) One who rules with glory

Volodymyr (Slavic) To rule with peace
Wolodymyr

Vulcan (Latin) In mythology, the god of fire
Vulkan, Vulckan

Vyacheslav (Russian) Form of Wenceslas, meaning "one who receives more glory"

W

Wade (English) To cross the river ford
Wayde, Waid, Waide, Waddell, Wadell, Waydell, Waidell, Waed

Wadley (English) From the meadow near the ford
Wadly, Wadlee, Wadli, Wadlie, Wadleigh

Wadsworth (English) From the estate near the ford
Waddsworth, Wadsworthe, Waddsworthe

Wafi (Arabic) One who is trustworthy
Wafie, Wafy, Wafey, Wafee, Wafiy, Wafiyy

Wahab (Indian) A big-hearted man

Wainwright (English) One who builds wagons
Wainright, Wainewright, Wayneright, Waynewright, Waynwright

Wakil (Arabic) A lawyer; a trustee
Wakill, Wakyl, Wakyle, Wakeel, Wakeele

Wakiza (Native American) A desperate fighter
Wakyza, Wakeza, Wakieza, Wakeiza

Walbridge (English) From the Welshman's bridge
Wallbridge, Walbrydge, Wallbrydge

Waljan (Welsh) The chosen one
Walljan, Waljen, Walljen, Waljon, Walljon

Walker (English) One who trods the cloth
Walkar, Walkir, Walkor

Wallace (Scottish) A Welshman, a man from the South
Wallach, Wallas, Wallie, Wallis, Wally, Wlash, Welch

Walter (German) The commander of the army
Walther, Walt, Walte, Walder, Wat, Wouter, Wolter, Woulter, Galtero, Quaid

Wamblee (Native American) Resembling an eagle
Wambli, Wamblie, Wambly, Wambley, Wambleigh, Wamblea

Wanikiy (Native American) A savior
Wanikiya, Wanikie, Wanikey, Waniki, Wanikee

Wanjala (African) Born during a famine
Wanjalla, Wanjal, Wanjall

Warford (English) From the ford near the weir
Warforde, Weirford, Weirforde, Weiford, Weiforde

Warley (English) From the meadow near the weir
Warly, Warleigh, Warlee, Warlea, Warleah, Warli, Warlie, Weirley

Warner (German) Of the defending army
Werner, Wernher, Warnher, Worner, Wornher

Warra (Aboriginal) Man of the water
Warrah, Wara, Warah

Warren (English / German) From the fortress

Warrick (English) Form of Varick, meaning "a protective ruler"
Warrik, Warric, Warick, Warik, Waric, Warryck, Warryk, Warryc

Warrigal (Aboriginal) One who is wild
Warrigall, Warigall, Warigal, Warygal, Warygall

Warwick (English) From the farm near the weir
Warwik, Warwyck, Warwyk

Wasswa (African) The first-born of twins
Waswa, Wasswah, Waswah

Wasyl (Ukrainian) Form of Vasyl, meaning "a king"
Wasyle, Wasil, Wasile

Watson (English) The son of Walter
Watsin, Watsen, Watsan, Watkins, Watckins, Watkin, Watckin, Wattekinson

Waylon (English) From the roadside land

Wayne (English) One who builds wagons
Wain, Wanye, Wayn, Waynell, Waynne, Guwayne

Webster (English) A weaver
Weeb, Web, Webb, Webber, Weber, Webbestre, Webestre, Webbe

Wei (Chinese) A brilliant man; having great strength

Wenceslas (Polish) One who receives more glory
Wenceslaus, Wenzel, Vyacheslav

Wendell (German) One who travels; a wanderer
Wendel, Wendale, Wendall, Wendele, Wendal, Windell, Windel, Windal

Wesley (English) From the western meadow
Wes, Wesly, Wessley, Westleigh, Westley, Wesli, Weslie, Wesleigh

Westby (English) From the western farm
Westbey, Wesby, Wesbey, Westbi, Wesbi, Westbie, Wesbie, Westbee

Weston (English) From the western town

Whit (English) A white-skinned man
White, Whitey, Whitt, Whitte, Whyt, Whytt, Whytte, Whytey

Whitby (English) From the white farm
Whitbey, Whitbi, Whitbie, Whitbee, Whytbey, Whytby, Whytbi, Whytbie

Whitfield (English) From the white field
Whitfeld, Whytfield, Whytfeld, Witfield, Witfeld, Wytfield, Wytfeld

Whitley (English) From the white meadow
Whitly, Whitli, Whitlie, Whitlee, Whitleigh, Whytley, Whytly, Whytli

Whitman (English) A white-haired man
Whitmann, Witman, Witmann, Whitmane, Witmane, Whytman, Whytmane, Wytman

Wildon (English) From the wooded hill
Willdon, Wilden, Willden

Wiley (English) One who is crafty; from the meadow by the water
Wily, Wileigh, Wili, Wilie, Wilee, Wylie, Wyly, Wyley

Wilford (English) From the willow ford
Willford, Wilferd, Willferd, Wilf, Wielford, Weilford, Wilingford, Wylingford

***William** (German) The determined protector
Wilek, Wileck, Wilhelm, Wilhelmus, Wilkes, Wilkie, Wilkinson, Will, Guillaume, Quilliam

Willow (English) Of the willow tree
Willowe, Willo, Willoe

Wilmer (German) A strong-willed and well-known man
Wilmar, Wilmore, Willmar, Willmer, Wylmer, Wylmar, Wyllmer, Wyllmar

Winston (English) Of the joy stone; from the friendly town
Win, Winn, Winsten, Winstonn, Wynstan, Wynsten, Wynston, Winstan

Winthrop (English) From the friendly village
Winthrope, Wynthrop, Wynthrope, Winthorp, Wynthorp

Winton (English) From the enclosed pastureland
Wintan, Wintin, Winten, Wynton, Wyntan, Wyntin, Wynten

Wirt (Anglo-Saxon) One who is worthy
Wirte, Wyrt, Wyrte, Wurt, Wurte

Wit (Polish) Form of Vitus, meaning "giver of life"
Witt

Wlodzimierz (Polish) To rule with peace
Wlodzimir, Wlodzimerz

Wolfric (German) A wolf ruler
Wolfrick, Wolfrik, Wulfric, Wulfrick, Wulfrik, Wolfryk, Wolfryck, Wolfryc

Wolodymyr (Ukrainian) Form of Volodymyr, meaning "to rule with peace"
Wolodimyr, Wolodimir, Wolodymeer, Wolodimeer

Woorak (Aboriginal) From the plains
Woorack, Woorac

***Wyatt** (English) Having the strength of a warrior
Wyat, Wyatte, Wyate, Wiatt, Wiatte, Wiat, Wiate, Wyeth

Wyndham (English) From the windy village
Windham

Xakery (American) Form of Zachery, meaning "the Lord remembers"
Xaccary, Xaccery, Xach, Xacharie, Xachery, Xack, Xackarey, Xackary

Xalvador (Spanish) Form of Salvador, meaning "a savior"
Xalvadore, Xalvadoro, Xalvadorio, Xalbador, Xalbadore, Xalbadorio, Xalbadoro, Xabat

Xannon (American) From an ancient family
Xanon, Xannen, Xanen, Xannun, Xanun

Xanthus (Greek) A blond-haired man
Xanthos, Xanthe, Xanth

***Xavier** (Basque / Arabic) Owner of a new house / one who is bright
Xaver, Xever, Xabier, Xaviere, Xabiere, Xaviar, Xaviare, Xavior

Xenocrates (Greek) A foreign ruler

Xesus (Galician) Form of Jesus, meaning "God is my salvation"

Xoan (Galician) Form of John, meaning "God is gracious"
Xoane, Xohn, Xon

Xue (Chinese) A studious young man

Yael (Israeli) Strength of God
Yaele

Yagil (Hebrew) One who rejoices, celebrates
Yagill, Yagyl, Yagylle

Yahto (Native American) Having blue eyes; refers to the color blue
Yahtoe, Yahtow, Yahtowe

Yahweh (Hebrew) Refers to God
Yahveh, Yaweh, Yaveh, Yehowah, Yehweh, Yehoveh

Yakiv (Ukrainian) Form of Jacob, meaning "he who supplants"
Yakive, Yakeev, Yakeeve, Yackiv, Yackeev, Yakieve, Yakiev, Yakeive

Yakout (Arabian) As precious as a ruby

Yale (Welsh) From the fertile upland
Yayle, Yayl, Yail, Yaile

Yanai (Aramaic) God will answer
Yanae, Yana, Yani

Yankel (Hebrew) Form of Jacob, meaning "he who supplants"
Yankell, Yanckel, Yanckell, Yankle, Yanckle

Yaotl (Aztec) A great warrior
Yaotyl, Yaotle, Yaotel, Yaotyle

Yaphet (Hebrew) A handsome man
Yaphett, Yapheth, Yaphethe

Yaqub (Arabic) Form of Jacob, meaning "he who supplants"
Ya'qub, Yaqob, Yaqoub

Yardley (English) From the fenced-in meadow
Yardly, Yardleigh, Yardli, Yardlie, Yardlee, Yardlea, Yarley, Yarly

Yaromir (Russian) Form of Jaromir, meaning "from the famous spring"
Yaromire, Yaromeer, Yaromeere, Yaromyr, Yaromyre

Yas (Native American) Child of the snow

Yasahiro (Japanese) One who is peaceful and calm

Yasin (Arabic) A wealthy man
Yasine, Yaseen, Yaseene, Yasyn, Yasyne, Yasien, Yasiene, Yasein

Yasir (Arabic) One who is well-off financially
Yassir, Yasser, Yaseer, Yasr, Yasyr, Yassyr, Yasar, Yassar

Yegor (Russian) Form of George, meaning "one who works the earth; a farmer"
Yegore, Yegorr, Yegeor, Yeorges, Yeorge, Yeorgis

Yehonadov (Hebrew) A gift from God
Yehonadav, Yehonedov, Yehonedav, Yehoash, Yehoashe, Yeeshai, Yeeshae, Yishai

Yenge (African) A hard-working man
Yengi, Yengie, Yengy, Yengey, Yengee

Yeoman (English) A man-servant
Youman, Yoman

Yestin (Welsh) One who is just and fair
Yestine, Yestyn, Yestyne

Yigil (Hebrew) He shall be redeemed
Yigile, Yigyl, Yigyle, Yigol, Yigole, Yigit, Yigat

Yishachar (Hebrew) He will be rewarded
Yishacharr, Yishachare, Yissachar, Yissachare, Yisachar, Yisachare

Yiska (Native American) The night has gone

Yngve (Scandinavian) Refers to the god Ing

Yo (Cambodian) One who is honest

Yoav (Hebrew) Form of Joab, meaning "the Lord is my father"
Yoave, Yoavo, Yoavio

Yochanan (Hebrew) Form of John, meaning "God is gracious"
Yochan, Yohannan, Yohanan, Yochannan

Yohan (German) Form of John, meaning "God is gracious"
Yohanan, Yohann, Yohannes, Yohon, Yohonn, Yohonan

Yonatan (Hebrew) Form of Jonathan, meaning "a gift of God"
Yonaton, Yohnatan, Yohnaton, Yonathan, Yonathon, Yoni, Yonie, Yony

Yong (Korean) One who is courageous

York (English) From the yew settlement
Yorck, Yorc, Yorke

Yosyp (Ukrainian) Form of Joseph, meaning "God will add"
Yosip, Yosype, Yosipe

Yovanny (English) Form of Giovanni, meaning "God is gracious"
Yovanni, Yovannie, Yovannee, Yovany, Yovani, Yovanie, Yovanee

Yukon (English) From the settlement of gold
Youkon, Yucon, Youcon, Yuckon, Youckon

Yuliy (Russian) Form of Julius, meaning "one who is youthful"
Yuli, Yulie, Yulee, Yuleigh, Yuly, Yuley, Yulika, Yulian

Yuudai (Japanese) A great hero
Yudai, Yuudae, Yudae, Yuuday, Yuday

Yves (French) A young archer
Yve, Yvo, Yvon, Yvan, Yvet, Yvete

Z

Zabian (Arabic) One who worships celestial bodies
Zabion, Zabien, Zaabian

Zabulon (Hebrew) One who is exalted
Zabulun, Zabulen

Zacchaeus (Hebrew) Form of Zachariah, meaning "The Lord remembers"
Zachaeus, Zachaios, Zaccheus, Zackaeus, Zacheus, Zackaios, Zaccheo

Zachariah (Hebrew) The Lord remembers
Zacaria, Zacarias, Zaccaria, Zaccariah, Zachaios, Zacharia, Zacharias, Zacherish

*****Zachary** (Hebrew) Form of Zachariah, meaning "the Lord remembers"
Zaccary, Zaccery, Zach, Zacharie, Zachery, Zack, Zackarey, Zackary, Thackary, Xakery

Zaci (African) In mythology, the god of fatherhood

Zaden (Dutch) A sower of seeds
Zadin, Zadan, Zadon, Zadun, Zede, Zeden, Zedan

Zadok (Hebrew) One who is righteous; just
Zadoc, Zaydok, Zadock, Zaydock, Zaydoc, Zaidok, Zaidock, Zaidoc

Zador (Hungarian) An ill-tempered man
Zador, Zadoro, Zadorio

Zafar (Arabic) The conqueror; a victorious man
Zafarr, Zaffar, Zhafar, Zhaffar, Zafer, Zaffer

Zahid (Arabic) A pious man
Zahide, Zahyd, Zahyde, Zaheed, Zaheede, Zaheide, Zahiede, Zaheid

Zahir (Arabic) A radiant and flourishing man
Zahire, Zahireh, Zahyr, Zahyre, Zaheer, Zaheere, Zaheir, Zahier

Zahur (Arabic) Resembling a flower
Zahure, Zahureh, Zhahur, Zaahur

Zale (Greek) Having the strength of the sea
Zail, Zaile, Zayl, Zayle, Zael, Zaele

Zamir (Hebrew) Resembling a songbird
Zamire, Zameer, Zameere, Zamyr, Zamyre, Zameir, Zameire, Zamier

Zander (Slavic) Form of Alexander, meaning "a helper and defender of mankind"
Zandros, Zandro, Zandar, Zandur, Zandre

Zane (English) form of John, meaning "God is gracious"
Zayne, Zayn, Zain, Zaine

Zareb (African) The protector; guardian
Zarebb, Zaareb, Zarebe, Zarreb, Zareh, Zaareh

Zared (Hebrew) One who has been trapped
Zarede, Zarad, Zarade, Zaared, Zaarad

Zasha (Russian) A defender of the people
Zashah, Zosha, Zoshah, Zashiya, Zoshiya

^**Zayden** (Arabic) Form of Zayd, meaning "To become greater, to grow"
Zaiden

Zeke (English) Form of Ezekiel, meaning "strengthened by God"
Zekiel, Zeek, Zeeke, Zeeq

Zene (African) A handsome man
Zeene, Zeen, Zein, Zeine

Zereen (Arabic) The golden one
Zereene, Zeryn, Zeryne, Zerein, Zereine, Zerrin, Zerren, Zerran

Zeroun (Armenian) One who is respected for his wisdom
Zeroune, Zeroon, Zeroone

Zeth (English) Form of Seth, meaning "one who has been appointed"
Zethe

Zion (Hebrew) From the citadel
Zionn, Zione, Zionne

Ziv (Hebrew) A radiant man
Zive, Ziiv, Zivi, Zivie, Zivee, Zivy, Zivey

Ziyad (Arabic) One who betters himself; growth
Ziad

Zlatan (Croatian) The golden son
Zlattan, Zlatane, Zlatann, Zlatain, Zlatayn, Zlaten, Zlaton, Zlatin

Zoltan (Hungarian) A kingly man; a sultan
Zoltann, Zoltane, Zoltanne, Zsolt, Zsoltan

Zorion (Basque) Filled with happiness
Zorian, Zorien

Zoticus (Greek) Full of life
Zoticos, Zoticas

Zsigmond (Hungarian) Form of Sigmund, meaning "the victorious protector"
Zsigmund, Zsigmonde, Zsigmunde, Zsig, Zsiga

Zubair (Arabic) One who is pure
Zubaire, Zubayr, Zubayre, Zubar, Zubarr, Zubare, Zubaer

Zuberi (African) Having great strength
Zuberie, Zubery, Zuberey, Zuberee, Zubari, Zubarie, Zubary, Zubarey

Zubin (English) One with a toothy grin
Zubine, Zuben, Zuban, Zubun, Zubbin

Zuzen (Basque) One who is just and fair
Zuzenn, Zuzan, Zuzin

Zvonimir (Croatian) The sound of peace
Zvonimirr, Zvonimeer

My Favorite Names